PLUTARCH was one of the last of the classical Greek historians. He was born in about A.D. 45 at Chaeronea in Boeotia, where he later had a school, and in middle age he took up a priesthood at near-by Delphi.

When Nero visited Greece in A.D. 66, Plutarch was a student at Athens. He became a philosopher, a man capable of lecturing and discussing on many learned topics, and wrote a large number of essays and dialogues on philosophical, scientific and literary subjects (the *Moralia*). He adopted the philosophical standpoint of a Platonist, and frequently attacked both Stoics and Epicureans. He wrote his historical works somewhat late in life, and his *Parallel Lives* of eminent Greeks and Romans is probably his best-known and most influential work (their translation by North was used by Shakespeare as a source for his Roman plays).

Plutarch travelled in Egypt and also went to Rome, where he had many distinguished friends. The Emperor Hadrian honoured him with a government appointment in Greece, yet he always remained strongly attached to his native Chaeronea. His death probably occurred some years after A.D. 120.

IAN SCOTT-KILVERT is Director of English Literature at the British Council. He has also translated, for the Penguin Classics, Plutarch's *The Rise and Fall of Athens: Nine Greek Lives* and *The Age of Alexander*.

MAKERS OF ROME

NINE LIVES BY PLUTARCH

CORIOLANUS

FABIUS MAXIMUS

MARCELLUS

CATO THE ELDER

TIBERIUS GRACCHUS

GAIUS GRACCHUS

SERTORIUS

BRUTUS

MARK ANTONY

Translated with an Introduction by
Ian Scott-Kilvert

PENGUIN BOOKS

Penguin Books Ltd, Harmondsworth, Middlesex, England
Penguin Books, 625 Madison Avenue, New York, New York 10022, U.S.A.
Penguin Books Australia Ltd, Ringwood, Victoria, Australia
Penguin Books Canada Ltd, 2801 John Street, Markham, Ontario, Canada L3R 1B4
Penguin Books (N.Z.) Ltd, 182–190 Wairau Road, Auckland 20, New Zealand

—

This translation first published 1965
Reprinted 1968, 1972, 1975, 1977, 1978

—

—

Made and printed in Great Britain
by Hazell Watson & Viney Ltd,
Aylesbury, Bucks
Set in Monotype Bembo

CONTENTS

* * *

INTRODUCTION

* *
*

THE present selection has been drawn up on principles similar to those adopted in my volume of Greek Lives, *The Rise and Fall of Athens.* Instead of following Plutarch's arrangement of grouping Greeks and Romans in pairs, I have selected eight representative figures whose careers range from the earliest years of the Republic to the establishment of the Empire under Octavius Caesar. Among these I have included the three Shakespearean heroes, Coriolanus, Brutus, and Mark Antony, whose biographies, besides their dramatic appeal, are particularly interesting examples of Plutarch's fondness for a semi-fictional rather than a factual treatment of history.

Two themes dominate the cycle of Plutarch's Roman Lives, the valour and tenacity of the Roman people in war, and their genius for political compromise. The creators of the *pax Romana* were first of all the children of Mars, and so Plutarch depicts them, often defeated but never subdued, and in the end triumphant over one dreaded enemy after another, the Volscians, the Gauls, Pyrrhus and his elephants, the Carthaginians and their matchless cavalry. Lastly the army moves into politics, the enemies of the Republic become her own legions led by their contending generals, and the clash of arms is only finally stilled when, after the victory of Actium, Octavius Caesar symbolically closes the ever-open doors of the temple of Janus.

This brings us to Plutarch's second motif, the problems of statecraft and the struggle for power between patrician and plebeian, the Senate and the popular leaders. It is here, for all the ruthlessness of Roman public life, that Plutarch pays tribute to the political instinct, the ability to close ranks in a moment of crisis, which eventually raised this tribal confederation of Italian farmers to the mastery of the world – and the absence of which proved the ruin of the Greek city-state. The tragedy of Greece and the triumph of Rome form the political poles of the Lives viewed as a whole, and Plutarch passes judgment on his fellow-countrymen in a memorable passage from the *Life of Flamininus*:

For if we except the victory at Marathon, the sea-fight at Salamis, the battles of Plataea and Thermopylae, and Cimon's exploits at Eurymedon . . . Greece fought all her battles against and to enslave herself. Every one of her trophies stands as a memorial to her own shame and misfortune, and she owed her ruin above all to the misdeeds and the rivalries of her leaders.

The peculiarly Roman virtues as Plutarch sees them – best exemplified perhaps in the careers of Fabius, Marcellus, and Sertorius – include not only courage and the power of leadership, but also generosity and forbearance, the qualities which create harmony between rulers and ruled. But the real source of Roman supremacy and object of Plutarch's admiration is 'the idea of Rome', a spiritual heritage undreamed of in Greece, which at moments of supreme crisis seems to descend upon the city's fallible representatives, to work through them and to shape their ends. Heine expresses something of this conception in his *Reisebilder*:

They were not great men, but through their position they were greater than the other children of earth, for they stood on Rome. Immediately they came down from the Seven Hills they were small. The greater Rome grew, the more this idea dilated; the individual lost himself in it: the great men who remain eminent are borne up by this idea, and it makes the littleness of the little men more pronounced.

Some such notion is surely in Plutarch's mind on the many occasions when he finds a supernatural power at work in the crises of Roman history. Time and again he returns to this theme, in Valeria's sudden intuition that only the women of Rome can move Coriolanus, in Fabius's power to inspire his countrymen's resistance after the débâcle of Cannae, in the delayed news of victory which destroys Brutus at Philippi; and he reiterates his belief in a divine providence which seems to stand guard over the fortunes of Rome.

All these issues are coincidentally, but none the less dramatically, brought together in the first biography of this series, the *Life of Coriolanus*, which seems to present the destiny of Rome in microcosm. The infant state, which had won its freedom as a republic less than twenty years before, is threatened at once from within and without. Rome possesses jealous neighbours, but more serious still, the mass of her citizens, because of the hardships suffered in incessant wars and the debts imposed on them by the propertied classes, are unwilling to fight in her defence. Yet in the end the city is saved by a sense of restraint for which each of the opposing factions can claim some credit. The patricians concede the tribunate and even sacrifice their champion Coriolanus rather than resort to civil war; the tribunes are ready to commute the death sentence on Coriolanus, and Volumnia's final appeal throws aside not only the interests of her class, but even of her son. The moral is drawn in the concluding chapter, when the Volscians, who have given way to their passion for vengeance, quickly reap their reward. In this Life, too, Plutarch demonstrates more clearly than usual that he is interested not so much in establishing historical facts as in investigating character and tracing a dramatic pattern of events. The character of Coriolanus is one of his most elaborate psychological studies, a portrait of the 'choleric man' which especially fascinated the Renaissance: but historically speaking Coriolanus is an almost wholly legendary personage.

To the twentieth-century reader Brutus may well appear the odd man out among Plutarch's heroes. If we would not go so far as Dante in consigning him to the lowest circle of the *Inferno*, modern opinion is inclined to judge him as a pedant, a prig, and a misguided idealist, who succeeded in justifying to himself the murder of his friend, only to discover that public opinion never demanded the act, and that his fellow conspirators were not the men he took them to be. Yet the fact which strikes us as peculiarly repugnant, that Brutus should have stabbed the man who had not only done him many kindnesses but also saved his life, was regarded by the ancients as the highest proof of his disinterestedness. We need to remember that Plutarch is always inclined to judge the actions of statesmen in terms of their personalities and to equate political conduct with the standards of private life. From this point of view Brutus stands out among the protagonists in the final drama of the Republic: he alone is the devoted husband, the philosopher in action, the model of private virtue, and the man whose actions are consistently guided neither by passion nor by self-interest but by principle. Nevertheless he can scarcely serve as an example of the qualities which Plutarch wishes to exalt. His life, as his biographer records it, is essentially a private not a public history, and indeed the resolve to form the conspiracy seems to have been the only major political decision of his career. The tragedy of the noblest Roman of them all was that he should ever have been manoeuvred by his friends and his own sense of his historic role into a position of leadership.

The *Life of Antony* is in many ways the most ambitiously conceived and the most brilliantly executed of the entire series. Nowhere else do we find a woman of the stature of Cleopatra, and the sweep of the narrative touches the very bounds of the Roman Empire itself, from the Alpine snows to the deserts of Parthia and from the plains of Philippi to the palaces of Alexandria. One of Keats's letters to Haydon gives us the effect in a nutshell:

> When a schoolboy the abstract idea I had of a heroic painting – was what I cannot describe. I saw it somewhat sideways, large, prominent, round and colour'd with magnificence – somewhat like the feel I have of Antony and Cleopatra. Or of Alcibiades leaning on his crimson couch in his galley, his broad shoulders imperceptibly heaving with the sea. (*8 April 1818*)

Middleton Murry suggests that for a Greek the theme of Antony's fatal dalliance with Cleopatra was 'a supreme example of the magic by which conquered Greece led captive its fierce conqueror.' However this may be, there is no doubt that the story captured Plutarch's own imagination as none other, and that in passages such as the famous description of Cleopatra in her barge at Cydnus his sentences glow with an opulence such as we find nowhere else in the Lives. Egypt was the first country which Plutarch visited on his travels, and the *Life of Antony* abounds with touches of personal reminiscence, as if the author felt the theme to be as close to him as contemporary history.

And indeed we are apt to forget the distance which separates Plutarch from his subjects. He is as it were a backward-looking writer standing on the last range which divided the pagan civilization from the Christian. His lifetime of some seventy-five years stretches from the middle forties A.D. to the beginning of Hadrian's reign.* It is the period at which the blend of Greek and Roman culture reached its highest point of development: almost all the major writers had done their work and Plutarch's writings are in many ways a summing up of that synthesis. He lacks the startlingly original and impersonal quality of Periclean literature, just as that literature lacks his intimacy on the one hand and the breadth of his tolerance and philanthropy on

* For a fuller account of Plutarch's life, see my introduction to the companion Penguin Classic: *The Rise and Fall of Athens.*

the other. He was no Thucydides applying a ruthlessly objective analysis to uncover the historical process. He was a lover of tradition, and his prime object was at once to cherish and understand the greatness of the past and to reassert it as a living ideal.

The form of Plutarch's writings suggests that his gifts were for the essay rather than the full length history. Apart from the biographies his other major work, the *Moralia*, is a collection of comparatively short treatises which cover an immense range of subjects, literary, ethical, political, and scientific. There is a distinct correspondence between the two, the *Moralia* celebrating the thought of the past as the Lives celebrate its action, and each throws a great deal of light upon the other. Plutarch never attempted any single work on a large scale and his themes are not developed organically, but rather as a series of factual statements followed by comments. Both in the *Moralia* and the Lives his main object is didactic. When he turned to history, he set out not only to convince the Greeks that the annals of Rome deserved their attention, but also to remind the Romans that Greece had possessed statesmen and soldiers who could challenge comparison with their own.

The order of composition of the Lives is still much disputed, but there are signs that they were written in four distinct groups. One series contained the Lives of Sertorius and Eumenes, Cimon and Lucullus, Lysander and Sulla, Demosthenes and Cicero, Agis and Cleomenes and Tiberius and Gaius Gracchus, Pelopidas and Marcellus, Phocion and Cato the Younger, and Aristides and Cato the Elder. This series Plutarch undertook, he tells us, at the request of his friends. A second group was composed for his own satisfaction, and it consisted of great men selected as object-lessons in a particular virtue: Pericles and Fabius Maximus, Nicias and Crassus, Dion and Brutus, Timoleon and Aemilius Paulus, Philopoemen and Titus Flamininus, Themistocles and Camillus, Alexander and Julius Caesar, Agis and Pompey, Pyrrhus and Marius, and Solon and Publicola. A third group was chosen to comprise those whose career may serve as a warning. It contains Demetrius and Mark Antony, and Alcibiades and Coriolanus, and here, not surprisingly, Plutarch achieves from the literary point of view three of his most brilliant successes. Lastly he turned to the semi-mythical and wrote of the founding fathers and legislators of Greece and Rome, Theseus and Romulus and Lycurgus and Numa.

By Plutarch's time a conventional form of biography already existed. It began with an account of the subject's birth, family, and education, went on to delineate his character and recount the most important and typical events of his career, and concluded with an account of his posterity and influence. Plutarch followed this organization of his material fairly closely, but he employed it with far greater skill and variety than his predecessors. He freed his Lives from the rhetorical and argumentative nature of Greek biography and from the ponderous eulogy of the Roman *laudatio*; above all he impressed upon them the charm of his personality and the depth of his insight into human nature. He was a conscientious collector of material and he draws upon a wide range not only of Greek but of Roman sources. His knowledge of Roman history, law, and institutions is often extremely sketchy, yet in spite of these deficiencies he can arrive, in the case of the Gracchi, for example, at a far more dispassionate verdict than the altogether better informed Cicero. His task, as he saw it, working over material which was already familiar in outline to his readers, was not so much to evaluate facts as to create an inspiring portrait. And so, like a portrait painter, we find him choosing a characteristic but sometimes dramatized pose for his subjects. He is a great master of the *ben trovato* and his comment on the story of Solon and Croesus explains the procedure which he follows again and again:

When a story is so celebrated and vouched for by so many authorities and, more important still, when it is so much in keeping with Solon's character and bears the stamp of his wisdom and greatness of mind, I cannot agree that it should be rejected because of the so-called rules of chronology....

Certainly it is when Plutarch's imagination is most strongly engaged that it is most likely to supplant the facts, and nowhere is this truer than in his portrait of Antony and Cleopatra. Rather than encumber the narrative with a lengthy discussion of these matters I have summarized them in a separate appendix.

But in general Plutarch's overriding purpose is to bring out the moral pattern in his hero's career, the movement from virtue to vice or the contrary, for he believed that a man cannot stand still in virtue, and that if he does not advance he will be driven back. He brought to history a Platonist's conviction that knowledge is virtue and that cause and effect are only truly operative in the sphere of Ideas: hence he tends to describe his statesmen's policies in terms of their personalities and to judge public conduct by the ethical standards of private life. He is apt to forget that a statesman is far more often faced with a conflict of opposing interests than with a straightforward choice between right and wrong, and he seems to regard the past as a self-contained world rather than as a continuum, which merges imperceptibly into present and future.

On the other hand it is just this boundless interest in the individual character which has given the Lives their enduring popularity from age to age. Plutarch has an unerring sense of the drama of men in great situations. His eye ranges over a wider field of action than any of the classical historians. He surveys men's conduct in war, in council, in love, in the use of money – always in Greek eyes a vital test of a man's capacities – in religion, in the family, and he judges as a man of wide tolerance and ripe experience. Believing implicitly in the stature of his heroes, he has a genius for making greatness stand out in small actions. We think of Alexander handing his physician the paper denouncing him as an assassin, and in the same gesture drinking off the physic the man had prepared for him, or of Antony sending Enobarbus's treasure after him: these and countless other scenes Plutarch has engraved upon the memory of posterity for all time. It was surely this power of his to epitomize the moral grandeur of the ancient world which appealed most strongly to Shakespeare and Montaigne, which inspired the gigantic outlines of such typically Renaissance heroes as Coriolanus and Mark Antony, and which later prompted Mme Roland's remark that the Lives are the pasturage of great souls.

I

CORIOLANUS

[*fl. c.* 490 B.C.]

* *
*

1. The patrician house of the Marcii at Rome produced many men of distinction. One of them was Ancus Marcius, the grandson of Numa on his daughter's side, who succeeded to the throne after the death of Tullus Hostilius. Publius and Quintus Marcius, the men who provided Rome with its best and most abundant supply of water, also belonged to this family, as did Censorinus, who, after he had twice been appointed censor by the Roman people, persuaded them to pass a law which prohibited any man from holding this office for a second term.

Gaius Marcius, the subject of this Life, lost his father when he was young, and was brought up by his mother, who never remarried. His example shows us that the loss of a father, even though it may impose other disadvantages on a boy, does not prevent him from living a virtuous or a distinguished life, and that it is only worthless men who seek to excuse the deterioration of their character by pleading neglect in their early years. On the other hand this same Gaius Marcius's career bears witness to the truth of the view that a naturally generous and noble disposition, if it lacks discipline, will produce both good and evil fruits at once, in the same way as a naturally fertile soil, if it does not receive the proper tilling. Coriolanus's energy of mind and strength of purpose constantly led him to attempt ambitious exploits, the results of which were momentous for Rome, but these qualities were combined with a violent temper and an uncompromising self-assertion, which made it difficult for him to cooperate with others. People could admire his indifference to hardship, to pleasure and to the temptations of money – which they dignified by the names of courage, moderation, and probity –

but when he displayed the same qualities in his dealings with his fellow-citizens, they were offended and found him harsh, ungracious, and overbearing. It is my belief that of all the blessings which men enjoy through the favour of the Muses, there is none so great as that process of taming and humanizing the natural instincts which is wrought through education and study, so that by submitting ourselves to reason we acquire balance and learn to avoid excess. On the other hand, we must remember that the Romans of those days prized above all else the kind of virtue which finds its expression in warlike and military achievements. We have an interesting piece of evidence for this in the fact that there is only one word in the Latin vocabulary which signifies virtue, and its meaning is *manly valour*: thus the Romans made courage stand for virtue in all its aspects, although it only denotes one of them.

2. Marcius was passionately fond of warlike feats and contests and began at once to handle arms even in his early boyhood. He believed that mere weapons are of little value in themselves, unless the soldier's natural capacities and physique are first properly developed and always kept ready for use. Accordingly he trained his body so thoroughly for every type of combat that he acquired not only the speed of an athlete, but also such muscular strength for wrestling and close combat that few opponents could escape his grasp. At any rate those who from time to time tested their prowess against his in feats of courage and daring used to attribute their defeat to his immense physical strength, which they found impossible to overcome and which no amount of exertion could wear out.

3. He served his first campaign while he was still little more than a boy. This was at the time when Tarquinius Superbus, after he had been expelled from the kingship of Rome and had fought many unsuccessful battles, resolved to stake everything upon a final throw. Tarquinius's army had been recruited mainly from the tribes of Latium, but many men from other districts of Italy had rallied to his cause and were marching against Rome, not so much because of any personal attachment to Tarquinius, but through fear and jealousy of the growing power of the Romans. In the battle which followed,* during which fortune changed sides several times, Marcius, who was

* Supposedly the battle of Lake Regillus, 498 B.C.

fighting bravely under the eye of the dictator, saw a Roman soldier struck down close by. He immediately ran up, placed himself in front of the wounded man, and killed his assailant. Later, after the Romans had won the battle, Marcius was one of the first to be crowned by the general with a garland of oak leaves.

This is the civic crown which, according to Roman custom, is awarded to a man who has saved the life of a fellow-citizen in battle. There are several possible explanations for the choice of this tree. It may have been intended as a compliment to the Arcadians, the tribe led by king Evander, who were the original founders of Rome and who, according to an oracle of Apollo, were known as acorn eaters: or it may have been a matter of mere convenience, because the Romans could easily find plenty of oak trees wherever they fought a campaign. Again, it may have been considered that an oaken wreath, which is sacred to Jupiter as the guardian of Rome, was the most fitting reward for a man who had saved the life of a fellow-citizen. Besides this the oak bears the most shapely fruit of any wild tree, and it is the strongest of all those that grow under cultivation. In the early days of the human race it supplied both food and drink from its acorns and from the honey found inside them, and it enabled men to catch a great number of grazing creatures and of birds for their meat, since it produced the mistletoe from which they made bird-lime for their snares. Legend has it that in this battle which I have described, Castor and Pollux appeared in the field, that immediately after the fighting they were seen in the Forum, their horses foaming with sweat, and that they announced the victory by the fountain where their temple now stands. For this reason the fifteenth of July, the day of the victory, was afterwards declared a festival dedicated to the Dioscuri.

4. It would seem that to win distinction and high honours too early in life is apt to stifle the ambitions of young men in whom the desire to excel does not go very deep, for then their thirst or appetite for fame, never very intense, is quickly satisfied. But for those strong-willed spirits, with whom ambition is a ruling passion, the honours they receive serve only to spur them to greater efforts: the fire within them glows, and they respond as if some mighty wind were urging them on in pursuit of their ideal. They do not think of themselves as being rewarded for what they have already achieved, but rather as

pledging themselves to the future: in this way they feel ashamed of the possibility of falling short of the reputation they have already won, and constantly strive to make their latest actions excel it. It was in this spirit that Marcius set himself to surpass his own record in courage. And since he was always eager to attempt fresh exploits, he added one deed of valour to another and heaped spoils upon spoils, so that his later commanders found themselves vying with their predecessors in the effort to commend him in ever higher terms and to pay him the honours he deserved. And indeed of all the many campaigns and battles which the Romans fought at that time, there was not one from which Marcius returned without laurels or some mark of distinction.

But while other men displayed their courage to win glory for themselves, Marcius's motive was always to please his mother. The delight that she experienced when she saw him crowned, and the tears of joy that she wept as she embraced him – these things were for him the supreme joy and felicity that life could offer. And this, no doubt, was the feeling which Epaminondas wished to express when he said, so the story goes, that he counted it the greatest blessing of his whole career that his father and mother should have lived to hear of his victory at Leuctra. But he was fortunate enough to have had both his parents to rejoice and share in his triumph, whereas Marcius, who believed that he ought to lavish on his mother all the filial affection which would normally have belonged to his father, could never do enough to praise and honour Volumnia. It was his mother's will and choice which dictated his marriage, and he continued to live in the same house with her, even after his wife had borne his children.

5. Marcius's prowess as a soldier had already earned him a great reputation and influence in Rome, when a serious political conflict broke out. The quarrel was between the Senate, which supported the interests of the rich, and the common people, who complained of the many grievous injustices which they had suffered at the hands of the moneylenders. Those who possessed a modest income had their property seized as security or compulsorily sold and suddenly found themselves destitute, while those who had no means at all were arrested and imprisoned, and this was done regardless of the many wounds and hardships they had suffered in the wars fought to defend their country. The last of these campaigns had been against the

Sabines: the people had gone out to fight after their richest creditors had expressly assured them that they would be treated with consideration, and the Senate had passed a decree that this undertaking would be guaranteed by the consul Marcus Valerius. But after they had fought with great courage and defeated the enemy, their creditors showed themselves as remorseless as ever, while the Senate did not even pretend to remember its promises, but again allowed them to be seized as security for their debts and dragged off to prison. It was not long before violent demonstrations and riots began to break out in the city, and the enemy soon took advantage of these disturbances to invade and devastate the countryside: but when the consuls called upon all those who were of military age to take up arms, not a man responded. In this crisis the ruling class were again divided among themselves as to how they should act. Some believed that they ought to make concessions to the poor, and that the state of the law was too strict and ought to be relaxed. Others opposed any leniency of this kind, and one of them was Marcius. He did so not because he attached any great importance to the matter of the people's debts, but rather because he regarded this as an insolent and presumptuous attempt on the part of the commons to overthrow the laws, and he sternly warned the magistrates that if they had any foresight they would put a stop to this threat without further ado.

6. The Senate held a number of meetings within the space of a few days to debate this question, but they failed to reach a decision. Thereupon the people suddenly assembled in a body, and after encouraging each other in their resolution marched out of the city, seized the hill which is now known as the Sacred Mount, and established themselves beside the river Anio.* They did not attempt any violence or revolutionary action, but merely shouted aloud as they marched along that they had long ago been driven out of their own city by the wealthy classes. Any part of Italy, they said, would provide them with air to breathe, water to drink, and a place to lay their bones, and this was all they possessed if they stayed in Rome, except for the privilege of being wounded or dying in wars fought for the protection of the rich. These proceedings frightened the Senate, and they therefore selected from among their older members those who were the most moderate and reasonably disposed towards the people,

* Some three miles outside the walls of Rome.

and sent them out to negotiate. Their chief spokesman was Menenius Agrippa. He began by appealing to the people to come to terms; next he put before them a frank defence of the Senate's position, and he concluded his speech with a well-known fable. Once upon a time, he told them, all the parts of the human body revolted against the belly. They accused it of being the only member which sat idly in its place and contributed nothing to the common good, while the others suffered great hardships and performed great services, all for the sake of keeping its appetites supplied. But the belly only laughed at them for being so simple as not to understand that while it received all the body's nourishment, it also sent it out again and distributed it to every organ. 'So you see, my fellow-citizens,' he went on, 'this is exactly the part that the Senate plays. It is there that the various proposals and affairs of state are studied and transformed into action, and the decisions which we take bring results which are useful and profitable to you all.'

7. In the end they succeeded in resolving their differences, but only after the people had asked and been granted by the Senate the right to elect five men to act as protectors of any citizen who might be in need of help: it is these officers who are now known as the tribunes of the people. The first men to be elected to this office were Junius Brutus and Sicinius Vellutus, who had led the people when they marched out of Rome. Then as soon as the city had been restored to unity, the people immediately hurried to enlist and enthusiastically offered the consuls their services for the war. Marcius was vexed that the people should have won a political victory at the expense of the aristocracy, but when he saw that many of the nobility shared his feelings, he reminded them that they must on no account be outdone in patriotism by the commons. On the contrary, they should prove that their superiority to the people lay in their valour rather than in their political strength.

8. At this time Rome was at war with the Volscian people, and the most important city in their territory was Corioli. Cominius the consul laid siege to it, whereupon the Volscians became alarmed that it might be captured and gathered their forces from all quarters to defend it, their intention being to force a battle in front of the city and then attack the Romans from both sides at once. To counter this

plan Cominius divided his army into two groups. He himself advanced to meet the relieving force, while Titus Lartius, one of the bravest Roman soldiers of that time, was left in charge of the siege operations. The men of Corioli, who now felt contemptuous of the weakness of the besieging force, made a sortie, attacked the Romans, and in the first engagement routed them and chased them back to their entrenchments. At this point Marcius collected a small body of men and hurried to the rescue. He cut down the leading ranks of the enemy, checked their advance, and in a loud voice summoned the Romans to return to the fight. Marcius went into action, as Cato insisted that a soldier should do, not only with a strong sword-arm, but with a powerful voice and a ferocious expression, so that his very appearance struck terror into the enemy and made him an almost irresistible opponent. Many of the Romans now rallied to support him and the enemy fell back in panic. Not content with this, Marcius pressed on and finally drove the men of Corioli in headlong flight up to the very gates of their city. Here he saw the Romans beginning to slacken their pursuit. They had now come within range of a shower of missiles which were being discharged from the walls, and none of them dared to think of mingling with the crowds of fugitives and so forcing their way into the city. But Marcius stood firm and exhorted them to make the attempt, cheering on his companions and shouting out that fortune had now thrown open the city to the pursuers no less than to the pursued. Only a handful of men volunteered to follow him, but putting himself at their head he fought his way through the enemy, rushed the gates, and broke into the city before a single man dared to oppose him. However, when the Volscians saw that only a handful of Romans all told had made their way inside, their courage returned and they attacked the intruders. In the hand to hand fighting that followed, Marcius, finding himself surrounded by a struggling mass in which friend and foe were inextricably intermingled, hewed his way out with a speed, a daring, and a sheer fury of attack which passed all belief. He bore down all resistance before him, so that some of his opponents took refuge in the farthest parts of the city, while others threw down their arms, and finally Lartius was able to lead in his troops without striking a blow.

9. After Corioli had been captured in this way, many of the Roman soldiers fell to looting and pillaging the city. This enraged Marcius

and he declared angrily that it was disgraceful for these soldiers, at the very moment when the consul Cominius and their fellow-citizens might be engaged in a battle with the Volscian army, to be roaming the streets of Corioli looking for plunder or hiding from danger under the pretext of collecting the spoils of war. Only a few paid any attention to his protest, whereupon he gathered together those who were willing to follow him and started out along the road which he had learned Cominius's army had taken. As they marched, he urged on his companions, begged them not to slacken their pace, and offered up prayer after prayer to the gods that they might not be too late for the battle, but arrive in time to share the trials and dangers of their fellow-countrymen.

In those days it was a custom among the Romans, when they were on the point of going into action and were preparing to gird up their tunics and take their shields in their hands, to make at the same time an unwritten will naming their heirs in the presence of three or four witnesses, and this was what Cominius's soldiers were doing when Marcius came up with them. Some of the men were dismayed at first, when they saw him arrive covered with blood and sweat and leading no more than a handful of men. But when he ran up to the consul with a jubilant expression, stretched out his hand, and gave him the news that Corioli had been captured, and when Cominius embraced him and kissed him, the soldiers took courage. Some of them actually heard him speak of the victory, while others guessed what had happened, and finally they all shouted to the consul to lead them into action. Marcius then asked Cominius what was the enemy's order of battle and where their best troops had been stationed. The consul said he believed that the finest and bravest soldiers in the Volscian army were the men of Antium and that they were posted in the centre, whereupon Marcius answered: 'I beg and demand of you to place us opposite them.' The consul was filled with admiration at his spirit and granted his request.

As soon as the armies came within range of each other and spears began to fly, Marcius ran out ahead of the Roman line. The Volscians opposite him could not face his charge, and the Romans broke through at the point where he had attacked. But the troops on either side wheeled inwards and surrounded him with their weapons, so that the consul became alarmed for his safety and despatched some of his personal bodyguard to the rescue. A furious battle raged around

Marcius and men fell thick and fast, but Cominius's troops never slackened the pressure of their attack and finally drove the enemy from the field. When they started in pursuit, they urged Marcius, who by this time was stumbling with fatigue and the pain of his wounds, to retire to the camp. His only reply was that the victor has no business to be weary, and he immediately set off on the heels of the flying enemy. In the end the entire Volscian army suffered a crushing defeat, many were killed, and large numbers taken prisoner.

10. On the following day Lartius's troops joined them and the whole army was paraded before the consul. Cominius then mounted the rostra, and after offering up the thanks that were due to the gods for two such glorious successes, he addressed himself to Marcius. He began by paying tribute to his extraordinary exploits, some of which he had seen for himself in the battle, while the others had been reported to him by Lartius. An enormous quantity of booty as well as prisoners and horses had been captured, and out of these spoils he ordered Marcius to choose a tenth share for himself before anything was distributed to the rest of the army, and over and above all this he presented him with a charger equipped with a splendid harness as a special prize for his valour. The Romans cheered this speech, whereupon Marcius stepped forward and declared that he gladly accepted the horse and was grateful for the consul's words of praise. But he felt that he must decline the other rewards, because they seemed to him to represent not so much an honour as a payment for his services, and so he would be content to take his single share like the rest. 'But there is one special favour,' he went on, 'which I beg may be granted me. There is a friend of mine among the Volscians, whose guest I have been. He is a just and kindly man, but now he has become a prisoner, and so has lost all his wealth and happiness and been reduced to the condition of a slave. He has suffered many misfortunes, but I should like to rescue him from one at least – the fate of being sold into bondage.'

These words were greeted with even louder applause, for there were even more admirers of Marcius's indifference to personal gain than of the courage he had shown on the battlefield. The very men who had felt a certain jealousy towards him on account of the extraordinary honours which he had been paid, now considered that he deserved great rewards for the very reason that he would not accept them, and they were more impressed by the virtue which enabled him to despise such prizes than by the exploits for which he had earned them. For it is a nobler achievement to have mastered the use of wealth than the use of weapons, but it is nobler still to have no need for it.

11. When the cheers which followed Marcius's speech had died down, Cominius spoke again and said: 'Fellow soldiers, we cannot force a man to accept these gifts against his will, but there is another reward which he can scarcely refuse when it is offered him. I propose that we give him this and pass a vote that he shall henceforth be named Coriolanus, although you might think that his gallantry at Corioli had already earned him the title.' This was the origin of his third name, Coriolanus, and the story makes it clear that Gaius was his personal name, that his second name, in this instance Marcius, was the common name of his family or clan, while the third was added afterwards and was given because of some exploit, stroke of fortune, physical peculiarity, or notable virtue. In the same way the Greeks in times past used to give men names that were derived from some action, for example *Soter* (The Deliverer) and *Callinicus* (The Victorious); or from a physical feature, such as *Physcon* (The Bloated) and *Grypus* (The Hook-nosed); or from some outstanding excellence such as *Euergetes* (The Benefactor) or *Philadelphus* (The Brotherly); or from a stroke of good fortune such as *Eudaimon* (The Lucky), the name given to the second king of the dynasty of Battus. On the other hand some of the Greek rulers have had names given them in irony, such as Antigonus *Doson* (The Maker of Promises) and Ptolemy *Lathyrus* (The Vetch). The Romans used surnames of this kind even more frequently. For example one of the Metelli was named *Diadematus* (The Man with a Crown), because he suffered for a long time from a running sore and was always to be seen with a bandage around his forehead. Another member of the Metellus family was named *Celer* (The Swift), because he managed to provide for the people funeral games in which gladiators took part within such a short time after his father's death that the speed and urgency of his preparations were considered extraordinary. To this day some Roman children take their names from the circumstances of their birth. Thus a boy may be called Proculus if he is born while his father is away from home, or Postumus if his father is dead, or, if twins are born of whom one

survives while the other dies, he is called Vopiscus. Again the Romans often give names because of physical peculiarities, and they choose not only such epithets as Sulla (The Pimply), Niger (The Black), and Rufus (The Red) but also Caecus (The Blind) and Claudius (The Lame). And indeed it is a wise practice to accustom men not to regard blindness or any other physical disability as a disgrace or a matter for reproach, but to answer to these names as if they were their own. However this is not the place for me to pursue this subject.

12. The war was no sooner over than the leaders of the popular party began to stir up fresh quarrels. They had no fresh cause for complaint nor any just ground for making accusations, but they exploited the various evils which had inevitably grown out of the earlier disputes and disturbances, and made these their excuse for opposing the aristocratic party. The greater part of the countryside had been left unplanted and untilled, and the war had allowed no opportunity to arrange for supplies to be imported from other territories. The result was a severe shortage of food, and when the popular leaders saw that there were no provisions in the market, and that even if there had been the people had no money to buy them, they spread malicious stories to the effect that the rich had deliberately created the famine to revenge themselves on the people.

At this moment there arrived a delegation from the people of Velitrae, who offered to hand over their city to the Romans and begged them to send out colonists to live in it. They had been attacked by a plague which had ravaged their country so terribly that barely a tenth of the whole population had survived. Those who could consider the matter without prejudice thought that this appeal from the people of Velitrae had come at a most fortunate moment, since the scarcity of food made it necessary to reduce the population at Rome, and at the same time they hoped that this seditious agitation would be broken up if the unruly elements and those who were most easily roused by the popular leaders could be purged away like some unhealthy discharge from the body. Accordingly the consuls selected a number of citizens of this type, who were known to be discontented, and ordered them to go and colonize Velitrae, while others were conscripted for a campaign against the Volscians. The consuls' intention was to keep them too well occupied to create disturbances at home, but they also hoped that when patricians, plebeians, rich and poor alike once more found themselves bearing arms together in the same camp and exerting themselves for the common good, they would learn to show more goodwill and to treat one another with greater tolerance.

13. However, Sicinius and Brutus, the popular leaders, immediately intervened. They protested bitterly that this apparently harmless scheme of sending out a colony was the cover for a most dastardly outrage. In reality the authorities were thrusting these poor citizens into a plague pit by sending them to a city where the air was full of infection and the stench of unburied corpses, and where they would live under the auspices of a strange god who was angry with his own people. And finally, as if the consuls were not satisfied with killing off some of their fellow-citizens by famine and exposing others to plague, they must also plunge the Roman people into a war of their own making: indeed it would seem that they were determined that the city should suffer every possible misfortune merely because it refused to remain enslaved to the rich. These speeches aroused such feelings of indignation among the people that they refused to obey the consuls' orders to enlist and were filled with suspicion against the proposed colony.

The Senate was at a loss what to do, but in the meanwhile Marcius had come to feel that he was a man of importance. He cherished lofty ambitions, and since he knew that he had earned the admiration of some of the most influential men in the state, he openly took the initiative in opposing the popular leaders. Accordingly the colony was sent out, and the men who were chosen by lot to occupy it were forced to go on pain of severe penalties. Finally, when the people flatly refused to take part in the campaign against the Volscians, Marcius organized a force made up of his own clients and as many other men as he could persuade to join him, and launched a raid on the territory of Antium. There he found large stocks of corn and captured great numbers of prisoners and of cattle. He kept none of these spoils for himself, but marched his troops back to Rome laden with booty of every kind. This success quickly produced a change of heart among the rest of the people. They envied their more fortunate fellow-citizens, but were filled with anger against Marcius. They deeply resented the rapid growth of his power and reputation, because they believed that it would be used against the interests of the people.

14. Not long afterwards, however, Marcius stood for the consulship, and then the people relented and reflected what a shame it would be to insult and humiliate a man who had no superior either for the nobility of his birth or for his courage, and who had rendered so many notable services to the state. Now it was the custom at Rome that the candidates for office should address their fellow citizens and appeal to them personally for their votes, and they would walk about in the Forum dressed in a toga, but without a tunic underneath it. They did this in some cases to emphasize their humility by the simplicity of their dress, or else, if they had wounds to show, to display the evidence of their courage. Certainly the people's insistence that their candidates should present themselves ungirt and without a tunic had nothing to do with any suspicion of bribery, for it was not until long afterwards that the abuse of buying and selling votes crept in and money began to play an important part in determining the elections. Later on, however, this process of corruption spread to the law courts and to the army, and finally, when even the sword became enslaved by the power of gold, the republic was subjected to the rule of the emperors. For it has rightly been said that the man who first offers banquets and bribes to the people is the first to destroy their liberties. In Rome this evil seems to have crept in stealthily and gradually, and it was many years before it became apparent. We do not know, for example, who was the first man to bribe the people or the courts of law, whereas at Athens Anytus, the son of Anthemion, has been named as the first man to give money to jurymen. He did this when he was being tried on a charge of treason for his failure to relieve Pylos.* However, this was at a time when the golden age still prevailed at Rome and the Forum was dominated by men of uncorrupted virtue.

15. So when Marcius displayed the scars he bore from the many battles in which for seventeen successive years he had covered himself with glory in the defence of Rome, the people were put to shame by these

* This outpost in the south-western Peloponnese had been captured by the Athenians, successfully fortified and held against all attacks in 425 B.C., early in the Peloponnesian War. The Spartans besieged and recaptured it in 410 B.C. after an Athenian fleet had failed to relieve it.

proofs of his valour and agreed among themselves that they would elect him consul. But when the polling day arrived and Marcius made an ostentatious entry into the Forum escorted with great ceremony by the entire Senate, while the patricians who surrounded him were clearly more determined than ever to secure a victory, the people's momentary feelings of goodwill towards him quickly subsided and their mood changed to one of envy and resentment. These sentiments were strengthened still further by the fear that if a man who wielded so much influence among the patricians and was so intensely aristocratic in his sympathies should ever hold the chief office of state, he might deprive the people of every liberty that they possessed.

For these reasons the people did not vote for Marcius. When the other candidates had been declared elected, the senators were bitterly indignant and felt that it was they rather than Marcius who had been humiliated, while he revealed that he was quite incapable of patience or self-control when faced with a reverse. He had always given free rein to the impulses of pride and aggression in his nature, as if there were some inherent grandeur and nobility in these qualities, and had never allowed himself to be ruled by reason and discipline so as to develop the combination of gravity and tolerance which is so indispensable a virtue for a statesman. He never understood that a man who aspires to play a part in public affairs must avoid above all things that tendency to self-assertion which is, in Plato's phrase, the companion of solitude, but rather must mingle with men, and even cultivate the capacity to submit to injury, which some people so contemptuously deride. Marcius, on the other hand, was as artless as he was obstinate, and believed that it is under all circumstances a brave man's duty to bear down and overwhelm all opposition: it never occurred to him that it might be a sign of weakness to be unable to restrain the anger which bursts out like an abscess from the wounded and suffering spirit, and so he went away full of indignation and rancour towards the people. The younger patricians, that section of the community which was most conscious of the nobility of its birth and most ostentatious in flaunting it, had always been fanatically devoted to Marcius and they now rallied to his support, although in a manner that did him no good, since their expressions of sympathy and indignation served only to make his resentment more bitter. They had long regarded him as their leader, and while on active service they had found him a most congenial instructor in the art of war, since he inspired them to vie with one another in acts of courage, and to rejoice in their successes without envying those of others.

16. Meanwhile a large consignment of grain arrived in Rome. Much of this had been purchased in Italy, but an equal amount had been sent as a gift by Gelo, the tyrant of Syracuse. The people were greatly encouraged, as they hoped that this windfall would put an end not only to the scarcity of food but also to the quarrel between patricians and plebeians. The Senate was promptly assembled, and the people waited eagerly outside the doors to hear the result of the debate. They expected that the price of grain would now fall to a reasonable figure and that the gift to the state would be distributed free of charge, and indeed this was the course recommended by a number of the senators. But when Marcius rose to speak, he violently attacked those who upheld the people's interests and denounced them as demagogues and traitors to the aristocracy. He argued that they were fostering to their own ultimate peril the pernicious seeds of insolence and insubordination which had been sown among the masses. They should never have allowed these to take root in the first place, and above all they should never have conceded to the people such a powerful magistracy as the tribunate. As it was, the masses had now become formidable. Every demand which they put forward was granted, and no decision was ever imposed upon them against their will: they defied the authority of the consuls and were governed only by their own champions of misrule whom they dignified by the title of rulers. So for the Senate to sit there and decree bounties and free distributions of grain for the whole population, just as they do in Greece, where the will of the people is apparently supreme, would amount to nothing less than to support them in their defiance of the constitution and would bring about the ruin of the whole state. 'The people will not regard these concessions,' he went on, 'as a reward for the campaigns in which they refused to serve, nor for the secessions whereby they betrayed their country, nor for the slanders against the Senate which they have been so ready to believe. The conclusion they will certainly draw is that you are handing out these doles and gratuities because you are afraid of them and want to flatter them, and you will then find that there will be no limits to their disobedience nor to the disputes and agitations they will stir up. In short, to take the step which you propose would be sheer madness: what we should do, if we have any sense,

is to abolish the office of tribune outright, since its only effect is to undermine the authority of the consuls and cause dissension in the city. The truth is that Rome is no longer a single commonwealth as once it was. It has been broken in two, and I do not believe that the two parts will ever knit again, or become of one mind, or cease to inflame and torment one another.'

17. These arguments and others in the same strain had a powerful effect upon the younger senators, so that Marcius succeeded to an extraordinary degree in inspiring them with his own passionate convictions. He also had most of the richest men on his side, and finally his supporters all cried out that he was the only man in Rome who would never be influenced either by the threat of force or the desire to flatter. In spite of this, however, some of the older senators opposed him, because they could foresee where his policy might lead them. And it led, in fact, straight to disaster. For the tribunes had been present at the debate, and as soon as they saw that Marcius's motion was likely to be carried, they rushed out and joined the crowd, shouting out loudly and calling upon the people to rally at once and stand by their own magistrates. There followed a stormy meeting of the Assembly, and when Marcius's words were repeated in public the people were so carried away with fury that their first impulse was to break into the Senate-house. However, the tribunes concentrated their attack on Marcius by laying a formal accusation against him, and he was then summoned by messenger to appear before the people and defend himself. When he contemptuously dismissed the officials who served this summons, the tribunes themselves went, accompanied by the aediles, to bring him by force and began to lay hands on his person. Thereupon the patricians crowded round him, forced back the tribunes, and actually struck the aediles.

By this time nightfall put an end to the general tumult, but as soon as it was day the angry populace began to hurry in from all directions and gather in the Forum. When the consuls saw this they became seriously alarmed for the city's safety. They summoned a meeting of the Senate and urged them to consider what sympathetic proposals and conciliatory resolutions they could put forward to appease and pacify the people. They appealed to the House to remember that this was no time for standing on their dignity or for a jealous assertion of their rights, but that they were facing a moment of great crisis in the affairs of Rome, which demanded a policy of moderation and humanity. The majority of the senators accepted this advice, whereupon the consuls went out and did their best to reason with the people and calm their indignation, answering dispassionately the charges which had been brought against the Senate and rebuking the people for their own violence only in the mildest terms. On the question of the price of corn and the way in which it should be supplied, they declared that there would no longer be any cause for dispute.

18. At this news the majority of the people allowed their anger to subside, and to judge from the serious and orderly attention with which they listened, they were well on the way to being won over. The tribunes then rose and announced that since the Senate was now acting with such moderation, the people were prepared in their turn to make any reasonable concessions. They insisted, however, that Marcius should answer the following charges: could he deny that he had incited the Senate to set aside the constitution and abolish the privileges of the people? Had he not refused to obey the people's order that he should appear before them? And finally had he not insulted and beaten the aediles in the Forum, and thereby done everything in his power to bring about a civil war by provoking his fellow-citizens to resort to arms? In making this demand they had two objects in mind. If Marcius were to curb his haughty temper, which would be quite contrary to his nature, and throw himself upon the people's mercy, he would be publicly humiliated: if on the other hand he followed his normal instincts, he would do something which would make the breach irreparable. It was the second eventuality which they hoped for, and they had correctly judged their opponent's character.

Marcius came and stood before the people as if he intended to offer a defence of his conduct, and his hearers listened to him in dead silence. But instead of the apologetic language which they had expected, he began to speak with an offensive bluntness, which soon developed into an outright attack upon the commons. At the same time both the tone of his voice and the expression on his face conveyed a fearlessness which betokened a total disdain and contempt for his audience, and at this the people lost all patience and began to show their mounting indignation and anger at his words. Thereupon Sicinius, the most outspoken of the tribunes, after conferring for a few moments with his colleagues, formally proclaimed that the tribunes of the people had condemned Marcius to death, and he ordered the aediles to take him immediately to the top of the Tarpeian rock and throw him over the precipice. But when the aediles came to lay hands on him, many people even among the plebeians felt that this was a terrible and outrageous act, while the patricians, who were beside themselves with grief and horror, hurried to the rescue, crying out loudly as they ran. Some of them thrust away the officers who were arresting him and got Marcius into their midst: others stretched out their hands, since words or cries were lost amid the general tumult, to implore the people to show mercy. Before long the friends and relatives of the tribunes saw that it would be impossible to carry out his punishment, unless they were prepared to kill large numbers of patricians. They therefore persuaded the tribunes to revoke the cruel and unprecedented penalty which their sentence carried and not to use violence or put Marcius to death without a trial, but to hand him over and let his case be decided by the vote of the people. After this Sicinius, adopting a calmer tone, asked the patricians what they meant by snatching Marcius away from the people when a resolution had been passed to punish him. The patricians countered by asking, 'What do you mean by dragging away one of the foremost men in Rome without a trial, to execute a barbarous and illegal sentence?' 'Well, on that score at least you will have no cause for complaint or grievance against the people,' retorted Sicinius, 'they agree to your request that the man should have his trial. As for you, Marcius, you are summoned to appear on the third market day from now to satisfy the citizens of your innocence, if you can, and they will then judge your case by vote.'

19. The patricians were content to accept this solution for the moment and returned to their homes with a feeling of satisfaction, taking Marcius with them. But during the period which elapsed before the third market day – which the Romans hold every ninth day and so call *nundinae* – an expedition was sent against the city of Antium, and this encouraged them to hope that the trial might never take place after all. They calculated that the campaign might last long enough for the people to become amenable, and that their anger might be appeased or subside altogether once their minds were taken up by the war. However, a settlement was soon reached with the people

of Antium and the citizens returned home. The patricians were now filled with alarm and held frequent meetings to discuss how they could avoid surrendering Marcius without at the same time giving the popular leaders the excuse to stir up new disorders. Appius Claudius, who was generally regarded as one of the bitterest opponents of the popular cause in Rome, solemnly declared that the Senate would not only destroy itself but would utterly betray its duty to the state if it allowed the people to use their voting powers to pass judgment on patricians. On the other hand, the older senators and those most sympathetic to the claims of the people contended that they would not use this power harshly or severely, but would show their moderation and humanity once it was granted them. They considered that it was not a question of the people's despising the Senate, but of believing that they were despised by it, and hence that they would feel themselves so much honoured and compensated by the privilege of being able to try a senator, that they would lay aside their resentment as soon as this prerogative came into their hands.

20. Accordingly when Marcius saw that the Senate was torn between its regard for himself and its fear of the people, he asked the tribunes what were the terms of the accusation against him, and on what charge he would be tried if they brought him before the people. They told him that he was to be charged with usurpation of the authority of the republic, and that they would prove him guilty of attempting to set himself up as an absolute ruler in Rome. At this he rose to his feet and declared that he would immediately appear before the people to defend himself on that score, that he offered himself freely to any form of trial, and that if convicted he would submit to any form of punishment. 'But,' he went on, 'be sure that you confine yourselves to the charge you have mentioned, and do not go back on your word to the Senate.' The tribunes agreed and it was upon these conditions that the trial took place.

But when the people assembled, the tribunes' first move was to insist that the votes should be cast not by centuries* but by tribes.

* The Assembly by centuries (*comitia centuriata*), the traditional method of voting in the early republic, was essentially a military grouping of the people, and, since it was based on property qualifications, weighted in favour of the upper classes. A majority within each century counted as a single block vote; there was a total of 193 centuries, of which the knights and the five highest property ratings comprised 98 – a clear majority.

By this manoeuvre they ensured that the well-to-do and reputable citizens who served the state in its wars would be outnumbered by the poorest classes, who cared nothing for considerations of honour, but liked to meddle in politics. Secondly, they ignored the charge of usurpation, which was impossible to prove, and repeated their attack upon the speech which Marcius had made in the Senate, when he had opposed the reduction of the price of grain and urged that the tribunate should be abolished. But they also introduced a new charge into the indictment, which concerned the distribution of the spoils captured at Antium. They alleged that Marcius had not paid into the public treasury the money raised from the sale of the plunder, but had divided it among the volunteers who had taken part in the operation with him. It was this accusation which disconcerted Marcius more than any other. He had never expected it, and for the moment was completely at a loss for a reply which would convince the people. Instead he began to praise the soldiers who had fought in the campaign, but this served only to provoke an uproar among those citizens who had not, and who were far more numerous. Finally when the people came to vote he was condemned by a majority of three tribes and was sentenced to perpetual banishment.

The news of Marcius's condemnation was greeted with an outburst of public rejoicing such as had never been witnessed even for a victory over a foreign enemy, and the people departed to their homes in a mood of triumph, while the senators were correspondingly downcast and despondent. They bitterly regretted that they had not done everything in their power to oppose the trial, whatever the consequences, rather than allow the people to assume such authority and then abuse it so outrageously. At this moment there was no need for any of the privileges of dress or other signs of rank to distinguish the two classes: it was clear at once that the exultant look belonged to the plebeians and the downcast to the patricians.

21. The only exception was Marcius himself, who was neither dismayed nor humbled by the news. In his outward appearance, demeanour, and expression he appeared to be the only man among all the patricians upon whom his misfortunes made no impression. But this apparent composure was based neither upon logic, equanimity, nor any intention of enduring his fate meekly. It was the product of a concentrated fury and indignation, which, although this is not

generally understood, is really an expression of intense pain. For when grief turns to anger, it is devoured, so to speak, by the flame which it generates, and any notion of humility or passive acceptance is utterly cast out. And so, just as a sick man seems to burn with fever, so the angry man seems to be full of energy, because he is suffering from a kind of inflammation, a swelling, and a throbbing of the spirit. This was Marcius's state of mind, as was soon made apparent by his behaviour.

His first action was to go home, where his mother and his wife greeted him with tears and lamentations. He took them in his arms, told them that they must bear this blow of fate with patience, and, without any further delay, set off for the city gates. Although the entire body of patricians turned out to escort him, Marcius took no possessions with him into exile, nor did he utter a single request, but merely walked out of the city accompanied by three or four of his clients. For a few days he stayed alone at a country estate, while a host of conflicting impulses crowded into his brain, urged on by his anger: none of these was inspired by any praiseworthy or constructive purpose, but simply by the desire to revenge himself on the Roman people. Finally he decided to incite one of the neighbouring countries to wage a destructive war against them, and the people whom he chose to approach first were the Volscians. He knew that they had great resources both in money and in fighting men, and he was confident that the recent defeats they had suffered had not so much weakened their power as increased their hostility, and made them long to renew their quarrel with the Romans.

22. There was at Antium a man named Tullus Aufidius, who because of his wealth, his courage, and his noble birth enjoyed the position and respect almost of a king among the Volscian people. Marcius knew that this man hated him more bitterly than any other Roman. They had often hurled threats and challenges at one another in the battles they had fought, and out of the rivalry and boasting which ambition often provokes among young warriors, a private and personal animosity had grown up between them, which went far beyond the hostility that prevailed between their respective peoples. At the same time Marcius sensed that Tullus possessed a certain magnanimity, and also that there was no other Volscian who was so passionately determined to revenge himself on the Romans: in short

Marcius acted as a living illustration of that famous saying of Heracleitus, 'It is hard to fight with anger, for whatever it wants, it will pay the price, even at the cost of life itself.' So Marcius dressed himself in clothes which completely transformed his normal appearance, and like Odysseus,

Into the enemy's city he stole disguised . . . .*

23. It was evening when he arrived in the town, and although many people passed him in the streets, none of them recognized him. When he had found his way to Tullus's house, he quickly entered, took his place by the hearth† in silence, and covering his head seated himself there without uttering a word. The people of the house were astonished at his behaviour but did not venture to disturb him – for there was an air almost of majesty about his bearing and his silence – but they told Tullus, who was at supper, of this mysterious event. Tullus rose from the table, walked over to the stranger, and asked who he was and why he had come. At this Marcius uncovered his face and after a moment's pause, he said: 'If you do not recognize me even now, Tullus, or if you cannot believe your own eyes, then I must act as my own accuser. I am Gaius Marcius, the man who has done you and the Volscian people more harm than any other, and the name of Coriolanus which I bear makes it impossible to deny the fact. This title is the one and only reward I have received for all the toils and perils I have endured, and it is a badge of my enmity to your country. This at least can never be taken away, but everything else has been stripped from me by the jealousy and insolence of the people, and the cowardice and treachery of the magistrates and the members of my own class. I have been driven out of Rome as an exile, and now I sit as a suppliant at your hearth. But I have not come to ask for safety nor protection – for why should I have risked my life in Antium if I were afraid to die – but to take revenge on the men who have banished me, and already I have made a beginning by putting myself in your hands. My brave Tullus, if you are eager to fight your enemies again, take advantage of my disgrace, and make my misfortune the Volscian people's good fortune. I shall fight even better

* *Odyssey* IV, 246.

† The hearth was considered sacred, since it housed the domestic gods, and it was here that a suppliant naturally sought asylum.

for you than I have fought against you, because the most dangerous opponents of all are those who know their enemies' secrets. But if you are tired of war, I have no desire to live, nor will there be any advantage in saving the life of a man who has for so long been your implacable enemy, but who now, when he offers you his services, turns out to be useless to you.'

When Tullus heard these words he was overjoyed, and giving him his right hand, he said: 'Rise up, Marcius, and take courage. In coming here you have brought us a great gift, and you may rest assured the Volscians will not be ungrateful.' Then he entertained Marcius at his table with every mark of kindness, and they spent the next few days discussing plans for the coming war.

24. Meanwhile Rome was in a state of turmoil. Marcius's banishment had done much to arouse a feeling of hatred for the people among the patricians, and at the same time soothsayers, priests, and private individuals all reported a succession of prodigies which were too significant to ignore. One of them was as follows. There was a certain Titus Latinus, not a prominent citizen, but a quiet and sensible man, who was by no means addicted to superstition nor to pretentious exaggeration of his experiences. He had a dream in which Jupiter appeared to him and commanded him to tell the Senate that the dancer whom they had chosen to lead the god's procession was a bad performer and thoroughly displeasing to him. Titus reported that the first time he saw this vision he paid little attention to it. Since then it had appeared to him a second and third time, and still he had taken no action. But not long after he had seen his son, a boy of great promise, sicken and die, and he himself had lost the use of his limbs. He related these events to the Senate after he had been brought there in a litter, and no sooner had he spoken, it is said, than he felt the strength returning to his body, and he rose to his feet and walked away without any help.

The senators were astonished at his story and made an inquiry into the circumstances. They discovered that a certain householder had handed over one of his servants to his fellow-slaves with orders that he should be flogged through the market-place and then put to death. While they were carrying out this punishment and were torturing the wretched man, whose pain made him writhe and twist his body into all kinds of hideous contortions, it so happened that the sacred procession in honour of Jupiter came up behind. Many of those who took part in it were roused to indignation by this inhuman spectacle and the agonized movements of the victim, but nobody came to his rescue: all they did was to utter reproaches and abuse against a master who could inflict such a cruel punishment. In those days the Romans in general treated their slaves with great kindness; the masters worked and even took their meals side by side with them, and because they knew them so well, were more considerate towards them. For example, if a slave had committed a fault, it was considered a severe punishment for him to be made to take up the piece of wood which supports the pole of a wagon and carry it round the neighbourhood. Any slave who was seen undergoing this punishment was disgraced and was no longer trusted either in his own or the neighbouring households. Henceforward he was known as a *furcifer*, for what the Greeks call a prop or support, is rendered in Latin by the word *furca*.

25. So when Latinus described his dream to the senators, and they were completely at a loss to identify this bad or unpleasing dancer who had headed the procession, some of them, because of the unusual nature of the punishment, remembered the slave who had been flogged through the Forum and afterwards executed. Accordingly, after the agreement of the priests had been obtained, the slave's master was punished, and the procession and the public ceremonies in honour of the god were enacted a second time.

This incident illustrates the foresight of Numa, who in general showed the greatest wisdom in specifying the correct procedure for religious ceremonies, and who very properly laid down the following regulation to ensure the people's reverent attention. Whenever the magistrates or priests perform any religious function, a herald goes before them crying out in a loud voice '*Hoc age*'. The phrase means 'Mind this', and it is intended to remind the people to give their whole attention to the sacred rites and not to allow any pressure of business or worldly preoccupations to disturb them, the implication being that men's attention is seldom fixed, and most of their duties are, in a sense, extorted from them and effected under constraint. The Romans are also well accustomed to repeating sacrifices and processions, not only for the kind of reason I have described, but on far more trivial grounds. For example, if one of the horses which pull the sacred vehicles (which are known as *tensae**) should become exhausted and stumble, or if the charioteer should take hold of the reins with his left hand, they decree that the procession must begin again. And at later periods of their history they have been known to perform a single sacrifice thirty times over, because some omission or mistake was believed to have taken place. Such is the piety and reverence of the Roman people in religious matters.

26. All this while Marcius and Tullus were secretly conferring with the leading men of Antium, and urging them to go to war with Rome while the city was still torn by party strife. At first the Volscians' sense of honour restrained them from seizing this advantage, because they had only recently concluded a truce and accepted a cessation of hostilities for two years. But then the Romans themselves provided a pretext by issuing at the public games a proclamation – prompted apparently by some suspicion or slanderous report – to the effect that all Volscians must leave the city before sunset. Some authorities† maintain that Marcius himself tricked the Romans into this action by sending a man to the consuls in Rome to plant the false rumour that the Volscians had laid a plot to attack the Romans during the public games and set fire to the city. At any rate this proclamation made the Volscian people more hostile than ever towards the Romans. Tullus did his utmost to magnify the incident and stir up the people's anger, and finally he persuaded them to send ambassadors to Rome with the demand that the territory and the cities annexed from the Volscians in the late war should be restored to them. When they heard these proposals the Romans became angry in their turn, and retorted that the Volscians might be the first to take up arms, but the Romans would be the last to lay them down. Thereupon Tullus summoned a general assembly, and after the people had voted for war, he advised them to call in the help of Marcius. He urged them not to bear him any grudge for the harm he had done them, but to rest assured that he would be even more valuable as an ally than he had been deadly as an enemy.

* A kind of litter used for conveying the images of the gods to the Circus.

† Dionysius of Halicarnassus, VIII, 3. In the essay in which Coriolanus is compared with his parallel, Alcibiades, Plutarch himself seems to accept this charge.

27. Accordingly Marcius was summoned and proceeded to address the people. His speech demonstrated that he was just as formidable an orator as his exploits had already proved him to be a soldier, and convinced them that in the art of war his intelligence was no less remarkable than his courage. They therefore appointed him joint commander with Tullus and gave him full powers to conduct the campaign. But as he feared that the Volscians would take so long to mobilize and equip themselves that he would lose the most favourable moment to attack, he left instructions for the magistrates and other principal citizens to raise troops and collect supplies. Meanwhile, without waiting for the formalities of enlistment, he recruited a band of volunteers from among the most adventurous spirits and made a sudden raid upon Roman territory. He achieved complete surprise and secured so much plunder that the Volscians could neither use it up in their camp nor carry it away with them. However to Coriolanus the quantity of supplies which he captured and the damage or destruction which he inflicted upon the enemy's territory were the least important results of the expedition: its principal consequence, and indeed his main purpose in undertaking it, was to blacken the reputation of the patricians in the eyes of the Roman people. For while he despoiled and devastated all other properties, he took the strictest precautions to guard the estates of the nobles, and would allow no damage to be done nor anything to be carried away from them. This led to bitter recriminations and clashes between the rival factions in the capital: the patricians accused the people of having unjustly banished a man of great ability, while the people retorted with the charge that their opponents were trying to get their revenge by encouraging Marcius to attack his own country, and were now revelling in the spectacle of others being made to suffer from the enemy's depredations, while their own property and sources of wealth outside the city were left completely untouched. After Marcius had achieved his purpose of sowing fresh dissensions among the Romans, and at the same time greatly increased the confidence of the Volscians and taught them to despise their enemies, he brought his troops safely back to their base.

28. Meanwhile the Volscians had mobilized their entire strength with great speed and enthusiasm. The army they had raised turned out to be so large that they decided to leave some of the troops to

garrison their cities, while the main body marched against the Romans. Marcius now left Tullus to decide which of these armies he wished to command. Tullus's reply was that as Marcius was clearly as brave a man as himself and had always enjoyed better fortune in his battles, he should lead the army that was to take the field, while Tullus remained behind to guard the Volscian cities and provide the supplies for the fighting troops. So Marcius, this time with a larger force under his command, opened his campaign by attacking Circeii, a town which was a colony of Rome. Here the people surrendered without resistance and he did them no harm. He then proceeded to ravage the region of Latium, as he expected that the Romans would risk a battle to defend the Latins, who were their allies and had despatched a succession of envoys imploring their help. But at Rome the people showed no desire to fight, the consuls were reluctant to risk a campaign during the few weeks which remained of their term of office, and so the Latins' appeal was dismissed. Marcius then led his troops against the various Latin cities. Those which offered resistance, namely Tolerium, Lavicum, Pedum, and, later on, Bola, he captured by assault, enslaved their inhabitants, and plundered their property. But he showed great consideration for the cities which came over to his side of their own accord, and to make sure that his troops inflicted no damage upon them against his orders, he pitched his camp at a distance from them and kept away from their territory.

29. When he finally captured the town of Bola, which is no more than twelve miles from Rome, great quantities of treasure fell into his hands, and he put almost the whole adult population to the sword. After this success, even the Volscians who had been detailed to garrison their own cities refused to remain any longer at their posts, seized their arms, and flocked to join Marcius, declaring that he was their only general and that they would recognize no other commander. His name and fame spread throughout the whole of Italy, and people asked one another with amazement how the valour of a single man could, by the mere act of changing sides, bring about such an extraordinary transformation in the fortunes of two peoples.

Meanwhile, in Rome, affairs were in utter disorder. The people refused to fight and spent all their time in devising party intrigues, making seditious speeches, and blaming one another, until the news came that the enemy had besieged Lavinium. It was here that the sacred relics of the ancestral gods of the Romans were stored, and it was indeed the birthplace of the Roman nation, being the first city ever founded by Aeneas. The news produced a complete and astonishing change of heart among the people, and an equally remarkable and unexpected one among the patricians. The people were now anxious to revoke the sentence of banishment against Marcius and invite him to return, but the Senate, after they had met and debated this proposal, decided to reject it. It is possible that they were determined out of sheer spite to oppose any measure which the people put forward, or that they did not wish Marcius to owe his recall to the people's favour. Or it may have been that their anger had turned against Marcius himself, because he had now proved that he was the enemy of every class, in spite of the fact that he had been injured only by one, and was well aware that the most powerful and influential men in Rome sympathized and had suffered with him. When this resolution was made known to the people, they were helpless to proceed further, since they had no power to enact a law without a previous decree of the Senate.

30. The news of the Senate's actions served only to make Marcius more resentful than ever. In his anger he immediately raised the siege of Lavinium, marched upon Rome, and pitched his camp at the so-called Fossae Cluiliae, which are only five miles outside the city. Although the sight of his army spread dismay and panic among the citizens, it at least put an end to their quarrels, since nobody, whether consul or senator, dared to oppose the people's desire to recall Marcius. On the contrary, when the Romans saw their womenfolk running distractedly through the streets and the old men prostrating themselves as they wept and prayed before the shrines of the gods, and knew that there was not a man in the city who was capable of inspiring them with courage or devising a plan of defence, then everybody agreed that the people had been right to attempt a reconciliation with Marcius, and the Senate utterly wrong to give vent to its anger and its memories of past wrongs at the very moment when it would have been wise to put such emotions aside. Accordingly it was unanimously resolved to send a delegation to Marcius to offer him the right to return to his country and implore him to put an end to the war. The men whom the Senate chose to make this appeal were all connected with Marcius either as friends or as

kinsmen, and they expected at their first interview to be warmly welcomed by a man whom they knew well or who was at least a relative. Nothing of the kind happened. After being led through the enemy's camp, they were brought before Coriolanus, who was seated in high state surrounded by the leading men of the Volscians, and who greeted them with an intolerably stern and arrogant expression. He then ordered them to explain the purpose of their visit, which they did in courteous and reasonable language and in a suitably conciliatory manner. When they had finished, he answered them harshly. He began by pouring out his bitter resentment at the injustices he had suffered: then in his capacity as commander of the Volscians he demanded that the Romans should restore the cities and the territory which they had annexed in the recent war, and at the same time pass a decree granting the Volscians the same civil rights as had recently been conceded to the Latins. Finally he told them that there could be no lasting peace between the two nations unless it were based upon just and equal rights. He gave them thirty days to consider these terms, and as soon as the envoys had departed he withdrew his troops from Roman territory.

31. There were a number of the Volscians, who had for some time envied his success and felt uneasy at the influence he had acquired, and this action provided them with their first opportunity to attack him. Among these was Tullus, not because he had been personally wronged in any way by Marcius, but because, being only human, he was angry to find his reputation totally eclipsed and himself ignored by the Volscians, who now felt that Marcius was everything to them, and that the other leaders ought to be thankful for whatever measure of power and authority he allowed them to share. It was in this way that the first seeds of complaint and denunciation were scattered in secret, and Marcius's opponents began to meet and compare their grievances. They called his withdrawal from Roman territory an act of treachery, not because he had betrayed cities or armies, but because he had thrown away an opportunity, which is the deciding factor as to whether these or any other prizes are won or lost. The fact was that he had given the Romans a breathing-space of thirty days, and in war it is always possible for a decisive change to take place in a far shorter time.

However, during this month of suspense Marcius was anything

but idle. He attacked the Romans' allies, raided and devastated their territories, and captured seven of their largest and most populous cities. All this while the Romans never ventured to send help to their friends. Their spirits were cowed, and they showed so little inclination for the war that you might have thought their limbs were paralysed or benumbed. When the thirty days had expired and Marcius appeared for the second time before Rome with his whole army, they sent another delegation to implore him to relent, withdraw the Volscian troops from their territory, and then put forward whatever terms he thought best for both parties. The Romans would not give way out of fear, but if he considered that certain concessions ought to be made to the Volscians, all these would be granted if they laid down their arms. Marcius's reply was that as commander of the Volscians he could not discuss this offer, but that as a man who was still a citizen of Rome, he strongly advised them to put themselves into a humbler frame of mind, reconsider what justice required of them, and come back in three days' time with a ratification of his original demands. If they should decide otherwise, they must know that it would not be safe for them to enter his camp again with nothing but empty phrases.

32. When this delegation had returned to Rome and made its report to the Senate, it was plain to all that the ship of state was being tossed on the billows of a fearful tempest, and since the waves seemed about to overwhelm it, it was decided to let go the sheet anchor. A decree was passed that the whole order of priests, the celebrants or custodians of the sacred mysteries, and those who practised the ancient and ancestral art of divination from the flight of birds, should go in procession to Marcius, all of them dressed in the vestments used for the performance of their various functions, and should solemnly entreat him in the same manner as before to declare a truce and then discuss with his own countrymen what terms should be offered to the Volscians. Marcius went so far as to admit this deputation to his camp, but this was the limit of his tolerance. He spoke and behaved to them as harshly as before and curtly reminded them that the Romans must either offer a settlement which complied with his original terms, or else resign themselves to war.

When the priests returned, the Romans decided that they would remain quietly inside their city, doing no more than guarding the walls and repelling the enemy if they attempted an assault. They resolved to put their trust above all in time and the accidents of fortune, since they could see no means of saving themselves by their own efforts. The city was full of confusion, terror, and rumours of disaster, until at last something happened which resembled one of those incidents such as Homer often describes, although people are usually unwilling to believe them. When some great and unusual action is about to take place, the poet declares in his lofty manner:

> Then in his mind the grey-eyed Athene planted this notion*

or again

> Then some immortal changed his resolve by making him ponder†
> The thought of what men might say

or again

> Either because he suspected, or the god enjoined him to act‡

People are apt to despise Homer, and to think that by introducing miraculous exploits and fantastic tales he makes it impossible to believe in the power of men to decide their course of action. But the truth is that Homer does nothing of the kind, for whenever an action is natural, normal, and the result of deliberation, he attributes this to our own powers, as we see in the phrase which he often uses

> Then I took counsel within my stout heart. . . .§

or again

> Such were his words, and Peleus's son was sorely afflicted,||
> So that within his rough breast two counsels strove for decision

or again

> . . . but she could never¶
> Lure the noble Bellérophon out of his upright resolve.

On the other hand, when he wishes to describe some prodigious or extraordinary exploit, whose accomplishment demands an element of supernatural possession or a sudden rush of heroic courage, Homer

* *Odyssey* XVIII, 158.
† Not identifiable in Homer.
‡ *Odyssey* IX, 339.
§ *Odyssey* IX, 299.
|| *Iliad* I, 188–9.
¶ *Iliad* VI, 161–2.

does not represent the god as depriving a man of his choice of action, but rather as guiding it, or, on other occasions, not as implanting the impulse itself but rather the idea which inspires the impulse. Thus he does not suggest that the deed is involuntary, but rather that the hero's will is set in motion, while courage and hope are added to strengthen it. And indeed, unless we are to rule out completely the idea that the gods can initiate or influence our actions, in what other way can they give us their help or support? They certainly do not manipulate our bodies or control the movements of our hands or feet. Instead, they make us aware of motives, or present images to the imagination, or thoughts to the mind, and in this way they either arouse the powers of decision and action in our natures, or else restrain or divert them.

33. During these days of crisis in Rome various groups of women went to all the temples in the city, but the greatest number and the most nobly born offered up their prayers at the shrine of Jupiter Capitolinus. One of these was Valeria, a sister of the great Publicola, who had rendered the state such immense services, both in war and in political life. Publicola had died some years before, as I have mentioned, but Valeria was still living and enjoyed great honour and respect in Rome, since her life was seen to be in every way worthy of her noble birth. This woman, then, suddenly experienced one of those intuitions such as I have described, and recognizing with an insight which must surely have been divinely inspired what would be the best course, rose from her knees and called upon the other women to accompany her to the house of Marcius's mother, Volumnia. She entered, and when she saw Volumnia sitting with her daughter-in-law Vergilia, holding Marcius's children on her lap, she called her companions round her and said: 'Volumnia and Vergilia, we have come to you as women to women, not because we have been ordered here by the Senate or the consuls, but because our god, as I believe, has listened to our prayers and put into our hearts the inspiration that we should turn to you. We are here to implore you to attempt something which will not only be the salvation of ourselves and the whole Roman people, but which will bring you, if you agree, a greater glory than was earned even by the daughters of the Sabines, when they converted their fathers and their husbands from mortal enmity to friendship and peace. Come now, and go

along with us to Marcius: join us in entreating him to show compassion, and help us to bear this true and just testimony for your country, that although she has suffered great wrongs from him, she has never, even in her anger, done or thought of doing harm to you, but restores you safe into his hands, even though he may grant her no better terms on that account.'

When Valeria had finished speaking, the other women added their voices to hers in appealing to Volumnia, who then answered as follows: 'My friends, we share with you the misfortune which has come upon the whole Roman people, but we have another of our own. We have lost the glory and the virtue which Marcius once possessed, and we are forced to see him as a man who is imprisoned rather than protected by the arms of our enemies. And yet the greatest misfortune of all is that Rome has grown so weak that she must rest her hopes of safety upon us. I do not know whether Marcius will show any regard for us, since he has none for his country, which he once loved better than his mother, his wife, and his children. But in any case take us, make what use of us you can, and lead us to him. If we can do nothing else, we can die offering up our prayers for our country.'

34. With this she took Marcius's children and Vergilia, and set out with the other women for the Volscian camp. They were a pitiful sight, and even the enemy greeted them with a respectful silence. It so happened that at that moment Marcius was seated on a tribunal with his chief officers around him. When he first caught sight of the procession of women approaching, he was filled with amazement. Then he recognized his mother walking at their head, and although he struggled hard to maintain his remorseless and inflexible resolve, he found himself overcome by his feelings. He could not bear to receive the women sitting, but jumped down from the tribunal and ran to meet them. He greeted his mother first and clasped her for a long while in his arms, and then when he embraced his wife and children he could hold back neither his tears nor his affection any longer, but allowed himself to be swept away by a flood of emotion.

35. When he had thus relieved his pent-up feelings and understood that his mother wished to tell him something, he called together

the Volscian leaders and they heard Volumnia speak as follows: 'My son, even if we were to say nothing, the wretchedness of our dress and our appearance should make you understand in what misery we have lived at home, ever since you were banished. But now you must know that we who have come to you here are the unhappiest women alive, for Fate has made that sight which should have been the most joyful into the most terrible of all, when Volumnia is compelled to see her son and Vergilia her husband turning his arms against the walls of his native city. And even to pray to the gods, which others may find a comfort in their misfortunes, has become impossible for us, since we cannot ask them in the same breath to make our country victorious and to keep you safe. When we pray for you, we are calling down a curse upon Rome, such as the bitterest of her enemies could desire, and your wife and children are compelled to sacrifice either their native land or yourself. As for me, I shall not wait for the war to decide this issue for me. If I cannot prevail upon you to prefer friendship and harmony to enmity and strife, and thus become the benefactor of both countries rather than the scourge of one of them, then you must know – and let there be no doubt of this – that you shall never attack Rome unless you trample first upon the dead body of the mother who bore you. I do not choose to wait for the day when I shall be forced to watch my son either led in triumph by his fellow-citizens or triumphing over them. If I were to ask you to save your country by ruining the Volscians, then I admit, my son, that you would be faced with a cruel choice, since it is neither honourable for a man to destroy his fellow-citizens, nor just to betray those who have trusted him. But as it is, all we ask is to be delivered from the disaster that threatens us. If this is done, it will prove the salvation of both nations, but it will bring more honour and glory to the Volscians. They have shown themselves the superior in arms, and this fact puts them in the position of being the givers of the two greatest blessings, peace and friendship, while they themselves will receive no less. If this happy issue comes to pass, you will have done more than any man to bring it about; if not, you alone will bear the blame from both sides. And although the chances of war are always uncertain, this much is sure: if you conquer Rome, you will be your country's evil genius, but if you are defeated, the world will say that to satisfy your revenge, you did not hesitate to bring disaster upon your friends and benefactors.'

36. While Volumnia was speaking, Marcius listened without uttering a word, and after she had finished he stood for a long while in silence, until she asked him: 'Why have you nothing to say, my son? Is it right to sacrifice everything to anger and resentment, but wrong to give way to your mother when she pleads with you in such a cause as this? A great man has no need to remember every wrong he has suffered, but a man who is both good and great should remember the benefits that children receive from their parents, and he should repay these by honouring and respecting them. Surely no man ought to value gratitude more highly than yourself, since you are so relentless in punishing ingratitude? And yet, although you have done much to punish your country, you have shown no gratitude to your mother. So it would have been an act of reverence on your part to grant what I asked without any pressure, when I came to plead in such a just and honourable cause; but since I cannot persuade you, I must use my last resource.' As she spoke, she and his wife and children threw themselves at his feet. At this Marcius cried out: 'Mother, mother, what have you done?' Then he raised her up and tenderly pressed her hand. 'You have won your victory,' he told her, 'you have saved Rome, but you have destroyed your son. This is my defeat, even though none but you could have defeated me.' He spoke privately for a few moments more to his mother and his wife, then sent them back to Rome as they wished. The next morning he marched the Volscian army out of Roman territory.

The Volscians themselves were variously affected by what had happened. Some of them blamed both the man and what he had done, others, who were in favour of a peaceful solution of the quarrel with Rome, approved of both, while others again, although they were angry at his action, could not regard him as a traitor, and thought it excusable to have yielded to such irresistible pressure. At any rate none refused to accept his orders and they all followed him obediently, although they did this rather because they admired his courage than because they any longer accepted his authority.

37. As for the Roman people, the end of the war revealed even more clearly the full extent of the terror and the sense of danger which had oppressed them while it lasted. As soon as they observed from the walls that the Volscian army was withdrawing, every temple in Rome was thrown open and the citizens decked themselves with

garlands and offered up sacrifices as if they were celebrating a victory. But the Senate and the whole people showed their joy most of all in the honours and marks of affection which they paid to the women, who, they declared, had proved themselves beyond any doubt to be the saviours of the city. However, when the Senate passed a decree to the effect that any honour or privilege which they asked for themselves should be granted by the magistrates, their only request was that a temple should be erected to the Fortune of Women. They offered to pay the costs of building this, provided that the state would undertake to carry out at the public expense all the sacrifices and other honours which are due to the gods. The Senate praised their public spirit, but nevertheless ordered the temple and its statue to be built at the expense of the state. In spite of this the women raised money themselves and set up a second image of the goddess, and the Romans say that as this statue was placed in the temple, it was heard to utter the words, 'Women, your gift of me is acceptable to the gods.'

38. According to the tradition that has come down to us, these words were not merely uttered but repeated, but to say this is to ask us to accept what is almost incredible and probably never happened. It is not difficult to credit that statues may have appeared to ooze with sweat, shed tears, or exude something which resembles drops of blood, since wood and stone often gather a mould which produces moisture, and not only display various colours themselves, but take on other tints from the atmosphere, and there is nothing to prevent us from believing that heaven sometimes employs such portents to foreshadow the future. It is also possible that statues may give out a sound which resembles a groan or a sigh, which is caused by a fracture or splitting of the particles of which they may be composed, and produces a louder noise if it takes place inside. But the notion that articulate speech, so clear and abundant and precise, could proceed from a lifeless object goes beyond the bounds of possibility, since neither the human soul, nor even a god, has ever spoken or conversed without possessing a body which is organically constructed and fitted with the various vocal members. But in a case where history compels our assent by providing a large number of convincing witnesses, we are forced to conclude that the imaginative faculty of the soul undergoes an experience which was not really a sensation,

but can persuade people that it was one, just as, for example, when we are asleep we believe that we see and hear, although in reality we do neither. However, those who possess a deep sense of reverence for the divine and cherish religion so strongly that they cannot disbelieve or reject phenomena of this sort, find a powerful support for their faith in the miraculous nature of the divine power, and the fact that its ways are not as ours. Yet the divine bears no resemblance to the human either in its nature or the scope of its activity or the skill or strength of its operations, nor is there anything incompatible with reason in the fact that it should achieve what is beyond our power, or execute what is impracticable for us: on the contrary, since it differs from us in every respect, it is in its works above all that it is unlike and remote from us. However, as Heracleitus remarks, most of the attributes of the divine escape our understanding through lack of faith.

39. Now when Marcius returned to Antium from his expedition, Tullus, who had long hated and felt jealous of him, began to make plans to remove his rival immediately, for he was afraid that if Marcius escaped him now, he was never likely to give him another such advantage. He therefore gathered together a large body of supporters to oppose Marcius, and then summoned him to lay down his command and render an account to the Volscians of his conduct as their general. Marcius was alarmed at the prospect of returning to private life while Tullus remained in authority and continued to exercise a powerful influence upon his countrymen, and so he answered that as he had received his command from the whole Volscian people, it was to them that he should surrender it, if this was their will; meanwhile he was ready to give an account of his generalship to the people of Antium, if they desired it. So an assembly was summoned, and the popular orators, as had been arranged, did their utmost to rouse the people against him. But when Marcius rose to reply, even the rowdiest elements in his audience fell silent and allowed him to speak freely, while the best of the men of Antium and those who were content with the peace made it clear that they were well disposed towards him and would judge his case fairly. Tullus now began to be afraid of the effect of his opponent's defence, for he was an orator of great power and the services he had originally rendered to the Volscians far outweighed his recent offence: indeed

the whole indictment against him was really a proof of how much they owed him, for they would never have become conscious of a grievance at not capturing Rome if Marcius's efforts had not brought them so close to success.

So the conspirators decided that there must be no delay and that they could not afford to wait to discover the feelings of the people. The boldest of them raised the cry that the Volscians must not listen to this traitor, nor allow him to keep his command and play the tyrant among them. Then they rushed upon him in a body and cut him down, and not a man stepped forward to defend him. But it soon became apparent that the conspirators did not carry the people with them. From every one of their cities crowds flocked to Antium to see Marcius's dead body, and he was buried with full honours, and his tomb hung with arms and trophies as the monument of a hero and a successful general.

When the Romans heard of his death, they took no action either to honour his memory or to condemn it, but simply gave their permission to the women of his family to wear mourning for him for ten months, as was the custom when any of them lost a father, a son, or a brother. This was the longest period that was allowed for mourning and it was fixed by Numa Pompilius as I have mentioned in his Life.

It was not long before the Volscians had cause to regret Marcius's death. First of all they had a dispute with the Aequi, who were their allies and friends, over which of the two nations should command their armies, and carried the quarrel to the point of bloodshed. Next they were defeated by the Romans, and in this battle Tullus was killed and the flower of the Volscian army perished. After this disaster they were content to accept the most humiliating terms, become the subjects of Rome, and pledge themselves to obey her commands.

2

FABIUS MAXIMUS

[*c.* 275–203 B.C.]

* *
*

1. Such was the man that Pericles* proved himself to be in his most memorable actions as they have come down to us. Now our history turns to the *Life of Fabius*.

It was a nymph, according to one legend, or a woman of the country according to another, who lay with Hercules by the river Tiber and bore him Fabius. This man was the founder of the family of the Fabii, which was to become one of the greatest and most distinguished in Rome. Another tradition has it that the original members of the family were called Fodii in ancient times, because of their practice of trapping wild beasts in pits – and even up to the present day ditches are known in Latin as *fossae* and the verb to dig is *fodere*. Then in the course of time and through the change of two letters, according to this theory, they became known as Fabii. At any rate the family produced a large number of eminent men, the greatest of whom was Rullus, who for this reason was given the surname of Maximus. The fourth in descent from him was the Fabius who is the subject of this Life.

He was nicknamed Verrucosus because of a small wart which grew on his upper lip, and while he was still a child people called him Ovicula or lambkin, because of his grave and gentle nature. He grew up with a quiet and placid disposition, showed an extraordinary caution even when he was indulging in childish pleasures, and learned his lessons slowly and laboriously; and these characteristics, combined with his docile, almost submissive behaviour towards his

* Plutarch's Greek parallel for Fabius was Pericles, the Athenian leader, who, at the beginning of the Peloponnesian War, likewise pursued a defensive strategy in the face of violent criticism, and constantly strove to restrain his impetuous colleagues.

companions, led those who did not know him thoroughly to suppose that he was dull and stupid. It was only a few who could see beyond these superficial qualities and discern the greatness of spirit, the lion-like temper, and the unshakeable resolution which lay in the depths of his soul. But as time went on and his mind was stirred by the demands of the life of action, he soon proved to all alike that this apparent lack of energy was really due to his freedom from over-mastering passions and that his caution proceeded from a soundly based judgement, while the fact that he never acted on impulse and was not easily persuaded meant that he was steadfast and resolute in all circumstances. He took note early in life both of the greatness of Rome's power and of the numerous wars that threatened it, and so he trained his body for fighting, since he considered its fitness to be his natural armour. At the same time he practised public speaking as an instrument with which to sway the people, and created a style which was a perfect expression of his way of life. His oratory carried no superfluous ornaments nor empty forensic graces, but it was full of the solid sense which characterized the man, and was reinforced by an abundance of maxims and generalizations which recalled the weighty judgements of Thucydides. One of his speeches has actually been preserved: he delivered it as a funeral oration over his son, who died after he had held the office of consul.

2. In the first of his five consulships Fabius won a triumph over the Ligurians.* He won a pitched battle, inflicting heavy losses on them, whereupon they withdrew into the Alps and ceased to ravage and plunder the Italian provinces which lay on their frontier. Fifteen years later Hannibal broke† into Italy, won his first victory at the battle of the river Trebia, and pressed on through Etruria, ravaging the countryside as he went. The inhabitants of Rome were filled with terror and dismay at the news of his advance and a number of portents were observed, some of them commonplace enough, such as peals of thunder, but others as inexplicable as they were unfamiliar. Thus it was reported that shields began to sweat blood, that at Antium the ripe ears of corn bled when they were cut by the reapers, that blazing

* 233 B.C.

† The word is worth singling out, as it is intended to suggest the amazement with which the Romans learned that Hannibal had crossed the Alps, a route which they had never dreamed he would take.

red-hot stones rained down from the sky, and that at Falerii the heavens were seen to open and many tablets to fall one of which was inscribed with the words, 'Mars is brandishing his weapons'.

However, none of these prodigies could daunt the consul Gaius Flaminius, who, besides being an ambitious and hot-tempered man, had been encouraged by the victories which he had won against all expectation only a few years before. On that occasion, although the Senate had disagreed with his plan and his colleague had vehemently opposed it, he had engaged the Gauls in a pitched battle and defeated them.* Fabius himself was not much disturbed by these portents which alarmed so many of his countrymen, because he considered them too strange to be easily understood. He was much more impressed by the reports of the small size of Hannibal's force and of how poorly it was supplied, and he urged the Romans to have patience and on no account to engage a commander who led an army that had been hardened in many contests for this very purpose of forcing a decisive battle. Instead they should send help to their allies, keep their subject cities under control, and allow Hannibal's strength, which must now be at its peak, to waste away like a flame which flares up brightly but has little fuel to sustain it.

3. But Flaminius refused to listen to these arguments. He declared that he would not allow the campaign to be conducted near Rome, nor would he, like Camillus of old, fight a battle for the city within her very walls,† and he therefore gave orders to the military tribunes to lead out the army. But as he leaped on to his horse, the animal was for no apparent reason seized with a fit of trembling and shied violently, so that Flaminius was unseated and thrown to the ground on his head. Even this did nothing to divert him from his purpose: he proceeded to march out to meet Hannibal according to his original plan, and drew up his army near Lake Trasimene in Tuscany.

When the two armies were locked in battle, at the critical moment

* In 224 B.C. Flaminius was inferior in numbers, neglected to take the auspices, and refused to open the Senate's dispatches before the action: the victory was won mainly through the skill of some of his subordinates. See also *Life of Marcellus*, ch. 4.

† The allusion is to the probably legendary battle which Camillus fought to raise the siege of Rome by the Gauls, about 390 B.C.

in the action, an earthquake took place which destroyed several cities, diverted rivers from their channels, and split off great fragments of cliffs, and yet in spite of the violence of the catastrophe none of those who were engaged in the battle noticed it at all. Flaminius himself fought with heroic strength and courage, but was cut down at last, and around him perished the flower of his army. The rest were routed and a tremendous carnage followed. Fifteen thousand Romans were killed and as many more taken prisoner. Hannibal was anxious to bury Flaminius's body with military honours as a tribute to his valour, but it could not be found and it was never discovered how it had disappeared.

Now when the Romans had been defeated in the first action of the campaign at the river Trebia, neither the general who wrote the dispatch nor the messenger who carried it gave a straightforward account of the battle: it was represented as being a disputed and uncertain victory. But as soon as Pomponius the praetor learned of this second defeat, he summoned an assembly of the people, faced them, and gave them the news in plain words, without any attempt to evade or disguise it. 'Men of Rome,' he said, 'we have been defeated in a great battle, our army has been destroyed, and the consul Flaminius is dead. You must consider now what we are to do to save ourselves.' His speech fell upon the great expanse of faces turned towards him like a sudden storm-blast upon the surface of the sea. The whole city was thrown into an uproar, and in such a mood of panic no man could take a grip on his thoughts and reflect calmly. But at length the whole people found themselves driven to the same conclusion, namely that the situation demanded the absolute authority of a single man (or, as the Romans call it, a dictatorship), who would wield this power with the utmost energy and without fear, and that Fabius Maximus was the only man fitted for this task. He alone, they believed, possessed a spirit and a dignity of character which were equal to the greatness of the office, and, besides this, he was of an age at which the strength of the body is fully capable of executing the decisions of the brain, while boldness is tempered with discretion.*

4. Accordingly the people passed a decree to this effect and Fabius

* One might expect this description to refer to the prime of life, but Fabius was by this time fifty-eight.

was declared dictator.* He in turn appointed Marcus Minucius to be his master of horse,† and then at once asked the Senate's permission to use a horse while he himself was on active service. I should explain that according to an ancient law the dictator was forbidden this privilege. The reason may have been that since the army had always been organized so that its main strength lay in the infantry, the Romans believed that their commander should always station himself with the phalanx and never leave it, or possibly that since the dictator's power is in other respects as great as a tyrant's, they considered that in this detail at least he should be shown to be dependent on the people. At any rate Fabius was anxious to impress the people immediately with the importance and grandeur of his office, so as to make them more docile and obedient to his orders. He therefore appeared in public attended by the full body of twenty-four lictors‡ carrying their fasces. And when the surviving consul came to meet him, he sent an officer with orders that he should dismiss his lictors, lay down the insignia of his office, and meet the dictator as a private citizen.

After this he made the best of beginnings, that is by turning his attention to religious matters, and he left the people in no doubt that their defeat had not been brought about by any cowardice on the part of their soldiers, but by their general's neglectful and contemptuous attitude towards religious observances. By this means he persuaded them that instead of becoming frightened of their enemies they should give their minds to honouring and propitiating the gods. He did not attempt to implant a spirit of superstition, but he invoked the people's piety to strengthen their courage, and he sought to dispel their fear of the enemy by instilling the faith that the gods were on the side of Rome. At the same time many of the so-called Sibylline Books, which contain secret advice of great importance to the state, were brought out to be consulted, and it is said that some of the oracular pronouncements which they contained actually corresponded to the chance happenings and events of the time. What was discovered in this way could not be made public, but the dictator came before the people and made a vow in their presence to sacrifice to the gods

* Only a consul possessed the constitutional power to appoint a dictator. As the surviving consul Servilius was still with the army, the people appointed Fabius to be 'pro-dictator'.

† Minucius was in fact appointed by the Assembly and was a popular, not an aristocratic choice, a fact which explains much that follows.

‡ Each consul was allowed twelve lictors.

a whole year's increase, that is, all the young produced in the coming spring by the goats, the pigs, the sheep, and the cattle from every mountain, plain, river, and meadow within the bounds of Italy.* He also pledged himself to celebrate a musical and dramatic festival, and spend on it the sum of 333 sestertia, 333 denarii, and a third of a denarius exactly. This sum in Greek money amounts to 83,583 drachmae and two obols.† It is difficult to discover the reason why this precise amount was specified, unless it was perhaps to honour the spiritual power of the number three: this is a perfect number by nature, and is also the first of odd numbers, the beginning of quantity, and contains within itself the first differences and the elements of every number.

5. By encouraging the people in this way to fix their thoughts upon religious matters, Fabius contrived to strengthen their confidence in the future. For his part, however, he trusted entirely to his own efforts to win the victory, since he believed that the gods grant men success according to the courage and wisdom that they display, and in this frame of mind he turned his attention to Hannibal. He was determined not to fight a pitched battle, and since he had time and manpower and money on his side, his plan was to exhaust his opponent's strength, which was now at its peak, by means of delaying tactics, and gradually to wear down his small army and meagre resources. With this object in view he always bivouacked in mountainous country, where he was out of reach of the enemy's cavalry, and at the same time hung menacingly over the Carthaginian camp. If the enemy stayed still, he did the same. If they moved, he would make a detour, descend a little distance from the heights, and show himself just far enough away to prevent himself from being forced into an action against his will, but near enough to create the suspicion from the very slowness of his movements that he might be about to attack. But the Romans soon became contemptuous of these time-killing tactics and Fabius began to be despised in his own camp, while the enemy – with one exception – were convinced that he was a nonentity who was utterly devoid of warlike spirit. The exception was Hannibal. He, and he alone, perceived his opponent's shrewdness

* Such an offering was known as a *ver sacrum* (sacred spring).

† At a rough calculation about £3,500, taking the drachma as worth about 10d.

and divined the strategy which Fabius had laid down for the war. He therefore made up his mind that he must use every trick to lure or force the enemy into battle, or else the Carthaginian cause was lost, since his men were being prevented from exploiting their superiority in training, while their manpower and resources, in which they were inferior to the Romans, were being steadily exhausted to no purpose. And so he brought into play all the arts and stratagems of war and tried every one in turn, like a skilful wrestler, who watches for his opportunity to secure a hold on his adversary. First he would attack Fabius's army directly, then try to throw it into confusion, then draw him on from one place to another, all in the effort to lure him away from the safety of his defensive tactics. Fabius, however, had complete faith in his plan, followed it out consistently, and refused to be drawn. But he was provoked by his master of horse, Minucius, a headstrong officer who longed for action regardless of the circumstances, and who tried to increase his popularity by raising empty hopes and working up his men's spirits to a state of wild enthusiasm. The soldiers mocked at Fabius and contemptuously called him Hannibal's governess,* but they thought Minucius a great man and a general worthy of Rome. This encouraged the master of horse to indulge his boastful arrogance more than ever and to make fun of Fabius's tactics of encamping on high ground, where, as he put it, the dictator took great trouble to provide them with splendid seats to witness the spectacle of Italy being laid waste with fire and sword. He was also fond of asking Fabius's friends whether he thought he was leading the troops up to heaven, since he had evidently ceased to take any interest in events on earth, or whether he was enveloping them in clouds and mist simply to escape from the enemy. Fabius's friends reported these remarks, and urged him to wipe out such aspersions on his courage by risking a battle. His answer was: 'In that case I should be an even greater coward than they say I am, if I were to abandon the plans I believe to be right because of a few sneers and words of abuse. There is nothing shameful in experiencing fear for your country's sake. But the man who allows himself to be frightened by the opinions of others or by their slanders or abuse, proves

* There is no precise English equivalent to convey the scorn implied in the word *paedagogus*: to a Roman the word signified a male slave employed to attend children on their walks or back and forth from school. 'Tutor' would imply a more intellectually advanced relationship.

that he is unworthy of such a high office as this, since he makes himself the slave of the very men whom it is his duty to restrain and overrule when they go astray and their judgement deserts them.'

6. Not long after this Hannibal committed a serious blunder. He wished to put some distance between Fabius's army and his own, and to occupy a stretch of open country* where he could find good pasturage. He therefore gave orders to his guides that they should lead the army immediately after the evening meal into the district of Casinum. But they did not take in the name correctly because of his foreign pronunciation, with the result that they hurried on his troops into the neighbourhood of Casilinum, through the midst of which there flows a river which the Romans call Vulturnus. The whole region is surrounded by mountains, but there is a narrow defile which leads down to the sea. Here the river overflows so as to form marshes and high sand dunes, and finally discharges itself into the sea on to a beach, where there is no anchorage because of the heavy breakers. While Hannibal was marching down into this valley, Fabius took advantage of his knowledge of the roads to send his troops round and block the pass with a detachment of four thousand infantry. He posted the rest of his army in a strong position on the neighbouring heights, and then with the lightest and most active of his troops attacked the Carthaginian rear-guard, killed about eight hundred of them, and threw the whole army into disorder. Hannibal quickly recognized his mistake and the danger of his position and he promptly crucified the guides who had led him there, but he could see no means of forcing his way out or dislodging the enemy from the mountain passes which they held securely. At last when his men were beginning to lose heart and sink into despair because they believed that they were surrounded on all sides by dangers from which there was no escape, he hit on a trick to deceive the enemy. This was what he did.

He gave orders for his troops to take some two thousand of the oxen which they had captured, and to fasten to each of their horns a torch consisting of a bundle of twigs or dry faggots. Then at a given

* Hannibal's intention was to march into the plains of Campania. He hoped that the spectacle of the most fertile land in Italy being laid waste before his eyes might at last lure Fabius into a battle.

signal after nightfall his men were to light the torches and drive the cattle along the defiles and towards the passes where the Romans were posted. As soon as these orders had been carried out, by which time it was already dark, he had the rest of his army ready to move, and proceeded to advance at a slow pace. At first, so long as the flames were low and were only burning the wood, the cattle moved on steadily towards the mountains as they were driven up the slopes, while the shepherds and herdsmen who looked down from the neighbouring heights stared with amazement at the flames which streamed from the tips of their horns, and imagined that this must be a whole army marching in close column and carrying innumerable torches. But when the horns had been burned down to the quick and the flames reached the raw flesh, the cattle began to shake and toss their heads in agony and covered one another with showers of sparks and embers. Soon they began to stampede, and then, mad with pain and fear, galloped off on a wild career down the slopes, with their foreheads and tails ablaze and setting fire to a great part of the forest as they passed. All this was a terrifying sight to the Romans guarding the passes. The flames appeared to come from numbers of men running to and fro and brandishing torches in their hands, and the Romans were thrown into the utmost confusion and alarm, since they believed that they were completely surrounded and that the enemy were about to attack from all directions at once. Their courage deserted them and they fled from their posts, fell back on the main body of the army which was stationed on the heights, and abandoned the defiles. In a moment Hannibal's light troops came up and seized the passes, and the rest of the Carthaginian army marched safely through, heavily loaded with plunder.

7. Fabius discovered the trick which had been played on him before the night was over, for some of the cattle had been caught by the Romans during their stampede. But he was afraid of falling into an ambush in the dark, and so kept his men under arms, but did not allow them to move. As soon as it was light, however, he pursued the enemy and harried their rear-guard. There were many hand-to-hand encounters over difficult ground and much confused fighting. At last Hannibal detached from his advance guard a body of his Spanish light infantry, fast-moving troops who were agile and practised mountaineers. They fell upon the heavily armoured Roman infantry,

killed many of them, and forced Fabius to retreat. This episode brought down more abuse and contempt upon Fabius than anything that had happened before. He had refused the challenge of an outright trial of strength in the hope of overcoming Hannibal through superior judgement and foresight, but it was in these very qualities that the Carthaginian had manifestly out-generalled and defeated him.

Hannibal was anxious to increase the general resentment against Fabius still further. Accordingly when he arrived at his country estates, he gave orders that these should be spared while all the surrounding property should be ravaged and burned, and even had a guard put on them to make sure that nothing should be removed and no damage done. When the news reached Rome it provoked a fresh wave of indignation against Fabius. The tribunes of the people kept up a stream of denunciation against him, most of which was instigated and encouraged by Metilius. He did this not out of any personal animosity towards Fabius, but because he was a relative of Minucius, the master of the horse, and believed that if he could lower Fabius's reputation, he would be raising his subordinate's. The Senate was also displeased with the dictator, and censured him in particular for the terms he had made with Hannibal about the exchange of prisoners of war. The two commanders had agreed to exchange prisoners man for man, and if either side held more than the other, the surplus prisoners were to be redeemed at a ransom of two hundred and fifty drachmas each. When the exchange had been carried out man for man, it was found that Hannibal still had two hundred and forty Romans left. The Senate decided that it would not provide the ransoms for these, and blamed Fabius for having acted improperly and against the interests of the state in attempting to rescue men who had fallen into captivity only because of their own cowardice. When Fabius heard this news, he did not allow his countrymen's anger to disturb him, but since he had no ready money of his own and could not tolerate the idea either of cheating Hannibal or of abandoning the Roman prisoners to their fate, he sent his son to Rome with instructions to sell his estates and bring him the money immediately at the camp. The young man carried out the sale and returned without delay, whereupon Fabius dispatched the ransoms to Hannibal and recovered the prisoners. Many of these men later offered to repay him, but he would accept nothing and insisted that the debt should be cancelled for every one of them.

8. After this he was recalled to Rome by the priests to be present at various sacrifices as the duties of his office demanded, and he then handed over the command to Minucius with orders not to become involved in a battle nor to engage the enemy in any way. Fabius not only issued these orders as dictator, but he repeated them to his deputy as his personal advice and request. Minucius paid little attention to any of these warnings, and immediately began to test the enemy's strength. One day he noticed that Hannibal had dispatched the greater part of his army on a foraging expedition. He promptly attacked the remainder, drove them back into their entrenchments with heavy losses, and spread panic among the rest, who were afraid that he would now lay siege to their camp: then when Hannibal concentrated his forces again inside the camp, Minucius succeeded in withdrawing his troops without loss. This engagement vastly increased Minucius's own arrogance and high opinion of himself and filled his soldiers with rash confidence. An inflated report of the action quickly reached Rome, and Fabius's comment when he heard it was that he feared the consequences of Minucius's success much more than his failure. Nevertheless the people were delighted at the news and hurried exultantly to a meeting in the Forum. There the tribune Metilius mounted the rostra and delivered a rabble-rousing speech, in which he glorified Minucius and denounced his superior. He attacked Fabius not merely as an effete and spiritless leader but even as a traitor, and he included in the same accusation many of the ablest and most distinguished men in the state. First of all they had led Rome into the war, he said, to destroy the power of the people, and then they had promptly delivered the city into the hands of a single dictator who was answerable to no man, and who by his dilatory tactics would allow Hannibal ample time to establish himself and summon another army from Libya, since he could claim that he now held Italy in his power.

9. When Fabius addressed the people, he wasted no time in defending himself against the tribune's charges. He merely said that the sacrifices and other religious rites must be carried out as quickly as possible, to enable him to return to the army and punish Minucius for having attacked the enemy against his orders. These words produced a great commotion among the people, since they now understood the danger in which Minucius stood. The dictator has the power to imprison

and even to inflict capital punishment without trial, and they believed that Fabius, who was normally the mildest of men, had at last been provoked to an extent which would render him harsh and implacable. This thought alarmed them so much that nobody dared to speak except for Metilius, who could rely upon his personal immunity as a tribune of the people, for this is the only office which is not deprived of its prerogatives by the appointment of a dictator, but survives intact when all the rest have their functions suspended. So he now made an impassioned appeal to the people. He implored them not to abandon Minucius, nor to allow him to suffer the penalty which Manlius Torquatus inflicted on his son,* whom he had beheaded after he had been awarded the laurel crown for an act of the utmost gallantry, and urged instead that they should deprive Fabius of his dictatorial powers and entrust the control of affairs to one who was able and willing to save his country.

The people were moved by these words, and yet, in spite of Fabius's unpopularity, they lacked the courage to compel him to lay down the dictatorship. Instead they voted that Minucius should be given an equal share in the command and should carry on the war with the same powers as the dictator, a division of authority for which there was no precedent in Roman history. A little later, it is true, a similar situation arose after the disaster at Cannae. On that occasion Marcus Junius, the dictator, was in command of the army, and it became necessary that the vacant places in the Senate should be filled, since so many senators had lost their lives in the battle, and so the people elected Fabius Buteo as a second dictator. But when he had taken up his office and discharged his task of selecting the men to fill the Senate, he immediately dismissed his lictors and the rest of his retinue, slipped into the crowd, and mingled with the people in the Forum, where he proceeded to occupy himself with his private concerns and transact business like any ordinary citizen.

10. When the people had conferred upon Minucius the same powers as the dictator's, they expected that Fabius would feel that he had been shorn of his authority and humiliated, but here they completely misjudged their man. The truth was that he did not regard their folly as being in any way a misfortune for himself. His attitude was like

* Manlius was consul when he had his son executed for disobeying his orders and engaging in single combat before a battle (340 B.C.).

that of Diogenes the philosopher, who when he was once told, 'The people are mocking you', retorted 'But I am not mocked', meaning that the only people who really suffer ridicule are those who allow it to influence them and are put out by it. So Fabius endured these vexations calmly and without stress, in so far as they concerned him personally, thus confirming the truth of the philosophical maxim that a truly good man can neither be insulted nor disgraced. And yet for his country's sake he could not but be distressed at the people's folly, since they had placed such opportunities in the hands of a man who was ruled by an insane ambition for military success. He feared that Minucius with his infatuated craving for empty glory and prestige might cause some irreparable disaster before he could be stopped, and he therefore left the city in great secrecy. When he arrived at the camp he found that Minucius's behaviour had become intolerable. He was overbearing and puffed up with conceit, and at once demanded to be given supreme command of the army on alternate days. Fabius refused this request, since he preferred to command a part of the army permanently rather than the whole of it by turns. He therefore took charge of the first and fourth legions himself and gave the second and third to Minucius, while the allied troops were equally divided between them. When Minucius put on haughty airs and boasted of the fact that the dignity of the highest and most powerful office in the state had been humbled and its authority reduced on his account, Fabius quietly reminded him that his real opponent, if he stopped to consider the matter, was not Fabius but Hannibal. But if he persisted in treating his colleague as a rival, let their rivalry concern itself with ensuring the safety of Rome. Minucius should take care that he, the man who had been honoured and proclaimed the victor by the people, should not be found to have served the Romans worse than the man who had been subdued and humiliated by them.

11. Minucius regarded this as an old man's disingenuous talk, and when he had taken command of the troops allotted to him, he moved into a separate camp. Meanwhile Hannibal, who had kept himself informed of these events, watched his opponent's movements closely. There was a hill between the Romans and the Carthaginians which could be occupied without difficulty, and which, once secured, offered a strong position for a camp and was well supplied in every

way. The plain which surrounded it appeared to be perfectly smooth and level, when seen from a distance, but in reality the ground was broken by many small ditches and hollows. For this reason, although it would have been easy to make a surprise advance and occupy the hill, Hannibal had preferred to leave it untouched in the hope of enticing the enemy into battle. As soon as he saw Minucius detach his forces from those of Fabius, he sent out scattered bodies of troops during the night with orders to hide themselves among the ditches and depressions in the ground. Then at first light he dispatched a few men to occupy the hill without any attempt at concealment, in the hope of luring Minucius into fighting for it.

His plan worked. First of all Minucius sent forward his light-armed troops, then his cavalry, and finally, when he saw that Hannibal was coming to the rescue of his men on the hill, he drew up his whole army and marched down into the plain. His men attacked courageously, advancing in the face of a hail of missiles from the hill, coming to close quarters there and holding their ground. Then Hannibal, seeing that his enemy was well and truly in the trap and had exposed his unguarded rear to the troops who were waiting in ambush, raised the signal. Thereupon his men sprang up from their hiding-places on all sides and attacked with loud shouts, cutting down the rear ranks of the enemy. An indescribable confusion and panic spread through the Roman army. Minucius himself felt his confidence gone and began to glance anxiously at his commanders in turn. None of them had the courage to stand their ground, and before long they broke and fled; but this proved a disastrous move, for the Numidian cavalry, who were now the masters of the field, galloped round the plain and cut down the fugitives as they vainly attempted to scatter.

12. None of this had escaped Fabius, who by now was well aware of the terrible danger that threatened the Romans. He had foreseen the consequences of Minucius's rashness, drawn up his own troops under arms and kept himself informed of the progress of the battle, not through the reports of scouts but from his own observations from a point of vantage in front of his camp. When he saw Minucius's army surrounded and thrown into confusion, and when the sound of their cries told him that the Romans were no longer holding their ground but had given way to panic and were in full retreat, he struck his thigh and with a deep sigh exclaimed to those around him, 'By

Hercules, Minucius has destroyed himself more quickly than I expected, and yet he was lucky that it did not happen sooner.' He then gave orders for the standards to advance with all speed and for the rest of the army to follow, and called out in a loud voice, 'My soldiers, every one of you must hurry forward. There is no time to lose. Think of Marcus Minucius. He is a brave man and loves his country. And if he has made a mistake in his anxiety to drive back the enemy, we will blame him for that another time.'

As soon as he appeared on the scene, he routed and scattered the Numidian cavalry who were galloping about the plain. Then he turned against the troops who were attacking the Roman rear, and killed all whom he met. The remainder gave way, before they were cut off and surrounded as the Romans had been, and made their escape. When Hannibal saw Fabius showing a vigour far beyond his years, as he forced his way through the thick of the battle up the hill towards Minucius, he knew that the battle had turned against him. He therefore broke off the action, signalled a retreat, and led the Carthaginians back to their camp, and for their part the Romans were equally grateful for a respite. It is said that as Hannibal marched back, he spoke jokingly to his friends about Fabius in some such words as these: 'Haven't I kept telling you that the cloud we have seen hovering over the mountain tops would burst one day like a tornado?'

13. When the battle was over and Fabius's men had stripped the spoils from the enemy's troops they had killed, the dictator retired to his camp without uttering a single overbearing or reproachful word in criticism of his colleague. Minucius, however, paraded his men and addressed them as follows: 'Fellow-soldiers, it is beyond the powers of mortal man to be placed in command of great enterprises and never to make a mistake, but it is a mark of courage and good sense to be able to profit from one's errors and treat a reverse as a lesson for the future. Let me confess then that although I have some slight excuse for blaming fortune, I have far more reason to praise her. In the short space of a single day I have been taught what it has taken me all my life to learn. I can now see that I am not capable of commanding others, but need a commander myself, and that for all these years I have been cherishing the ambition to rise above men whom I ought to have felt honoured to acknowledge as my superiors. Now in all other matters the dictator shall be your leader, but in

expressing our thanks to him I shall take the lead, and set an example by showing that I am ready to follow his advice and obey his orders.'

After these words he ordered the eagles to be raised aloft and all his men to follow them, and led the way to Fabius's camp. As soon as he arrived he went to the general's tent, while the whole army looked on in astonishment and wonder. When Fabius came outside, Minucius had the standards of the legions planted in front of him and addressed him in a loud voice as Father, while his soldiers greeted Fabius's men as Patrons, which is the title that freedmen use towards those who have given them their liberty. When silence had been restored, Minucius said: 'Dictator, on this day you have won two victories, one over Hannibal through your bravery, and the other over your colleague through your generalship and your generosity. With the first you saved our lives, and with the second you taught us a lesson, and just as Hannibal's superiority disgraced us, so yours has given us back not only our safety but our honour. I call you by the name of Father, because it is the most honourable that I can use, and yet even a father's kindness is not so great as the kindness I have received from you. My father gave me my life, but you have saved not only this but the lives of all the men under me.' As he ended, he embraced Fabius and kissed him, and the soldiers on both sides followed his example, so that the whole camp was filled with rejoicing and tears of happiness.

14. After this* Fabius laid down his office of dictator and consuls were once more elected. The first of these carried on the defensive tactics which Fabius had created, avoiding pitched battles but giving support to the allies and preventing them from going over to the enemy. But then came the year in which Terentius Varro was elected to the consulship.† He was a man of humble birth, who was remarkable chiefly for his obsequious flattery of the people, combined with his liking for impetuous action, and since his utter lack of experience was equalled only by his self-confidence, it soon became clear that he was prepared to risk everything on a single throw. He liked to thunder at the people in the Assembly that the war would make no progress so long as the Romans continued to employ men such as Fabius for their generals, but that he would defeat the enemy on the first day he set eyes on them. He did not confine himself to

* Fabius's term expired at the end of 217 B.C.

† 216 B.C.

making these speeches, but he enlisted and assembled a larger force than Rome had ever put into the field against any enemy. Eighty-eight thousand men were mobilized for his campaign and this caused the greatest alarm to Fabius and all the more thoughtful Romans, for they believed that if the city were to lose so many men in the prime of life, she would never recover from the blow.

Varro's colleague was Paulus Aemilius, a man who, despite his great experience of war, was unpopular with the people and was afraid of them because of a fine which they had once imposed on him. Accordingly Fabius did his utmost to exhort and encourage him to resist his colleague's impetuosity, explaining that, if he wished to serve his country, he would find himself contending just as much with Hannibal as with Varro. Varro, he said, was eager to fight because he did not know where his own strength lay, and Hannibal because he was too well aware of his own weakness. 'But you must believe me, Paulus,' he went on, 'when I say that I understand Hannibal's situation far better than Varro does, and I am certain that, if no battle takes place with him for a year, he will either perish in Italy, if he chooses to remain, or else be forced to depart. Remember that even now, when he is supposed to be supreme and to have gained complete control of the country, not one of his enemies has come over to his side, and he does not now possess even a third part of the army that set out from Carthage.' To this Paulus is said to have replied: 'If I had only myself to consider, I would rather fall by the spears of the enemy than be condemned again by the votes of my fellow-countrymen. But if our country is now in such danger, I will try to make sure that my conduct as a general satisfies Fabius rather than all the men who are pressing me to take the opposite course.' Having taken this resolve, Paulus set out for the campaign.

15. Varro insisted on observing the practice whereby each consul took command of the army on alternate days. He then pitched his camp opposite Hannibal's on the banks of the river Aufidus near the town named Cannae, and at daybreak hoisted the signal for battle, a scarlet tunic hung out over the general's tent. At first even the Carthaginians were dismayed, not only by the Roman commander's apparent boldness, but also by the strength of his army, which was more than double their own. Hannibal ordered his troops to prepare for action, while he himself with a few companions rode to the crest

of a gently rising slope, from which he could look down on the enemy as they formed their order of battle. When one of his companions, an officer of equal rank, remarked that the numbers of the enemy seemed amazingly large, Hannibal looked grave for a moment, and said: 'There is another thing you have not noticed, Gisco, which is even more amazing,' and when Gisco asked what this was, he replied, 'The fact that in all this enormous host opposite there isn't a single man called Gisco.' The joke caught the whole party off guard and they all began to laugh: then as they rode down from the high ground they repeated it to everyone they met, so that their high spirits quickly spread among the troops and the officers of Hannibal's staff were completely overcome with laughter. The Carthaginians took heart when they saw this, for they thought that their general must have a great contempt for the Romans if he could laugh and joke like this in the face of danger.

16. In the battle itself Hannibal made use of a number of stratagems. First he took advantage of the ground to post his men with the wind behind them. It was a scorching wind, which swept across the bare and sandy plains like a hurricane, whipping up choking clouds of dust and driving them over the Carthaginian lines straight into the faces of the Romans, who were thrown into confusion as they turned away to avoid the blast. His second ruse lay in his order of battle. His best and most warlike troops were stationed on the wings, while the weakest were concentrated in the centre, which he intended to use as a wedge projecting far ahead of the rest of the line. The orders given to the crack formations were as follows. The Romans would cut the Carthaginian centre to pieces, and as they pressed forward in pursuit, the centre would fall back forming a hollow, until the Romans had penetrated deep into their enemies' line of battle. At this moment the Carthaginian wings would wheel sharply inwards, attack the Romans from the flanks, and envelop them by closing in upon the rear.* It was this manoeuvre, it seems, which brought about the fearful carnage that followed. When the Carthaginian centre gave ground and the Romans surged forward in pursuit, Hannibal's line

* Plutarch's account of the fighting is written with a large degree of hindsight. The issue was finely balanced. If Hannibal's centre had been broken before the Numidian cavalry could attack from the rear, the battle would have been lost.

was transformed into a crescent; thereupon the commanders of the picked troops on the wings wheeled them swiftly to right and left and attacked the enemy on their unguarded flanks, so that the Romans were overwhelmed and slaughtered to a man, except for the few who escaped before their encirclement was complete.

It is said that the Roman cavalry also suffered an unexpected misfortune. Paulus's horse, it appears, was wounded and threw its rider, whereupon one man after another of his staff dismounted and came to help the consul on foot. When the main body of the cavalry saw this, they assumed that it was a general order, with the result that every man dismounted and engaged the enemy on foot. When Hannibal saw this he remarked, 'This is better than having them all delivered over to me bound hand and foot.' However, for episodes of this kind I may refer the reader to those historians who have reported the war in detail.

As for the two consuls, Varro galloped off with a few followers to the city of Venusia, but Paulus, caught in the surging torrent of the rout, covered with the barbs which still hung in his wounds, and overwhelmed both in body and spirit by the weight of his misfortune, sat with his back against a stone and waited for the enemy to dispatch him. His head and face were so streaked and disfigured with blood that scarcely anybody could recognize him; even his friends and attendants passed him by, unaware that this was their general. At last Cornelius Lentulus, a young patrician, caught sight of him and knew who he was. He jumped from his horse, led it up to Paulus, and besought the consul to take it and save himself for the sake of his fellow-citizens, who had never needed a brave commander so much as at that moment. But nothing could persuade Paulus to give way to his entreaty, and he compelled the young man, in spite of his tears, to mount his horse again. Then he rose to his feet, clasped Lentulus's hand, and said to him, 'Tell Fabius Maximus, and you yourself bear witness, that Paulus Aemilius followed his friend's advice to the end and stood by every one of the undertakings he had given, but he was overcome first by Varro and then by Hannibal.' When he had given Lentulus this message, he sent him away, and plunging into the midst of the slaughter, he met his death. It is said that fifty thousand Romans were killed in this battle and four thousand captured alive, while after the fighting no less than ten thousand were captured in the camps of the two consuls.

17. After this overwhelming success Hannibal's friends urged him to follow up his good fortune and force his way into Rome on the heels of the retreating enemy, and they assured him that, if he pressed on, he would be dining on the Capitol on the fifth day after his victory. It is not easy to say what consideration can have held him back.* It almost seems as if his evil genius or some divine power intervened at this moment to fill him with the timidity and irresolution which he now showed. This is why Barca the Carthaginian is reported to have said to him angrily, 'You know how to win a victory, Hannibal, but you have no idea how to exploit it.' In spite of this his victory brought about a tremendous change in his situation. Before it he had not controlled a single city, trading station, or seaport in Italy, and had found great difficulty in obtaining even a bare supply of provisions by foraging: he had not possessed any secure base of operations, but had been obliged to roam about the countryside with his army, as if it were a troop of brigands. But after Cannae he brought almost the whole of Italy under his control. Many of the largest tribes came over to him of their own accord, and he also persuaded Capua, which was the most important city after Rome, to give him her support.

'Misfortune tests the quality of our friends,' Euripides tells us, and the same test, it would seem, reveals the prudent general. The very strategy, which before the battle had been condemned as passive and cowardly, now came to be regarded as the product of a superhuman power of reasoning, or rather of a divine, almost miraculous intelligence, capable of penetrating the future and of prophesying a disaster which could scarcely be believed by those who experienced it. So it was upon Fabius that the Romans centred their last hopes. His wisdom was the sanctuary to which men fled for refuge as they might to a temple or an altar, and they believed that it was his practical capacity above all which had preserved the unity of Rome at this moment, and had prevented her citizens from deserting the city and dispersing, as had happened during the disasters of the Gallic invasion. For when the people had felt secure, it was Fabius who had appeared to be cautious and timid, but now, when all others were giving way to

* Many reasons have been suggested by various historians. Among the most obvious are that Hannibal's army by now mustered less than 20,000 men, that it was not equipped for a siege, and that the cavalry, which had played so important a part in his victories, would have been useless for attacking a fortified city.

boundless grief and helpless bewilderment, he was the only man to walk the streets with a resolute step, a serene expression, and a kindly voice. It was he who checked all womanish lamentations, and prevented those who wished to bewail their sorrows from assembling in public. On the other hand, he persuaded the Senate to continue to hold its meetings, stiffened the resolution of the magistrates, and made himself the strength and the moving spirit of all the offices of state, since every man looked to him for guidance.

18. He placed guards at the gates of Rome to prevent the frightened crowds from abandoning the city, and he regulated the times and the places at which it was permissible to lament the dead. Those who wished to go into mourning were ordered to do so in their homes for a period of thirty days, at the end of which all mourning was to cease and the city was to be purified of such rites. Since the festival of Ceres happened to fall within these dates, it was thought better to cancel both the sacrifices and the procession, since the small numbers and the dejection of those taking part could only bear a painful witness to the magnitude of the disaster; for it is the honours they receive from the fortunate which give most pleasure to the gods. However, all the rites which the augurs recommended to appease the anger of the gods or to avert inauspicious omens were duly performed. Besides this, Fabius Pictor, a relative of Fabius Maximus, was sent to consult the oracle at Delphi, and when two of the Vestal Virgins were found to have been seduced, one of them was buried alive, according to the traditional custom, and the other took her own life.

But perhaps what may impress us most of all today was the spirit of calm composure which the city displayed when Varro, the surviving consul, returned after his flight from the battlefield. He arrived in a state of the deepest dejection and humiliation, as a man who had brought a most terrible and disgraceful calamity upon his country, to find himself met by the Senate and the whole people, who welcomed him at the gates. As soon as calm had been restored the magistrates and senior members of the Senate, of whom Fabius was one, praised him because even in the midst of such a disaster he had never abandoned hope for the city, but had presented himself to take up the duties of government and to invoke the aid of the laws and of his fellow-citizens, confident that their salvation lay in their own hands.

19. When at length the citizens learned that Hannibal had turned aside after the battle and set off for other parts of Italy, their courage revived and they once more sent armies and generals into the field. The most remarkable of these were Fabius Maximus and Claudius Marcellus, both of whom earned high praise, although for qualities which were almost diametrically opposed. Marcellus, as I have related in his Life, was a brilliant leader who possessed a dynamic energy and audacity, a doughty fighting-man of the same breed as those noble warriors whom Homer calls 'high-mettled' and 'lovers of battle'. Accordingly he conducted his first operations against Hannibal in a spirit of enterprise and daring which matched Hannibal's own. Fabius, on the other hand, clung to his original ideas, and placed his faith in the principle that if nobody fought with Hannibal or even harassed him, his army would wear itself out and its fighting qualities would swiftly decline, like an athlete whose physique has been overtaxed and exhausted. This was the reason, so Poseidonius tells us, why their countrymen called Fabius the shield and Marcellus the sword of Rome, because the combination of the steadiness and caution of the one with the warlike ardour of the other proved the salvation of their country. In his frequent encounters with Marcellus it was as though Hannibal had to face a raging torrent, which battered and swept away his forces, while against Fabius, whose tactics were slow, silent, and yet relentless in their steady pressure, his strength was gradually and imperceptibly undermined and drained away. In the end he was reduced to a situation in which he was exhausted with fighting Marcellus, and afraid of Fabius because he could not fight him.

These men were his opponents almost continuously, either as praetor, consul, or pro-consul, for each of them was elected consul five times. However, while Marcellus was serving his fifth term as consul, Hannibal contrived to lure him into an ambush in which Marcellus was killed, but although he tried every kind of ruse and stratagem against Fabius, he never gained an advantage over him. Once, it is true, he was able to deceive him and very nearly inflicted a crushing defeat. He forged a number of letters which were supposed to have come from the leading citizens of Metapontum and sent them to Fabius. They offered to surrender the city if he would present himself there, and indicated that the conspirators were only waiting for him to come and show himself in their neighbourhood. Fabius was impressed by their letters, and resolved to detach a part of his army and set out for Metapontum by night. But when he found that the auspices were unfavourable, he decided to cancel his plan, and soon afterwards he discovered that the letters had been cleverly forged by Hannibal, who was waiting in ambush for him near the city, and we may perhaps attribute this escape to the favour of the gods.

20. When several of the Italian cities attempted to revolt and there were uprisings among the allies, Fabius believed that the best policy was to reason with them sympathetically and to dissuade and restrain them by lenient measures, without inquiring too closely into every case of doubtful loyalty or treating every suspected person harshly. It is said, for example, that when a certain Marsian soldier, a man of note among the allies both for the nobility of his birth and his courage, was found to be discussing with some of the soldiers the prospects of deserting to the enemy, Fabius showed no sign of anger, but admitted that the man had been unjustly passed over. This much, he said, was the fault of his commanders, who were apt to show favouritism rather than give courage its due when they awarded honours, but in future it would be the man's own fault if he did not come directly to Fabius whenever he wished to make a request. Having said this he presented him with a charger and other rewards for valour, and from that time onwards there was no more faithful nor devoted man in the army. Fabius thought it a shame that trainers of horses and dogs should be able to soften the obstinacy, discontent, and savage spirit of their charges by means of care, intimate knowledge, and a regular diet rather than by the use of whips or heavy collars, and yet that an officer who has the command of men should not base his discipline mainly upon kindness and gentleness, but should treat them with more harshness and violence than even farmers do with wild figs, olives, or pear trees, whose nature they can domesticate by careful cultivation, until they bear excellent olives and pears and figs.

In the same way when his officers reported to him that another soldier, this time a Lucanian, was repeatedly deserting his post and absenting himself from the camp, Fabius asked them their opinion of him in other respects. All of them then testified that it would be difficult to find a better soldier, and quoted several of his exploits in which he had shown extraordinary courage. When the general had inquired further into the cause of the man's disobedience, he found that the soldier was in love with a girl and frequently took the risk of making long journeys from the camp to meet her. Accordingly Fabius sent some of his men to arrest the girl without her lover's knowledge, and hid her in his own tent. Then he summoned the Lucanian to a private interview and told him, 'I know that you have many times spent the night outside the camp contrary to the customs and regulations of the Roman army. I also know that you have done good service in the past. In consideration of this I propose to overlook your present offence, but for the future I shall hand you over to the charge of someone who will be answerable for you.' Then to the soldier's amazement Fabius produced the girl and put her in his hands, saying: 'This is the person who has given her word that you will stay in the camp with us. Now you can prove by your conduct that you had no other discreditable motive, but that this girl and your love for her was the only reason that made you desert your post.' Such is the account that we have of this episode.

21. Fabius succeeded in recapturing* the city of Tarentum which the Romans had originally lost by treachery,† and here another love affair played its part. There was a young Tarentine in the Roman army whose sister was particularly devoted to him. The commander of the garrison stationed by Hannibal to defend the city, who was a Bruttian, had fallen deeply in love with this girl, and this fact encouraged her brother to hope that he might turn it to the advantage of the Romans. Fabius gave his consent to the scheme, and the young man made his way into the city under the pretence of having deserted the army to visit his sister. For the first few days of his stay the Bruttian remained at home, since the girl supposed that her brother knew nothing about their love affair. Then her brother said to her: 'When I was with the Roman army, there were rumours that one of the commanders of the garrison has been paying court to you. Who is he? If he is a man of high reputation who is well known for his courage, as I have been told, it makes little difference what country he belongs to, since war throws all our affairs into confusion and mixes all the nations together. It is no disgrace to yield to necessity. On the contrary, in these days when right has so little power, we must think ourselves lucky if might, supposing we are obliged to

* 209 B.C. † 212 B.C.

surrender to it, turns out not to be too disagreeable.' After this the girl sent for the Bruttian and introduced him to her brother, who quickly won the barbarian's confidence. Not only did he encourage the love affair, but it was clear that he persuaded his sister to show more tenderness and compliance to her lover than before. From here it was a simple step, since the Bruttian was not only a lover but a mercenary, to persuade him to transfer his allegiance to the Romans by the promise of a large reward which he would receive from Fabius.

This is the commonest version of the story. But some writers say that the woman who seduced the Bruttian from his allegiance was not a Tarentine but was herself a Bruttian, and that she had previously been Fabius's mistress. When she discovered that a fellow-countryman and acquaintance of hers was in command of the garrison, she informed Fabius, met and spoke with the man beneath the city walls, and gradually won him over to the Roman cause.

22. While this plot was being hatched, Fabius wished to devise a scheme to draw Hannibal away from the neighbourhood, and he therefore gave orders to the garrison of Rhegium to overrun and ravage the territory of the Bruttians and to take Caulonia by storm. This body of troops at Rhegium was eight thousand strong. Many of them were deserters, and they included the worst elements of the force which Marcellus had sent home from Sicily in disgrace: in fact they were men who were considered expendable and whose loss would cause the least possible harm or distress to Rome. Fabius hoped that by throwing out this force as a bait before Hannibal he would lure him away from Tarentum, and this was exactly what happened. Hannibal immediately hurried with his army to Bruttium to pursue them, and meanwhile Fabius moved in to besiege Tarentum. On the sixth day of the siege the young man, whose sister had helped him to concert his plan with the Bruttian commander, came to visit Fabius at night. He had seen and inspected the place where the Bruttian would be keeping watch to let in the besiegers and hand over the city. But Fabius was not prepared to make his plans entirely dependent on this act of treachery. Accordingly he himself led a body of troops to the appointed place, while the rest of the army launched a general attack on the walls by land and sea. Their assault was accompanied by a tremendous clamour and commotion, until most of the Tarentines had rushed to the support of the defenders.

Then the Bruttian gave Fabius the signal, whereupon he and his men scaled the walls and took possession of the city.

At this point, however, Fabius's ambition seems to have proved stronger than his principles, for he ordered his men to put the Bruttian contingent to the sword* before anyone else, so as to conceal the fact that he had captured the city by treachery. However, he not only failed to win the credit for this exploit, but he incurred the charge of bad faith and inhumanity. Besides the Bruttians many of the Tarentines were killed, thirty thousand of them were sold into slavery, their city was sacked by the Roman army, and the public treasury was enriched by the sum of three thousand talents. While everything else was being carried off as plunder, it is said that the officer who was drawing up a schedule of public property asked Fabius what were his orders concerning the gods, by which he meant the paintings and statues, and that Fabius replied, 'Let us leave the Tarentines their angry gods.'† However, he removed the gigantic statue of Hercules and had it placed on the Capitol, and close by he erected an equestrian statue of himself in bronze. Fabius showed himself to be far more arbitrary in these dealings than Marcellus, or rather he proved by the contrast between them that Marcellus was a man of extraordinary mildness and humanity, as I have indicated in his Life.‡

23. It is said that Hannibal had arrived within five miles of Tarentum when the city fell, and that in public he merely remarked, 'It seems that the Romans have found another Hannibal, for we have lost Tarentum in the same way that we took it.' But in private he admitted to his friends for the first time that he had long recognized that it was very difficult for them to conquer Italy with their present forces, and that he now believed it was impossible.

* Livy (XXVII, 16) implies that the slaughter of the Bruttians was occasioned by a traditional feud between themselves and the Romans and was not carried out at Fabius's orders.

† Livy contrasts the attitude of Fabius with that of Marcellus, who removed so many works of art from Syracuse in 212 B.C. 'Fabius killed the people but spared their gods; Marcellus spared the people but took their gods.' Fabius's phrase conceals two meanings. Tarentum had been founded by the Spartans, who liked to depict the gods in warlike poses (even their Aphrodite wore armour). Thus the Tarentine gods were angry in a double sense, and Fabius may have wished not only to spare the Tarentines yet another grievance, but also to preserve the Romans from the luxury of Greek statuary.

‡ See *Life of Marcellus* (ch. 21).

For this success Fabius celebrated a second triumph, which was even more magnificent than his first. The Romans saw that he was dealing with Hannibal like an experienced wrestler, and had mastered the technique of frustrating his opponent's moves, now that his grips and holds had lost their original force. The truth was that some of Hannibal's troops had become enervated by luxury and plunder,* while others had had their fighting qualities blunted and worn down by incessant campaigning.

Now there was a certain Marcus Livius, who had been in command of the garrison of Tarentum when Hannibal had persuaded the city to revolt. He had seized the citadel, however, and had never been dislodged from this position, but continued to hold out until the town was recaptured by the Romans. Livius was annoyed at the honours which were conferred on Fabius, and on this occasion he was so far carried away by his jealousy and ambition as to declare that it was not Fabius but he who was responsible for the capture of Tarentum. At this Fabius burst out laughing and retorted 'You are quite right, Livius. If you had not lost the city, I could never have recaptured it.'

24. One of the many marks of honour which the people bestowed upon Fabius was to elect his son as consul.† After he had taken up his office and was dealing with some business concerning the conduct of the war, his father, either because of his age and weakness, or perhaps because he was putting his son to the test, mounted his horse and rode towards him through the crowd of bystanders. The young man caught sight of him at a distance and refused to allow this affront to his office. He sent a lictor to order him to dismount and approach on foot if he had any business with the consul. Those who were present were offended at this command and turned their eyes towards Fabius in silence, while their looks expressed their indignation at such officious treatment of a man of his reputation. But Fabius himself leaped from his horse, and with open arms almost ran to his son and embraced him affectionately, saying, 'You are right, my son, both in your thought and your action. You understand the nature of the people who have chosen you to govern and the grandeur of the

* Hannibal had occupied the wealthy city of Capua after his victory at Cannae and made it his winter headquarters.

† In 213 B.C.

office you have received from them. This was the way in which we and our forefathers made Rome great, by putting the honour and the service of our country before those of our own parents and children.' And indeed there is a similar story concerning the great-grandfather of our Fabius. Even though he possessed the greatest reputation and influence of any man in Rome, had served five times as consul and had celebrated the most magnificent triumphs after the greatest wars of his time, nevertheless, when his son became consul and set out for the war,* he himself served as his subordinate. Then in the triumph that followed, while the son entered the city in a four-horse chariot, the father followed on horseback with the rest of the procession, and he took pride in the fact that while he had authority over his son as a private individual and was himself both in name and in reality the greatest man in the state, yet he was ready to submit himself to the law and the chief magistrate. This, of course, was not the only admirable thing about him.

Fabius had the misfortune to lose his son, but he bore this blow patiently like a wise man and a good father. It is the custom at Rome, whenever a famous man dies, for one of his relatives to pronounce a funeral oration. Fabius delivered this from his place in the Forum, and later wrote out the speech and distributed it among his friends.

25. Meanwhile Publius Cornelius Scipio had been sent to Spain, where he not only defeated the Carthaginians in a series of battles and drove them out of the country, but also brought many tribes over to his side, captured great cities, and achieved glorious deeds for Rome. When he returned to the capital, he was acclaimed and idolized as no Roman had ever been before, and was promptly elected consul. But since he recognized that the people expected and demanded some tremendous achievement from him, he came to the conclusion that the strategy of containing Hannibal in Italy was now out of date and had become an old man's task. His plan was that the Romans should pour troops into Libya, attack and ravage the territory of Carthage herself, and transfer the scene of the war from Italy to Africa, and he threw himself heart and soul into the task of arousing the people to support this policy. But now Fabius did his utmost to spread doubts and misgivings of every kind against the proposal. He argued that they were rushing into grave and unknown perils under

* In 212 B.C.

the leadership of a hot-headed young man, and he did not hesitate to say or do anything which he thought might dissuade his fellow-countrymen from adopting his opponent's policy. He succeeded in convincing the Senate, but the people believed that he was attacking Scipio out of jealousy of his exploits, and also because he was afraid that if Scipio achieved some brilliant and decisive success and either finished off the war or removed it from Italy, then he himself might be condemned as a lazy and cowardly general for having allowed the fighting to drag on for so many years.

It seems likely that Fabius's opposition originally sprang from his instinctive caution and prudence and that he was genuinely alarmed by the risks involved in Scipio's strategy, which indeed were great, but that in the course of time the effort to check his opponent's rising influence made his attitude more violent and extreme and introduced an element of personal rivalry and ambition into the conflict. He even tried to persuade Crassus, Scipio's fellow-consul, not to hand over the command of the army to his colleague but to lead it to Carthage himself, if the decision to invade Africa were adopted, and he also prevented the voting of any funds for the campaign. Scipio was left in the position of having to find the money himself, and he therefore collected it on his private account from the cities of Etruria, which were devotedly loyal to him. As for Crassus, he remained at home, partly because he was a peaceable man by nature and had no inclination to quarrel with his colleague, and partly on religious grounds, since he held the office of Pontifex Maximus, which obliged him to remain in Italy.

26. After this Fabius adopted a different set of tactics. He tried to prevent the young men who were anxious to serve under Scipio from taking part in the campaign. He complained at meetings of the Senate and the Assembly that it was not merely a question of Scipio's running away from Hannibal: he was proposing to sail off with the whole reserve of Italy's manpower, and he was deluding these young men with false hopes and persuading them to abandon their parents, their wives, and their city, while a conquering and still undefeated enemy threatened the very gates of Rome. He succeeded in alarming the Romans to such an extent with these arguments that they decreed that Scipio should only take with him the troops that were already in Sicily, together with a detachment of three hundred picked men, who

had served him loyally in Spain. In insisting on this policy Fabius was clearly dominated by the dictates of his own cautious nature.

However, no sooner had Scipio landed in Africa* than almost immediately news began to arrive in Rome of extraordinary achievements, brilliant exploits, and decisive victories. The reports were quickly substantiated by the immense spoils which followed these successes. The king of Numidia was captured, two of the enemy's camps were burned and destroyed together with great quantities of men, horses, and arms, and envoys were sent to Hannibal with urgent instructions that he must abandon his fruitless hopes in Italy and hasten home to the rescue of his native city. And yet when every tongue in Rome was applauding Scipio's victories, this was the moment which Fabius chose to demand that he should be recalled and a successor sent out. He did not attempt to justify this request, but merely repeated the familiar proverb to the effect that it was dangerous to entrust such immense operations to the fortune of one man, since it is difficult for any single man to enjoy good fortune at all times. This proposal offended most of Fabius's fellow-citizens, who felt that he was now acting out of mere peevishness and malice, or else that in his old age he had lost all his courage and confidence and was obsessed by an exaggerated fear of Hannibal. For even when Hannibal and his army had sailed away from Italy, Fabius still could not refrain from casting gloom over the general rejoicings and dashing his fellow-countrymen's spirits. The city, he prophesied, was now facing her final and most terrible ordeal, for they would find Hannibal a far more formidable enemy under the walls of Carthage than he had ever been in Italy, and Scipio would have to meet an army which was still reeking with the blood of many generals, dictators, and consuls. By means of such speeches he again succeeded in filling the city with dismay, and although the war had been transferred to Africa, yet its terrors seemed to have moved nearer than ever to Rome.

27. But not long afterwards Scipio defeated Hannibal himself in a pitched battle† and crushed the pride of Carthage underfoot. He gave his countrymen a joy that went far beyond all their hopes and, in restoring their supremacy,

Righted the ship that storms so long had tossed.

* In 204 B.C. † At Zama, 202 B.C.

Fabius Maximus, however, did not live to see the end of the war, nor did he ever hear of Hannibal's overthrow, nor witness the glorious and lasting prosperity of his country, for at about the time when Hannibal sailed from Italy, he fell sick and died.*

Epaminondas was buried by the Thebans at the public expense, because when he died, so the story goes, he was so poor that nothing was found in his house but a single obol. The Romans did not bury Fabius at the expense of the state, but every citizen contributed the smallest coin in his possession towards the funeral. This was not because he was so poor as to need their help, but rather because they felt that they were burying the father of the people. Thus in his death he received the honour and regard which he had earned by the conduct of his life.

* In 203 B.C.

3

MARCELLUS

[271–208 B.C.]

* *
*

1. Marcus Claudius, who five times held the office of consul of the Roman people, was the son of Marcus, and according to Poseidonius was the first of his family to be given the name of Marcellus, which means warlike. Much of his experience was concerned with the art of war and he possessed a powerful arm and a vigorous body. Fighting appealed to his temperament, and he was a daring soldier who bore himself with lordly assurance on the battlefield, but in other respects he was modest and humane. He had enough regard for Greek culture and literature to make him honour and admire those who excelled in them, but he himself never found the leisure to master or even study these subjects to the extent that he would have wished. For if ever there were men for whom, as Homer says,

> The gods decreed that from youth until ripe old age they should labour
> Fighting in arduous wars . . .*

they were the foremost Romans of his generation. In their youth they campaigned against the Carthaginians for the possession of Sicily: in their prime they fought the Gauls for the defence of Italy itself, and as veterans they found themselves matched once more against the Carthaginians, this time under Hannibal. In this way they never enjoyed the relief from active service which old age brings to most men, but because of their noble birth and their prowess in war they were constantly summoned to take up new commands.

2. Marcellus was a trained and expert soldier in every branch of fighting, but it was above all in single combat that he excelled: he

* *Iliad* XIV, 86–7.

never declined a challenge and he killed every opponent who challenged him. In Sicily he saved the life of his brother Otacilius, when he was in mortal danger, by covering him with his shield and killing his attackers. For these exploits he was awarded crowns and other decorations by his commanders, although he was still only a young man, and as his reputation increased, the people elected him to the office of curule aedile, and the priests chose him to be an augur. This is a branch of the priesthood to which the law assigns as one of its most important functions the observation and study of auguries, which arise from the flight of birds.

While he was aedile he was obliged to bring a disagreeable accusation before the Senate. He had a son, also named Marcus, who was just then in the flower of his youthful beauty, and who was admired by his fellow-countrymen as much for his modesty and his exemplary upbringing as for his good looks. Marcellus's colleague, Capitolinus, a dissolute man, whose passions were as shameless as they were uncontrolled, tried to seduce him. The boy at first repelled his advances by himself, but when they were repeated, he confided in his father. Marcellus was furious, and denounced the man before the Senate. Capitolinus tried by various shifts and evasions to quibble his way out of the charge, then appealed to the tribunes of the people, and finally, when they rejected his plea, flatly denied the accusation. As there had been no witnesses of his behaviour, the Senate decided to send for the boy. When he appeared before them and they saw how he blushed and wept, and how his feelings of shame were mingled with an unquenchable indignation, they decided that no further proof was necessary, but immediately condemned Capitolinus and fined him. Marcellus used the money from the fine to commission some silver libation bowls and dedicated these to the gods.

3. After the first Punic war had ended in its twenty-second year,* Rome once more found herself engaged in a struggle with the Gauls. The Insubrians were a Celtic people, who inhabit the part of Italy which lies at the foot of the Alps, and although they were strong in numbers, they not only mobilized their own forces, but called in the help of the Gallic mercenaries known as the Gaesatae. It seemed to be a piece of miraculously good fortune for Rome that this Gallic war did not break out while the struggle with Carthage was still in

* In 241 B.C.: the war with the Insubrians did not in fact begin until 225 B.C.

progress, but that the Gauls, like a third competitor, sat on one side awaiting their turn, and remained scrupulously inactive while the other two nations fought each other, and then only stripped for action when the victors were ready to receive their challenge. But even so the prospect of the war aroused the deepest fears among the Romans, partly because they would be engaging an enemy who lived so near their own frontiers and homes, and partly because of the traditional prestige of the Gauls, whom the Romans seem to have feared more than any other enemy. The Romans never forgot that it was this people who had once captured their city,* and afterwards they had passed a law that their priests should normally be exempt from military service, the exception being in the event of a fresh invasion by the Gauls. They gave further proof of their fears in their exceptional preparations for the war, for it is said that never before nor since were so many thousands of Romans called upon to bear arms at once, and also in the extraordinary sacrifices which they offered to the gods. The Romans do not practise any barbarous or outlandish rites, and in the humane sentiments which they cherish towards their divinities they come nearer than any other people to the Greeks: nevertheless at the outbreak of this war they felt obliged to follow out certain oracular instructions laid down in the Sibylline Books, and to bury alive two Greeks, a man and a woman, and likewise two Gauls in the place known as the Cattle-market;† and in accordance with these oracles they still to this day in the month of November perform certain ceremonies, which may not be spoken of nor witnessed by either Greeks or Gauls.

4. The opening battles of this war brought great victories and also great disasters to the Romans, but none of these proved decisive, until the two consuls Flaminius and Furius led a strong army against the Insubrians. But just as they set out, the river which flows through Picenum was seen to be running with blood: it was reported that three moons had been seen at the city of Ariminum, and at the same time the augurs, whose duty it was to observe the flight of birds during the consular elections, insisted that the omens had been inauspicious and hostile at the moment when the victorious candidates' names had been announced. Thereupon the Senate immediately had letters dispatched to the camp in which they summoned the

* In 390 B.C. † In the Forum Boarium at Rome.

consuls to return to the city as quickly as possible to lay down their office, and forbade them to undertake any action against the enemy so long as they remained in authority. When these letters were delivered, Flaminius refused to open them until he had first engaged the barbarians, routed them in battle, and overrun their territory. For this reason, when he returned to Rome laden with great quantities of booty, the people would not go out to meet him. Instead, because he had not immediately complied with the order recalling him, but had disobeyed the letters and treated them with insolent contempt, the people came near to denying him the honour of a triumph, and as soon as he had celebrated it, they compelled both him and his colleague to lay down their consulship and reduced him to the rank of private citizen. Such were the scruples of the Romans in referring all their affairs to the will of the gods, nor would they tolerate the smallest oversight in the observation of omens and traditional rites, even if the omission were followed by the most brilliant successes. In short they regarded it as more important for the safety of the state that their magistrates should honour religious observances than that they should defeat their enemies.

5. As an example of this belief I may quote the case of Tiberius Sempronius, a man whose reputation for courage and upright conduct was second to none in Rome, and who announced the names of Scipio Nasica and Gaius Marcius as his successors in the consulship. When these two men had already arrived in their provinces and taken up command of their armies, Sempronius came by chance upon a book which specified the various religious ceremonials, and discovered in it an instruction of which he had never even heard before. It was this. Whenever a consul has hired a house or a tent outside the city walls for the purpose of sitting there and taking the auspices by observing the flight of birds, and he is obliged for any reason to return to the city before sure signs have appeared, he must give up the house which he originally hired and take another, and must begin all his observations afresh. Tiberius had apparently been unaware of this instruction and had twice used the same house before proclaiming as consuls the men whose names I have mentioned. When he discovered his error he reported the matter to the Senate. The Senate decided that they could not treat even such a minor act of negligence lightly, but sent out letters to the consuls, who in turn

immediately left their provinces, returned to Rome with all speed and resigned their appointments. These events took place at a later date. But in the present instance two priests of the noblest families were deprived of their offices, Cornelius Cethegus because he failed to observe the proper procedure in presenting the entrails of a victim, and Quintus Sulpicius because, while he was sacrificing, the peaked cap, which is worn by the priests who are known as *flamines*, had fallen off his head. Again, because the squeak of a shrew-mouse was heard at the moment when Minucius the dictator was appointing Gaius Flaminius as his master of horse, the people thereupon deprived both men of their positions and put others in their places. Yet although they were so scrupulous in observing these minute details, they did not indulge in any kind of superstition, because they never permitted any change or departure from their ancient rites.

6. To return to our narrative. When Flaminius and his colleague Furius had resigned their offices, Marcellus was chosen as consul by the so-called *interreges*,* and after taking up the office he nominated Gnaeus Cornelius as his colleague. Now it has been alleged that although the Gauls put forward a number of conciliatory proposals, and although the Senate was in favour of concluding peace, Marcellus stirred up the people's indignation so as to persuade them to continue the war. In spite of this it appears that a peace was made, and that the Gaesatae broke it when they crossed the Alps and stirred up the Insubrians. The Gaesatae mustered thirty thousand men, while the Insubrians' numbers were even larger, and since they were now full of confidence in their strength, they immediately marched against Acerrae,† a town which was situated to the north of the river Po. Having arrived in this region, their king Britomartus detached a force of ten thousand Gaesatae and proceeded to ravage the country in the neighbourhood of the Po. When this news reached Marcellus, he left his colleague at Acerrae in command of all the heavy infantry and a third of the cavalry. Then taking with him the rest of the cavalry

* These officials were appointed when there were no consuls in office to supervise the consular elections. They held office for five days and if necessary appointed successors until the consulship was filled.

† Plutarch's account is somewhat misleading. The Romans had been besieging Acerrae and the Gauls had advanced to relieve it. Finding themselves unable to do so, they laid siege to Clastidium to create a diversion.

and six hundred of the most agile of his light infantry, he marched day and night without a halt until he came up with the ten thousand Gaesatae near Clastidium, a Gallic village which had submitted to Roman rule not long before. There was no time for him to rest or refresh his troops, since his arrival was quickly discovered by the barbarians. They felt nothing but contempt for his tiny force of infantry, and, since they were Gauls, had no great opinion of the Roman cavalry. The Gauls are particularly formidable at fighting on horseback, and in fact they have the reputation of excelling in this arm above any other, while on this occasion they also greatly outnumbered Marcellus. Headed by their king and shouting bloodcurdling threats at the tops of their voices, they immediately launched a furious charge, expecting to sweep the Romans away. But Marcellus was determined to prevent them from outflanking and encircling his small force; as he led his cavalry forward he made them fan out, and so extended his wings into a thin line until he was almost in contact with the enemy. Then, just as he was turning to launch a charge, his horse, startled by the enemy's ferocious shouts, suddenly wheeled about and carried him to the rear. Marcellus was alarmed that this sight might be taken as a bad omen and create confusion among the Romans, so he at once reined his horse to the left and forced the animal to face the enemy. At the same time he went through the movements of praying to the sun, as if it was for this purpose that he had wheeled his horse, for the Romans always turn in this way when they offer worship to the gods. Then just before he closed with the enemy, he is said to have vowed that he would sacrifice to Jupiter Feretrius the finest suit of armour to be found among the Gauls.

7. It was now that the king of the Gauls first saw Marcellus. He guessed from his badges of rank that this was the Roman commander, and riding far out in front of his men he made directly for him, shouting out a challenge and brandishing his lance. He stood out among the rest of the Gauls, not only for his size but for his complete suit of armour, which was embossed with gold and silver and decorated with brilliant colours and elaborate designs, so that it glittered like lightning. As Marcellus glanced along the enemy's ranks, he thought that this was the finest armour of all, and concluded that it must be the offering which he had vowed to the god. So he charged

the Gaul and pierced his breast-plate with his lance: the impetus of his horse hurled his opponent to the ground still living, and a second and a third blow immediately dispatched him. Thereupon Marcellus leaped from his horse and, laying his hands on the dead man's armour, he gazed up to heaven and cried aloud: 'Jupiter Feretrius, you who judge the great deeds of generals and captains in war and on the battlefield, I call upon you to witness that I, a Roman general and a consul, have killed with my own hand a general and a king, that I am the third Roman commander to do this, and that I dedicate to you the first and the finest of the spoils. I pray that you will grant us no less good fortune as we fight out the rest of this war.'

As he ended his prayer, the Roman cavalry charged and found themselves engaging not only the Gallic horsemen but also their supporting infantry, who attacked them at the same time. But in the end they won a victory which was as unparalleled as it was unexpected. Never before nor since, so we are told, had so few mounted troops overcome such a large combined force of cavalry and infantry. The Gauls lost the greater part of their army and their weapons and baggage were captured, after which Marcellus returned to join his colleague, who was holding out with difficulty against another Gallic army in the neighbourhood of their largest and most populous city. This was Mediolanum,* which the Cisalpine Gauls regard as the capital of their country, and they defended it with such spirit that Cornelius found his army had become the besieged rather than the besiegers. However, when Marcellus arrived and the Gaesatae learned that their king had been defeated and killed, they retired to their own territory. Mediolanum was captured and the Gauls surrendered the rest of their cities of their own accord and offered their submission to the Romans. They were granted peace on equitable terms.

8. The Senate decreed that only Marcellus should be granted a triumph. His procession produced a superb spectacle such as has seldom been seen in Rome, both for the splendour and riches of the spoils of war and for the gigantic size of the prisoners. But the most unusual and impressive sight of all was that of the general himself, when he appeared to carry the barbarian king's armour as an offering to the god. He had cut the tall, straight trunk of a young oak tree,

* The modern Milan.

trimmed it into the shape of a trophy, and upon this he had fastened and hung the spoils, with each part of the armour arranged in its proper position. When the procession began to move, he took up the tree himself, mounted his four-horse chariot, and in this way an image of victory, the finest and most glorious ever seen in his day, was borne in state through the city. His troops followed, clad in their most brilliant armour, and as they marched they sang odes composed for the occasion and paeans of victory in honour of the god and their general. In this way Marcellus traversed the city until he reached the temple of Jupiter Feretrius, where he dismounted and dedicated his offering. He was the third, and, up to our day, the last Roman to achieve this feat. The first was Romulus, who offered up the spoils of Acron of Caeninum; the second was Cornelius Cossus with the spoils of Tolumnius the Tuscan; after them Marcellus with the spoils of Britomartus, king of the Gauls; and since Marcellus no man. The god to whom the spoils were dedicated is called Jupiter Feretrius. Some people say that this surname is derived from the *pheretron*, or car in which the trophy was carried. The word is Greek, like many others which had at that time been absorbed into Latin. Others say that the epithet refers to Jupiter as the wielder of the thunderbolt, since *ferire* is the Latin word which means 'to strike'. Another explanation is that the word is derived from a blow given to the enemy, because even down to the present day, when the Romans are pursuing their enemies, they encourage one another by shouting the word *feri*, meaning 'strike!' The word for spoils in general is *spolia*, but these particular spoils are known as *spolia opima*. It has been pointed out, however, that Numa Pompilius in his commentaries mentions three categories of *opima*. He lays it down that those of the first degree are to be consecrated to Jupiter Feretrius, those of the second to Mars, and those of the third to Quirinus, and also that the reward for the first is to be three hundred asses, for the second two hundred, and for the third one hundred. However, the most generally accepted account is that the only spoils which rank as *opima* are those which are captured in a pitched battle before the fighting begins, when the general kills the opposing commander with his own hand. So much then for this subject.

The Roman people were so overjoyed at this victory and at the ending of the war that they sent the Pythian Apollo at Delphi a golden bowl as a thanks-offering. They also presented a generous share of the spoils to the allied cities, and sent many presents to Hiero the ruler of Syracuse, who was their friend and ally.

9. After Hannibal had invaded Italy, Marcellus was sent to Sicily in command of a fleet.* Then came the disastrous defeat at Cannae,† in which thousands of Romans were killed and only a few saved their lives by fleeing to Canusium. Everyone expected that Hannibal would immediately march on the capital, now that he had destroyed the flower of the Roman army. At this point Marcellus dispatched fifteen hundred men from his fleet to help to defend Rome, and then under orders from the Senate he went to Canusium, collected the soldiers who had taken refuge there, and made a sortie from their fortified camp to show Hannibal that he had no intention of abandoning the surrounding countryside. By this time the Romans had lost the greater number of their generals and prominent men in battle, while Fabius Maximus, who had earned the highest reputation for his reliability and shrewdness of judgement was blamed for his excessive caution, and his anxiety to avoid losses at any cost was attacked as mere cowardly passivity. The people regarded him as a general who was perfectly qualified to carry on a defensive campaign, but who could never move over to the offensive. They therefore turned to Marcellus, and in the hope of combining his boldness and energy with Fabius's caution and foresight, they sometimes elected both as consuls together and sometimes sent out one as consul and the other as pro-consul. Poseidonius says that Fabius was called the shield and Marcellus the sword of Rome. And indeed Hannibal himself declared that he feared Fabius as a schoolmaster and Marcellus as an opponent. The first prevented him from inflicting losses on the Romans: the second inflicted them on him.

10. One of the first consequences of Hannibal's victory at Cannae was that his troops became over-confident and careless of their discipline. Scattered groups of men would leave their camp and roam the countryside in search of plunder, whereupon Marcellus would swoop down and cut off these stragglers, and in this way he gradually weakened the Carthaginian army. Secondly he did much to relieve the situation of Neapolis and of Nola. In Neapolis he strengthened the resolution of the citizens, who were already staunch allies of

* In 218 B.C. † In 216 B.C.

Rome by their own choice. Nola, on the other hand, he found in a far more unsettled state, since the senate was unable either to control or to win over the people, who wished to ally themselves with Hannibal. One of the leading citizens, who was prominent not only for his aristocratic birth but also for his bravery in the field, was a man named Bantius. He had shown the greatest courage in fighting for the Romans at Cannae, where he had killed many Carthaginians, and when he was at last found among the heaps of the dead with his body riddled with barbs, Hannibal felt so much admiration for his gallantry that he not only released him without a ransom, but presented him with gifts of his own accord and entertained him as a personal friend. In return for this generous treatment Bantius became one of Hannibal's most ardent supporters, and proceeded to use all his influence to make the people revolt against Rome. Marcellus felt that it would be a crime to put to death a man of such brilliant achievements, who had fought side by side with the Romans in their greatest battles; and in addition to his natural kindliness of manner he possessed the knack of winning the confidence of men who are dedicated to the pursuit of honour. So one day when Bantius greeted him, he asked him who he was. Of course Marcellus knew this perfectly well, but he wanted an excuse to strike up a conversation with him. Then when the man answered, 'Lucius Bantius', Marcellus, pretending to be surprised and delighted, exclaimed: 'What, are you the same Lucius Bantius who is more talked of in Rome than any other man who fought at Cannae – the only soldier, so they say, who did not abandon Paulus Aemilius, the consul, but received in your own body most of the spears and arrows that were aimed at him?' When Bantius answered that he was the man and showed Marcellus some of his scars, the general went on: 'Well then, since you carry with you all these marks of your devotion to Rome, why did you not come to us at once? Do you think that we are slow to reward such courage in our friends, when even our enemies go out of their way to honour it?' After paying Bantius these compliments he embraced him, and soon afterwards presented him with a war horse and five hundred silver drachmas.

11. After this Bantius became a staunch supporter and ally of Marcellus, and played an important part in tracking down and denouncing the activities of Hannibal's partisans. These were very numerous, and

they organized a plot to seize the Roman baggage train as soon as the army marched out against the enemy. Marcellus therefore marshalled his troops inside the city, had the baggage placed near the various gates, and then issued a proclamation forbidding the citizens of Nola to approach the walls. In this way he made sure that there were no armed men to be seen, and Hannibal was tricked into leading his troops up to the walls without first putting them into battle order, as he supposed that fighting was going on inside the city. At this moment Marcellus ordered the gate behind which he was waiting to be thrown open. He had his best cavalry formations with him, and immediately launched them against the enemy. Soon after, his infantry sallied forth from another gate, and with loud shouts bore down upon the Carthaginians at the run. Finally while Hannibal was regrouping his forces to meet these attacks, a third gate was flung open, and through this the remainder of the Roman army poured out and attacked the enemy on all sides. This unexpected onslaught threw the Carthaginians into confusion, and they put up only a weak resistance against the first attack, because of the troops whom they could see in the distance bearing down upon them. Hannibal's troops were driven back to their camp with heavy losses both in killed and wounded, the first occasion on which they had ever been put to flight by the Romans. It is said that more than five thousand of them lost their lives against a bare five hundred on the Roman side. Livy, however, does not consider that the Carthaginians suffered a major defeat in this battle, nor does he say that they lost so many men, but he confirms that the victory brought great prestige to Marcellus, and had a wonderful effect in raising the spirits of the Romans after the disasters they had suffered. They could now feel that they were faced not by an invincible and irresistible enemy, but by one who was just as liable to suffer a defeat as themselves.

12. It was for this reason that when one of the consuls was killed,* the people called upon Marcellus to take his place. They did this even though he was absent from Rome at the time, and in spite of the wishes of the magistrates they postponed the election until he could return from the army. When he arrived he was elected consul by a unanimous vote. But it so happened that a peal of thunder was heard

* Lucius Postumius Albinus was defeated and killed by the Boii, a Gallic tribe, in 215 B.C.

at that moment, and the augurs regarded this as an inauspicious omen.* However, their fear of the people was such that they did not dare to oppose his election openly, and so Marcellus himself voluntarily resigned his office. But this did not mean that he laid down his military command: instead he was created pro-consul, returned to Nola, and began to take action there against the party which had sided with the Carthaginians. When Hannibal hurried to Nola to rescue his supporters and tried to bring about a pitched battle, Marcellus refused to be drawn; but as soon as Hannibal had allowed the greater part of his force to disperse on various plundering raids and was no longer expecting a battle, the Romans made a sortie and attacked him. Marcellus had armed his infantry with the long spears which are used in naval fighting, and had taught them to watch for their opportunity and hurl their weapons at the enemy from long range, as the Carthaginians were not trained in throwing the javelin and carried only short spears for hand to hand fighting. These tactics seem to have produced remarkable results. All the Carthaginians who were engaged in this battle with the Romans turned tail and fled at once. They lost five thousand dead and six hundred prisoners, while four of their elephants were killed and two captured alive. But the most significant event of all was that on the third day after the battle more than three hundred Spanish and Numidian horsemen deserted to the Romans. This was the first time that Hannibal had ever experienced such a disaster, for although he commanded a barbarian army composed of many separate and diverse nationalities, he had succeeded year after year in preserving a spirit which united all the troops serving under him. Nevertheless the men who deserted to the Romans remained completely loyal for the rest of the war both to Marcellus and to the generals who succeeded him.

13. In the following year after Marcellus had been elected consul for the third time,† he sailed to Sicily. Hannibal's successes in Italy had encouraged the Carthaginians to make another attempt to recover the island, especially as the affairs of Syracuse had been thrown into

* Marcellus was a plebeian, as was his colleague Sempronius. It was the patricians who put pressure upon the augurs to make this pronouncement, because they were unwilling to have two plebeians as consuls simultaneously.

† In 214 B.C. His colleague was Fabius Maximus.

confusion after the death of the tyrant Hieronymus.* Indeed the situation there had already compelled the Romans to dispatch an army under the praetor Appius Claudius. As soon as Marcellus had taken over the command of this force, great numbers of Romans, whose predicament I shall now describe, presented themselves at his camp to petition him. Of the Roman army which had faced Hannibal at Cannae some had fled from the battlefield, while so many had been taken prisoner that it was believed that the Romans did not have enough men left to defend the walls of the capital. Yet in spite of this the citizens' resolve remained so firm and their spirit so unconquerable that although Hannibal offered to release his prisoners of war for a small ransom, the people voted against their return. Instead they allowed some to be put to death and others to be sold into slavery outside Italy. As for the large number of survivors who had saved themselves by running away, they sent them to Sicily and forbade them to set foot again in Italy so long as the war against Hannibal lasted. These were the men who crowded around Marcellus as soon as he arrived, threw themselves at his feet, and implored him with tears and lamentations to admit them once more to honourable military service: they swore that they would prove by their actions that the defeat they had suffered had been caused by misfortune not by cowardice. Marcellus took pity on them and wrote to the Senate asking for permission to enlist these men so as to make up the losses in his own army as they occurred. A lengthy debate followed, at the end of which the Senate's verdict was that the Romans did not need the services of cowards, but that if Marcellus nevertheless wished to employ them, they must not be awarded any of the usual honours or prizes for valour. This decree angered Marcellus, and when he returned to Rome after the end of the war in Sicily, he reproached the Senate because they had not allowed him in consideration of his many great services to rescue this large body of citizens from their wretched situation.

* Hiero II, the patron not only of Archimedes but also of the poet Theocritus, ruled Syracuse for over fifty years. For most of this time he was a loyal ally of the Romans, whom he assisted in the first Punic war. He died in 216 B.C. His fifteen-year-old grandson Hieronymus, who succeeded him, was obliged by the council of regency to support the Carthaginian cause and was soon afterwards murdered, whereupon the Carthaginian faction led by Hippocrates seized power in 214 B.C.

14. But to return to the campaign in Sicily. Marcellus was first of all confronted with an outrage committed by Hippocrates, the commander of the Syracusans. This man, in order to secure the support of the Carthaginians and make himself tyrant, slaughtered many of the Romans living in Leontini, whereupon Marcellus stormed and captured the city. He did no harm to the native inhabitants, but had all the deserters whom he captured flogged and beheaded. At this Hippocrates first sent a report to Syracuse that Marcellus was massacring all the inhabitants of Leontini, and when this rumour had created a panic in the city, he suddenly attacked and captured it. Marcellus responded by moving his whole army up to Syracuse. He encamped close by and sent envoys into the city to give the people the true account of what had happened at Leontini, but this manoeuvre proved ineffective and the Syracusans refused to listen to them, as Hippocrates and his supporters were now in control. Marcellus's next action was to attack the city by land and sea simultaneously, the land forces being commanded by Appius, while Marcellus directed a fleet of sixty quinquiremes, which were equipped with many different kinds of weapons and missiles. In addition he had built a siege-engine which was mounted on a huge platform supported by eight galleys lashed together, and with this he sailed up to the city walls, confident that the size and the imposing spectacle of his armament together with his personal prestige would combine to overawe the Syracusans. But he had reckoned without Archimedes, and the Roman machines turned out to be insignificant not only in the philosopher's estimation, but also by comparison with those which he had constructed himself. Archimedes did not regard his military inventions as an achievement of any importance, but merely as a by-product, which he occasionally pursued for his own amusement, of his serious work, namely the study of geometry. He had done this in the past because Hiero, the former ruler of Syracuse, had often pressed and finally persuaded him to divert his studies from the pursuit of abstract principles to the solution of practical problems, and to make his theories more intelligible to the majority of mankind by applying them through the medium of the senses to the needs of everyday life.

It was Eudoxus and Archytas who were the originators of the now celebrated and highly prized art of mechanics. They used it with great ingenuity to illustrate geometrical theorems, and to support by means of mechanical demonstrations easily grasped by the senses propositions which are too intricate for proof by word or diagram. For example, to solve the problem of finding two mean proportional lines, which are necessary for the construction of many other geometrical figures, both mathematicians resorted to mechanical means, and adapted to their purposes certain instruments named mesolabes taken from conic sections. Plato was indignant at these developments, and attacked both men for having corrupted and destroyed the ideal purity of geometry. He complained that they had caused her to forsake the realm of disembodied and abstract thought for that of material objects, and to employ instruments which required much base and manual labour. For this reason mechanics came to be separated from geometry, and as the subject was for a long time disregarded by philosophers, it took its place among the military arts.

However this may be, Archimedes in writing to Hiero, who was both a relative and a friend of his, asserted that with any given force it was possible to move any given weight, and then, carried away with enthusiasm at the power of his demonstration, so we are told, went on to enlarge his claim, and declared that if he were given another world to stand on, he could move the earth. Hiero was amazed, and invited him to put his theorem into practice and show him some great weight moved by a tiny force. Archimedes chose for his demonstration a three-masted merchantman of the royal fleet, which had been hauled ashore with immense labour by a large gang of men, and he proceeded to have the ship loaded with her usual freight and embarked a large number of passengers. He then seated himself at some distance away and without using any noticeable force, but merely exerting traction with his hand through a complex system of pulleys, he drew the vessel towards him with as smooth and even a motion is if she were gliding through the water. The king was deeply impressed, and recognizing the potentialities of his skill, he persuaded Archimedes to construct for him a number of engines designed both for attack and defence, which could be employed in any kind of siege warfare. Hiero himself never had occasion to use these, since most of his life was spent at peace amid festivals and public ceremonies, but when the present war broke out, the apparatus was ready for the Syracusans to use and its inventor was at hand to direct its employment.

15. When the Romans first attacked by sea and land, the Syracusans were struck dumb with terror and believed that nothing could resist the onslaught of such powerful forces. But presently Archimedes brought his engines to bear and launched a tremendous barrage against the Roman army. This consisted of a variety of missiles, including a great volley of stones which descended upon their target with an incredible noise and velocity. There was no protection against this artillery, and the soldiers were knocked down in swathes and their ranks thrown into confusion. At the same time huge beams were run out from the walls so as to project over the Roman ships: some of them were then sunk by great weights dropped from above, while others were seized at the bows by iron claws or by beaks like those of cranes, hauled into the air by means of counterweights until they stood upright upon their sterns, and then allowed to plunge to the bottom, or else they were spun round by means of windlasses situated inside the city and dashed against the steep cliffs and rocks which jutted out under the walls, with great loss of life to the crews. Often there would be seen the terrifying spectacle of a ship being lifted clean out of the water into the air and whirled about as it hung there, until every man had been shaken out of the hull and thrown in different directions, after which it would be dashed down empty upon the walls. As for the enormous siege-engine which Marcellus brought up, mounted on eight galleys as I have described, and known as a *sambuca* because of its resemblance to the musical instrument of that name, a stone weighing a hundred pounds was discharged while it was still approaching the city wall, immediately followed by a second and a third. These descended on their target with a thunderous crash and a great surge of water, shattered the platform on which the machine was mounted, loosened the bolts which held it together, and dislodged the whole framework from the hulks which supported it. Marcellus, finding his plan of attack thus brought to a standstill, drew off his ships as quickly as possible and ordered his land forces to retire.

After this he held a council of war and formed a new plan to move up as closely as possible to the walls under cover of darkness. The Romans calculated that the cables which Archimedes used for his siege-engines imparted such a tremendous velocity to the missiles they discharged that these would go flying over their heads, but that at close quarters, where a low trajectory was required, they would be ineffective. However, Archimedes, it seems, had long ago foreseen such a possibility and had designed engines which were suitable for any distance and missiles to match them. He had had a large number of loopholes made in the walls, and in these he placed short-range weapons known as scorpions, which were invisible to the attacker, but could be discharged as soon as he arrived at close quarters.

16. So when the Romans crept up close to the walls expecting to surprise the enemy, they were again greeted by a hail of missiles. Huge stones were dropped on them almost perpendicularly, and it seemed as if they were faced by a curtain of darts along the whole length of the wall, so that the attackers soon fell back. But here too, even while they were hurrying, as they hoped, out of danger, they came under fire from the medium-range catapults which caused heavy losses among them: at the same time many of their ships were dashed against one another, and all this while they were helpless to retaliate. Archimedes had mounted most of his weapons under the cover of the city walls, and the Romans began to believe that they were fighting against a supernatural enemy, as they found themselves constantly struck down by opponents whom they could never see.

17. Marcellus, however, escaped unhurt from this assault and afterwards made fun of his own siege-experts and engineers. 'We may as well give up fighting this geometrical Briareus,'* he said, 'who uses our ships like cups to ladle water out of the sea, who has whipped our *sambuca* and driven it off in disgrace, and who can outdo the hundred-handed giants of mythology in hurling so many different missiles at us at once.' For the truth was that all the rest of the Syracusans merely provided the manpower to operate Archimedes's inventions, and it was his mind which directed and controlled every manoeuvre. All other weapons were discarded, and it was upon his alone that the city relied both for attack and defence. At last the Romans were reduced to such a state of alarm that if they saw so much as a length of rope or a piece of timber appear over the top of the wall, it was enough to make them cry out, 'Look, Archimedes is aiming one of his machines at us!' and they would turn their backs and run. When Marcellus saw this, he abandoned all attempts to

* A mythical giant who possessed a hundred hands.

capture the city by assault, and settled down to reduce it by blockade.

As for Archimedes, he was a man who possessed such exalted ideals, such profound spiritual vision, and such a wealth of scientific knowledge that, although his inventions had earned him a reputation for almost superhuman intellectual power, he would not deign to leave behind him any writings on his mechanical discoveries. He regarded the business of engineering, and indeed of every art which ministers to the material needs of life, as an ignoble and sordid activity, and he concentrated his ambition exclusively upon those speculations whose beauty and subtlety are untainted by the claims of necessity. These studies, he believed, are incomparably superior to any others, since here the grandeur and beauty of the subject matter vie for our admiration with the cogency and precision of the methods of proof. Certainly in the whole science of geometry it is impossible to find more difficult and intricate problems handled in simpler and purer terms than in his works. Some writers attribute this to his natural genius. Others maintain that a phenomenal industry lay behind the apparently effortless ease with which he obtained his results. The fact is that no amount of mental effort of his own would enable a man to hit upon the proof of one of Archimedes's theorems, and yet as soon as it is explained to him, he feels that he might have discovered it himself, so smooth and rapid is the path by which he leads us to the required conclusion. So it is not at all difficult to credit some of the stories which have been told about him; of how, for example, he often seemed so bewitched by the song of some inner and familiar Siren that he would forget to eat his food or take care of his person; or how when he was carried by force, as he often was to the bath for his body to be washed and anointed, he would trace geometrical figures in the ashes and draw diagrams with his finger in the oil which had been rubbed over his skin. Such was the rapture which his work inspired in him, so as to make him truly the captive of the Muses. And although he was responsible for many discoveries of great value, he is said to have asked his friends and relatives to place on his tomb after his death nothing more than the shape of a cylinder enclosing a sphere, with an inscription explaining the ratio by which the containing solid exceeds the contained.*

* Cicero mentions that when he was quaestor in Sicily in 75 B.C. he found Archimedes's tomb, which the Syracusans had allowed to fall into neglect (*Tusculan Disputations* V, 64).

18. Such was Archimedes's character, and in so far as it rested with him, he kept himself and his city unconquered. But while Syracuse was being blockaded, Marcellus did not remain idle. He captured Megara, one of the most ancient of the Greek settlements in Sicily, and he also stormed Hippocrates's camp at Acrillae, and killed more than eight thousand of his men, launching his attacks while the enemy were still digging their entrenchments.* Besides this he overran a large part of Sicily, persuaded a number of cities to revolt from the Carthaginians, and defeated his opponents wherever he encountered resistance. Some while afterwards he captured a man named Damippus, a Spartan who had attempted to escape from Syracuse by ship. The Syracusans were anxious to ransom him, and during the numerous meetings and negotiations that followed, Marcellus noticed a particular tower which was carelessly guarded and into which he could infiltrate men unobserved, since the wall in its immediate vicinity was easy to climb. During his visits to parley with the Syracusans he had the height of the tower carefully measured and scaling ladders prepared. Marcellus chose a moment when the Syracusans were celebrating a feast-day in honour of Artemis and had given themselves up to drinking and other festivities. Before they knew what he was about, he had not only seized the tower but also occupied the adjacent wall with his troops and forced his way through the Hexapyla, the gate at the north-west corner of the city. When the citizens discovered what had happened, and while they were running to and fro in confusion and attempting to muster their forces, Marcellus ordered his trumpets to be sounded from all sides at once. The Syracusans fled from the sound in terror and imagined that the whole city had already been captured. But in fact they still held Achradina, which is the largest, handsomest, and most strongly defended quarter, because it had been fortified on the landward side, where it adjoins the other districts of the city, the northern part of which is known as Neapolis and the southern as Tyche.

19. When these districts had been captured, Marcellus made his entry at daybreak through the Hexapyla amid the congratulations of his officers. It is said that as he looked down from the heights upon

* The Carthaginians had meanwhile landed an army at Heraclea near Agrigentum. In an attempt to join forces the Syracusans had sent out part of their garrison under Hippocrates, but Marcellus intercepted him.

the great and magnificent city below, he wept as he thought of its impending fate, and of how its appearance would be transformed in a few hours' time when his army had sacked it. For his troops had demanded their plunder and not one of his officers dared to resist them, indeed many of them had urged that they should set fire to the city and raze it to the ground. Marcellus refused to tolerate this suggestion, but much against his will he allowed his men to carry off property and slaves. However, he gave strict orders that they must not lay a hand on free citizens, nor kill, outrage, or enslave any Syracusan.

And yet in spite of having shown such moderation, he felt that the city had been subjected to a pitiable fate, and even in the moment of triumph he was filled with sorrow and compassion as he saw the brilliant prosperity of so many generations being swept away in a few short hours. It is said that as much wealth was carried away from Syracuse as at a later date from Carthage. Not long afterwards* the rest of the city was captured by treachery and given over to plunder, except for the royal property, which was handed over to the Roman treasury.

But what distressed Marcellus most of all was the death of Archimedes. As fate would have it the philosopher was by himself, engrossed in working out some calculation by means of a diagram, and his eyes and his thoughts were so intent upon the problem that he was completely unaware that the Romans had broken through the defences, or that the city had been captured. Suddenly a soldier came upon him and ordered him to accompany him to Marcellus. Archimedes refused to move until he had worked out his problem and established his demonstration, whereupon the soldier flew into a rage, drew his sword, and killed him. According to another account, the Roman came up with a drawn sword and threatened to kill him there and then: when Archimedes saw him, he begged him to stay his hand for a moment, so that he should not leave his theorem imperfect and without its demonstration, but the soldier paid no

* Plutarch, as his habit often is, has telescoped events. Marcellus began the siege of Syracuse in 214 and captured Tyche and Neapolis early in 212, but Achradina and the island of Ortygia continued to hold out with the help of a Carthaginian fleet and garrison. A plague attacked both Roman and Carthaginian troops in the autumn of that year. The Carthaginian fleet sailed home to obtain fresh supplies, but on its return was unable to round Cape Pachynus, the southern extremity of Sicily. At the end of the year Achradina surrendered and Ortygia was betrayed to Marcellus.

attention and dispatched him at once. There is yet a third story to the effect that Archimedes was on his way to Marcellus bringing some of his instruments, such as sundials and spheres and quadrants, with the help of which the dimensions of the sun could be measured by the naked eye, when some soldiers met him, and believing that he was carrying gold in the box promptly killed him. At any rate it is generally agreed that Marcellus was deeply affected by his death, that he abhorred the man who had killed him as if he had committed an act of sacrilege, and that he sought out Archimedes's relatives and treated them with honour.

20. The Romans were regarded by other peoples as masters of the art of war and formidable adversaries on the battlefield, but they had so far given little indication that they could show kindness or humanity or the civil virtues in general, and Marcellus seems to have been the first to demonstrate to the Greeks that the Romans possessed a stronger sense of justice than they themselves. He behaved with such fairness to all who came into contact with him and conferred so many benefits both upon cities and private individuals that, if the peoples of Enna or Megara or Syracuse were subjected to any harsh treatment, it was generally believed that the fault for this lay with the vanquished rather than the victors. Here I will quote one example out of many. There is a Sicilian town named Engyion, which is of no great size, but is very ancient and is celebrated because of the appearance there of the goddesses who are known as Mothers. Tradition has it that the local temple was built by Cretans, and the people used to keep on show there a number of spears and bronze helmets, some of them inscribed with the name of Meriones,* and others with that of Odysseus, who are reputed to have dedicated these to the goddesses. The people were ardent supporters of the Carthaginians, but their most prominent citizen, whose name was Nicias, did his utmost to persuade them to go over to the Romans, arguing his case in bold and outspoken language in the public assembly, and attacking his opponents' policy as unsound. His enemies became alarmed at his growing influence and prestige, and planned to kidnap him and hand him over to the Carthaginians. Nicias soon became aware of their plot and of the fact that he was being secretly watched, and so he purposely

* A Cretan warrior at the siege of Troy, who was well-known for his helmet, which was decorated with boar's tusks.

let fall in public a number of irreverent references to the Mothers, and went out of his way to show that he could neither believe in the generally accepted legend about their appearances nor even respect it. This action delighted his enemies, since he seemed to be providing them with excellent grounds for the punishment they had in store for him. But just as they had completed their preparations to seize him, a public assembly was held, and during the debate, while Nicias was actually offering some advice to the people, he suddenly threw himself to the ground. Then, after waiting for a few moments amid the silence and astonishment which naturally followed this action, he raised his head, turned it about, and began to speak in a low and trembling tone, which little by little he made shriller and more intense. Finally, when he saw that the whole assembly had been struck dumb with horror, he threw off his cloak, tore open his tunic, and leaping up half-naked rushed towards the exit of the theatre, crying out that he was pursued by the Mothers. So strong was his fellow-citizens' awe of the gods that not one of them dared to lay a hand on him or stand in his path. Instead everyone made way for him as he dashed to the city gates, imitating as he ran the shrieks and gestures that might be expected of a man who was possessed and out of his wits. At the same time his wife, who had been let into the secret and was helping him play his part, took her children with her and prostrated herself as a suppliant before the shrines of the goddesses. Then under pretence of looking for her husband as he wandered about the countryside, she made her way safely out of the city without any hindrance, and in this way they all escaped to Marcellus's camp at Syracuse. The leading men of Engyium went on to insult the Romans and commit various acts of hostility against them, and at length Marcellus captured the town, had them put in chains, and was about to execute them. At this point Nicias, who was standing by, burst into tears and clasping Marcellus's hands and knees pleaded with him to spare the lives of his fellow-countrymen, beginning with his enemies. Marcellus relented, set them all free, and refrained from punishing their city, while he also presented Nicias with a large estate and a number of gifts. At least this is the story which we have from Poseidonius the philosopher.

21. When the Romans recalled Marcellus to carry on the war against Hannibal in Italy, he took back with him most of the statues and

other offerings which the Syracusans had dedicated to the gods, including their finest works of art; for he intended that these should not only decorate his triumph but also adorn the capital. Before this date Rome neither possessed nor indeed was even aware of such elegant and exquisite creations, nor was there any taste for a graceful and delicate art of this kind. Instead the city was filled with the bloodstained arms and spoils of barbarian tribes, and crowned with the monuments and trophies of victorious campaigns, so that to the unwarlike visitor or the aesthete she offered almost nothing to gladden or reassure the eye. Indeed just as Epaminondas speaks of the Boeotian plain as 'a dancing-floor of Ares', and Xenophon refers to Ephesus as 'an arsenal of war', so it seems to me that one might have summed up the Rome of those days in Pindar's phrase as 'a sanctuary of Ares who revels in war'. At any rate Marcellus greatly pleased the common people, because he adorned the capital with works of art which possessed the Hellenic grace and charm and truth to nature. On the other hand it was Fabius Maximus who earned the approval of the older generation, because after he had captured Tarentum he neither disturbed nor removed a single monument of this kind. He carried off all the money and valuables which had belonged to the city, but allowed all the statues to remain in their places, and on this occasion made the remark which has since become famous: 'Let us leave the Tarentines these angry gods of theirs!'* Such people blamed Marcellus in the first place for bringing discredit upon the name of Rome, because he paraded not only men but gods like captives in his triumphal procession; and secondly because hitherto the people had been accustomed to spend their time either in fighting or in agriculture and had never tasted luxury or leisure, so that their character had been as Euripides describes that of Hercules,

Rough and unpolished, but great on great occasions.

Now, on the contrary, he was teaching them to become lazy and glib connoisseurs of art and artists, so that they idled away the greater part of the day in clever and trivial chatter about aesthetics. In spite of such criticisms, Marcellus spoke with pride of what he had done and he liked to claim even to Greeks that he had taught the ignorant Romans to admire and honour the glories of Greek art.

* See *Life of Fabius Maximus*, ch. 22.

22. Marcellus's enemies opposed the granting of a triumph to him, on the grounds that the campaign in Sicily was not yet finished, and that a third triumph would arouse undue envy. The general therefore gave way of his own free will and agreed to lead the main procession to the Alban Mount,* and to enter the city only with the minor ceremony, which the Greeks call an *eva* and the Romans an *ovatio.* The general who leads this does not ride in a four-horsed chariot heralded by trumpets and wearing a crown of laurel, as happens in a major triumph, but walks in the procession in shoes, escorted by a large company of flute-players and wearing a crown of myrtle, so that his appearance is peaceable and friendly rather than menacing. This is a clear proof, it seems to me, that in ancient times it was not so much the importance of a general's achievement as the manner in which he had accomplished it which decided whether a major triumph or an ovation was granted him. Those who had conquered by fighting a battle and killing their enemies entered the city with the martial and awe-inspiring pomp of the formal triumph, after crowning their men and their weapons with abundant wreaths of laurel, as was also the custom whenever they purified the army with lustral rites. On the other hand the generals who had had no occasion to appeal to arms, but had brought everything to a successful issue by means of diplomacy, persuasion, and negotiation were granted by the law the honour of conducting this peaceful and festive procession in the manner of a paean of thanksgiving. For the flute is an instrument of peace and the myrtle is beloved of Aphrodite, who of all the gods and goddesses is the most averse to violence and war. The name of *ova* for this minor triumph is not derived from the Greek *evasmos,* as is generally supposed (for the major triumph is also accompanied by songs and cries of *eva!*), but the word has been twisted by the Greeks into a form that bears a meaning in their language, because they are convinced that the ceremony is also partly intended to honour Dionysus, among whose names are those of *Evius* and *Thriambos.* The true explanation, however, is a different one, namely that it was customary for the general if taking part in the major triumph to sacrifice an ox, and if in the minor a sheep. Now the Latin for sheep is *ovis* and this is why the minor triumph is called *ova.* It is also worth mentioning

* This meant that his army did not enter the city. The Alban Mount was some thirteen miles south-east of Rome.

here that the instructions laid down by the law-giver of Sparta are exactly the opposite of those observed by the Romans. In Sparta the returning general, if he had overcome the enemy by deception or persuasion, sacrificed an ox, and if by force of arms a cock. For although the Spartans were the most warlike of peoples, they believed that an exploit achieved by means of argument and intelligence was greater and more worthy of a human being than one effected by mere force and courage. As to which of these opinions is to be preferred, I leave it to the reader to decide.

23. While Marcellus was serving his fourth term as consul,* his enemies persuaded the Syracusans to come to Rome, lay accusations against him, and denounce him before the Senate for having perpetrated terrible injustices contrary to the terms of their surrender. It so happened that when they arrived, Marcellus was engaged in performing a sacrifice on the Capitol, but as the Senate was still sitting, the Syracusans immediately presented themselves before it and begged that their grievances might be heard and justice granted them. Marcellus's fellow-consul was indignant that his colleague should be accused in his absence and tried to have them ejected from the chamber, but as soon as Marcellus heard of their arrival, he hurried to the Senate-house. Then, seating himself as consul in his curule chair, he began to dispatch the regular business of the day. When this was finished, he came down from his chair and taking his stand as a private citizen in the place where those who had been put on trial customarily offered their defence, he called upon the Syracusans to press their charges. The dignity and assurance of his manner thoroughly disconcerted them, and they were abashed to find that the man who had been irresistible in the field was still more formidable and unassailable in his consular robe of purple. But at length, with the encouragement of Marcellus's opponents, they began their impeachment and urged their plea for justice, in the course of which they indulged in much lamentation for the fate of their city. The substance of their complaint was that, in spite of their being friends and allies of the Roman people, they had suffered harsher treatment at Marcellus's hands than that which other generals had meted out even to conquered enemies. Marcellus retorted that they had com-

* In 210 B.C.

mitted many hostile acts against the Romans, for which they had received no punishment whatsoever, except for the kind of damage from which it is impossible to protect a population when a city is taken by storm. The fact that their city had been captured, he added, was due to their own wilful refusal of his repeated offers of terms. They certainly could not plead that they had been forced into war by tyrannical rulers, for they had themselves elected these very rulers with the object of going to war.

After both sides had been heard and the Syracusans according to the usual custom had withdrawn, Marcellus handed over the presidency of the Senate to his colleague, left the chamber with his accusers, and stood outside the doors. His appearance remained perfectly normal and showed not a trace of apprehension for the verdict nor of anger against the Syracusans: he simply waited with the utmost serenity and self-control to hear the outcome of the case. When the votes had been cast and he was declared not guilty, the Syracusans threw themselves at his feet. They implored him with tears in their eyes to put away his anger against the delegates before him and to take pity on the rest of the city, which never forgot a kindness and would henceforth be eternally grateful to him. Marcellus was moved by this appeal: he pardoned the envoys, and thereafter became a constant benefactor to their city. He had already restored to them their freedom, the right to be governed by their own laws, and what remained of their property, and these concessions were confirmed by the Senate. In return the people conferred many of their highest honours upon him, and in particular they passed a law that whenever Marcellus or any of his descendants should land in Sicily, the Syracusans should wear garlands and offer sacrifices to the gods.

24. Soon after this he again took the field against Hannibal. Ever since the defeat at Cannae, the other consuls and generals had relied almost without exception upon the strategy of avoiding an engagement at all costs, and certainly none had had the courage to risk a pitched battle with the enemy. Marcellus, however, chose precisely the opposite course, because he was convinced that, long before the period allowed for wearing down Hannibal's strength had elapsed, Italy herself would have bled to death. He believed too that Fabius, by constantly insisting upon safety at all costs, was pursuing the wrong method to heal his country's affliction: the danger was that Rome was already

drooping under her burdens, and that if they continued to wait as he proposed, the end of the war might well coincide with her total collapse. Fabius, as he saw it, was like one of those timid physicians who shrink from applying drastic remedies and imagine that a disease has subsided, when it is really the patient's powers of resistance which have been exhausted.

Accordingly his first move was to regain control of the principal Samnite cities which had revolted. There he found large sums of money and stocks of grain, and he also captured the Carthaginian detachments amounting to three thousand soldiers whom Hannibal had stationed to defend them. Next, after Hannibal had defeated and killed the pro-consul Gnaeus Fulvius in Apulia together with eleven military tribunes, and had cut to pieces the greater part of his army, Marcellus sent letters to Rome telling the citizens to take heart, since he was already on the march and would see to it that Hannibal's triumph was short-lived. Livy remarks that when these letters were read they did not do much to reassure the Romans, but rather increased their alarm. They reflected that the risk which lay ahead of them was even greater than the defeat they had just suffered, in proportion as Marcellus was a better general than Fulvius.

However, Marcellus, according to his promise, at once marched after Hannibal and made contact with him in Lucania. There he found him entrenched in a strong position on high ground near the city of Numistro, and so he encamped in the plain. On the following day Marcellus was the first to draw up his troops in battle order, and a great battle ensued which, although desperately contested, remained indecisive. The fighting began at nine o'clock in the morning and was only broken off with difficulty after nightfall. But at daybreak Marcellus once more led out his army, formed up his men amid the heaps of dead, and challenged Hannibal to fight again to decide the victory. This time Hannibal declined battle, whereupon Marcellus, after stripping the enemy's dead and burying his own, continued to pursue the Carthaginians. He won the highest admiration for his skill in this campaign, because although Hannibal repeatedly set ambushes for him, Marcellus escaped every one and had the better of their skirmishing encounters. For this reason when the time for the consular elections approached, the Senate decided that it was advisable to summon the other consul from Sicily rather than to recall Marcellus at the moment when he was grappling with Hannibal. When the consul arrived, the Senate instructed him to declare Quintus Fulvius dictator. The reason for this procedure was that a dictator cannot be chosen either by the people or by the Senate. Instead, one of the consuls or praetors appears before the assembled people and nominates the man whom he himself has selected. This is the derivation of the word *dictator*, for the verb *dicere* in Latin signifies to 'name' or 'declare'. Some writers, however, maintain that the dictator is so called because he does not put any question to the vote or to a show of hands, but issues his decrees and pronouncements on his own authority and according to his own judgement, and it is noteworthy that the orders of magistrates, which the Greeks call *diatagmata*, are called by the Romans *edicta*.

25. However, when Marcellus's colleague arrived from Sicily, he wished to nominate a candidate other than Fulvius as dictator, and in order to avoid being forced to act against his own judgement he sailed back to Sicily by night. In this situation Quintus Fulvius was nominated as dictator by the people, and the Senate wrote to Marcellus requesting him to support this measure. He did so, proclaimed Quintus Fulvius dictator, and in this way confirmed the people's choice, while he himself was elected pro-consul for the following year.* Then, after conferring with Fabius Maximus, it was agreed that while Fabius should besiege Tarentum, Marcellus should follow Hannibal closely, divert his attention, and prevent him from making any move to relieve the city. Accordingly he set out and came up with the Carthaginians at Canusium. Although Hannibal constantly shifted his camp and avoided a battle, Marcellus never lost contact with him, and at last attacked him when he had encamped, and by harassing him with skirmishers succeeded in drawing him out of his entrenchments. Hannibal advanced and Marcellus received his attack, but nightfall put an end to the fighting. The next morning Marcellus again took the field, and formed up his troops in battle order. At this Hannibal in great anxiety called the Carthaginians together and appealed to them to fight as they had never done before. 'You see,' he told them, 'that even after all the great victories we have won, we shall not be able to breathe in peace or enjoy the leisure we have earned

* 209 B.C.

by our superiority in arms, until we have driven this fellow away.'

After this the two armies met, and during the fighting Marcellus seems to have made an ill-judged manoeuvre which cost him the battle.* He found his right wing hard pressed and ordered one of his legions to advance to the front to support it, but this change of formation threw his ranks into confusion and allowed the enemy to carry off the victory, the Romans losing two thousand seven hundred men. Marcellus then withdrew his troops into his fortified camp, called them together, and reprimanded them, telling them that he could see many Roman weapons and bodies, but not a single Roman worthy of the name. They asked his pardon, whereupon he said that he could not give this when they had been driven off the field, but only after they had made themselves masters of it. However, he assured them that he would fight again on the next day, so that the first news to reach Rome would be of their victory, not of their rout. As he dismissed the troops, he gave orders that the cohorts which had been defeated should be issued with rations of barley instead of wheat. His words made so deep an impression, that although many of his soldiers had suffered painful and dangerous wounds in the fighting, it is said that every man in the army felt Marcellus's reproaches more keenly than his own hurts.

26. At daybreak Marcellus had the scarlet tunic hung out, which is the usual signal for offering battle. At their own request the disgraced units were posted in the front of the line, and the military tribunes led out the rest of the army and deployed it in battle order. When Hannibal learned this, he exclaimed, 'Hercules, what do we do with a man who refuses to accept either good fortune or bad? This is the only general who gives his enemy no rest when he is victorious, nor takes any himself when he is defeated. We shall never have done with fighting him, it seems, because he attacks out of confidence when he is winning, and out of shame when he is beaten.' Then the two armies engaged, and when Hannibal saw that the issue was evenly balanced, he gave orders for his elephants to be brought up to the front and launched against the Roman line. The shock of their charge broke up the formation of the front ranks and caused great disorder,

* According to Livy the manoeuvre was not so much ill-judged as badly executed. The right wing gave ground more quickly than it should have done, and the eighteenth legion was slow to move up in support.

but one of the military tribunes snatched up a standard, and, facing the elephants, struck the leading beast with the iron spike and forced it to wheel about. The elephant collided with the animal immediately behind, and threw it and the rest of the column into confusion. Marcellus saw this and at once ordered his cavalry to charge at full speed into the struggling mass, so as to increase the enemy's disorder. The cavalry made a brilliant charge and pursued the retreating Carthaginians, cutting them down until they reached their own camp, but it was the plunging of their dying and wounded elephants which caused the greatest slaughter among the enemy. More than eight thousand Carthaginians are said to have lost their lives, while of the Roman force three thousand were killed, and almost all the survivors wounded. It was this fact which allowed Hannibal to break camp during the night and put a long distance between himself and the Romans. Marcellus was unable to pursue him because of the large numbers of his own wounded, and he later withdrew at a leisurely pace into Campania and spent the summer at Sinuessa, allowing his soldiers to regain their strength.

27. Hannibal, on the other hand, now that he had disengaged himself from Marcellus, felt confident enough to let his troops roam as freely as if they were disbanded, and he sent them raiding, plundering, and burning throughout the length and breadth of Italy. Meanwhile Marcellus had fallen into disfavour at Rome, and his enemies persuaded Publicius Bibulus, one of the tribunes of the people, a clever speaker and a violent party politician, to bring an accusation against him. This man frequently harangued the assembly, and tried to persuade them to hand over the command of Marcellus's army to another general. 'Marcellus,' he said, 'exchanged a few passes with the enemy, but now he has left the arena and retired to the hot baths to refresh himself.' When he heard of this, Marcellus left his legates in charge of the army and travelled to Rome to answer the slanders brought against him and defend his good name. There he found that an indictment based on these calumnies had already been drawn up. A day was appointed for the trial, and after the people had assembled in the Circus Flaminius, Bibulus rose and delivered his impeachment. Marcellus's own defence was short and simple, but a number of the most prominent and distinguished Romans paid glowing tributes to his generalship and upheld his actions in the most outspoken terms.

They reminded the people that if they condemned Marcellus for cowardice, they would prove themselves to be far worse judges than Hannibal, for Marcellus was the one general whom the Carthaginian always sought to avoid, in fact he employed every trick he knew to elude him and engage the others. These speeches had such an effect that Bibulus's hopes were completely frustrated, and in the end Marcellus was not only acquitted of the charges against him, but was actually elected consul for the fifth time.*

28. As soon as he had taken up his office, he succeeded in bringing under control a dangerous situation in Etruria, where the people were on the verge of revolt, and he then visited and pacified the cities of the region. After this he wished to dedicate to Glory and to Valour a temple which he had built out of the spoils he had captured in Sicily, but this scheme was frustrated by the priests, who refused to agree to a single temple's being occupied by two deities: Marcellus was vexed by the priests' opposition, but he regarded it as an ominous sign and so began to build another temple adjoining the first. And indeed that year was filled with prodigies which caused him anxiety. Several temples were struck by lightning and the gold offerings in the shrine of Jupiter were gnawed by mice. There were also reports that an ox had uttered human speech, and that a boy had been born with an elephant's head; and, worse still, when various rites and sacrifices were performed to expiate these prodigies, the seers encountered unfavourable omens and therefore kept him in Rome, although he chafed at inaction and was fretting to be gone, for no man was ever so consumed by a single passion – to match himself against Hannibal in a decisive battle. His one dream by night, his single topic of discussion with his friends and colleagues, and his sole prayer to the gods was that he might meet Hannibal fairly in the field. I truly believe that his heart's desire would have been to have the two armies surrounded by a wall or a rampart where they could fight out the issue. And but for the fact that he was already loaded with honours, and had given ample proof that in respect of good sense and maturity of judgement he could stand comparison with any general in history, I should have said that he had fallen a victim to a boyish obsession which was quite out of keeping with his years, for

* For 208 B.C.

by the time that he entered upon his fifth consulship he had already passed the age of sixty.*

29. However, when at last the sacrifices and rites of purification recommended by the soothsayers had been performed, he took the field with his colleague and set himself to harass Hannibal's army in its camp between Bantia and Venusia, trying by every possible means to bring his opponent to battle. Hannibal refused to be drawn, but when he learned that the Romans had detached a force to attack the Epizephyrian Locrians, he laid an ambush in the hills near Petelia and killed two thousand five hundred of their men. This action filled Marcellus with an overwhelming desire to get to grips with the enemy and he moved his forces still closer to Hannibal.

Between the two camps there was a hill which appeared to offer a useful point of vantage, and was thickly covered with trees and shrubs. Its slopes provided look-out posts which commanded a view of both camps, and streams could be seen flowing down the sides. The Romans were astonished that Hannibal, who had had the first choice of such a strong natural position, had not occupied it, but had left it for the enemy. It appears that in fact he did consider it a good site for a camp, but an even better one for an ambush, and it was for this purpose that he chose to use it. He concealed a force of javelin-throwers and spearmen among the woods and hollows, as he felt certain that the Romans would be allured to the place because of its obvious natural advantages, and in the event his calculations were exactly fulfilled. In their camp the Romans immediately began to talk about the necessity of occupying the feature, and they enlarged on the advantages they would gain over their enemies by encamping on it, or at the very least by fortifying it. Accordingly Marcellus decided to ride forward with a few horsemen and reconnoitre the site. But before doing this he sent for his soothsayer and offered up a sacrifice, and when the first victim had been killed, the soothsayer showed him that its liver had no head. When he sacrificed for the second time, the head of the liver turned out to be unusually large, while all the other indications appeared exceptionally auspicious, and this seemed to dispel the misgivings aroused by the first offering.

* In 208 B.C. It is worth noting that this Life describes only the last quarter of Marcellus's career. By the time of the Gallic campaign described in chs. 6–8 he was already forty-six.

However, the soothsayers declared that this sequence of events disturbed them even more, because when unusually forbidding or threatening omens are immediately followed by others which are exceptionally favourable, the unexpectedness of the change is in itself a matter for suspicion. But since, in Pindar's words

Not fire, not walls of iron can hinder fate*

Marcellus rode out, taking with him his colleague Crispinus, his son, who was a military tribune, and two hundred and twenty horsemen in all. None of these, as it happened, was a Roman: they were all Etruscans, with the exception of forty men of Fregellae, who had given Marcellus many proofs of their loyalty and courage. On the crest of the hill, which was thickly wooded, the enemy had posted a look-out. He could not be seen by the Romans, but could observe every movement in their camp. This man signalled the approach of the reconnoitring party to the troops who were hiding in ambush, and they allowed Marcellus to ride close up to them. Then all of a sudden they sprang to their feet, surrounded his party, flung their javelins, stabbed with their spears, pursued those who ran away, and fell upon those who stood their ground. These were the forty men of Fregellae, who after the Etruscans had galloped off at the first onslaught, rallied round the two consuls and fought to defend them. Finally Crispinus, who had been hit by two javelins, wheeled his horse and fled, while Marcellus was run through the side with a broad-bladed spear, the Latin name for which is *lancea*. Then the few survivors among the Fregellans left Marcellus lying where he had fallen, rescued his son who had been wounded, and made their escape back to the camp. In this skirmish there were hardly more than forty men killed, but five lictors and eighteen horsemen were taken prisoner and Crispinus died of his wounds a few days later. To have lost both their consuls in a single action was a disaster without a parallel in the whole of Roman history.

30. Hannibal took little interest in the fate of the other soldiers, but when he heard that Marcellus had been killed, he immediately hurried to the spot and stood for a long time by the dead body, admiring its strength and beauty. He uttered not a single boastful word, nor did he show any sign of exultation, such as might be expected of a man

* Fragment 232.

who has just rid himself of a bitter and formidable enemy. But after he had expressed his wonder at the unexpectedness of Marcellus's death, he removed his signet ring,* but gave orders that his body should be treated with honour, wrapped in a fine robe, adorned, and burned. After this he collected the ashes in a silver urn, crowned it with a gilded wreath, and sent it to Marcellus's son. But on the way a party of Numidians fell in with the men who were escorting the urn. They tried to seize it by force, and when the others resisted, they fought and in the struggle the ashes were scattered far and wide. When Hannibal heard this, he remarked, 'I might have known that nothing can be done against the will of the gods.' He ordered the Numidians to be punished, but made no further effort to collect or return the remains, since he evidently felt that the strange manner in which Marcellus had met his death and been denied a proper burial indicated that some divine purpose was at work. This, at any rate, is the account which we find in Cornelius Nepos and Valerius Maximus, but according to Livy and Augustus Caesar the urn was returned to Marcellus's son and buried with splendid ceremony.

Besides the monuments which Marcellus dedicated in Rome there was a gymnasium at Catana in Sicily which bore his name, and statues and votive tablets from among the plunder of Syracuse were set up in the temple of the gods named the Cabiri in Samothrace, and in the temple of Athena at Lindos. On his statue there, according to Poseidonius, the following epigram was inscribed:

Stranger, this man you behold was the guiding star of his country,
  Claudius Marcellus by name, born of a glorious line;
Seven times consul, he led the armies of Rome into battle,
  Death and destruction he dealt to all who invaded his land.

The author of these verses has counted his two pro-consulates as well as his five consulates. His descendants continued to distinguish themselves down to the time of that Marcellus, the nephew of Augustus Caesar, whose parents were Caesar's sister Octavia and Gaius Marcellus. He died while he was holding the office of aedile at Rome, soon after he had married the emperor's daughter Julia. It was in his honour and to his memory that Octavia dedicated a library and Augustus built a theatre, both of which bear his name to this day.

* Hannibal evidently hoped to make use of this ring to deceive some of the neighbouring cities, but the Romans forestalled him.

4

CATO THE ELDER

[234–149 B.C.]

* *
*

1. Marcus Cato's family is said to have originated from Tusculum, although he himself was brought up and spent his life – before he devoted himself to politics and soldiering – on a family estate in a country of the Sabines. None of his ancestors appears to have made any mark in Roman history, but Cato himself praises his father Marcus as a man of courage and a capable soldier. He also mentions that his grandfather Cato was several times decorated for valour in battle, and was awarded by the state treasury for his gallantry the price of the five horses which had been killed under him in battle.

The Romans were in the habit of describing as 'new men' all those whose ancestors had never risen to high office,* but who were beginning to become prominent through their own efforts, and Cato soon acquired this title. He himself used to say that he was certainly new to honours and positions of authority, but that as regards deeds of valour performed by his ancestors, his name was as old as any. Originally his third name was not Cato, but Priscus: he earned the name Cato later in his life on account of his remarkable abilities, for the Romans apply to a man of outstanding wisdom and experience the epithet *catus*.

In appearance he was red-haired and possessed piercing grey eyes, as we learn from the author of this rather malicious epigram,

> Red-haired, grey-eyed, snapping at all comers, even in Hades,
> Porcius, Queen Persephone will turn you away from the gate.

* The principal offices of state, such as the consulship and praetorship, carried with them the so-called *jus imaginum*, the right of having oneself represented in painting or statuary. A 'new man' possessed such an effigy only of himself, a noble had them of his ancestors.

Ever since his early youth he had trained himself to work with his own hands, serve as a soldier, and follow a sober mode of living, and hence he possessed a tough constitution and a body which was as strong as it was healthy. He also developed his powers of speech, which he regarded almost as a second body, and, for the man who has no intention of leading an obscure or idle existence, as an indispensable instrument which serves not only the necessary but also the higher purposes of life. So he practised and perfected his oratory in the towns and villages near Rome, where he acted as an advocate for all who needed him, and he earned the reputation first of being a vigorous pleader and then an effective orator. As time went on the gravity and dignity of his character revealed themselves unmistakably to those who had dealings with him, and marked him out as a man who was clearly qualified for employment in great affairs and a position of leadership in the state. Not only did he provide his services in lawsuits without demanding a fee of any kind, but he did not seem to regard the prestige acquired in these contests as the principal object of his efforts. On the contrary he was far more anxious to distinguish himself in battles and campaigns against Rome's enemies, and his body was covered with honourable wounds before he had even reached manhood. He says himself that he served in his first campaign when he was seventeen years old at the time when Hannibal, at the height of his success, was laying all Italy waste with fire and sword.* In battle he was a formidable fighter, who stood his ground resolutely and confronted his opponents with a ferocious expression. He would greet the enemy with a harsh and menacing war-cry, for he rightly believed and reminded others that such an appearance often frightens the enemy even more than cold steel. When he was on the march he used to carry his own armour and weapons on foot, and would be followed by a single attendant who looked after his food and utensils. It is said that he never lost his temper with this man, nor found fault with him when he served up a meal, in fact he would often join in and share the task of preparing food, so long as he was free from his military duties. On active service he drank nothing but water, except that occasionally when he was parched with thirst he would ask for vinegar, or when his strength was exhausted add a little wine.

* In 217 B.C.

2. Near his estate was a cottage which had belonged to Manius Curius,* a redoubtable soldier of the past who had celebrated three triumphs. Cato often visited the place, and the small size of the farm and the house itself inspired him to meditate upon its owner, who although he had become the greatest Roman of his day, had conquered the most warlike tribes and driven Pyrrhus out of Italy, continued to till this little patch of land with his own hands and to live in this cottage, even after he had celebrated his three triumphs. It was here that the ambassadors of the Samnites had found him sitting in front of his hearth boiling turnips. They offered him large sums of gold, but he sent them away, telling them that a man who could be satisfied with such a meal did not need gold. He added that he believed it more honourable to conquer those who possessed gold than to possess it himself. Cato would return home with his mind full of these reflections: then he would look afresh at his own house and servants and review his mode of life, and would undertake still more work with his own hands and cut down any sign of extravagance.

When Fabius Maximus captured the city of Tarentum,† it happened that Cato, who was still quite a young man, was serving under his command. Cato was billeted with a man named Nearchus, who belonged to the sect of the Pythagoreans, and this made him curious to learn something of their theories. When he heard Nearchus expounding the doctrine, which Plato also upholds, 'that pleasure is to be condemned as the greatest incentive to evil, that the body is the greatest hindrance to the development of the soul, and that the soul can only release and purify herself by employing reason to divorce and deliver her from physical sensations', he became more and more attracted to these ideals of simplicity and self-discipline. Beyond this, we are told, he did not study Greek until late in life, and he did not begin to read Greek books until he was an old man. Then he improved his oratory to some extent from the study of Thucydides, and still more from Demosthenes. But in spite of his limited acquaintance with the language, his writings are often enriched by ideas and

* Manius Curius Dentatus gained his triumphs for victories in the Samnite War (298–90 B.C.) and over the Greek king Pyrrhus (275 B.C.). He also became famous for his pronouncement that a virtuous citizen should be content with seven acres of land (the size of an estate prescribed after the expulsion of the kings).

† In 209 B.C.

anecdotes borrowed from the Greek, and many of his maxims and proverbs are literally translated from it.

3. There was at Rome at this time a certain Valerius Flaccus, a member of one of the oldest patrician families and a man of great political influence, who combined a keen eye for excellence while it was in the bud with the generosity to foster it and bring it to full flower. He owned the estate next to Cato's, and learned from his neighbour's servants of their master's frugal and self-sufficient way of living. They told him to his amazement that it was Cato's practice to set out early on foot to the market-place of the local town; there he would plead the causes of all who required his services and later in the day return to his farm. Then he would set to work among his own labourers, wearing a sleeveless smock in winter and stripped to the waist in summer, and would sit down with them to eat the same bread and drink the same wine. After they had told him other stories of Cato's just dealings and his moderation, and quoted some of his shrewd sayings, Valerius invited his neighbour to dinner. He soon discovered when he came to know him that his nature was gentle and possessed a charm of its own, and that like a plant it needed to be cultivated and given room to expand: accordingly Valerius encouraged him and at length prevailed upon him to take part in public life at Rome. Once he had settled there his performance as an advocate quickly attracted admirers and friends, while at the same time Valerius's patronage brought him both honour and influence, so that it was not long before he was appointed military tribune and later quaestor. From this point he quickly rose to such heights of fame and distinction that his name came to be associated with Valerius's own in the highest offices of state, and he served as his colleague first as consul and later as censor.

Among the elder statesmen he attached himself most closely to Fabius Maximus. At that time Fabius enjoyed the highest reputation and wielded the greatest power of any man in Rome, yet it was not these distinctions but rather the man's character and his way of life which Cato chose as his ideal. And it was the same considerations which persuaded him to oppose the great Scipio, later known as Africanus. This distinguished man, although at that time barely in his thirties, was already becoming a serious rival to Fabius, and was generally believed to be jealous of him. When Cato was posted to

Africa to serve as Scipio's quaestor for the invasion of Carthage,* he saw that his commander was not only indulging in his usual lavish personal expenditure, but was also squandering extravagantly high pay upon his troops. He protested to Scipio and told him bluntly that the most important issue was not the question of expense, but the fact that he was corrupting the native simplicity of his men, who, as soon as they had more money than they needed for their everyday wants, would spend it on luxuries and the pleasures of the senses. Scipio retorted that when his plan of campaign was proceeding as it were under full sail he had no use for a niggling quaestor, and that he would be called upon to account to the Roman people not for the money he had spent but for the battles he had won. Cato therefore left Scipio's army, which was then being assembled in Sicily. He proceeded at once to Rome and helped Fabius to denounce the general before the Senate. They attacked Scipio's waste of immense sums of money and his childish fondness for public games and theatrical performances, as if he had been appointed the impresario of some festival, not a commander on active service. As a result of these accusations tribunes were sent out with authority to recall Scipio to Rome, if the charges were proved to be true. However, Scipio was able to impress upon the tribunes that success in war depends upon the size of the preparations made for it, and furthermore that he could indulge in agreeable diversions with his friends during his hours of leisure without allowing his sociability to make him neglectful of his serious duties. At any rate his defence convinced the tribunes, and he set sail for Africa.

4. All this while Cato's speeches continued to add greatly to his reputation, so that he came to be known as the Roman Demosthenes, but what created an even more powerful impression than his eloquence was his manner of living. His powers of expression merely set a standard for young men, which many of them were already striving their utmost to attain. But a man who observed the ancestral custom of working his own land, who was content with a cold breakfast, a frugal dinner, the simplest clothing, and a humble cottage to live in, and who actually thought it more admirable to renounce luxuries than to acquire them – such a person was conspicuous by his rarity. The truth was that by this date the Roman republic had

* In 204 B.C.

grown too large to preserve its original purity of spirit, and the very authority which it exercised over so many realms and peoples constantly brought it into contact with, and obliged it to adapt itself to an extraordinary diversity of habits and modes of living. So it was natural enough that everybody should admire Cato when they saw others prostrated by their labours or enervated by their pleasures, while he remained unaffected by either. What was even more remarkable was that he followed the same habits, not merely while he was young and full of ambition, but even when he was old and grey-headed and had served as a consul and celebrated a triumph, and that he continued, like some champion athlete, to observe the rules of his training and maintain his self-discipline to the end.

He tells us that he never wore a garment which cost more than a hundred drachmas,* that even when he was praetor or consul he drank the same wine as his slaves, that he bought the fish or meat for his dinner in the public market and never paid more than thirty asses for it, and that he allowed himself this indulgence for the public good in order to strengthen his body for military service. He also mentions that when he was bequeathed an embroidered Babylonian robe, he immediately sold it, that none of his cottages had plastered walls, that he never paid more than 1,500 drachmas for a slave, since he was not looking for the exquisite or handsome type of domestic servant, but for sturdy labourers such as grooms and herdsmen, and that when they became too old to work, he felt it his duty to sell them rather than feed so many useless mouths. In general he considered that nothing is cheap if it is superfluous, that what a man does not need is dear even if it cost only a penny, and that one should buy land for tilling and grazing, not to make into gardens, where the object is merely to sprinkle the lawns and sweep the paths.

* The changes which have taken place in the value and purchasing power of money even within the past generation make any attempt to compare classical and modern currencies largely illusory. But it is worth mentioning that the following rough equivalents were current among scholars at the beginning of the present century:
6 obols – 1 drachma
1 drachma – 10d.
4 asses – 1 sesterce
4 sesterces – 1 denarius
1 denarius – 9d.

According to this reckoning Cato's maximum prices (by Victorian values) would have been about £4 for a garment, 1s. 5d. for a meal, and £60 for a slave.

5. Some people attributed these actions to sheer meanness of spirit on Cato's part, while others upheld them on the grounds that he practised this austere and close-fisted way of life so as to correct and restrain the extravagance of others. For my own part I regard his conduct towards his slaves in treating them like beasts of burden, exploiting them to the limits of their strength, and then, when they were old, driving them off and selling them, as the mark of a thoroughly ungenerous nature, which cannot recognize any bond between man and man but that of necessity. And yet we see that kindness possesses a far wider sphere of action than justice, for it is in the nature of things that law and justice are confined to our dealings with our fellow men, whereas kindness and charity, which often flow from a gentle nature like water from an abundant spring, may be extended even to dumb animals. A kindly man will take good care of his horses even when they are worn out in his service, and will look after his dogs not only when they are puppies, but when they need special attention in their old age.

When the people of Athens were building the Parthenon, they turned loose those mules which had worked the hardest, put them out to grass, and declared them to be exempted from any further service. One of these, so the story goes, came back to the site of its own accord, trotted by the side of its companions which were hauling wagons up the Acropolis in harness, and even led the way as though encouraging and urging them on, whereupon the Athenians passed a decree that the animal should be fed at the public expense for the rest of its life. The graves of Cimon's race-horses too, a set of mares with which he won three victories at Olympia, can still be seen near the tombs of his family. There are many instances of dogs which have become the faithful companions and friends of their masters: perhaps the most famous of all was Xanthippus's dog,* which swam by the side of his trireme to Salamis when the Athenians were abandoning Athens, and was buried with honour on the promontory, which is to this day called Cynossema, or the Dog's Mound.

We ought never to treat living creatures like shoes or kitchen utensils to be thrown away when they are broken or worn out in our service, but rather cultivate the habit of behaving with tenderness and consideration towards animals, if only for the sake of gaining practice in humanity when we come to deal with our fellow-men.

* See *Life of Themistocles*, ch. 10.

For my part, I would not sell even my draught ox simply because of his age, far less turn out an old man from the home and the way of life to which he has grown accustomed for the sake of a few paltry coins, especially since he would be of no more use to the buyer than he was to the seller. But Cato goes so far as to boast of such economies, and says that he left behind him in Spain even the charger which he rode during his campaigns as consul, so as to save the state the cost of its transportation. Now whether these actions are to be judged as examples of greatness or of pettiness of spirit is a question which the reader must decide for himself.

6. However, in other respects, Cato's self-restraint deserves the highest commendation. For example, when he commanded an army he never drew for himself and his staff more than three Attic bushels of wheat a month, and for his horses less than a bushel and a half of barley a day. When he became governor of Sardinia,* whereas his predecessors had been in the habit of charging the cost of their tents, beds, and clothing to the public funds, and extorting immense sums from the province to pay for large retinues of servants and friends and for sumptuous banquets and entertainments, he substituted an unheard-of economy in his administration. He imposed no charges whatever on the public treasury and visited the various cities on foot, followed by a single public servant, who carried his robe and his cup for pouring libations. But although in these matters he treated the people under his authority with tolerance and a strict regard for economy, in other respects he governed with an exemplary dignity and severity. He was inexorable in the administration of justice, and direct and peremptory in the execution of his orders, so that the authority of Rome was never more feared nor more loved than during his term of office.

7. These are also the qualities which distinguish Cato's oratory. It was at once elegant and forceful, agreeable and vehement, playful and severe, epigrammatic and combative. In the same way Plato remarks of Socrates that superficially he impressed the people as an uncouth man with a face like a satyr, who was rude to everyone he met, but that his inward nature was deeply serious, and full of thoughts which touched his listeners' hearts and moved them to tears. For this reason I

* In 198 B.C.

find it hard to understand those who say that the closest parallel to Cato's oratory is to be found in the speeches of Lysias.* However, this kind of question must be decided by those who are better qualified than myself at defining the characteristics of Roman oratory. I shall now relate a few of Cato's memorable sayings, since I believe that it is often a man's words rather than his appearance which throw light on his character.

8. On one occasion when he wished to dissuade the Roman people from raising what he considered to be a quite unjustifiable clamour for a free distribution of corn, he began his speech with the words, 'It is difficult, my fellow-citizens, to argue with the belly, since it has no ears.' Then when he was attacking the extravagance of the day, he remarked, 'How can we expect to save a city, where people are prepared to pay more for a fish than for an ox?' On another occasion he declared, 'The Roman people are like sheep: you cannot budge one of them on its own, but when they are in a flock, they all follow their leaders as a single body. In the same way, when you come together in the assembly, you allow yourselves to be led by men whose advice you would never think of following in your private affairs.' On the subject of the influence of women, he said, 'All mankind rule their wives, we rule all mankind, and our wives rule us.' However, this saying is borrowed from Themistocles,† who when he found his son constantly giving him orders which really originated from his wife, told her; 'My dear, the Athenians rule the Greeks, I rule the Athenians, you rule me, and our son rules you. So he must be careful not to abuse his power, because it is greater than anyone else's.'

'The Roman people', he pointed out on another occasion, 'fix the value not only of dyes and colours, but also of men's occupations. For just as dyers make most use of the colours which they see are most popular, so your young men study and apply themselves to the subjects which they think will earn credit with you.' He also put it to the people that if they had won their empire by means of virtue and self-restraint, they should not allow themselves to fall away from these qualities, but that if it was through self-indulgence and vice,

* Lysias was considered a master of the plain style. A friend of Plato, he was a professional pleader who wrote many speeches for litigants, and excelled at matching them to the age and circumstances of his clients.

† *Life of Themistocles*, ch. 18.

they should try to bring about a change for the better, since these qualities had already made them great enough. Those who were perpetually ambitious to hold high office, he compared to men who did not know their way, and who expected to be attended all the time by lictors, in case they should go astray. He also found fault with the people for constantly electing the same men to the most important positions. 'It can only be supposed,' he said, 'either that you do not think the office itself is of much consequence, or else that you believe there are very few men capable of filling it.' Speaking of one of his enemies, who was notorious for his dissolute and disreputable life, Cato said, 'That man's mother thinks of it as a curse, not a blessing, if anyone prays that her son should survive her.' And on another occasion, he pointed to a man who had sold his ancestral estate, which was near the sea, and pretending to admire him for possessing greater strength than the sea itself, he said, 'The sea could only wash away a small part of his fields, but this man has drunk up every one of them without any difficulty at all.'

When king Eumenes of Pergamum paid a state visit to Rome, the Senate received him with extraordinary honours, and the most prominent citizens in Rome vied with one another in showing him attention, whereupon Cato made a point of treating him with suspicion and reserve. 'But surely,' someone said to him, 'Eumenes is an excellent man and a friend of Rome.' 'That may be,' replied Cato, 'but nevertheless a king is an animal that lives on human flesh.' He maintained that none of the kings who had enjoyed so great a reputation could be compared with Epaminondas or Pericles or Themistocles or Manius Curius or Hamilcar Barca. His enemies, he used to say, hated him because he got up early every day and devoted himself to public affairs but neglected his own. Another saying of his was that he would rather do what was right and go unrewarded than do wrong and go unpunished, and that he was prepared to forgive everybody's mistakes except his own.

9. The Romans once sent three ambassadors to Bithynia, one of whom suffered from gout, another had had his skull trepanned, and the third was generally regarded as a fool. Cato ridiculed these appointments, and said that the Romans were sending out a delegation which could not muster a pair of feet, nor a head, nor a heart. Scipio Africanus once approached him at Polybius's request.

to enlist his support on behalf of the Greek exiles from Achaea.* The question was debated at great length in the Senate, some speakers contending that the men should be allowed to return home, and others that they should continue to be detained in Italy. At last Cato rose and asked: 'Have we nothing better to do than to spend an entire day sitting here and discussing whether some poor old Greeks are to be buried by our grave-diggers or their own?' The Senate then decreed that the men should be allowed to return home, but a few days later Polybius tried to have another proposal laid before the Senate, whereby the exiles would have the honours and positions which they had formerly held in Achaea restored to them, and he asked Cato's opinion as to whether this petition was likely to succeed. Cato smiled and told him that what he was suggesting was rather as though Odysseus had wanted to go back into the Cyclops' cave to fetch a cap and belt he had left behind.

'Wise men,' he used to say, 'profit far more from the example of fools than the other way round. They learn to avoid the fools' mistakes, whereas fools do not imitate the successes of the wise.' He said that he liked to see young men blush rather than turn pale, and that he had no use for a soldier who used his hands on the march and his feet when it came to fighting, or one who snored louder in his sleep than he shouted in battle. There was an excessively fat Roman of whom he made fun by saying: 'How can a body like this be of any service to the state, when everything in it from the gullet to the groin is devoted to the belly?' When a certain epicure wished to enjoy his company and sent him an invitation, he excused himself by saying that he could not spend his time with a man whose palate was so much more highly developed than his heart. He also remarked once that a lover's soul lives in the body of his beloved. As for regrets, he said that there were only three actions in his life of which he repented. The first was to have entrusted a secret to a woman, the second to have paid for his sea passage to a place instead of walking there, and the third to have remained intestate for a whole day. Speaking to an old man who was leading a depraved life, he remarked,

* In 167 B.C. after the defeat of the kingdom of Macedon by the Romans at Pydna, which marked the end of Greek independence, a thousand prominent Achaeans were deported to Italy, where they remained for seventeen years. At the end of this time the three hundred survivors, one of whom was Polybius, were permitted by a special decree of the Senate to return home.

'Old age is vile enough as it is: do not add to it the deformity of vice.' To a tribune of the people who was reputed to be a poisoner, had introduced an iniquitous bill, and was trying to force its passage, he said, 'Young man, I do not know which will do us more harm, to drink your potions or to enact your bills.' And when he himself was attacked by a man who led an infamous and dissolute life, he retorted: 'We can never fight on equal terms: you are so hardened to abuse that you can return it just as easily as you suffer it, whereas for me it is as unusual to hear as it is unpleasant to utter.' These are some examples of his memorable sayings.

10. After he had served as consul with his close friend Valerius Flaccus,* he was allotted the province which is known as Hither Spain. While he was engaged in subduing some of the tribes by force and winning over others by diplomacy, he was attacked by a huge army of barbarians and was in danger of being driven ignominiously out of the province. In this situation he appealed to a neighbouring tribe, the Celtiberi, to join forces with him. When they demanded two hundred talents as the price for their assistance, Cato's Roman officers thought it an intolerable humiliation that Romans should actually pay barbarians to come to their rescue. But Cato took the view that there was nothing shocking in this. If the Romans won, they could pay their allies out of the spoils of the campaign, not out of public funds, and if they lost there would be nobody left either to ask for the reward or to pay it. In the battle which followed he won an overwhelming victory, and the rest of the campaign was brilliantly successful. Polybius records that in the space of a single day, the walls of all the cities on the Roman side of the river Baetis were razed to the ground on Cato's orders, and yet these were very numerous and full of excellent fighting men. Cato himself tells us that he captured more cities than he stayed days in Spain. And this is no idle boast, since in fact the number taken amounted to four hundred.

His soldiers enriched themselves greatly during this campaign, and over and above their plunder he presented each of them with a pound of silver, saying that it was better that many of the Romans should return home with silver in their pockets than a few with gold. As for himself, he states that he took no share whatever of the spoils of war, apart from what he ate and drank. 'I do not blame those who seek

* In 195 B.C.

to make their fortune in this way,' he added, 'but I would rather compete for bravery with the bravest than for money with the richest, or for covetousness with the most greedy.' At any rate he not only kept his own hands clean, but insisted that his staff should also be free from any taint of profiteering. He had five personal attendants with him while he was on active service. One of these, whose name was Paccius, bought three boys at a public sale of prisoners of war, but when he found that Cato had learned of this transaction, he went and hanged himself rather than face his master. Cato sold the boys and returned the money he received for them to the public treasury.

11. While Cato was still serving in Spain, Scipio Africanus, who was a personal opponent of his and wished to check the sequence of his successes and take the administration of Spanish affairs out of his hands, contrived to have himself appointed to succeed Cato as governor of the province. He therefore travelled to Spain as quickly as he could and cut short Cato's term of office. However Cato took with him five cohorts of infantry and five hundred horsemen as an escort for his return journey, and on his march to Rome subdued the tribe of the Lacetani* and put to death six hundred deserters, whom they surrendered to him. Scipio was furious at this action, whereupon Cato replied with mock humility that Rome would truly be at her greatest when men of noble birth refused to yield the prizes of valour to those of humbler position, and when plebeians such as himself dared to contend with their superiors in birth and distinction. But in spite of Scipio's disapproval, the Senate decreed that none of Cato's measures should be revoked or altered, so that Scipio's term of office, which he had so eagerly sought, was conspicuous for its inactivity and lack of initiative, and it was his own rather than Cato's reputation which suffered.

Cato on the other hand was honoured with a triumph.† But he neither abandoned nor relaxed his efforts, as is so often the case with men whose ambition is directed towards fame rather than virtue, and who as soon as they have attained the highest honours, served as consul, and celebrated a triumph, promptly withdraw from public

* A tribe inhabiting the north-east of Spain in the neighbourhood of the modern Barcelona.

† In 194 B.C.

affairs and devote the rest of their careers to a life of ease and pleasure. Instead, Cato behaved like a man who is all athirst for glory and reputation on his first entry into public life, and in this spirit he once more sprang into action and offered his services to his friends and his fellow-countrymen both in the courts of law and in the field.

12. This was how he came to serve as legate under Titus Sempronius the consul, and helped him to subdue the region of Thrace and the territories bordering the Danube. Later he was a military tribune under Manius Acilius during his campaign in Greece against Antiochus the Great, who next to Hannibal was the most formidable opponent the Romans ever encountered. Antiochus first reconquered almost all the territory in Asia which had previously been ruled by Seleucus Nicator, and subdued many warlike barbarian tribes, and finally his elation at these conquests led him to attack the Romans, whom he regarded as the only nation worthy to cross swords with him. He used the restoration of Greek liberties as a specious pretext for his invasion, although in fact the people had no need for this gift, since the Romans had only recently freed them from the domination of Philip of Macedon. At any rate Antiochus crossed with an army into Greece,* which was at once thrown into a turmoil of hopes and fears, and corrupted by the prospects of royal favour held out by the demagogues whom Antiochus had won over. Accordingly Manius despatched envoys to the various cities. In most of these Titus Flamininus succeeded in quelling the efforts of the agitators and in restoring the people to their allegiance, as I have described in detail in his Life, but Cato was responsible for bringing over Corinth, Patras, and Aegium to the side of Rome.

He also stayed for a considerable time in Athens, and we are told that a certain speech of his has survived which he delivered to the Athenian people in Greek. In this he told them of his admiration for the virtues of the ancient Athenians, and of his delight at seeing a city as beautiful and as magnificent as theirs. All this is untrue, since Cato in fact spoke to the Athenians through an interpreter. He was quite capable of addressing them in their own language, but he clung to Roman forms and made a point of ridiculing those who admired everything that was Greek. For example, he made fun of the Roman author Postumius Albinus, who wrote a history in Greek and asked

* In 192 B.C.

his readers to make allowances for his ignorance of the language. Cato remarked that they might have made allowances if he had been compelled to undertake the task by a decree of the Amphictyonic Council. Cato himself claims that the Athenians were greatly impressed by the speed and the concision of his address, for the interpreter took a long time and a great many words to communicate what he expressed briefly, and in general he concludes that the Greeks speak from the lips, but the Romans from the heart.

13. Now Antiochus had blocked the narrow pass of Thermopylae* with his army and strengthened the natural defences of the position by means of walls and trenches, and there he sat, confident that it was impossible to attack him in Greece. And in fact the Romans did give up hope of forcing the pass by a frontal assault. However, Cato, remembering the famous outflanking march whereby the Persians had turned Leonidas's defences, took a large force and set off under cover of darkness. They had climbed to a considerable height, when their guide, who was a prisoner of war, lost the way and wandered helplessly along tracks which either gave out or ended in sheer precipices, until the soldiers were thoroughly disheartened and on the verge of despair. At this point Cato, recognizing the danger of their position, ordered the troops to halt, while he himself with a single companion named Lucius Manlius, who was an expert mountaineer, went forward to reconnoitre the path. This he did with great difficulty and danger, as it was a moonless pitch-dark night, and the rocks and trees hindered them by preventing them from seeing distinctly where they were going. At last they came upon a path which they believed led down to the enemy's camp. As they returned, they left marks upon some of the most conspicuous rocks on the heights of Mount Callidromus, and at last found their way back to the main body. Then they led the troops forward up to the signs, and started on the downward path. But when they had gone only a little way, the track again gave out, and a yawning precipice stretched below their feet. Once more fear and bewilderment descended on the troops, since it was impossible for them to know or to see that they were almost upon the enemy whom they sought. But presently the darkness began to fade, they believed that they could hear voices close by, and soon they actually caught sight of Greek entrenchments and

* In 191 B.C.

an outpost near the foot of the cliffs. Cato then halted his troops and called up the men of Firmum for a private conference: this was a contingent which he had always found to be especially daring and reliable.

When they had run up and gathered round him, he told them: 'I need to capture one of the enemy alive and find out who this advance guard consists of and what is its strength, the order of battle of the main body, and what preparations they have made to resist us. But to get your prisoner you will have to move without a second's hesitation, as quickly and as boldly as a lion leaping on a timid herd.' When they had listened to Cato's orders, the Firmians set off at a rush, just as they were, poured down the mountain-side, and hurled themselves upon the enemy's sentinels. The surprise was complete and the whole outpost was thrown into confusion and scattered at once. The Firmians seized one man, arms and all, and hurried him back to Cato. He soon discovered from the prisoner that the enemy's main body was encamped in the pass with the king himself, while the detachment which held the approach from the heights above consisted of six hundred picked Aetolians. Now that he knew the weakness of the advance guard and the carelessness of their dispositions, Cato was filled with confidence. He drew his sword, and with a battle-cry and a great blast of trumpets led his men into the attack. When the enemy saw the Romans pouring down upon them from the cliffs, they immediately fled and took refuge with the main body, filling it with confusion and dismay.

14. Meanwhile Manius on the lower ground flung his whole army into the pass and stormed the enemy's fortifications. Antiochus was struck in the mouth by a stone, which shattered his teeth and made him wheel his horse in agony, and before the shock of the Roman charge his troops gave way at every point. There was little enough hope of escape, since the mountain tracks were hard to follow and led over difficult ground, while deep marshes on the one side and steep cliffs on the other threatened any who slipped and fell; but in spite of everything the routed troops tried to force their way through the narrow pass towards these dangers, and trampling upon one another in their terror of the Romans' swords, many of them perished miserably.

It would seem that Cato never stinted his own praise, and could never resist following up a great achievement with a correspondingly boastful description of it, so he gives a characteristically inflated account of this battle. He says that those who saw him pursuing and cutting down the enemy felt that Rome owed more to Cato than he to his city, and that the consul Manius himself, flushed with victory, threw his arms around him in a long embrace and cried aloud in sheer joy that neither he nor the whole Roman people could ever repay Cato for his services to the state. Immediately after the battle he was dispatched to Rome to carry the news of his own exploits. He sailed with a favourable wind to Brundisium, crossed the peninsula in a single day, and after travelling four days more reached Rome on the fifth day after his landing. His arrival filled the whole city with rejoicing and sacrifices, and inspired the people with the proud belief that they could conquer every land and every sea.

15. These actions which I have described were the most remarkable achievements of Cato's military career. In his political life he seems to have concerned himself most of all with the impeachment and trial of wrongdoers. He undertook many prosecutions himself, gave his help to others in bringing theirs, and in some instances incited his fellow-citizens to open proceedings, as in the case of Petillius's prosecution of Scipio. Scipio's response, as a member of one of the greatest families in Rome and a man of lofty spirit, was to trample these accusations underfoot, and when Cato found that he could not obtain a conviction on a capital charge, he dropped the case. But he joined the accusers of Scipio's brother Lucius, and was active in securing his condemnation to pay a heavy fine to the state. Lucius was unable to meet this and therefore became liable to imprisonment, and it was only with difficulty and after the intervention of the tribunes that he was set free.*

There is also a story of a young man, who had brought an action against an enemy of his dead father, and succeeded in obtaining his disfranchisement. When the case was over and he was leaving the Forum, Cato greeted him and said: 'This is the kind of sacrifice we should offer up to the spirits of our parents, not lambs nor kids, but

* The case was brought in 187 B.C. and the charge was concerned with the sum of 500 talents received by Lucius from Antiochus as pay for his troops. Cato contended that Lucius Scipio was obliged to render an account of this transaction to the state.

the condemnation and then the tears of their enemies.' Yet Cato himself did not escape with impunity. Whenever in his political career he gave his enemies the slightest ground to attack him, he was repeatedly prosecuted and sometimes in danger of being condemned. It is said that nearly fifty impeachments were brought against him, the last when he was eighty-six years of age. It was on this occasion that he uttered the famous remark, 'It is hard for a man who has lived through one generation to be called upon to defend himself before another', but even this action was not his last, for four years later at the age of ninety* he impeached Servius Galba, and indeed one might say of him as of Nestor that his life spanned three generations, and he was active in each one of them. He fought many political contests with Scipio Africanus, as I have described above, and he lived to continue them with Scipio the Younger, who was Africanus's grandson by adoption, his father being that Aemilius Paulus who conquered Perseus and the Macedonians.†

16. Ten years after his consulship Cato became a candidate for the censorship.‡ This office was regarded as the crowning honour of Roman civic life, and in a sense the culminating achievement of a political career. Its powers were very extensive and they included the right to inquire into the lives and manners of the citizens. The Romans did not think it proper that anyone should be left free to follow his personal preferences and appetites, whether in marriage, the begetting of children, the regulation of his daily life, or the entertainment of his friends, without a large measure of surveillance and control. They believed that a man's true character was more clearly revealed in his private life than in his public or political career, and they therefore chose two officials, one from among the so-called patricians and the other a plebeian, whose duty it was to watch, regulate, and punish any tendency to indulge in licentious or voluptuous habits and to depart from the traditional and established way of living. These officers were known as censors, and they had authority to degrade a Roman knight or to expel a senator who led a vicious or disorderly life. They also carried out and maintained a general census of property, kept a register of all the citizens according to their social and political classification, and exercised various other important powers.

* Plutarch's chronology is at fault here. Cato died in his eighty-sixth year.

† At the battle of Pydna (168 B.C.).

‡ In 184 B.C.

Accordingly, when Cato became a candidate, almost all the most prominent and influential members of the Senate joined forces to oppose him. Those of them who belonged to the most ancient families were actuated by jealousy, since they regarded it as an insult to the nobility that men of totally undistinguished origin should be raised to the highest positions of honour and power, while others, who were conscious of having committed shameful misdeeds or departed from traditional customs, dreaded the austerity of Cato's disposition and felt sure that he would prove harsh and inexorable in his use of power.

So after conferring together and drawing up their plans, they put up no less than seven candidates to oppose Cato, and these men at once set themselves to court the people's votes by promising that they would show great leniency while in office, imagining that the commons desired a lax and indulgent régime. Cato, on the other hand, did not deign to offer any concessions whatever. He openly threatened wrongdoers in his speeches from the rostra, proclaimed that what the city needed was a drastic purification, and exhorted the people, if they had any sense, to choose a physician who would prescribe not the most painless but the most strenuous course of treatment. He himself was such a one, he told them, among the plebeians, and among the patricians they should elect Valerius Flaccus. Flaccus was the only colleague, he insisted, with whom he could make some progress in cutting away and cauterizing the hydra-like luxury and degeneracy of the age. As for the rest of the candidates, it was clear that the only object of their efforts was to force their way into the office and pervert its functions, since they were afraid of those who would administer them with justice. On this occasion the Roman people showed itself to be truly great, and hence worthy of great leaders. They did not allow themselves to be deterred by Cato's inflexibility nor even by his arrogance. On the other hand they rejected his smooth-spoken opponents, who had promised to do everything to please them, and they elected Flaccus together with Cato. Indeed they treated Cato not as if he were a candidate for office, but already installed in it, and exercising his authority.

17. As soon as he was elected, Cato appointed his friend and colleague Lucius Valerius Flaccus to be leader of the Senate, and he also expelled several of its members, including a certain Lucius Quintius. This man had been consul seven years before and – a distinction which counted

for more even than the consulship – was the brother of the Titus Flamininus who had overcome king Philip of Macedon.* The reason for his expulsion was as follows. There was a youth who had been Lucius's favourite ever since his boyhood. He kept him constantly at his side, even taking him on his campaigns, and allowed him to enjoy more honour and influence than any of his closest friends and relatives. While Lucius was serving as governor of his consular province, he held a drinking party. On this occasion the youth was reclining, as he usually did, next to Lucius and serving up flattery to his patron, who was in any case all too easily led astray by drink. 'I am so devoted to you,' the boy told him, 'that once, when there was to be a gladiatorial show in Rome, I missed it to hurry out here and join you, even though I have always longed to see a man killed.' Lucius, who was anxious to demonstrate his affection, answered, 'I am not going to have you lying there holding a grudge against me on that account. I will soon put the matter right.' At this he gave orders for a criminal who had been condemned to death to be brought into the banquet, and for a lictor to stand by him with an axe. Then he again asked his favourite whether he wanted to see a man struck dead, and when the boy said he did, he ordered the prisoner to be beheaded. This is the account which most writers give of the incident, and when Cicero in his *Dialogue On Old Age* introduces Cato as telling the story, he gives the same details. According to Livy, however, the man who was executed was a Gaulish deserter, and Lucius did not have him beheaded by a lictor, but struck the blow with his own hand, and he also mentions that this version of the story is repeated in a speech of Cato's own. When Lucius was expelled from the Senate in this way, his brother Titus was indignant and appealed to the people, demanding that Cato should explain the reasons for his action. Cato then did so and told the whole story of the drinking party. Lucius tried to deny the affair, but when Cato challenged him to a formal inquiry and a judicial wager on the result, he declined. After this everybody recognized that he had been justly punished. But some time later, when a public spectacle was put on in the theatre, Lucius walked past the seats reserved for men of consular rank, and took his place as far away as possible among the least distinguished members of the audience. This action made the people take pity on him, and they began to raise a clamour until they obliged him to change his seat,

* At Cynoscephalae in 198 B.C.

thus restoring his dignity so far as they could and alleviating the humiliation he had suffered.

Cato also expelled another senator, Manilius – despite the fact that public opinion had marked him out as a strong candidate for the consulship – on the ground that he had embraced his wife by daylight in the presence of his daughter. For his own part, Cato declared, he never embraced his wife except when a loud peal of thunder occurred, and it was a favourite joke of his that he was a happy man whenever Jove took it into his head to thunder.

18. Cato also had Lucius Scipio expelled from the equestrian order, even though the man had enjoyed the honour of a triumph. But on this occasion he was sharply criticized since it was believed that he had acted out of personal spite, and that his principal object had been to insult the memory of Lucius's brother, the great Africanus. But what annoyed people more than anything else were his efforts to cut down extravagance and luxury. These habits could not be abolished outright, since most of the people were already to some extent infected by them, and so Cato attempted an indirect approach. He had an assessment made of all clothing, carriages, women's ornaments, furniture, and plate: whatever exceeded 1,500 drachmas in value was rated at ten times its worth and taxed accordingly, as he wished to ensure that those whose possessions were the most valuable should also pay the highest taxes. He then imposed a tax of three asses for every thousand assessed in this way, so that when owners of property found themselves burdened with these charges, and saw that people who enjoyed the same income but led frugal and simple lives paid far less in taxes, they might give up their extravagant habits. However, the result of these measures was to earn him the hatred not only of those who put up with the taxes to enjoy their luxuries, but also of those who sacrificed the luxuries to avoid the taxes. The truth is that most people feel that they are being deprived of their wealth if they are prevented from displaying it, and it is the superfluities, not the necessities of life, which really afford the opportunity for such display. This is the phenomenon which so much astonished Ariston the philosopher, as we are told: he could not understand why men should regard it as a happier state to possess what is superfluous rather than what is essential. We may remember the story of Scopas the Thessalian, one of whose friends asked him for an object which was of no

great use to him, and pointed out, to justify his request, that he was not asking for anything which was really necessary or useful; whereupon Scopas replied: 'But it is just these useless and superfluous things which make me enjoy my wealth.' From this we see that the craving for wealth is not a passion that comes naturally to us, but is imposed by the vulgar and irrelevant opinions of the outside world.

19. Cato paid not the slightest attention to the protests which his measures aroused, but proceeded to make them more rigorous than ever. He cut off the pipes by which people were in the habit of diverting some of the public water supply into their houses and gardens: he had any houses which encroached on public land demolished, reduced the contracts for public works to the lowest, and raised the rent for public lands to the highest possible figure. All these proceedings made him intensely unpopular. Titus Flamininus and his friends organized a party to oppose his programme, prevailed upon the Senate to cancel the contracts which he had arranged for the building of temples and other public works, and encouraged the boldest of the tribunes to prosecute him before the people and fine him two talents. He also met with vehement opposition from the Senate when he had built in the Forum at public expense a basilica below the Senate-house, which came to be known as the Basilica Porcia.

But for all his unpopularity with the rich, Cato's activities as censor seem to have been wholeheartedly admired by the Roman people. At any rate when they erected a statue to his honour in the temple of Hygieia, what they chose to commemorate was not his military campaigns nor his triumph but, according to the inscription, the fact that 'when the Roman state was sinking into decay, he became censor and through his wise leadership, sober discipline, and sound principles restored its strength'. And yet at one time Cato used to ridicule those who took pleasure in receiving honours of this kind. Such people could never understand, he said, that the effigies in which they took so much pride were nothing more than the work of sculptors and painters, whereas the finest image of himself, as he saw it, was the one which his fellow-citizens carried in their hearts. And if anyone showed surprise that there were so many statues which commemorated men of no distinction, but none of himself, he would answer, 'I had far rather that people should ask why there is no statue of me than why there is one.' In short he believed that a good citizen should not accept even the praise that he had earned, unless this could benefit the state.

On the other hand we should recognize that no man ever did more to heap praises upon himself. Cato tells us for example that when men were reproved for misconduct of one kind or another, they would say: 'It is not fair to blame us: we are not all Catos.' And again that men who tried to imitate his habits but went about it clumsily were known as 'left-handed Catos'. He also mentions that the Senate at moments of great crisis looked to him as sailors do to their pilot, and that they would often postpone their most important business, if he could not be present. These claims, it is true, are confirmed by other writers, for his whole course of life, his eloquence, and his age all combined to invest him with immense authority among the Romans.

20. He was also a good father, a kind husband, and a most capable manager of his own household, since he was far from regarding this side of his affairs as trivial or allowing it to suffer from neglect. For this reason I think I should give some examples of his conduct in his private life. He chose his wife for her family rather than her fortune, for he believed that while people of great wealth or high position cherish their own pride and self-esteem, nevertheless women of noble birth are by nature more ashamed of any disgraceful action and so are more obedient to their husbands in everything that is honourable. He used to say that a man who beats his wife or child is laying sacrilegious hands on the most sacred thing in the world. He considered that it was more praiseworthy to be a good husband than a great senator, and was also of the opinion that there was nothing much else to admire in Socrates of old, except for the fact that he was always gentle and considerate in his dealings with his wife, who was a scold, and his children, who were half-witted. When his son was born, Cato thought that nothing but the most important business of state should prevent him from being present when his wife gave the baby its bath and wrapped it in swaddling clothes. His wife suckled the child herself and often did the same for her slaves' children, so as to encourage brotherly feelings in them towards her own son. As soon as the boy was able to learn, his father took charge of his schooling and taught him to read, although he had in the household an educated slave called Chilo who was a schoolmaster and taught many other boys. However, Cato did not think it right, so he tells us, that

his son should be scolded or have his ears pulled by a slave, if he were slow to learn, and still less that he should be indebted to his slave in such a vital matter as his education. So he took it upon himself to teach the boy, not only his letters, but also the principles of Roman law. He also trained him in athletics, and taught him how to throw the javelin, fight in armour, ride a horse, use his fists in boxing, endure the extremes of heat and cold, and swim across the roughest and most swiftly flowing stretches of the Tiber. He tells us that he composed his history of Rome, writing it out with his own hand and in large characters, so that his son should possess in his own home the means of acquainting himself with the ancient annals and traditions of his country. He also mentions that he was as careful not to use any indecent expression before his son as he would have been in the presence of the Vestal Virgins, and that he never bathed with him. This last seems to have been the general custom among the Romans, and even fathers-in-law avoided bathing with their sons-in-law, because they were ashamed to show themselves naked. In later times, however, the Romans adopted from the Greeks the practice of stripping in the presence of other men, and they in turn taught the Greeks to do the same even in the presence of women.

Such was Cato's approach to the noble task of forming and moulding his son for the pursuit of virtue. The boy was an exemplary pupil in his readiness to learn, and his spirit was a match for his natural goodness of disposition. But since his body was not strong enough to endure extreme hardship, Cato was obliged to relax a little the extraordinary austerity and self-discipline of his own way of life. However, his son, in spite of a delicate physique, became an excellent soldier, and fought with great distinction under Aemilius Paulus at the battle of Pydna,* when the Romans defeated king Perseus. During the fighting his sword was either struck out of his hand or else slipped from his grasp when it became moist with sweat. The young man felt deeply ashamed at losing it, and so he turned to some of his companions and, rallying them to his side, charged the enemy again. The fighting was fierce, but at length he succeeded in clearing a space, and there he came upon the weapon amid the heaps of arms and corpses, where the bodies of friends and enemies lay piled high upon one another. Paulus, his commander, was greatly impressed by the young Cato's courage, and a letter has come down to us

* In 168 B.C.

written by the father to his son, in which he praises him in the highest terms for his gallantry and for the sense of honour which he showed in recovering his sword. He afterwards married Tertia, a daughter of Paulus and hence the sister of Scipio the Younger, as he afterwards became known, and the distinction of this alliance with so noble a family was quite as much due to his own achievements as to his father's. In this way Cato was justly rewarded for the care which he had devoted to his son's education.

21. Cato possessed a large number of slaves, whom he usually bought from among the prisoners captured in war, but it was his practice to choose those who, like puppies or colts, were young enough to be trained and taught their duties. None of them ever entered any house but his own, unless they were sent on an errand by Cato or his wife, and if they were asked what Cato was doing, the reply was always that they did not know. It was a rule of his establishment that a slave must either be doing something about the house, or else be asleep. He much preferred the slaves who slept well, because he believed that they were more even-tempered than the wakeful ones, and that those who had had enough sleep produced better results at any task than those who were short of it. And as he was convinced that slaves were led into mischief more often on account of love affairs than for any other reason, he made it a rule that the men could sleep with the women slaves of the establishment, for a fixed price, but must have nothing to do with any others.

At the beginning of his career, when he was a poor man and was frequently on active service, he never complained of anything that he ate, and he used to say that it was ignoble to find fault with a servant for the food that he prepared. But in later life, when he had become more prosperous, he used to invite his friends and colleagues to dinner, and immediately after the meal he would beat with a leather thong any of the slaves who had been careless in preparing or serving it. He constantly contrived to provoke quarrels and dissensions among his slaves, and if they ever arrived at an understanding with one another he became alarmed and suspicious. If ever any of his slaves was suspected of committing a capital offence, he gave the culprit a formal trial in the presence of the rest, and if he was found guilty he had him put to death.

When he began to devote himself more energetically to making money, he came to regard agriculture as a pastime rather than as a source of income, and he invested his capital in solid enterprises which involved the minimum of risk. He bought up ponds, hot springs, land devoted to producing fuller's earth, pitch factories, and estates which were rich in pasture-land or forest. All these undertakings brought in large profits and could not, to use his own phrase, be ruined by the whims of Jupiter. He also used to lend money in what is surely the most disreputable form of speculation, that is the underwriting of ships. Those who wished to borrow money from him were obliged to form a large association, and when this reached the number of fifty, representing as many ships, he would take one share in the company. His interests were looked after by Quintio, one of his freedmen, who used to accompany Cato's clients on their voyages and transact their business. In this way he drew a handsome profit, while at the same time spreading his risk and never venturing more than a fraction of his capital.

He would also lend money to any of his slaves who wished it. They used these sums to buy young slaves, and after training them and teaching them a trade for a year at Cato's expense, they would sell them again. Often Cato would keep these boys for himself, and he would then credit to the slave the price offered by the highest bidder. He tried to encourage his son to imitate these methods, and told him that to diminish one's capital was something that might be expected of a widow, but not of a man. But he certainly went too far when he ventured once to declare that the man who deserved the highest praise, indeed who should be honoured almost as a god, was the one who at the end of his life was found to have added to his property more than he had inherited.

22. Cato was an old man when Carneades the Academic and Diogenes the Stoic arrived in Rome as ambassadors from Athens. They had been sent to plead that the Athenians should be released from a sentence which had imposed on them a fine of five hundred talents. The people of Oropus had brought an action, the Athenians had allowed the case to go by default, and the people of Sicyon had pronounced judgement against them.* When these philosophers

* The Athenians had plundered the city of Oropus. The dispute was referred to the Sicyonians for arbitration, and their verdict was that the Athenians, who did not attempt to defend themselves, should be fined five hundred talents.

arrived, all the young Romans who had any taste for literature hurried to frequent their company, and listened to them with delight and wonder. Above all they were spellbound by the grace and charm with which Carneades expressed himself. He was the ablest of the Greeks and his performance did not belie his reputation. His discourses attracted large and admiring audiences, and before long the city was filled as if by a rushing, mighty wind with the sound of his praises. The report spread that a Greek of extraordinary talents had arrived, who could subdue all opposition beneath the spell of his eloquence, and who had so bewitched all the youth of the city that they seemed to have abandoned all their other pleasures and pursuits and to have run mad after philosophy.

Most of the Romans were gratified by this, and were well content to see their sons embrace Greek culture and frequent the society of such estimable men. But Cato, from the moment that this passion for discussion first showed itself in Rome, was deeply disturbed. He was afraid that the younger generation might allow their ambitions to be diverted in this direction, and might come to value most highly a reputation that was based upon feats of oratory rather than upon feats of arms. So when the prestige of the philosophers continued to rise still higher, and no less eminent a man than Gaius Acilius volunteered to act as their interpreter for their first audience with the Senate, Cato made up his mind to find some plausible excuse for clearing the whole tribe of philosophers out of the city. Accordingly he rose in the Senate and criticized the authorities for having kept in such long suspense a delegation composed of men whose powers of persuasion were so remarkable that they could obtain any verdict that they wished. 'We ought to come to a decision as soon as possible,' he declared, 'and take a vote on their proposal, so that these distinguished men may return to their seats of learning and lecture to the sons of Greece, but leave the youth of Rome to give their attention to the laws and the magistrates, as they have done in the past.'

23. Cato did not take this action, as some people believe, out of personal animosity towards Carneades, but rather because he was opposed on principle to the study of philosophy, and because his patriotic fervour made him regard the whole of Greek culture and its methods of education with contempt. He asserts, for example, that Socrates was a turbulent windbag, who did his best to tyrannize over

his country by undermining its established customs and seducing his fellow-citizens into holding opinions which were contrary to the laws. He made fun of Isocrates as a teacher of rhetoric, saying that his disciples went on studying with him until they were old men, so that they were only able to practise the tricks they had learned and plead their cases in the court where Minos sat in judgement in Hades. And in the effort to turn his son against Greek culture, he allowed himself an utterance which was absurdly rash for an old man: he pronounced with all the solemnity of a prophet that if ever the Romans became infected with the literature of Greece, they would lose their empire. At any rate time has exposed the emptiness of this ominous prophecy, for in the age when the city rose to the zenith of her greatness, her people had made themselves familiar with Greek learning and culture in all its forms.

However, Cato's dislike of the Greeks was not confined to philosophers: he was also deeply suspicious of the Greek physicians who practised in Rome. He had heard of Hippocrates's celebrated reply, when he was called upon to attend the king of Persia for a fee amounting to many talents, and declared that he would never give his services to barbarians who were enemies of Greece. Cato maintained that all Greek physicians had taken an oath of this kind, and urged his son not to trust any of them. He himself had compiled a book of recipes and used them for the diet or treatment of any members of his household who fell ill. He never made his patients fast, but allowed them to eat herbs and morsels of duck, pigeon, or hare. He maintained that this diet was light and thoroughly suitable for sick people, apart from the fact that it often produced nightmares, and he claimed that by following it he kept both himself and his family in perfect health.

24. However his self-sufficiency in these matters seems to have been justly punished, for he lost both his wife and his son by disease. He himself, so far as physical health and strength were concerned, possessed an iron constitution, and was able for many years to resist the onset of old age. Even when he was far advanced in years he continued to indulge his sexual appetite, and he finally took a second wife long after he had passed the age to marry. This was how it came about. After the death of his first wife, he arranged a marriage between his son and Aemilius Paulus's daughter, who was also the sister of Scipio the Younger; but while he himself remained a widow-

er, he consoled himself with a young slave girl, who came to his room secretly to sleep with him. This intrigue soon came to light, as might be expected in a small household which contained a young daughter-in-law, and on one occasion, when the girl seemed to flaunt her presence altogether too impudently on her way to Cato's room, the old man could not fail to notice that his son kept silent, glanced at her with intense dislike, and then turned away in disgust. As soon as Cato understood that his behaviour annoyed his children, he did not blame or find fault with them at all. Instead, as he was walking towards the Forum with his clients in the usual way, he called out to one of them whose name was Salonius. This man had been one of his secretaries and now regularly escorted him, and Cato asked him in a loud voice whether he had by now found a suitable husband for his young daughter. The man said that he had not, and had no intention of settling the matter without first consulting his patron. 'Very well,' replied Cato, 'I have found a suitable son-in-law, unless you happen to object to his age: there is nothing wrong with him in other respects, but he is a very old man.' Salonius at once urged him to take the matter into his own hands and betroth the girl to whomever he thought best, since she was under his patronage and would always depend upon his good offices. Thereupon Cato, without further ceremony, told him that he wished to marry the girl himself. At first Salonius, naturally enough, was astounded at the proposal, since he supposed that Cato was well past the age to marry, and also that his own family was far too humble to be allied with a house which had earned consular rank and triumphal honours; but once he saw that Cato was in earnest he gladly accepted, and as soon as they arrived at the Forum, the betrothal ceremony was carried out.

While the preparations for the marriage were being made, Cato's son collected some of his friends, went to visit his father, and asked whether he had done anything to harm or annoy him, to have a stepmother foisted upon him in this way. 'Heaven forbid, my boy,' answered Cato, 'you have been a model son to me, and I have no fault of any kind to find with you. It is simply that I want to leave behind me more sons like you of my blood, and more citizens like you to serve my country.' However, this remark is said to have been made many years earlier by Pisistratus, the tyrant of Athens, whose sons were already grown men when he married Timonassa of Argolis, by whom we are told he had two more children, Iophon and

Thessalus. Cato also had a son by his second marriage, whom he named Salonius after his father-in-law, but his first-born son died during his praetorship. Cato often mentions him in his books as having been a good and courageous man, and it is said that he endured his loss with all the calm of a philosopher, nor did he take any less keen an interest in public affairs than before. Unlike Lucius Lucullus and Metellus Pius at a later date, he never became so enfeebled by old age as to abandon public service or to regard political activity as an oppressive duty: still less did he follow the example of Scipio Africanus before him, who because of the attacks of those who envied the glory he had won, turned his back on the Roman people and determined to spend the rest of his life in untroubled retirement. Somebody is said to have advised Dionysius, the ruler of Syracuse, that absolute power is the best winding-sheet for a man to die in, and in the same way it was Cato's belief that the service of the state was still the most honourable employment for old age. But whenever he had leisure, his favourite recreations consisted of writing books and farming.

25. He wrote discourses on an immense number of subjects and also histories. When he was a young man he applied himself seriously to farming because of his poverty – in fact he remarks that at that time he knew only two ways of acquiring money, by farming and by saving – but in later life he regarded agriculture as a hobby and a subject to study in theory. He also wrote a treatise on farming, which includes various recipes for making cakes and preserving fruit, so anxious was he to show that he possessed a superior and independent knowledge of every subject. His table too was never so abundantly stocked as when he was in the country. He always invited his friends and acquaintances from the neighbourhood, and showed himself a gay and spirited host. And indeed his company was so agreeable that it was greatly sought after, not only by his contemporaries but even by the younger generation, for his experience was wide and he had read and heard a great deal that was worth repeating. He believed that a good table was the best place for making friends, and at his own the conversation often dwelt on the praises of brave and honourable men, but he also made it a rule to refrain from mentioning those who were worthless or disreputable. Such persons were taboo in Cato's company, either by way of praise or blame.

26. Some people consider that the last of his political achievements was the destruction of Carthage.* In the military sense it was the younger Scipio who brought this about, but the fact that the Romans went to war at all was very largely the consequence of Cato's advice. This was how it happened. Cato was sent out on a diplomatic mission to investigate the causes of a dispute between the Carthaginians and Masinissa the king of Numidia, who were at this time† at war. Masinissa had been a friend of the Roman people from the first,‡ whereas the Carthaginians had entered into treaty relations with Rome only after the defeat which they had suffered at the hands of Scipio Africanus, and this settlement had stripped them of their empire and compelled them to pay a heavy tribute to Rome. Nevertheless it was at once apparent to Cato that the city was by no means crushed nor impoverished as the Romans imagined. He found it teeming with a new generation of fighting men, overflowing with wealth, amply stocked with weapons and military supplies of every kind, and full of confidence at this revival of its strength. He drew the conclusion that this was no time for the Romans to occupy themselves with regulating the affairs of Masinissa and the Numidians, but that unless they found means to crush a city which had always borne them an undying hatred and had now recovered its power to an incredible extent, they would find themselves as gravely threatened as before. He therefore returned with all speed to Rome, and warned the Senate that the overwhelming defeats and misfortunes which the Carthaginians had suffered had done much to diminish their recklessness and over-confidence, but little to impair their strength, and that they were likely to emerge not weaker but more experienced in war. He was convinced that this present dispute with the Numidians was merely the prelude to an attack upon Rome, and that the peace and the treaty which existed between them were a convenient fiction to cover a period of suspense, until a suitable moment should arrive to begin a war.

27. As he ended this speech it is said that Cato shook out the folds of his toga and contrived to drop some Libyan figs on the floor of the Senate-house, and when the senators admired their size and beauty,

* In 146 B.C. † In 150 B.C.

‡ Numidia had, in fact, been allied to Carthage during most of the second Punic war, but went over to Rome in its closing stages.

he remarked that the country which produced them was only three days' sail from Rome. Afterwards he adopted a still more forceful method of driving home his point: whenever his opinion was called for on any subject, he invariably concluded with the words, 'And furthermore it is my opinion that Carthage must be destroyed!' On the other hand Publius Scipio Nasica made a point of adding the phrase, 'And in my view Carthage must be spared!' Scipio had already observed, no doubt, that the Roman people was by this time indulging in many excesses, and that the insolence occasioned by its prosperity prompted it to cast aside the control of the Senate and force the whole state to follow in whichever direction the impulses of the masses might lead. He was therefore in favour of keeping the fear of Carthage hanging over the people as a check upon their arrogance, and he evidently also believed that although Carthage was not strong enough to threaten the Romans, she was not so weak that they could afford to despise her. But this was precisely the danger that Cato feared, namely that at a time when the Romans were intoxicated and carried away by their new-found power, they should allow a city which had always been great and had now been sobered by calamity to continue to threaten them. He believed that it was best to free the Romans from any fear of outside danger, so that they could devote themselves wholeheartedly to reforming their own shortcomings and abuses at home.

This is the way in which Cato is said to have brought about the third and last war against Carthage. He died almost immediately after it had begun,* leaving a prophecy that it would be ended by a man who was still young, but who had already as a military tribune given remarkable proofs of his intelligence and daring in his encounters with the enemy. When his exploits were reported in Rome, Cato is said to have quoted the line from Homer, in which Circe speaks of the prophet Tiresias in the underworld,

> Only his wisdom abides; the rest glide around him like shadows.†

This prophecy Scipio soon confirmed by his actions. Cato left one son by his second wife, whose surname I have mentioned was Salonius, and one grandson the child of his first son, who was already dead. Salonius died while he was in office as praetor, but his son Marcus later became consul. This Marcus was the grandfather of

* In 149 B.C. † *Odyssey* x, 495.

Cato the philosopher,* who for his courage and uprightness of character and the fame which these qualities brought him was one of the most remarkable men of his time.

* This was the Cato who opposed Julius Caesar in the great debate on the conspiracy of Catiline, later became one of the last champions of the Republican cause, and finally, after his colleague's defeat by Caesar at the battle of Thapsus, committed suicide at Utica (46 B.C.).

5

TIBERIUS GRACCHUS

[163–133 B.C.]

* *
*

1. Now that I have fulfilled the first part of my task in relating the story of the lives of the Spartan kings Agis and Cleomenes,* it remains to consider an equally tragic history, the fate of the Roman pair, Tiberius and Gaius Gracchus, which I have chosen as a parallel. They were the sons of Tiberius Sempronius Gracchus, a man who although he had held the office of censor, served twice as consul and celebrated two triumphs, was even more renowned for his personal character than his achievements. It was for this reason that, after the death of Scipio Africanus, the conqueror of Hannibal, even though Tiberius had not been a friend of his and had in fact opposed him in politics, he was nevertheless considered worthy to marry Scipio's daughter Cornelia. There is a story that Tiberius once caught a pair of snakes on his bed and that the augurs, after giving thought to this prodigy, told him that he must neither kill both reptiles nor let both go: their interpretation was that he must deal with each separately, and that if he killed the male serpent this would bring about his own death, if the female, Cornelia's. Gracchus loved his wife, and considered that as he was far advanced in years, while his wife was still young, it was better that he should die, and so he killed the male

* Agis ruled Sparta from 244 to 240 B.C. He attempted to redress the distribution of wealth and of land by reviving some of the ancient institutions of Lycurgus. He was deposed and executed at the age of twenty-four. Cleomenes, whose reign lasted from 236 to 222 B.C., also attempted reforms on the Lycurgan pattern. He was defeated by Antigonus of Macedon in 222 B.C., fled to Egypt, and committed suicide there two years later. Gracchus senior was consul in 177 and 163 and censor in 169 B.C. He was awarded triumphs for his victories in Further Spain and Sardinia.

serpent and let the female escape. He died soon afterwards,* leaving Cornelia with twelve children by him.

Cornelia took charge both of the children and of her husband's property, and proved herself a woman of such discretion and noble ideals and so devoted a mother that Tiberius was considered to have made no unreasonable choice in electing to die in place of such a wife. For when Ptolemy,† the king of Egypt, asked for her hand in marriage and invited her to share his crown she refused, and remained a widow. While she was still a widow she lost all her children but three, a daughter who married Scipio Africanus the younger,‡ and two sons, Tiberius and Gaius, who are the subjects of this Life. These boys Cornelia brought up with such care and such ambitious hopes that, although by common consent no Romans have ever been more naturally gifted, they were considered to owe their virtues even more to their education than to their heredity.

2. We notice that the figures of Castor and Pollux, as they are represented in sculpture and painting, show certain differences in their physique, as between the boxer and the runner. In the same way with these two young Romans; in spite of their strong resemblance to one another in courage and self-discipline as well as in generosity, eloquence, and idealism, there also developed some strong contrasts which manifested themselves both in their actions and in their political careers, and it will not be out of place for me to set forth these differences before going farther.

First of all Tiberius was gentle and composed, alike in his cast of features, expression, and demeanour, whereas Gaius was highly strung and impassioned. Thus, when they addressed the people, Tiberius always spoke in a decorous tone and remained standing in

* About 150 B.C.

† This seems likely to have been Ptolemy VI, Philometor, rather than the unattractive Ptolemy VII, Euergetes, also known as Physcon (big-bellied), who deposed his elder brother Philometor in 163 B.C. Both brothers visited Rome and probably met Cornelia during her husband's lifetime.

‡ This Scipio was the son of Lucius Aemilius Paulus, the conqueror of Macedonia, and was adopted by Publius Cornelius Scipio, the son of the hero of the Second Punic War. He acquired the title of Africanus as a result of his generalship in the Third Punic War (149–146 B.C.), in which Carthage was finally crushed. His marriage to Sempronia, Tiberius Gracchus's sister, was not a success.

the same position, whereas Gaius was the first Roman to stride up and down the rostra and wrench his toga off his shoulder, in the same way that Cleon the Athenian is said to have been the first of the demagogues to tear open his cloak and slap his thigh. Gaius's oratory tended to electrify his audience and was impassioned to the point of exaggeration, whereas Tiberius was more conciliatory and appealed to men's sense of pity. Tiberius's style was pure and his language chosen with extreme care, whereas Gaius's was plausible and exuberant. In the same way as regards their table and mode of life, Gaius, although austere if judged by the standards of his contemporaries, was yet somewhat ostentatious and addicted to new fashions by comparison with his brother. We have some evidence for this in the accusation brought against him by Drusus of buying silver dolphins at the price of 1,250 drachmas a pound.* The same differences which appeared in their styles of speaking were also reflected in their characters. Tiberius was mild and reasonable, while his brother was harsh and impulsive, and often, against his better judgement, allowed himself to be so far carried away by anger while he was speaking that his voice would rise to a high pitch, he would lapse into abuse, and lose the thread of his argument. To guard against such digressions he employed a well-educated slave named Licinius, who stood behind him with an instrument which was intended to correct the tones of his voice and give them their proper pitch. Whenever he noticed that Gaius's voice was becoming harsh or broken with passion, he would sound a soft note, and as soon as Gaius heard this he would immediately moderate his anger, tone down his voice, and show that his emotions were under control.

3. These were the differences between the two brothers, but in respect of bravery in the face of the enemy, justice in their dealings with the subject peoples, scrupulous attention to their public duties, and restraint in the pleasures they allowed themselves, both were exactly alike. Tiberius, however, was nine years older than his brother, which meant that their political careers were separated by an interval, and it was this factor rather than any other which turned out to be the fatal weakness in their undertakings. They did not rise to political prominence at the same time, with the result that their powers were exerted separately, whereas if only they had

* These were probably ornaments attached to some piece of furniture.

been combined the effect would have been irresistible. I must therefore describe their careers individually and shall deal with the elder brother first.

4. By the time that Tiberius arrived at manhood, he had already earned such a reputation that he was considered worthy to be elected to a priesthood in the college of augurs,* but he owed this distinction to his personal merits rather than his noble birth. This was proved by the action of Appius Claudius, a man who had held the offices of censor and consul, who by reason of his rank had been raised to the position of leader of the Senate,† and who for the loftiness of his spirit surpassed all the Romans of his time. When the augurs held a banquet on the occasion of the young man's election to office, Appius greeted Tiberius warmly, expressed his regard for him, and went on to offer him his daughter's hand in marriage. Tiberius gladly accepted and the betrothal was agreed at once. Later when Appius returned home, he called out excitedly to his wife from the doorway where he was standing, 'Antistia, I have betrothed our Claudia!' His wife answered in surprise, 'Why so suddenly? Why are you in such a hurry, unless you have found Tiberius Gracchus for a husband?' I know that some writers relate this story of Tiberius's father and Scipio Africanus, but most of them follow the version which I have given, and Polybius mentions that, after Scipio Africanus's death, Cornelia's relatives chose Tiberius in preference to any other husband and gave her to him in marriage, which indicates that her father had left her unaffianced and unbetrothed.

Soon afterwards the young Tiberius served for a period in Africa‡ under Scipio Africanus the younger, who had married his sister. There, according to the Roman custom,§ he shared a tent with his

* There were nine augurs, who co-opted a new member when a vacancy arose.

† An honorary distinction which at this period of Roman history was conferred upon the man considered most suitable by the censors.

‡ In 146 B.C. at the end of the Third Punic War, in which Scipio brought about the final subjugation of Carthage and earned the title of Africanus.

§ It was usual for a number of young Romans of good family to be attached to the general's staff to learn the art of war. Their association with the commander and admission to his table and his friendship depended upon how they acquitted themselves in the field.

commander, and it was not long before he learned to appreciate Scipio's character. The older man was a model of the soldierly virtues and provided a constant example to imitate and rival these qualities in action. Tiberius soon came to surpass all the young Romans of his age in discipline and courage: indeed he was the first to scale the enemy's wall, according to Fannius, who writes that he himself climbed up with Tiberius and shared in the exploit. Tiberius won the affections of many of his comrades while he was with the army and was greatly missed when he returned to Italy.

5. After the Carthaginian war he was elected quaestor, and it fell to his lot to serve in the operations against Numantia under the consul Gaius Mancinus,* a man by no means undeserving in his personal qualities, but perhaps the unluckiest Roman ever to hold the office of general. At any rate, amid the various unexpected misfortunes and military reverses which marked this campaign, Tiberius's courage and intelligence shone out all the more brightly, and not only these qualities but also – which was more admirable still – the respect and honour in which he continued to hold his commander, who, under the weight of successive reverses, even forgot that he was a general. After he had been defeated in several major battles, Mancinus attempted to abandon his camp and withdraw his army by night, but the Numantines discovered his intention and promptly seized his camp, attacked his men as they fled, and cut the rearguard to pieces. They then proceeded to encircle his men and drive them on to difficult ground from which there was no escape. By this time Mancinus had given up all hope of breaking through to safety, and he therefore sent envoys to the enemy to propose a truce and arrange terms for a peace; but the Numantines declared that they would trust no Roman except Tiberius and demanded that Mancinus should send him. They did this not only out of their regard for Tiberius's personal qualities – for he had a great reputation among the Numantine troops – but also because they remembered his father Tiberius. He had fought against the Spaniards and subdued many of their tribes, but had made a peace with the Numantines and had always ensured that the Roman people kept its terms with the strictest justice. So Tiberius was duly sent to confer with the enemy's leaders. He gave way on some points and extracted concessions on others, and in the end arrived

* Consul in 137 B.C.

at an agreement which undoubtedly saved the lives of twenty thousand Roman citizens, not to mention their slaves and camp followers.

6. Nevertheless the Numantines took possession of all the property which had been left in the camp and treated this as plunder. Among these spoils were Tiberius's ledgers, which contained the written records of his transactions as quaestor, and which he was most anxious to recover. Accordingly, when the Roman army was already well on its way, he went back to Numantia accompanied by three or four of his friends. There he called out the magistrates and asked them to return his tablets, to prevent his enemies from seizing this opportunity to slander his good name because of his inability to account for his administration. The Numantines were delighted that this accident had enabled them to do him a service. They invited him to enter the city, and as he stood considering the matter, they came nearer, clasped his hands, and begged him no longer to regard them as enemies but rather as friends whom he could trust. So Tiberius decided to fall in with their wishes, since he was anxious both to recover the tablets and also to avoid offending the Numantines by appearing to distrust them. When he entered the city, the Numantines' first action was to set out a meal for him, and they pressed him in the friendliest fashion to sit down and eat with them. Next they returned his ledgers, and urged him to take whatever else he wanted from the spoils. Tiberius refused everything, however, except for some incense which he was in the habit of using for public sacrifices, and after saying good-bye with warm expressions of friendship, he took his leave.

7. When he returned to the capital, he found that the whole transaction had aroused a storm of indignation, and was being denounced as a disaster and a disgrace to the name of Rome. On the other hand the relatives and friends of the soldiers, who formed a large proportion of the citizen body, came flocking to Tiberius, blamed the general for everything that was dishonourable in the affair, and insisted that it was through Tiberius's efforts that the lives of so many citizens had been saved. However, those who condemned the conduct of the campaign most harshly, urged that this was an occasion for the people to follow the precedent set by their ancestors, who had stripped and delivered up to the Samnites those very generals who had been

content to buy their safety on dishonourable terms.* What was more, this punishment had been extended to cover everyone who had taken any part in the terms of surrender, namely the quaestors and military tribunes, and in this way the people had made these officials responsible for the subsequent repudiation and violation of the agreement with the Samnites. But it was on this occasion more than on any other that the people chose to demonstrate their goodwill and affection towards Tiberius. They voted that the consul should be delivered up to the Numantines stripped and in chains, but for Tiberius's sake all the other officers were spared. It appears that Scipio, who at this time was the most powerful and influential man in Rome, also played his part in rescuing them, but in spite of this he was blamed by Tiberius and his friends for not saving Mancinus from punishment,† and also for not insisting that the agreement which his friend and kinsman Tiberius had negotiated with the Numantines was duly ratified. It seems most likely that whatever difference arose between the two men was caused by Tiberius's personal ambition, and by the friends and sophists who encouraged him. But certainly this estrangement produced no irreconcilable breach between them, and in my opinion Tiberius would never have suffered the fate which finally overtook him if Scipio had been in Rome at the time of his political campaign. However, as events turned out, Scipio was already at Numantia and was carrying on the war there when Tiberius brought forward his programme of agrarian reform.‡ The occasion for this was as follows.

8. Whenever the Romans annexed land from their neighbours as a result of their wars, it was their custom to put a part up for sale by auction: the rest was made common land and was distributed among the poorest and most needy of the citizens, who were allowed to cultivate it on payment of a small rent to the public treasury. When

* In 321 B.C. the Roman army had been trapped by the Samnites in the pass known as the Caudine Forks, and compelled to submit to the humiliation of passing under the yoke. The Senate rejected the terms of surrender, on the ground that such a treaty could not be made without the consent of the Roman people.

† Mancinus himself supported the proposal and he was handed over, but the Numantines refused to accept him.

‡ Scipio left for Numantia in 134 B.C. Tiberius's death and the capture of Numantia both took place in the following year.

the rich began to outbid and drive out the poor by offering higher rentals, a law was passed which forbade any one individual to hold more than 500 *jugera** of land. For a while this law restrained the greed of the rich and helped the poor, who were enabled to remain on the land which they had rented, so that each of them could occupy the allotment which he had originally been granted. But after a time the rich men in each neighbourhood by using the names of fictitious tenants, contrived to transfer many of these holdings to themselves, and finally they openly took possession of the greater part of the land under their own names. The poor, when they found themselves forced off the land, became more and more unwilling to volunteer for military service or even to raise a family. The result was a rapid decline of the class of free small-holders all over Italy, their place being taken by gangs of foreign slaves, whom the rich employed to cultivate the estates from which they had driven off the free citizens. Scipio's friend Gaius Laelius attempted to reform this abuse, but when he found himself opposed by the property-owning class, he took fright at the conflict which his programme seemed likely to arouse and abandoned his efforts, as a result of which he was given the name of 'the wise', or 'the prudent', for the Latin word *sapiens* seems to be able to carry either meaning. Tiberius, on the other hand, went straight to the root of the matter as soon as he had been elected tribune. He was encouraged in his plans, as most writers report, by Diophanes the orator and Blossius the philosopher. Diophanes was an exile from Mitylene, but Blossius was a native Italian from Cumae, and had been a close friend of Antipater of Tarsus at Rome, who had paid him the honour of dedicating to him some of his philosophical writings. Some writers consider that Cornelia was at least partly to blame for Tiberius's death, since she often reproached her sons with the fact that the Romans still referred to her as the mother-in-law of Scipio, but not yet as the mother of the Gracchi. Others maintain that Tiberius was also influenced by his jealousy of a certain Spurius Postumius. This man was of the same age as Tiberius and a close rival as a public speaker. So when Tiberius returned from the campaign against Numantia and found that his adversary had far outdistanced him in fame and influence and had attracted general admiration, it seems likely that he resolved to outdo him by introducing a challenging political programme, which would arouse great

* About 310 acres: The law was the *Lex Licinia* of 366 B.C.

expectations among the people. However, his brother Gaius has written in a political pamphlet that while Tiberius was travelling through Etruria on his way to Numantia, he saw for himself how the country had been deserted by its native inhabitants, and how those who tilled the soil or tended the flocks were barbarian slaves introduced from abroad; and that it was this experience which inspired the policy that later brought so many misfortunes upon the two brothers. But it was above all the people themselves who did most to arouse Tiberius's energy and ambitions by inscribing slogans and appeals on porticoes, monuments, and the walls of houses, calling upon him to recover the public land for the poor.

9. He did not, however, draft his law by himself, but consulted a number of the most eminent and respected citizens, among them Crassus the Pontifex Maximus, Mucius Scaevola the jurist, who was then consul, and Appius Claudius who was Tiberius's own father-in-law. And certainly many will agree that no law directed against injustice and avarice was ever framed in milder or more conciliatory terms. For the men who deserved to be punished for breaking the law, and who should have been fined as well as obliged to surrender the land which they had been illegally enjoying, were merely required to give up their unjust acquisitions – for which they were compensated – and to allow the ownership to pass to those citizens who most needed the land. But even though this act of restitution showed such tenderness for the wrongdoers, the people were content to forget the past so long as they could be assured of protection against injustice for the future. The wealthy classes and the landowners, on the other hand, were bitterly opposed to these proceedings: they hated the law out of sheer greed, and its originator out of personal resentment and party prejudice, and they did their utmost to turn the people against the reform by alleging that Tiberius's object in introducing a redistribution of land was really to undermine the foundations of the state and stir up a general revolution.

However, these tactics achieved nothing. Tiberius was fighting for a measure which was honourable and just in itself, and he was able to summon up an eloquence which would have done credit to a far less worthy cause. The result was that whenever he mounted the rostra and pleaded the case of the poor with the people crowding around him to listen, the effect of his words was overwhelming and no other orator could stand against him.

'The wild beasts that roam over Italy,' he would tell his listeners, 'have their dens and holes to lurk in, but the men who fight and die for our country enjoy the common air and light and nothing else. It is their lot to wander with their wives and children, houseless and homeless, over the face of the earth. And when our generals appeal to their soldiers before a battle to defend their ancestors' tombs and their temples against the enemy, their words are a lie and a mockery, for not a man in their audience possesses a family altar; not one out of all those Romans owns an ancestral tomb. The truth is that they fight and die to protect the wealth and luxury of others. They are called the masters of the world, but they do not possess a single clod of earth which is truly their own.'

10. To such oratory as this, the utterance of a noble spirit, delivered with genuine passion to a people profoundly moved and fully aroused to the speaker's support, none of Tiberius's adversaries could make an effective reply. So they abandoned any attempt to oppose him by argument and sought the help of Marcus Octavius,* one of the tribunes of the people, a serious young man of steady character, discreet and a close friend of Tiberius. For this reason Octavius at first declined their advances out of regard for Tiberius, but in the end the unremitting pressure of so many powerful and influential men proved too much for him, and so he set himself to oppose Tiberius and found means to obstruct the passage of the law. Now in this situation the decisive power rests with the dissentient tribune; for if a single tribune interposes his veto, the wishes of the rest are of no avail. These tactics angered Tiberius, and he thereupon withdrew his conciliatory law and introduced one which was more gratifying to the people and harsher to the illegal owners of land: it demanded that they should vacate the land which they had acquired in defiance of the earlier laws, but this time it offered no compensation.

So day after day the two speakers fought out this issue on the rostra,

* An ancestor of the Octavius who later became the emperor Augustus. As mentioned in the *Life of Coriolanus* (ch. 7) the tribunes were established in 494 B.C., but it was not long before the rich learned the technique of frustrating their actions by winning over one of their number. The opposition of a single tribune rendered his colleagues powerless.

but although each exerted his powers of expression to the utmost in the effort to defeat his opponent, neither, we are told, ever resorted to abuse, nor in the heat of passion let fall a word of disparagement of the other. For it is not only in the midst of Bacchic orgies, as Euripides writes, but in the control of personal ambitions and passions that a noble nature and a sound upbringing serve to compose and govern the mind. Moreover, when Tiberius learned that Octavius was himself affected by the law as the owner of large tracts of public land, he begged him to withdraw his opposition and offered to pay Octavius the value of his holding out of his own resources, although he was by no means a rich man. But Octavius refused his offer, whereupon Tiberius issued an edict prohibiting all the other magistrates from transacting any public business until the people had cast their vote either for or against his law. He also placed his private seal on the temple of Saturn* so as to prevent the quaestors from drawing money out of the treasury or paying it in: at the same time he gave public notice that a penalty would be imposed upon any praetor who disobeyed the edict; the result of this was to alarm the magistrates so much that they suspended all their various functions. The response of the property-owning faction was to dress themselves in mourning and walk about in the Forum with a dejected appearance calculated to arouse compassion, but at the same time they secretly formed a conspiracy against Tiberius and hired a band of cut-throats to assassinate him. Tiberius for his part – and this soon became common knowledge – took to wearing a dagger under his toga, of the kind which is used by robbers and is known as a *dolon*.

11. When the appointed day arrived and Tiberius was summoning the people to cast their votes, the party of the rich seized the voting urns,† and the whole proceedings were thrown into confusion. However, Tiberius's supporters were numerous enough to force the issue and they were mustering their strength to do this when Manlius and Fulvius, two men of consular rank, fell on their knees before Tiberius, clasped his hands, and implored him to stop the proceedings. Tiberius sensed that the situation had now reached a crisis, and out of respect for two such distinguished men asked them

* This temple was used at that time as the state treasury.

† The urns from which lots were drawn in order to decide the order in which the tribes would vote.

what they wished him to do. They replied that they had no competence to advise on so important a matter, but they earnestly entreated him to refer the whole problem to the Senate, and to this proposal Tiberius agreed.

However, the meeting of the Senate produced no solution because the rich were able to dominate the proceedings, and so Tiberius, since he could find no other way of putting his law to the vote, resorted to a measure which was neither constitutional nor just: he had Octavius deprived of his tribuneship. But before taking this action, he addressed Octavius in affectionate terms, clasped his hands, and pleaded with him in public to give way and gratify the wishes of the people, who after all were demanding nothing more than their just rights, and who would receive little enough in return for the dangers and sufferings which they endured to protect the state. Finally when Octavius rejected his appeal, Tiberius told him that, since they were colleagues in office who possessed equal authority but found themselves opposed on matters of vital importance, it was impossible for them to complete their term of office without an open conflict, and that he could see only one remedy for this situation, namely for one or the other to resign his position. He urged Octavius that the people should first give their vote on his own case, and promised that he would immediately retire into private life, if this was what the citizens desired. But Octavius rejected this proposal too, whereupon Tiberius announced that he would put the matter of Octavius's deposition to the vote, unless his opponent were to change his mind after reflection.

12. Upon this understanding he dissolved the Assembly, but on the following day when the people had gathered again, he mounted the rostra and made yet another attempt to persuade Octavius. Finally, when his opponent still remained immovable, Tiberius proposed a motion depriving Octavius of his tribuneship and called upon the citizens to cast their votes at once. Now there were thirty-five tribes,* and when seventeen of them had voted and the addition of one more would compel Octavius to become a private citizen once again, Tiberius stopped the voting and once more appealed to his opponent, throwing his arms around him, kissing him in full view of the

* The vote of each tribe counted as one, and was decided by the majority within the tribe.

people, and fervently entreating him not to allow himself to suffer this humiliation, nor to oblige his fellow-tribune to incur the blame for introducing so harsh and odious a measure.

We are told that Octavius could not remain unmoved as he listened to this entreaty: his eyes filled with tears, and for a long while he did not utter a word. But presently when he looked up towards the rich men and landowners, who stood solidly grouped together, his awe of them and fear of losing their good opinion hardened his resolve, and he decided to risk the worst and tell Tiberius that he must do as he pleased. Accordingly the motion was passed, and Tiberius then ordered one of his freedmen to drag Octavius from the rostra. He was in the habit of employing his own freedmen instead of the public officers, and this made the sight of Octavius being ignominiously dragged along even more distressing. Worse still, the people then made a rush at the prisoner, and although his wealthy sympathizers ran all together to his help and spread out their hands to protect him, it was only with great difficulty that Octavius was pulled away and rescued from the mob. At the same time a faithful slave, who had planted himself in front of his master to protect him had his eyes torn out, in spite of the efforts of Tiberius, who as soon as he grasped what was happening, came running down and did his utmost to restrain the rioters.

13. After this, Tiberius's agrarian law was passed, and three men were appointed to survey and distribute the public land. These were Tiberius himself, Appius Claudius his father-in-law, and Gaius Gracchus his brother, who was not at that time in Rome, but was serving under Scipio in the campaign against the Numantines. Tiberius succeeded in carrying through all these measures peacefully and without opposition, and in addition he secured the election of a new tribune to replace Octavius. This man did not belong to any of the distinguished families: he was merely one of Tiberius's clients whose name was Mucius. The propertied classes, however, who were angered by all these measures and were becoming alarmed at the growth of Tiberius's power, took every opportunity of insulting him in the Senate. When he asked for a tent, which was normally provided at the public expense, for his work in dividing up the land, they refused to approve his request, although other men had often been granted this facility for much less urgent reasons, and in the

same way his daily allowance for expenses was fixed at nine obols.* The chief promoter of these affronts was Publius Nasica, who now abandoned himself completely to his hatred of Tiberius: he was one of the largest owners of public lands and felt bitterly resentful at being obliged to give them up.

These actions had the effect of enraging the people all the more, so that when a friend of Tiberius died suddenly and malignant spots appeared all over his body, the rumour spread that he had been poisoned. A huge crowd swiftly gathered to attend his funeral, and the people carried the bier on their shoulders and stood by to witness the last ceremonies. And here indeed it seemed that their worst suspicions were confirmed. For the corpse burst open and discharged such a mass of corrupt matter that the funeral pyre was completely extinguished. When it was lit again, the body still would not burn until it had been removed to another place, and it was only after a great deal of effort that the flames could be made to take hold. Thereupon Tiberius, who wished to stir up the people's anger still further, dressed himself in mourning, brought his two children before the Assembly, and implored the people to take care of them and of their mother, thus implying that he had given up his own life for lost.

14. Soon after this† king Attalus Philometor died, and Eudemus of Pergamum brought to Rome his last will and testament, in which the Roman people were named as his heirs. Tiberius at once made a bid for popularity by introducing a law which provided that as soon as king Attalus's money arrived in Rome, it should be distributed among those citizens who had received allotments of public land so as to help them stock and cultivate their farms. As for the cities which lay within the bounds of Attalus's kingdom, Tiberius declared that the Senate had no right to decide their destiny, but that he himself would submit a plan to the people on this subject. No proposal could have been better calculated to give offence to the Senate,‡ and when Pompeius rose to speak he asserted that he was a neighbour

* About 1s. 3d. † Early in 133 B.C.

‡ The Senate naturally regarded itself as the competent authority in matters of foreign policy: here Tiberius may have been angling for the support of the knights. The Senate was traditionally opposed to expansion, the knights eager to acquire further provinces to exploit.

of Tiberius and therefore knew that Eudemus of Pergamum had chosen a diadem and a purple robe out of the royal treasures, and presented them to him in the expectation that he would soon become king of Rome. Quintus Metellus also reproached Tiberius by reminding him that whenever the elder Gracchus, his father, was returning home after a supper while he was censor, the citizens of Rome would put out their lights, so that there should be no suspicion that they were indulging beyond reason in entertainments or drinking-bouts. Tiberius, by contrast, was constantly lighted on his way at night by the poorest and rowdiest elements among the people. Titus Annius also joined in the debate. He enjoyed no great reputation either for uprightness of character or for moderation, but was regarded as unrivalled for his skill in cross-examination, and he now challenged Tiberius to a judicial wager; he contended that by deposing Octavius Tiberius had committed an act of contempt against the person of his fellow-tribune, which by law was sacred and inviolable. This speech was loudly applauded by many of the senators, whereupon Tiberius rushed out of the Senate-house, summoned a meeting of the Assembly, and ordered Annius to be brought before the people with the intention of denouncing him. However, Annius, who knew that he was no match for Tiberius either in reputation or as an orator, took refuge in the technique of which he was a master and called upon Tiberius to answer a few questions before the argument began. Tiberius agreed and after silence had been restored, Annius formulated this question: 'Let us assume that you wish to depose me and heap insults upon me, that I appeal to one of your colleagues in office, that he mounts the rostra to defend me, and that you then fly into a passion. Will you then deprive him of his office?' Tiberius, we are told, was so disconcerted by this question that although normally no man was quicker in repartee or bolder in action, yet on this occasion he could make no reply.

15. For the present, then, he dissolved the Assembly. At the same time he saw clearly that his treatment of Octavius had offended not only the aristocratic party but even the people, since it was generally felt that the tribunate was invested with a peculiar dignity, an august almost sacrosanct quality, which until that day had been jealously preserved, but had now been violated and destroyed. He therefore delivered a long speech to the people, and it will not be out of place

to recapitulate a few of his arguments here, so as to indicate something of Tiberius's subtlety and powers of persuasion. He declared that a tribune was sacred and inviolable because he was dedicated to the people and stood as their protector. 'But,' he went on, 'if a tribune should depart from his duty, oppress the people, cripple its powers, and take away its right to vote, he has by his own actions deprived himself of his honourable office by not fulfilling the conditions upon which he accepted it. Otherwise we should be obliged to allow a tribune the freedom even to demolish the Capitol or burn down the naval arsenal. If a tribune commits such actions as these he is still a tribune, even though a bad one, but if he annuls the powers of the people, he ceases to be a tribune at all. Is it not a flagrant contradiction, then, that a tribune should have power to send a consul to prison, while the people are unable to remove a tribune from authority, even when he uses it against the very men who put it in his hands: for remember that consuls and tribunes are both elected by the people. Now the office of king not only embraces within itself every kind of authority, but kings are also consecrated to the gods by having to perform the most important religious ceremonies. Yet in spite of this, when Tarquin acted wrongfully, the Roman state expelled him, and because of the lawless action of one man, the ancestral form of government, to which Rome owes her foundation, was abolished for ever. Again, is there anything so sacred or so venerable in all Rome as the order of Vestal Virgins who tend and watch over the undying fire? Yet if one of these breaks her vows, she is buried alive, for when they sin against the gods, they forfeit that inviolable sanctity which they possess on account of their service to the gods. In the same way a tribune who infringes the rights of the people has no just claim to retain the immunity which is granted to him for his services to the people, since he is destroying the very power which is the foundation of his own. And surely if it is legal for him to be elected to his office by a majority vote of the tribes, then it must be still more so for him to be deprived of it by a unanimous vote. Again, nothing is so sacred and inviolable as an offering which has been consecrated to the gods, but the people have never been prohibited from making use of them, or from moving or changing their position as they may choose. Accordingly, on this principle, it is legal for the people to transfer the tribunate, just as it is to transfer a sacred offering, from one person to another. Moreover, it is a fact that on many occasions men have resigned from the tribunate after taking an oath of disability, or have asked of their own free will to be relieved of their responsibilities, and from this it follows that it is not an inviolable institution, nor an office of which a man cannot be deprived.'

16. These were the principal arguments which Tiberius brought forward in defence of his action. Meanwhile his friends had taken note of the threats and the organized opposition which was gathering against him: they considered that he must be elected tribune again for the following year,* and so once more Tiberius set out to strengthen his position among the people by introducing a series of new measures. These included a reduction of the period of military service,† the right of appeal to the people from the verdicts of the juries, and the admission to the juries – which had hitherto been composed exclusively of senators – of an equal number of knights. In short, Tiberius's programme was designed to cripple the power of the Senate in every possible way, and it was inspired by motives of anger and party politics rather than by considerations of justice and the common good. While the voting was in progress it became clear to Tiberius's friends that their opponents would gain a majority, since many of the people could not be present.‡ So first of all they began to play for time by delivering speeches abusing Tiberius's fellow-tribunes, and next they dissolved the Assembly and adjourned the meeting until the following day.

Tiberius then went down into the Forum and pleaded with the citizens in a humble tone and with tears in his eyes. He went on to tell them that he was afraid that his enemies would break into his house at night and kill him, and in this way he touched the emotions of his audience so powerfully that many of them encamped outside his house and spent the night there on guard.

17. At daybreak there arrived at the house the man who brought the birds which the Romans use to take the auspices. He threw food in front of them, but with one exception the birds refused to leave

* This was unconstitutional by custom, though the people could create a new precedent.

† At that time from the age of seventeen to forty-six.

‡ The Assembly's vote was dominated by the rural tribes, of which there were thirty-one as against four urban tribes. But many of Tiberius's rural supporters were unable to attend because of the harvest.

their cage, although the keeper shook the bars vigorously; and the one which ventured outside would not touch its food, but merely lifted its left wing, stretched out a leg, and retired again into the cage. This episode reminded Tiberius of another which had taken place earlier. He possessed a helmet which he had won in battle, a splendid and elaborately chased piece of armour. Some snakes had crawled into this unobserved, laid their eggs, and hatched them out, and this made Tiberius still more uneasy about the signs from the birds. However, when he heard that the people were assembled on the Capitol he set out, but as he was leaving the house he stumbled against the threshold.* He struck his foot so violently that the nail of his big toe was split, and the blood ran out through his sandal. He had not gone far before some crows were seen fighting on the roof of a house to the left, and although many people were passing by, as was natural, a stone dislodged by one of the crows fell on Tiberius's own foot.† This made even the boldest of his followers hesitate. Nevertheless Blossius of Cumae, who was with him, declared that it would be a shame and an unbearable disgrace if Tiberius, a son of Gracchus, a grandson of Scipio Africanus, and a champion of the Roman people, should fail to answer his fellow-citizens' call for help because he was afraid of a raven: besides, his enemies would not only laugh at such a cowardly refusal, but would seize the opportunity to denounce him to the people as a man who was now playing the tyrant and treating them with contempt. At this moment a group of people ran up with a message from his friends on the Capitol, who urged him to hurry there, as events were now going in his favour. And indeed at first everything promised splendidly. As soon as the crowd saw him they raised a welcoming cheer, and as he climbed the hill they greeted him enthusiastically and gathered around him to prevent any stranger from approaching.

18. However, when Mucius began once again to summon the tribes to the vote, it was impossible to carry out the usual procedure, because of a disturbance which had arisen on the outskirts of the crowd, where Tiberius's supporters were pushing and jostling against their opponents, who were trying to force their way in and mingle with the rest.

* This was considered a bad omen.

† An indication that the omen concerned him.

superstition

At this moment Fulvius Flaccus, a senator, climbed into a conspicuous position, and since he could not make his voice heard at such a distance, he gesticulated with his hand to indicate that he wanted to say something in private to Tiberius. The latter called upon the crowd to make way for Flaccus, who with great difficulty struggled towards Tiberius and warned him that the Senate was sitting, and that the party of the rich were plotting to kill Tiberius themselves, since they could not persuade the consul to do so, and that they had armed a large number of their followers and slaves for this purpose.

19. Tiberius passed on this news to his supporters who were standing round him, and they at once girded up their togas. Then they broke up the staves which the officers use to keep back the crowd, distributed these, and prepared to defend themselves against their attackers. Those who were standing farther away were at a loss to know what was happening and asked what it meant. Thereupon Tiberius raised his hand to his head intending, since the people could not hear his voice, to signify that his life was in danger. But when his enemies saw this gesture, they rushed to the Senate and reported that Tiberius was asking for a crown, and that they had the proof of this in the signal he had just given. This created an uproar in the Senate, and Nasica demanded that the consul must now act to protect the state and put down the tyrant. The consul answered in conciliatory fashion that he would not be the first to use violence, and would put no citizen to death without a regular trial. On the other hand he declared that, if Tiberius should incite or oblige the people to pass any illegal resolution, he would not consider it to be binding. At this, Nasica sprang to his feet and shouted, 'Now that the consul has betrayed the state, let every man who wishes to uphold the laws follow me!' Then he drew the skirt of his toga over his head and strode out towards the Capitol. The senators who followed him wrapped their togas over their left arms and thrust aside anyone who stood in their path. Nobody dared to oppose them out of respect for their rank, but those whom they met took to their heels and trampled down one another as they fled.

The senators' followers were armed with clubs and staves, which they had brought from their houses. The senators themselves snatched up the legs and fragments of the benches which the crowd had broken in their hurry to escape, and made straight for Tiberius, lashing out at those who were drawn up in front of him. His protectors were quickly scattered or clubbed down, and as Tiberius turned to run, someone caught hold of his clothing. He threw off his toga and fled in his tunic, but then stumbled over some of the prostrate bodies in front of him. As he struggled to his feet, one of his fellow-tribunes, Publius Satyreius, as everybody agrees, dealt the first blow, striking him on the head with the leg of a bench. Lucius Rufus claimed to have given him the second, and prided himself upon this as if it were some noble exploit. More than three hundred men were killed by blows from sticks and stones, but none by the sword.

20. This is said to have been the first outbreak of civil strife in Rome, which ended in the bloodshed and death of citizens, since the expulsion of the kings. All the other disputes, although they were neither trivial in themselves nor concerned with trivial objects, were resolved by some form of compromise, with the Senate making concessions through fear of the people and the people out of respect for the Senate. Even on this occasion it was generally believed that Tiberius would have given way without difficulty if his opponents had attempted to persuade him, or would have surrendered without any need for violence or bloodshed, since his supporters at that time did not number more than three thousand. But the conspiracy which was formed against him seems to have had its origin in the hatred and malevolence of the rich rather than in the excuses which they put forward for their action: at any rate the brutal and lawless fashion in which Tiberius's enemies treated his dead body certainly points to this conclusion. They refused his brother's request for permission to take up the body and bury it at night: instead they threw it into the Tiber together with the rest of the dead. And this was not all. Some of Tiberius's supporters were banished without a trial, while others were arrested and executed, Diophanes the rhetorician among them. A certain Gaius Villius was shut up in a vessel with vipers and other poisonous snakes and put to death in this way. Blossius of Cumae was brought before the consuls, and when he was questioned concerning his part in the events, he answered that he had acted in every instance on Tiberius's orders. At this Nasica asked him, 'What would you have done then if Tiberius had ordered you to set fire to the Capitol?' Blossius replied at first that Tiberius would never have given such an order, but when the same question was put to him time

after time by his interrogators, he answered, 'If Tiberius had given such an order, then it would have been right for me to carry it out, for he would never have done such a thing unless it were for the good of the people.'

At any rate Blossius was acquitted and afterwards attached himself to the party of Aristonicus* in Asia: later, when Aristonicus's cause collapsed, he committed suicide.

21. After these events the Senate made an effort to conciliate the people. They allowed the distribution of public land to proceed, and proposed that the people should elect a new commissioner to succeed Tiberius. A ballot was taken and the choice fell on Publius Crassus, who was related to the Gracchi, for his daughter Licinia was Gaius's wife. Cornelius Nepos maintains that Gaius's wife was not Licinia, but the daughter of that Brutus who was awarded a triumph over the Lusitanians, but most writers agree with the account that I have given. Meanwhile, the people were still deeply aggrieved at the murder of Tiberius, and it was clear that they were only awaiting an opportunity to take their revenge. Nasica was already threatened with impeachment, and the Senate became so alarmed for his safety that they passed a resolution to send him to Asia, although they had nothing for him to do there. Whenever he appeared in public, people made no attempt to conceal their loathing, but shouted and hurled abuse at him: they called him a tyrant who carried a curse on his head, and had defiled the most hallowed and awe-inspiring sanctuary in Rome with the blood of a man whose person should have been sacred and inviolable. So Nasica left Italy secretly, in spite of the fact that he had the most important and sacred duties to keep him there, for he was Pontifex Maximus.† He wandered from place to place, a despised outcast, and not long afterwards died at Pergamum.

But we need hardly be surprised that such hatred should have been felt for Nasica, when even Scipio Africanus the Younger, who seems to have been as deeply and as justly beloved by the Roman

* The illegitimate son of Attalus III of Pergamum, Aristonicus resented his brother Philometor's bequest of the kingdom to the Romans, and tried to recover it by force. After a brief success against the Romans, he was captured and executed in 130 B.C.

† The Pontifex Maximus was elected for life, and could neither resign from nor be deprived of his office.

people as any man in their history, came near to losing their affection on Tiberius's account: the reason for this was first of all that when the news of Tiberius's death reached him at Numantia, he exclaimed, in Homer's words:

> So may all who engage in such lawless conspiracies perish*

and secondly that, when at a later date Gaius and Fulvius asked him before the Assembly what he thought of Tiberius's fate, his answer left no doubt that he disapproved of the dead man's policies. This so much angered the people that they began to shout interruptions while he was speaking, a thing which they had never done before, and Scipio in his turn was provoked into abusing his audience. All this I have described in greater detail in my *Life of Scipio*.†

* *Odyssey* I, 47. Athena's comment on the fate of Aegisthus, the murderer of Agamemnon.

† One of Plutarch's lost Lives. There are indications that he paired Scipio Africanus the Younger (the victor of the Third Punic War) with his favourite Greek hero, Epaminondas.

6

GAIUS GRACCHUS

[153–121 B.C.]

* *
*

1. After his brother's death Gaius Gracchus at first withdrew completely from the Forum and played no part in public life. He may have been afraid of his political enemies, or he may have wished to make them appear still more detestable in the eyes of the people. At any rate, he stayed quietly at home, like a man who had been humbled for the present, and who intended for the future to remain aloof from political life. Indeed some people even went so far as to attack him on the grounds that he disapproved of Tiberius's policy and had repudiated it. But it must also be said that he was still scarcely more than a boy, since he was nine years younger than Tiberius, who had not reached thirty when he died. But as time went on his character gradually revealed itself. He had no inclination for a life of idleness, nor for effete amusements, nor for the pleasures of the table, nor was he interested in making money. But by developing his powers of oratory, as if these were the wings which would carry him to the heights of public life, he clearly showed that he had no intention of remaining inactive. And when a friend of his named Vettius had to stand his trial and Gaius undertook his defence, the force of his eloquence aroused the people to an ecstatic, almost frenzied enthusiasm and made the efforts of the other pleaders appear quite childish by comparison. So the long dormant fears of the aristocratic party revived once more, and there was much anxious talk to the effect that Gaius must be prevented from becoming a tribune.

However, it now fell to his lot, quite by chance, to be sent to Sardinia* as quaestor to the consul Orestes. Gaius's enemies were delighted and he himself was by no means displeased. He enjoyed military service and was certainly quite as well trained for it as for

* In 126 B.C.

speaking in the courts. And although he still hesitated to embark upon a political career and appear on the rostra, he found it impossible to resist the appeals of his friends and of the people that he should enter public life, and he therefore welcomed this opportunity to leave the city. Yet in spite of these facts it is often alleged that Gaius was an out-and-out demagogue, who was far more eager to win the good opinion of the masses than his brother Tiberius had ever been. But the truth is quite different, namely that Gaius seems to have been drawn into public life by necessity rather than choice. We also have the testimony of Cicero the orator, who says that Gaius had begun by shunning any prospect of office and had decided to live in retirement, when his brother appeared to him in a dream and said, 'Why do you hesitate, Gaius? There is no escape. Fate has decreed the same destiny for us both, to live and die in the service of the people.'

2. Once in Sardinia, Gaius soon proved his merits in many different fields. He surpassed all his contemporaries not only in operations against the enemy and in just dealings with the subject peoples, but also in the loyalty and respect which he showed towards his commander, while in self-restraint, frugality, and attention to his duties he excelled even his seniors. The winter in Sardinia was severe and unhealthy for the army, and the Roman commander requisitioned clothing for his troops from the local cities, whereupon the inhabitants sent a petition to Rome begging that they should be relieved of this imposition. The Senate granted their plea and ordered the general to find some other method of providing for his men. The general was at a loss and meanwhile the soldiers were suffering acutely from the cold, so Gaius Gracchus made a tour of the cities himself and persuaded them of their own free will to send clothing and relieve the army's plight. This action was duly reported to Rome and alarmed the Senate, who supposed that it marked the beginning of another attempt to win the support of the masses. So, first of all, when a delegation arrived from king Micipsa of Numidia with the news that because of his regard for Gaius Gracchus he had sent a consignment of grain to the Roman commander in Sardinia, the senators took offence and refused to receive the envoys. Secondly, they passed a decree that fresh troops should be sent out to relieve those who were serving in Sardinia, but that Orestes should continue at his post, the object of this arrangement being to ensure that Gaius

would also be kept there because of his position as quaestor. Gaius was enraged when he learned of this, and immediately embarked for Rome. When he appeared there unexpectedly, not only did his enemies attack him, but even the people thought it strange that he, a quaestor, should have abandoned his post before his commander, the consul. However, when Gaius was accused before the censors, he asked for permission to defend himself, and so completely won over the sympathies of his hearers that by the time he left the court they were convinced that he had been grossly maligned. He pointed out that he had served in the army for no less than twelve years, although other men were obliged to serve for only ten,* and that he had spent more than two years as quaestor, although the law allowed him to return after one. He also claimed that he was the only man in the army who had brought out a full purse with him, and taken it back empty. The rest of his comrades had drunk up the wine jars which they took out with them to Sardinia, and brought them back to Rome crammed with gold and silver.

3. After this his enemies laid further accusations and indictments against him: they charged him with having incited the Italian allies to revolt, and with having taken part in the conspiracy at Fregellae,† which at that time had just been denounced at Rome. Here again Gaius was able to clear himself completely, and once he had proved his innocence he immediately began to campaign for election as tribune. All the most distinguished men in Rome without exception joined forces to oppose him, but such an immense multitude poured into the city from various parts of Italy to support his candidature that many of them could find no lodging; and since the Campus Martius was too small to hold them, they climbed up to the attics and housetops to declare their support for Gaius.‡ In spite of this the nobility were so far successful in imposing their will on the people and frustrating Gaius's hopes that he was not returned first as he expected, but fourth in the poll. But once he had taken up office, he

* The cavalry were obliged to serve for ten, the infantry for twenty years.

† An important colony some seventy miles south-east of Rome which rebelled in 125 B.C., possibly because of the rejection of Flaccus's proposal to grant it Roman citizenship. The rebellion was put down by the Lucius Opimius who was later to become Gaius Gracchus's mortal enemy.

‡ This probably meant only vocal support. Many people who did not possess a vote thronged to Rome to watch and, if possible, influence the elections.

quickly asserted his predominance over the other tribunes, for he was incomparably the finest orator in Rome and the grief he had suffered encouraged him to speak out fearlessly, whenever he lamented the fate of his brother. He seized every occasion to lead the people back to this subject and remind them of what had happened to Tiberius. In particular he contrasted their cowardly behaviour with the actions of their ancestors, when the latter had declared war on the people of Falerii for the sake of the tribune Genucius who had been insulted by them, or when on another occasion they had condemned Gaius Veturius to death, because he was the only man who had refused to make way for a tribune as he was passing through the Forum. 'But you stood by and watched,' he told them, 'while these men beat Tiberius to death with clubs, and while his dead body was dragged through the midst of the city to be thrown into the Tiber. And afterwards those of his friends who were caught were put to death without a trial. And yet it is a long-established custom among us that, if any man is charged with a capital offence and does not answer the summons, then a trumpeter must go to the door of his house in the morning and summon him forth by the sound of the trumpet, and not until this has been done are the jurors permitted to vote upon his case. These were the kind of safeguards and precautions which our ancestors believed to be necessary when a citizen's life was at stake.'

4. After he had roused the people's emotions with sentiments such as these – and he possessed a powerful voice and spoke with overwhelming conviction – Gaius Gracchus proceeded to introduce two laws. The first laid it down that if the people had deposed any magistrate from his position, this man should be disqualified from holding office a second time, while the second empowered the people to prosecute any magistrate who had banished a citizen without trial.*

* This law was more far-reaching than Plutarch implies. It reaffirmed the ancient principle which protected a citizen's life against the summary jurisdiction of the magistrates and placed it under that of the assembled people. In earlier times, at moments of national emergency, the ultimate powers of life and death were temporarily vested in a dictator, but since this office had not been filled for generations, its authority had been tacitly assumed by the Senate. Thus one of the aims of Gaius's law was to challenge the legality of the Senate's action in putting Tiberius to death without trial, and subsequently executing others among his supporters.

The first of these was clearly aimed at disqualifying Marcus Octavius, whom Tiberius had deposed from the tribunate, while the second affected Popilius Laena, who as praetor had banished Tiberius's supporters. Popilius made no attempt to stand his trial, and immediately fled from Italy, but the first law was revoked by Gaius himself, who declared that he had spared Octavius at the request of his mother Cornelia. This action pleased the people and they gave their consent to the withdrawal of the measure, for they honoured Cornelia just as much for her sons as they did for her father. Later on they erected a bronze statue of her with the inscription 'Cornelia, mother of the Gracchi'. Some of Gaius's phrases have come down to us from an occasion on which he was attacking one of his enemies in the coarse and pungent style which he used in the Forum. 'What is this? Do you dare to insult Cornelia, the mother of Tiberius?' And since the man who had uttered the abuse was suspected of being a homosexual, Gaius went on, 'You have a nerve to compare yourself with Cornelia. Have you borne any children like hers? At any rate everyone in Rome knows that you have slept with a man far more recently than she has!' Gaius was never squeamish in his choice of words, and there are plenty of similar examples to be found in his writings.

5. He now introduced a number of laws which he hoped would not only find favour with the people, but would also undermine the authority of the Senate.* One of these concerned the public lands

* Plutarch does not indicate the connexions between these very diverse laws. But it seems likely that they formed part of a programme which was deliberately aimed at breaking the control of the political system exercised by the rich. This class was able to control the Assembly (*comitia tributa*), because, with each tribe exercising a single block vote determined by the majority, the voting power of the urban proletariat was concentrated within four tribes. The rural tribes, on the other hand, numbered thirty-one. The landowners could register themselves and their freedmen and 'clients' in these, and this organized body of supporters of vested interests could normally dominate the Assembly, since the small farmers seldom travelled to Rome in large numbers and never stayed there for long. The system had, of course, originally been devised to prevent the interests of the farmers from being swamped by those of the urban masses. Gaius's plan was to organize an opposition consisting of the knights, the city populace, and the Italian allies. His programme appealed to the allies through the proposal to extend the suffrage, and to the masses through the laws dealing with military service and the price of grain. The appeal of the jury-reforms to the knights lay in the fact that the courts in

which he proposed to divide up among the poor citizens. Another related to the army, and laid it down that soldiers should be supplied with clothing at the public expense without any corresponding deduction being made from their pay, and that nobody should be conscripted below the age of seventeen. Yet another was devoted to the allies, and extended to the Italians the same voting rights as were already enjoyed by Roman citizens. A fourth dealt with supplies of grain and reduced the price at which it was to be sold to the poor, while the fifth regulated the appointment of jurymen. It was this law which did more than any other to reduce the power of the Senate. Up to this date only senators had been entitled to serve as jurors in criminal cases and it was this privilege above all which had made them feared both by the common people and by the equestrian order. The effect of Gaius's law was to add to the three hundred members of the Senate a further three hundred drawn from the equestrian order and to arrange that juries should be drawn from the whole six hundred. Gaius is said to have made even more strenuous efforts than usual to secure the passage of this law. But what was especially noticeable in his campaign was that, whereas in the past all popular leaders, whenever they rose to speak, had turned their faces to the right towards the Senate-house and the part of the Forum which is known as the Comitium, he now created a new precedent by turning, whenever he addressed the people, to the left towards the Forum proper, and he made a regular habit of this procedure. Thus, by a slight change of posture and deviation from the normal practice, he raised an issue of immense importance and in a sense transferred the whole character of Roman politics from an aristocratic to a democratic basis; for what his action really implied was that orators should address themselves to the people and not to the Senate.*

6. The people not only passed this law, but also charged Gaius with the selection of the jurors who were to be drawn from the equestrian

question were empowered to try offences such as bribery at elections or corruption in public administration, which might involve senators or provincial governors. This offered the knights a potential hold over such governors, whose cooperation they needed in extracting profits from their activities as tax-gatherers.

* Compare the opposite procedure adopted by the Thirty Tyrants at Athens (*Life of Themistocles*, ch. 19).

order, so that he found himself invested with almost monarchical powers, and even the Senate agreed to accept his advice. But whenever he gave this, it was always to support measures which reflected credit on that body, as for instance the extremely just and honourable resolution which was passed on the subject of the corn sent by Quintus Fabius the pro-praetor from Spain. Gaius prevailed upon the Senate to sell the corn and return the money to the cities which had originally supplied it, and, not content with this, he had Fabius censured for making the authority of Rome intolerably oppressive to a subject people. This decree, besides making Gaius popular in the provinces, added greatly to his reputation.

He also introduced legislation which provided for the founding of colonies,* the construction of roads,† and the establishment of public granaries. He himself acted as director and supervisor of every project and never flagged for a moment in the execution of all these different and elaborate undertakings. On the contrary, he carried out each of them with an extraordinary speed and power of application, as if each concern were the only one he had to manage, so that even those who disliked and feared him most were amazed at his efficiency and his capacity to carry through every enterprise to which he set his hand. As for the people, the very sight of Gaius never failed to impress them, as they watched him attended by a host of contractors, craftsmen, ambassadors, magistrates, soldiers, and men of letters, all of whom he handled with a courteous ease which enabled him to show kindness to all his associates without sacrificing his dignity, and to give every man the consideration that was his due. In this way he gave the clearest possible proof that those who had represented him as a tyrannical, overbearing, or violent man were uttering nothing but malicious slanders. He was in fact a more effective popular leader in his personal dealings with men and his handling of business than he was in his speeches from the rostra.

7. The construction of roads was the task into which he threw

* Up to this date settlements of Roman citizens had been planted mainly with the object of defending newly won territory. Gaius Gracchus saw in them the possibility of providing further allotments of land for the poor of Rome and Italy.

† The roads likewise had hitherto been built mainly for strategic purposes. Gaius understood the importance of opening up the communications of the more fertile districts for the support and development of Italian agriculture.

himself most enthusiastically, and he took great pains to ensure that these should be graceful and beautiful as well as useful. His roads were planned so as to run right across the country in a straight line, part of the surface consisting of dressed stone and part of tamped-down gravel. Depressions were filled up, any watercourses or ravines which crossed the line of the road were bridged, and both sides of the road were levelled or embanked to the same height, so that the whole of the work presented a beautiful and symmetrical appearance. Besides this he had every road measured in miles – the Roman mile is a little less than eight furlongs – and stone pillars erected to mark the distances. Other stones were set up at shorter intervals on both sides of the road so that horsemen should be able to mount from these without help.

8. These services won him the wholehearted devotion of the people, and they were prepared to do almost anything in the world to show their goodwill. One day he mentioned in a speech that he intended to ask a favour of them, which he would value beyond words if they would grant it, though he would bear no ill will if they refused. Most people interpreted this as an allusion to the consulship, and expected that he would offer himself for election to the tribunate and the consulship at the same time. But when the consular elections were at hand and everyone was in a fever of anticipation that he would announce his candidature, he appeared leading Gaius Fannius into the Campus Martius and canvassed on his behalf together with Fannius's friends. This action turned the scale in Fannius's favour. He was duly elected consul and Gaius tribune for the second time, even though he had not presented himself as a candidate and did not campaign for office: he owed his election, in fact, entirely to the people's enthusiasm.

However, it soon became apparent that the Senate was uncompromisingly opposed to him, and when Fannius's goodwill also began to cool, Gaius devised a new series of laws to rally the people to his side. In particular he proposed that new colonies* should be founded at Tarentum and Capua and that the full rights and privileges

* These colonies were urban and commercial in character, rather than agricultural. They were intended to relieve the congestion of Rome and other cities where the masses, because of the abundance of slave-labour, were largely unemployed.

of Roman citizens should now be extended to the Latins.* It was at this point that the Senate, in their fear that Gracchus's influence would soon become irresistible, resorted to new and unconventional tactics in an effort to detach the people's support. They now adopted the method of competing with Gaius for the favour of the masses and granting their wishes regardless of the best interests of the state.

One of Gaius's colleagues in the tribunate was Livius Drusus. This was a man who possessed all the advantages of birth and upbringing, and who, in strength of character, in wealth, and oratorical power could compete with those who had raised themselves by such gifts to the highest and most honoured positions in the state. Accordingly, the aristocratic party approached him and invited him to attack Gaius and join forces with them in opposing him. Their plan was that he should on no account resort to violence nor risk any open clash with the people, but rather use his power to please them and grant concessions when it would have been more honourable to incur unpopularity by refusing them.

9. So Livius agreed to work for these objects and use his powers as tribune to serve the Senate's interests. He then proceeded to draw up laws which were neither creditable in themselves, nor beneficial to the community, since his sole object – like the rival demagogues in Aristophanes' comedy *The Knights* – was to outbid his opponent in flattering and gratifying the people. All this clearly indicated that the Senate did not disapprove of Gaius's policy in itself, but that it would stop at nothing to humiliate him personally and destroy him. Thus, for example, when Gaius introduced a measure to found two colonies, which were to be composed of the most reliable citizens, they accused him of trying to ingratiate himself with the people; but when Livius proposed to found twelve and send out three thousand of the poorest citizens to each, they approved his scheme wholeheartedly. Again, when Gaius distributed public land among those citizens whose need was greatest, on condition that each man should pay a small rent to the public treasury, they protested angrily and charged him with

* This measure proved to be the fatal weakness in Gaius's programme. The extension of political rights to the Latin communities throughout Italy was bound to involve concessions and sacrifices on the part of the various classes in Rome, and the patricians, the knights, and the masses were united in distrusting and opposing this policy.

currying favour with the masses; but when Livius proposed to relieve the tenants of even this token contribution, they were quite ready to support him. And when Gaius proposed to grant equal voting rights to the Latins, the aristocratic party professed to be deeply offended, but they approved a bill of Livius's which laid it down that no Latin should be beaten with rods even during his military service. Meanwhile, whenever Livius addressed the people, he made a point of explaining that he was introducing these measures on the authority of the Senate, who always felt a special regard for the people's welfare, and indeed this was perhaps the one positive benefit which resulted from his legislation, namely that it created more kindly feelings among the people towards the Senate. Before this they had suspected and hated the patricians, but Drusus succeeded in softening these bitter feelings and dissolving their memories of past wrongs by assuring them that it was at the instance of the nobles that he had embarked upon his policy of conciliating the people and meeting their wishes.

10. What did most to establish confidence in Livius's personal integrity and goodwill towards the people was the fact that he never appeared to propose any law for his own benefit or to further his private interests. It was always other men whom he sent out to take charge of new colonies, and he was careful to take no part in the administration of public funds, whereas Gaius always put himself at the head of such schemes and kept the most important functions in his own hands. So when* Rubrius, one of his fellow-tribunes, introduced a bill for the establishment of a colony on the site of Carthage, which had been destroyed by Scipio twenty-three years earlier, and it fell to Gaius's lot to supervise its foundation, he soon sailed off to Africa to take charge. Drusus promptly took advantage of his absence to make further headway against him, ingratiate himself with the people, and win their support, and for this purpose he found it especially useful to attack the character of Fulvius Flaccus. This man was a friend of Gaius and had been elected with him as a commissioner to supervise the distribution of public land, but he was a born agitator and hence was detested by the Senate, while others suspected him of stirring up discontent among the Italian allies and inciting

* In 123 B.C. After the final destruction of Carthage at the end of the third Punic War the ground where the walls had stood was ploughed up and the restoration of the city forbidden by solemn imprecations.

them to revolt. These charges were bandied about without any evidence or inquiry to support them, but Fulvius himself lent colour to such rumours, since his policies were not only unsoundly based, but carried with them the threat of revolution. It was inevitable that Gaius should attract some share of the hatred which Flaccus aroused, and it was this more than anything else which brought about his ruin. For example, when Scipio Africanus the Younger died without any known cause, except that the marks of various blows upon his dead body seemed to indicate that he had suffered violence, as I have described in his Life, it was Fulvius whom most people believed to be guilty of his murder, since he had been Scipio's enemy and had violently abused him in a speech delivered from the rostra on the very day of his death; but nevertheless Gaius did not escape suspicion. And yet what seems even more significant is that such an outrageous crime, committed against the foremost and greatest Roman of his day, was not even investigated, let alone punished, the reason being that the masses were opposed to any judicial proceedings being opened, for fear that if the murder were made the subject of an inquiry, the findings might implicate Gaius. However, these events took place several years earlier.*

11. Gaius had now travelled to Africa to supervise the foundation of the new colony on the site of Carthage, which he named Junonia – or Heraea in the Greek form – and during his visit many ominous portents are said to have occurred, which indicated the displeasure of the gods.† The leading standard was caught in a violent gust of wind, and although the bearer held on to it with all his strength, the shaft was snapped into pieces; the sacrificial victims lying on the altars were blown away by a hurricane and scattered beyond the stakes which marked the boundaries of the city, and the stakes themselves were attacked by wolves, who tore them out and scattered them a long way off. But in spite of these misfortunes, Gaius settled the boundaries of the colony, put its affairs in order within seventy days, and then returned to Rome, since he had heard that Fulvius was being

* In 129 B.C. Scipio had been a violent opponent of the Gracchan agrarian reforms.

† The foundation of a Roman colony was attended by solemn ceremonials and its anniversary was religiously observed. Hence these unfavourable omens could not easily be forgotten.

hard pressed by Drusus and that the situation demanded his presence. The reason for this was the threat to his own position, which now presented itself in the person of Lucius Opimius, a man of extreme oligarchical views who was a leading member of the Senate. Opimius had once before failed to secure election to the consulship, when Gaius had opposed him and exerted all his influence to support Fannius. But this time Opimius had built up a strong body of supporters, and it was generally believed that he would not only win the election but that as soon as he was in office he would set himself to destroy his opponent's power. Indeed Gaius's influence was already showing signs of decline, and his policies no longer appealed so strongly to the people, since there were now so many leaders competing for their favour, while the Senate itself readily gave way to their demands.

12. As soon as Gaius returned to Rome, his first action was to leave his house on the Palatine Hill and take up his quarters in the neighbourhood of the Forum. He felt that this was more in keeping with his democratic principles, since this was the quarter in which most of the humblest and poorest citizens lived. Next he put forward the rest of his proposed legislation, so as to have these measures ratified by the vote of the people. But when a great multitude began to gather in Rome from all parts of Italy to support him, the Senate persuaded the consul, who was then Fannius, to expel from the city all persons who were not Roman by birth. Thereupon a strange and exceptional proclamation was issued, which forbade any of the allies or friends of Rome to appear in the city during this period. Gaius responded by issuing a counter-edict in which he denounced the consul for this action, and promised the allies his support if they refused to leave the city. Nevertheless he failed to keep this promise, and when he saw one of his close friends being dragged away to prison by Fannius's lictors, he passed by without offering any help. This may have been because he was afraid to put his power to the test, knowing that it was already on the wane, or because he was unwilling, as he himself declared, to take any action which would give his enemies the excuse they wanted to bring about an open conflict and an outbreak of violence.

It so happened that at this moment he had also given offence to one of his fellow-tribunes for the following reason. A gladiatorial display had been arranged for the people to watch in the Forum, and most of the magistrates had had seats built around the arena, which they intended to hire to the spectators. Gaius insisted that these should be taken down so that the poor could watch the show without payment. But since his orders were ignored, he waited until the night before the event and then took all the workmen whom he had under his orders for public contracts and dismantled the seats, so that by the morning he was able to show the people a completely empty space. The people thought him a man for this, but his fellow-tribunes were furious and regarded it as a piece of interference of the most presumptuous and violent kind. In fact it was generally believed that this action cost him his election to the tribunate for the third time, because although he won a majority of the votes, his colleagues falsified the returns and the declaration of the result. There was some dispute as to exactly what happened, but certainly Gaius took his defeat too much to heart, and when he saw his enemies exulting over his failure, he told them in an ill-judged outburst of arrogance that they would laugh on the other side of their faces if they could see the doom which awaited them* as a result of his reforms.

13. At the same time Gaius's opponents secured Opimius's election as consul, and they at once proceeded to repeal many of his laws and also to interfere with the organization of the colony at Carthage. They did this in the hope of provoking Gaius into committing some act of violence, which would give them the excuse to destroy him. At first he bore this treatment patiently, but as time went on, he was goaded by his friends and above all by Fulvius into recruiting a body of supporters to oppose the consul. It was at this point, according to some accounts, that his mother helped him to organize resistance by hiring a number of foreigners and sending them to Rome disguised as harvesters, and these arrangements are said to be hinted at in various letters to her son. Other authorities, however, maintain that Cornelia strongly disapproved of these plans.

At any rate on the day when Opimius and his party had planned to revoke Gaius's laws, both factions posted themselves on the Capitol early in the morning. Then after the consul had offered up a sacrifice,

* It is conjectured that in using this metaphor Plutarch is alluding to the laughter of the doomed suitors, which Homer describes in *Odyssey* XX, 348.

one of his attendants, Quintus Antyllius, who was carrying away the entrails of the victims, shouted to Fulvius's supporters, 'Stand back, you rogues, and make way for honest citizens!' Some writers add that as he spoke these words he stretched out his bare arm towards them and made an insulting gesture. At any rate he was instantly set upon and stabbed to death with long writing-styluses, which were said to have been made expressly for this purpose.* The crowd was thrown into utter confusion by the murder, while the leaders of the two parties were affected in diametrically opposite ways. Gaius was deeply distressed and reproached his followers for having given their enemies the pretext they had been looking for all this time, while Opimius was triumphant, as if he could now seize a long-awaited opportunity, and he proceeded to urge the people to take revenge.

14. At this moment there was a heavy downpour of rain and the Assembly dispersed. Early next morning Opimius summoned a meeting of the Senate, and while he began to transact business, others placed the naked body of Antyllius on a bier and carried it – as had previously been arranged – through the Forum and past the Senate-house to the accompaniment of piercing cries and lamentations. Opimius, who knew perfectly well what was happening, pretended to be surprised at the noise, so that some of his listeners went out into the Forum. There, when the bier had been set down in the midst of the crowd, the senators began to express their horror at what they called an atrocious and monstrous crime, but the only effect which this had on the people was to stir up their hatred and make them execrate the aristocrats. The senators, they shouted, had murdered Tiberius Gracchus on the Capitol with their own hands and flung his body into the Tiber, and he was a tribune. Antyllius was nothing more than a servant, and although he had suffered more than he deserved, he had done a great deal to bring it upon himself: yet here he was, laid out in the Forum, while the entire Roman Senate stood weeping around him and was prepared to follow this hireling to the grave in order to destroy the one remaining champion of the people. After this the senators returned to the Senate-house and formally

* The Roman stylus was made of iron or bronze, and was sharp at one end and flat at the other. The point was used for writing on waxen tablets, and the flat end for erasing and smoothing the surface.

passed a decree instructing Opimius to preserve the safety of the state and to put down the tyrants.*

Thereupon Opimius gave notice to the senators to arm themselves, and every member of the equestrian order was commanded to bring with him two servants fully armed the next morning. Fulvius, on the other hand, also made his preparations and gathered together a large crowd of his followers, but Gaius, as he left the Forum, paused in front of his father's statue, gazed at it for a long time, and then with the tears rolling down his cheeks uttered a deep sigh and walked away. Many of those who saw this were seized with pity for Gaius: they blamed themselves for abandoning him and betraying him, and made their way to his house where they spent the night outside his door. Their behaviour was very different from that of the men who were guarding Fulvius. His followers passed an uproarious evening, shouting and drinking and boasting of what they would do. Fulvius himself, who was the first to become drunk, spoke and behaved in a way that was disgraceful for a man of his age. Gaius's supporters, on the other hand, were oppressed by the thought that a disaster was threatening their country and felt the deepest concern for the future, and so they remained silent and spent the night sleeping and keeping watch in turn.

15. When it was day, Fulvius's partisans aroused their leader with some difficulty from his drunken stupor, and armed themselves with the various trophies and spoils of war which decorated his house, and which he had captured after a victory won over the Gauls during his consulship. Then they set out to the accompaniment of much shouting and noisy threats to occupy the Aventine hill.† As for Gaius, he refused to arm himself, but set off in his toga, just as if he were on his way to the Forum, and took with him nothing but a short dagger. As he was leaving his door, his wife threw herself at his feet and placing one arm around her husband and the other round their little son, said to him, 'When you leave me today, Gaius, I know you are not setting out for the rostra to speak as a tribune or a lawgiver, nor

* This was the formal decree, *videant consules ne quid respublica detrimenti capiat*, which was only employed in extreme emergency (such as the occasion of the conspiracy of Catiline). Its effect was to proclaim martial law and suspend constitutional proceedings.

† The plebeian quarter of Rome.

for some glorious campaign, where if you should die, as all men must some day, you would leave me honour to console my grief. No, you are going to expose yourself to the men who murdered Tiberius, and you are right to go unarmed and to suffer wrong rather than inflict it on others. And yet our country will be none the better for taking your life, for injustice has triumphed in Rome, and it is violence and the sword which settle all disputes. If your brother had fallen before Numantia, his body would have been given back to us under the truce, but, as it is, I too may have to pray to some river or sea to yield up yours. What faith can we put in the gods or in the laws of men, when we have seen Tiberius murdered?' While Licinia was pouring out her sorrow, Gaius gently freed himself from her embrace and walked away with his friends without uttering a word. Licinia clutched vainly at his toga, then sank to the ground and lay for a long time speechless. At last her servants lifted her up unconscious and carried her to her brother Crassus's house.

16. When the popular party were all assembled together, at Gaius's suggestion Fulvius sent his younger son to the Forum carrying a herald's wand.* He was a handsome youth, and he now presented himself with the greatest deference and modesty, and with tears in his eyes delivered a message to the consul and the Senate which offered terms for an agreement. The majority of his listeners were by no means unwilling to negotiate, but Opimius insisted that Fulvius and Gracchus could not expect to discuss conditions with the Senate through an envoy. They must behave as citizens who were answerable to the laws, and come down and surrender themselves for trial, and only then could they ask for mercy. He ended by telling the young man that he must bring back his leaders' acceptance of these terms or not return at all. Gaius, so we are told, was willing to come and plead his case before the Senate, but, as no one else would agree, Fulvius sent back his son to intercede with the Senate as before. But Opimius was now eager to force the issue and he at once arrested the youth and put him under guard. He then advanced against Fulvius's party with a strong body of armed men supported by Cretan archers, who began to shoot at their opponents, wounded many of them, and threw them into such confusion that they fled in terror. Fulvius

* The staff which envoys or heralds carried in time of war, when they were sent to an enemy.

took refuge in a disused bath, where he was soon discovered with his eldest son, and both put to the sword. Gaius, it was observed, took no part in the fighting, but, sunk in grief and despair at the turn which events had taken, he fled for sanctuary to the temple of Diana. There he had intended to kill himself, but was prevented by two of his most faithful friends, Pomponius and Licinius, who snatched away his sword and urged him to save himself. It is said that Gracchus knelt down in the temple, and, stretching out his hands towards the goddess, prayed that in return for their ingratitude and treachery towards him the people of Rome should remain enslaved to their rulers for ever after; for at the news that an amnesty had been proclaimed, many of his supporters were already openly changing sides.

17. Gaius now tried to make his escape, but he was hotly pursued by his enemies and they were on the point of overtaking him at the wooden bridge over the Tiber. Here his two friends insisted that he should go on, while they turned to face his pursuers and continued to defend the bridge against all comers until both were killed. Gaius had no other companion in his flight but a slave named Philocrates. All the spectators along the road urged him to run faster, as though they were watching a race, but not a man came to his help or would even provide him with a horse, although he begged them to do so, for his enemies were close on his heels. He was still a little ahead of them when he reached a grove which was sacred to the Furies, and there his slave Philocrates first killed his master and then himself. Some writers report that both men were captured alive, but that the slave had flung his arms round Gaius so closely that no one could touch him until they had first dispatched Philocrates under a hail of blows. It is also said that a man cut off Gaius's head and was carrying it along, when it was snatched from him by one of Opimius's friends, Septimuleius, for it had been announced at the beginning of the battle that anyone who brought in the head of Gaius or Fulvius would be paid its weight in gold.* Septimuleius brought the head to Opimius stuck on the point of a spear, and when it was placed on the scales it weighed seventeen and two-thirds pounds. On this occasion Septi-

* This is said to have been the first occasion in Roman history when a reward was paid for a head, but unfortunately it was not the last. Sulla, Lepidus, Mark Antony, and Octavius Caesar all followed this barbarous practice in their proscriptions.

muleius had committed a fraud as well as an outrage, for he had removed the brain and poured molten lead into the cavity. The man who brought in Fulvius's head was considered to be of no account, and so got no reward at all. The bodies of Gaius, Fulvius, and the rest of their followers who lost their lives, to the number of three thousand in all, were thrown into the Tiber, their property was sold and the proceeds confiscated by the public treasury. Their wives were even forbidden to wear mourning, while Licinia, Gaius's wife, was deprived of her dowry. Most inhuman of all was the treatment meted out to Fulvius's younger son, who had neither lifted a hand against the patricians nor even been present during the fighting. He had attempted to bring about a truce before the battle, had then been arrested, and was put to death after the fighting was over. But the action which the people resented more bitterly than this or any other injustice was the building of a temple of Concord by Opimius.* They felt that he was claiming honour and exulting, in a sense even celebrating a triumph, over the massacre of all these Roman citizens. And so somebody at night carved this inscription on the temple,

This temple of Concord is the work of mad Discord.

18. Opimius was the first consul who arrogated to himself the powers of a dictator, and who condemned to death without trial three thousand Roman citizens, among them Fulvius Flaccus and Gaius Gracchus, the one a consul who had celebrated a triumph, and the other the foremost man of his age in virtue and reputation. Yet it is noteworthy that this same Opimius could not resist the temptation of fraud. When he was sent as a commissioner to Jugurtha, the ruler of Numidia, he accepted bribes from him, and after being convicted of these shameful charges spent his old age in disgrace, amid the hatred and insults of his fellow-countrymen. The people were cowed and humiliated by the collapse of the democratic cause, but they soon showed how deeply they missed and longed for the Gracchi. Statues of the brothers were set up in a prominent part of the city, the places where they had fallen were declared to be holy ground, and the first-fruits of the season were offered up there throughout the year. Many

* In 367 B.C. Camillus had built a temple of Concord to celebrate the reconciliation of patricians and plebeians. It was this which Opimius had now restored.

people even sacrificed to the Gracchi every day, and worshipped their statues as though they were visiting the shrines of gods.

19. Cornelia is said to have borne her misfortunes in a noble and magnanimous spirit, and to have said of the sacred places where her sons had been murdered that these tombs were worthy of the dead who occupied them. She went to live at the promontory called Misenum* and made no change in her normal mode of life. She had many friends and kept a good table which was always thronged with guests; Greeks and other learned men frequently visited her, and all the reigning kings exchanged presents with her. Her visitors and intimate friends would listen with pleasure as she recalled the life and habits of her father, the great Scipio Africanus, but what they admired most of all was to hear her speak of her sons without showing sorrow or shedding a tear, and recall their achievements and their fate to any inquirer, as though she were relating the history of the early days of Rome. This made some people think that old age or the weight of her misfortunes had affected her mind, and so far dulled her feelings as to make her incapable of suffering. Yet the truth is that such people are themselves too dull to understand how far a noble nature, an honourable ancestry and a virtuous upbringing can fortify men against grief, and that although fate may defeat the efforts of virtue to avert misfortune, it cannot deprive us of the power to endure it with equanimity.

* At the northern tip of the bay of Naples, a favourite area for the villas of wealthy Romans. Cornelia's house was famous and was later occupied by Marius, Lucullus, and the emperor Tiberius.

7

SERTORIUS

[c. 125–72 B.C.]

* *
*

1. When we reflect that time is infinite and Fortune for ever changing her course, it need hardly surprise us that certain events should often repeat themselves quite spontaneously. For if the number of those elements which combine to produce a historical event is unlimited, then Fortune possesses an ample store of coincidences in the very abundance of her material: if, on the other hand, their number is fixed, then the same pattern of events seems bound to recur, since the same forces continue to operate upon them. Now, there are some people who take pleasure in collecting by hearsay or from their reading examples of accidental occurrences, which appear to have been the result of calculation and forethought. They notice, for instance, that two men named Attis* have become celebrated in legend, the one a Syrian and the other an Arcadian, and that both were killed by a wild boar; that there were two Actaeons,† one of whom was torn to pieces by his dogs and the other by his lovers; that there were two Scipios, one of whom conquered Carthage in the Second Punic War, while the other destroyed it utterly in the Third; that the city of Troy was originally captured by Hercules on account of the horses which Laomedon had promised him, then by Agamemnon through the famous wooden horse, and finally by Charidemus, because a horse fell between the gates and prevented the Trojans from closing them quickly enough. Again, there are two

* The story of the Lydian Attis is told in Pausanias, VII, 175. The allusion to an Arcadian Attis is unknown.

† The first Actaeon was the legendary huntsman who caught sight of Artemis bathing, was changed into a stag, and devoured by his own hounds. The second was a young man beloved by Archias of Corinth, who tried to abduct him. His friends resisted and in the struggle Actaeon was torn to pieces.

cities which bear the same name as the most fragrant of plants, Ios (violet) and Smyrna (myrrh), and the poet Homer is said to have been born in the one and died in the other. Let me therefore add a contribution of my own to this collection. The most warlike of generals and those who have achieved most by a combination of cunning and natural ability have been one-eyed men, namely Philip of Macedon, Antigonus, Hannibal, and the subject of the present Life, Sertorius. We may say of him that he was more chaste towards women than Philip, more loyal to his friends than Antigonus, and more merciful to his enemies than Hannibal. None of his rivals surpassed him in intelligence, but every one of them did so in good fortune. Fortune he always found harder to deal with than his acknowledged enemies, and yet he proved that he was a match for the experience of Metellus, the daring of Pompey, the luck of Sulla, and the might of the whole Roman people, and this in spite of the fact that he spent much of his career as an exile and as a foreigner commanding barbarians.

Of all the Greek generals I think that the career of Eumenes of Cardia offers the closest parallel to his. Both men were born leaders, and both combined a warlike spirit with a genius for outwitting the enemy: both were banished from their own countries, commanded foreign troops, and suffered the same violent and unjust stroke of fortune in their deaths, since both were the victims of conspiracy and were assassinated by the very men whom they were leading to victory against their enemies.

2. Quintus Sertorius belonged to a family of some distinction in the Sabine city of Nussa. He lost his father when he was a child, and was carefully brought up by his widowed mother, to whom he seems to have been unusually devoted. Her name, we are told, was Rhea. His education included a grounding in the law, and his eloquence earned him a certain reputation at Rome when he was little more than a boy, but as a result of his brilliant exploits on the battlefield his ambitions soon turned towards a military career.

3. He had his first experience of war under Caepio during the campaign in which the Cimbri and the Teutones broke into Gaul, when the Romans suffered a crushing defeat and their army was routed.* After this battle, in spite of losing his horse and being severely woun-

* At the river Arausio in 105 B.C.: the Romans lost 80,000 men.

ded, Sertorius swam across the Rhône in the teeth of a strong current still carrying his shield and his breastplate: such was the strength of his body and so rigorously had he hardened it by training. Not long afterwards the same enemy moved forward in a new offensive.* The invaders marched in a horde scores of thousands strong and they threatened destruction to all, so that at such a moment it was no small thing for a Roman to keep his post and obey his general's orders. Marius was then in command, and Sertorius offered to go and reconnoitre the enemy's camp as a spy. He disguised himself in Celtic dress, mastered as many of the common phrases of the language as he was likely to need for a simple conversation, and then boldly went and mingled with the barbarians. There he used his eyes and ears to pick up the most important details of the enemy's dispositions and returned to Marius. For this act of valour he was duly decorated, and during the rest of the campaign he proved his courage and intelligence on so many occasions that he completely won Marius's confidence and was promoted to a position of high rank.

After the war against the Cimbri and Teutones was over, Didius the praetor sent him as a military tribune to Spain,† where he spent the winter in Castulo, a city of the Celtiberians. Here the Roman troops were living in the midst of such plenty that they threw off all discipline and spent much of their time drunk. The barbarians came to despise them and one night they summoned their neighbours, the Oritanians, to help them: they then attacked the Romans in their quarters and began to slaughter them. Sertorius slipped out with a few companions, rallied the soldiers who were making their escape, and surrounded the city. He found that a gate had been left open through which the attackers had stolen in, but he did not repeat their mistake. He posted a guard on it, and then, once he had gained control of every quarter of the town, he put to death every male who was old enough to bear arms. When the slaughter was over, he ordered all his men to take off their own armour and tunics, put on the clothes of the Spaniards, and follow him in this disguise to the city of the Oritanians who had made the attack. The barbarians were deceived by the Romans' appearance, and Sertorius found the gates of their city open, and caught a crowd of men coming out to greet what they imagined was the raiding-party of their friends and fellow-citizens returning from a successful night's work. Thereupon

* In 102 B.C.

† In 97 B.C.

the Romans killed most of the Oritanians by their city gates: the rest surrendered and were sold into slavery.

4. This exploit made Sertorius's name known throughout the length and breadth of Spain. As soon as he returned to Rome he was appointed quaestor of Cisalpine Gaul, where the situation was critical. The Marsic War* was just about to break out, and Sertorius was ordered to raise troops and provide arms. He carried out his task with such speed and enthusiasm, compared with the feeble and dilatory performance of his other young colleagues, that he won the reputation of a man who was destined for a career of great achievements. However, his promotion to the rank of commander did nothing to diminish his daring as a fighting soldier: on the contrary, he continued to carry out extraordinary feats of courage in battle and to expose himself unsparingly, with the result that he was wounded and lost the sight of an eye. This was an injury on which he always prided himself. Others, he used to say, could not always carry about with them the decorations they had received for their valour, but must leave their necklaces and spears and crowns behind, whereas he could wear the badge of courage wherever he went, and those who saw what he had lost saw the proof of his bravery at the same time. The Roman people also paid him the tribute he deserved. When he entered the theatre they greeted him with loud applause and cries of admiration, and this was an honour that was seldom granted even to men who were far advanced in years and distinguished in rank. In spite of this, when he stood for the tribuneship he was opposed by Sulla and lost the election, and this seems to have been the cause of his subsequent antagonism to Sulla.

Not long afterwards Marius was defeated by Sulla† and took refuge in Africa, while in the following year Sulla set out for his campaign against Mithridates. Of the two consuls then in office, Octavius was attached to Sulla and the aristocratic faction, while Cinna, who hoped to bring about another revolution, was doing his utmost to restore the declining fortunes of Marius and the democratic party. Sertorius

* In 90 B.C. Also known as the Social War: the Italian allies (*socii*) revolted when, after the assassination of the tribune M. Livius Drusus, they found themselves deprived of the prospect of obtaining the franchise by constitutional means.

† In 88 B.C.

gave his support to Cinna, more particularly because he saw that Octavius was a man of little initiative, who was inclined to distrust Marius's supporters. A great battle was fought between the consuls in the Forum from which Octavius emerged victorious, and Cinna and Sertorius fled after losing nearly ten thousand men. However, they succeeded in rallying to their side most of the troops who were still scattered throughout Italy, and with these reinforcements they soon made themselves a match for Octavius.*

5. Marius now sailed home from Libya and volunteered to serve as a private citizen under Cinna, who was still consul. The rest of his party were in favour of accepting this offer, but Sertorius opposed it. He may have reckoned that his own influence with Cinna would be weakened by the presence of another general so much more experienced than himself, or he may have been afraid of Marius's bloodthirsty and vindictive temper, suspecting that in the hour of triumph his rage would carry him far beyond the bounds of justice and throw all their affairs into confusion. So he pointed out to Cinna that since they had already overcome their enemies there remained little for them to do, and that if they accepted Marius's proposals, he would soon find ways of diverting all the power and prestige of their party into his own hands, since he found it difficult to share authority and was not to be trusted. Cinna replied that these arguments were sound enough, but that since he himself had invited Marius to join them, he did not see how he could turn him away, and indeed would feel ashamed to do so. Sertorius retorted, 'I had understood up to now that Marius had come to Italy on his own initiative, and so I was simply considering how far this would be useful to us. But since you had invited him, you had no right to discuss the problem of what to do with him, as if it were an open question. You should have welcomed him and employed him at once, for after you have given your word there is no room for further argument.' Cinna then sent for Marius, the army was divided into three corps, and the three men held joint command.

When the fighting was over,† Cinna and Marius indulged themselves in every kind of insolence and cruelty, so that even the horrors of war seemed to the Romans to have been a kind of golden age by comparison. Sertorius was the only man, we are told, who neither

* In 87 B.C. † In 87 B.C.

killed anyone for revenge, nor abused his authority in the hour of victory, but actually rebuked Marius and on several occasions appealed personally to Cinna to use his power more moderately. And finally it was Sertorius who dealt with the slaves whom Marius had recruited during the war and employed as a personal bodyguard to carry out his acts of tyranny. They had grown rich and become a powerful body of men, partly as a result of Marius's direct orders or of his tolerance of their behaviour, and partly through the outrages they had committed against their masters; for they had murdered many of these, and then raped their wives and violated their children. Sertorius decided that he could no longer tolerate their existence, and he had them surrounded in their camp and killed with javelins. This gang numbered no less than four thousand and were known as the Bardyaeans.*

6. Not long after this Marius died,† and two years later Cinna was murdered by his own troops. The younger Marius then succeeded by illegal means and against Sertorius's wishes in making himself consul. Men such as Carbo, Norbanus, and Scipio made futile attempts to block Sulla's advance upon Rome, and the cause of the popular party began to collapse everywhere, partly through treachery and partly through the cowardice and feebleness of its generals. In this situation there was no reason for Sertorius to stay in Rome and watch affairs go from bad to worse because of the incompetence of his superiors. Finally Sulla pitched his camp near Scipio's army, made friendly overtures as if he were about to negotiate for peace, and set about subverting his opponent's troops. Sertorius gave Scipio clear warning of what was happening, but was unable to convince him. So at last he gave up Rome for lost and set out for Spain, hoping that if he could arrive there before his enemies and establish himself securely he would be able to offer a refuge to his friends, who would soon be defeated in Italy.

He met heavy storms on his march through the mountains, and the barbarians demanded that he should pay them dues for his passage. His companions took offence at this and thought it a monstrous humiliation that a Roman pro-consul should pay tribute to a wretched tribe of barbarians, but Sertorius made light of what seemed to them a disgrace. He remarked that he was buying time, which to a man

* See *Life of Marius*, ch. 44. † In 86 B.C.

who has great objects in view is the most precious commodity in the world. So he pacified the barbarians by paying them, and then hurried on and made himself master of Spain. He found that its tribes were strong in numbers and possessed plenty of fighting men, but that because of the greed and insolence of the officials who were periodically sent out from Italy, the people had become bitterly resentful of the whole character of the Roman administration. So he set himself to win them over by entering into personal dealings with the chiefs and by reducing the taxes imposed on the people. But the measure which earned him more gratitude than any other was his decision to cease billeting his soldiers upon them, for he gave orders to his troops to make their winter quarters in tents outside the walls of the various cities, and he set the example by pitching his own there. However, he did not entirely rely upon the goodwill of the barbarians, but took the precaution of arming all the Roman settlers in the country who were of military age, and he also put in hand the manufacture of military engines and equipment of many kinds and the construction of triremes. In this way he kept the cities firmly under control, and showed himself lenient in his civil administration, but formidable in his preparations against his enemies.

7. When the news reached him that Sulla had captured Rome and that the cause of Marius and Carbo was lost,* he expected that it would not be long before a general and an army were on their way to fight out the issue with him. He therefore sent Julius Salinator with a force of six thousand infantry to block the passes of the Pyrenees. Soon after this Gaius Annius was sent out by Sulla, and when he saw that Salinator had taken up an impregnable position, he was at a loss to know what to do next and encamped at the foot of the mountains. However, at this point a certain Calpurnius, surnamed Lanarius, assassinated Salinator, whose soldiers then abandoned the heights of the Pyrenees. Annius proceeded to cross the mountains and marched on with his large force, brushing aside the weak resistance he encountered. Sertorius was not strong enough to oppose his advance and retreated with three thousand men to New Carthage.† There he embarked his troops, crossed the sea, and landed in North Africa in the territory of the Mauretanians. But while his soldiers were fetching

chased in to Libya

* In 82 B.C. † The modern Cartagena.

water, without having posted a guard, they were attacked by the barbarians, and after losing many men Sertorius set sail again for Spain. Here he was once more driven away from the coast, but, after joining forces with a number of pirate ships from Cilicia, he attacked the island of Pityussa,* overpowered the garrison which Annius had placed there, and forced a landing. Soon afterwards Annius arrived with a large fleet and a force of 5,000 infantry, whereupon Sertorius ventured to engage him in a full-scale naval battle, even though his own ships were fraily built and were designed for speed rather than for fighting. A strong west wind whipped up the sea and most of Sertorius's ships were driven on to the rocky shore because of their light construction. Sertorius himself and his few remaining vessels could neither put out into the open sea because of the gale, nor land because of the enemy, and so for ten days he was tossed about in a desperate struggle with high seas and violent winds and only succeeded with great difficulty in riding out the storm.

8. As the wind died down, he ran in among a group of scattered and waterless islands, where he spent the night. Then, setting sail from there and passing through the straits of Gades, keeping the Spanish coast on his right, he landed a little north of the delta of the river Baetis,† which flows into the Atlantic, and has given its name to the neighbouring parts of Spain.

Here he met a number of sailors who had recently returned from the Atlantic islands.‡ There are two of these, separated from one another by a narrow channel. They are twelve hundred and fifty miles from the African coast and are known as the Isles of the Blest. The rains are moderate and arrive only at long intervals, and for most of the year they enjoy soft breezes which scatter a heavy dew. Thus the islands not only possess a rich and fertile soil, which responds well both to ploughing and to planting, but they also produce fruits which grow of their own accord and are abundant and wholesome enough to support a whole people without the need for any human labour or effort. The seasons are temperate, and the transition between them so gentle that the air which surrounds these islands

* The Balearic island now known as Ibiza.

† The modern Guadalquivir.

‡ Opinion is divided as to whether this account refers to Madeira and Porto Santo, or to the Canaries group.

is always healthy and serene. For the northerly and easterly winds which blow from our part of the world launch themselves into empty space, and so dissipate and lose their force before they arrive at the islands, while those from the south and west, which envelop their shores from the seaward side, sometimes bring soft and scattered showers of rain, but more often merely cool them with moist breezes which gently and imperceptibly nourish the soil. For this reason it is generally believed even among the barbarians that these are the Elysian Fields and the abode of the blessed which Homer has made famous in the *Odyssey*.*

9. When Sertorius heard this report he was seized with an overwhelming desire to settle in the islands and live in peace there, safe from tyranny and endless wars. But his allies, the Cilician pirates, had no desire for peace or leisure; their interest was all in winning spoils and riches. So as soon as they discovered Sertorius's intention, they sailed off to Africa to restore Ascalis the son of Iptha to the throne of Mauretania. Sertorius did not allow this setback to make him abandon hope. Instead he decided to help the party which was opposing Ascalis. His object here was to inspire his followers with fresh hopes, offer them a new adventure, and so keep them united in spite of all their hardships. The Moors were pleased at his arrival and he quickly moved into action, defeated Ascalis in battle, and proceeded to besiege him. And when Sulla sent out Paccianus with an army to help Ascalis, Sertorius engaged him in battle, killed him, won over his army after their defeat, and captured the city of Tingis,† where Ascalis and his brothers had fled for refuge.

According to the Libyans, this city is the burial place of the giant Antaeus. Because of the enormous size of the tomb, Sertorius had been inclined to disbelieve this legend of the barbarians, and he therefore had it dug open. But when he came upon the body and discovered, so it is said, that it was sixty cubits long, he was dumbfounded, and after offering a sacrifice had the tomb filled up again. He then gave his own confirmation to the story and paid fresh honours to the memory of Antaeus. Now the people of Tingis have a legend that, after Antaeus's death, his wife Tinga came to live with Hercules and bore him a son named Sophax, who later became king of this country and gave his mother's name to the city. Sophax is also

* *Odyssey* IV, 563–8. † The modern Tangier.

said to have had a son, Diodorus, who brought many of the Libyan peoples under his rule, since he commanded a Greek army made up of the Olbians and Mycenaeans, who had been settled by Hercules in that region. But this story may well have originated from a desire to please King Juba, for no king was ever more devoted to historical research; at any rate, his ancestors are said to have been descendants of Sophax and Diodorus.

When Sertorius had established his authority throughout the country he gave fair treatment to all those who offered submission and put their trust in him: their property and cities were restored and they were reinstated in authority, while he accepted only such gifts as it was proper for them to offer.

10. While he was considering where he should turn his energies next, the people of Lusitania sent ambassadors and invited him to become their leader. They badly needed a commander of great reputation and experience, for they felt themselves threatened by the power of Rome, and when they learned more about Sertorius's character from the men who had served with him, they entrusted their safety to his hands alone. For Sertorius was a man, it is said, whose nature enabled him to resist pleasure and fear alike: he was unmoved in the face of danger, nor did he become over-elated with success. In the open field he was as bold as any commander of his time, while for any campaign which required secrecy of movement or a sudden initiative in seizing strong positions or crossing rivers, or for operations which demanded speed, the deception of the enemy, or, if necessary, the invention of falsehoods, he possessed a skill which amounted to genius. He showed himself generous in rewarding deeds of valour and at the same time merciful in punishing offences. On the other hand, towards the end of his life, his cruel and vindictive treatment of his hostages seemed to suggest that his humanity was not spontaneous, but was a quality which he displayed for the sake of effect whenever the need arose. And yet it seems to me that a virtue which a man embraces on principle and which is genuinely a part of his nature can never be transformed into its opposite by any mere stroke of fortune. I say this in spite of the fact that praiseworthy intentions and natural good qualities may change their character if they are subjected to great and undeserved misfortune, as the guiding genius of a man's life changes. And this, I believe, was the case with Sertor-

ius, so that, when his luck began to fail, adversity had the effect of embittering him against those who betrayed him.

11. However, at the period which I am now describing, he accepted the Lusitanians' invitation and set out from Africa. He took command of their affairs as general with absolute powers, proceeded at once to reorganize their country, and also brought the neighbouring parts of Spain under his control. Most of the tribes acknowledged his authority of their own accord, chiefly because of the way in which his rule combined mildness with efficiency: but he also employed various ingenious devices on occasion to beguile and charm the people, the chief of which was the affair of his fawn. The story goes as follows.

A countryman of that region named Spanus came upon a doe which had just given birth and was trying to escape the hunters. He could not overtake the mother, but he followed the fawn because he was struck by its unusual colour, which was all milk-white, and finally he caught it. It so happened that Sertorius had lately encamped in the neighbourhood, and whenever people brought him game or the produce of their farms, he would receive such gifts gladly and give a generous reward to anyone who favoured him in this way. So Spanus brought the fawn and made him a present of it, which Sertorius accepted. At first he did not take any special notice of the animal, but after a while he made it so tame and gentle that it would obey him whenever he called. It accompanied him on his walks, showed no fear of crowds or the uproar of camp life, and little by little he began to build up the impression that there was something sacred and mysterious about the creature. He declared that she was a gift from Diana and possessed the power of revealing secrets to him, for he knew that the barbarians are naturally prone to superstition. He also resorted to such devices as the following. Whenever he received secret intelligence that the enemy had invaded his territory or were attempting to persuade some city to revolt, he would give it out that the fawn had spoken to him in his sleep and warned him to keep his troops ready. Again, whenever he learned of any victory won by his generals, he would hide the messenger and bring out the fawn crowned with garlands to celebrate the arrival of good news: then he would encourage his men to rejoice and offer sacrifice to the gods, for they could rest assured that they would soon hear of some success.

12. Through devices such as these he made the people amenable to his plans, so that they obeyed his orders without hesitation, for they were convinced that they were being guided not by the mortal intelligence of a mere foreigner, but by a god; and indeed the facts could very well support their belief, for the growth of Sertorius's power was truly extraordinary. His army consisted of the two thousand six hundred men whom he called Romans, and a motley band of seven hundred Libyans, who had crossed over to Lusitania with him, reinforced by four thousand Lusitanian light infantry and seven hundred horsemen. With this force he carried on war with four Roman generals, whose combined strength amounted to a hundred and twenty thousand infantry, six thousand cavalry, two thousand archers and slingers, together with the resources of innumerable cities, while he at first controlled only twenty cities all told. And yet with such small beginnings and slender resources he not only subdued large tribes and captured many cities, but he triumphed time and again over the generals who were sent against him. He defeated Cotta in a naval battle near the straits of Gibraltar, routed Fufidius the governor of Baetica on the banks of the Baetis,* and killed two thousand Roman soldiers with him, while Sertorius's quaestor overcame Lucius Domitius, the pro-consul of Hither Spain.† Sertorius also killed Thoranius, one of the commanders whom Metellus sent against him with an army, and on Metellus‡ himself, the foremost Roman citizen and most distinguished general of his time, he inflicted a whole series of defeats, and reduced him to such straits that Lucius Manlius was obliged to march from south-western Gaul to rescue him and Pompey the Great was hastily dispatched from Rome with reinforcements. Metellus was, in fact, utterly baffled. He was confronted by a daring opponent who evaded every kind of open engagement, but who was always able, thanks to the agility and light equipment of his Spanish troops, to adapt his tactics to new conditions. Metellus, on the other hand, had gained his experience in pitched battles, fought in the orthodox fashion by men in full armour,

* Near the modern Cordoba.

† Spain was divided into two provinces, Hither Spain, the eastern half of the country, and Further Spain, the western. Fufidius was governor of the latter.

‡ This was Q. Metellus Pius, the son of the general who played a leading part in the Jugurthine War.

and had been accustomed to command a slow-moving phalanx, whose formation never varied in the course of a battle. Such troops were splendidly trained for repelling and bearing down an enemy in hand to hand fighting, but were quite incapable of climbing mountains, or keeping contact with the incessant attacks and withdrawals of light troops who faded away like the wind, nor could they endure hunger, as their enemies could, nor live under the open sky with neither a fire nor a tent.

13. Besides, Metellus was by this time well advanced in years, and after the many great battles he had fought was inclined to indulge in a relaxed and luxurious style of living, whereas Sertorius, now in the prime of life, was full of mettle, and his physique was capable of extraordinary feats of strength, rapid movement, and hard living. He never indulged in drinking-bouts, even in his hours of relaxation, and he had accustomed himself to endure great physical effort, long marches and continuous lack of sleep, supported all the while on a coarse and meagre diet. Besides this, since he was constantly on the move, or else hunting whenever he could spare the time, he became so familiar with the lie of the country and its accessible and inaccessible parts that he always knew how to find a way of escape in retreat, or to cut off the enemy when in pursuit.

The consequence was that by being prevented from fighting Metellus suffered all the disadvantages of defeat, while by constantly eluding his enemy Sertorius reaped all the advantages of victory. For example he would cut off his opponents' supplies of water and prevent them from foraging: then, if the Romans advanced, he would slip out of their way, but if they stayed in camp he would harass them. If they laid siege to a place, he would immediately appear and blockade them in turn by cutting off their supplies. In the end he succeeded in reducing the Romans to such despair by these tactics that, when he challenged Metellus to single combat, the soldiers shouted at their commander and urged him to fight, general against general and Roman against Roman, and when Metellus refused, they jeered at him. Metellus only laughed at this, and he was right, for a general, as Theophrastus says, should die like a general and not like a common soldier.

Metellus had noticed that Sertorius received a great deal of help from the tribe of the Langobritae, and that their capital city was vulnerable because of its lack of water. The townspeople possessed only one spring inside the city, and the streams which flowed through the suburbs and under the walls could be cut off by any besieging force. He therefore advanced against the city, expecting that, once his opponents had been deprived of water, he could finish off the siege in two days, and for the same reason he ordered his troops to carry rations for no more than five days. But Sertorius quickly came to the rescue, ordered two thousand skins to be filled with water, and offered a large reward for the delivery of each skin. Both Spaniards and Moors flocked to volunteer for the task, so that Sertorius was able to pick men who could move swiftly as well as possessing great physical strength, and he then dispatched them by a route through the mountains. Their orders were that after delivering the skins inside the city they should smuggle out the entire non-combatant population which could not take part in the defence, so that the water should last all the longer for the garrison. Metellus was much disturbed when he discovered this, since his soldiers had already used up their rations, and so he sent out Aquinus with a force six thousand strong to forage for provisions. But Sertorius learned of this move and set an ambush of three thousand men by the side of the road along which Aquinus was marching back. These men suddenly swarmed out of a shady ravine and fell upon Aquinus's troops from the rear, while Sertorius attacked from the front and routed his opponents, killing some and taking others prisoner. Aquinus escaped to Metellus, but not without first losing both his weapons and his horse, whereupon Metellus ignominiously withdrew from the siege amid the jeers of the Spaniards.

14. By such exploits as these Sertorius earned not only the barbarians' admiration but also their love, and at the same time by introducing Roman weapons and battle formations and signals he did away with their savage and frenzied displays of courage, and transformed their military strength into that of a disciplined army instead of a horde of brigands. He also allowed them generous quantities of gold and silver to decorate their helmets and ornament their shields, and accustomed them to wear flowered cloaks and tunics. He provided them with the money to buy all these things, and by appealing to their sense of rivalry and display he completely won their hearts. But what attached them to him most deeply of all was the

care he took of their children. He sent for all the boys of the noblest parentage from the various tribes and placed them in the large city of Osca,* where he appointed masters to teach them Greek and Roman letters. Thus to all appearances he was educating them with the assurance that when they had grown to manhood he would give them a share in administration and authority, whereas in reality he had made them his hostages. Meanwhile, their fathers were delighted to see their sons, dressed in their togas with purple borders, decorously attending their classes, while Sertorius paid their fees, frequently held examinations, awarded prizes to the best pupils, and presented them with the golden pendants which the Romans call *bullae*.

Now it was the custom in Spain for the bodyguard which was stationed around a commander to die with him, if he was killed in battle, and the barbarians in these parts call this action a 'consecration'. The other commanders had only a few of these guards or comrades in arms, but by this time there were thousands of men who followed Sertorius and had dedicated themselves to die with him in this fashion. The story goes that when his army was defeated near a certain city and the enemy were pressing hard upon them, the Iberians exposed themselves without a thought for their safety, rescued Sertorius, and, lifting him on to their shoulders one after another, carried him up to the walls. Then only when their general was safe did they make their escape, each man looking after himself.

15. And in fact it was not only the Spaniards who cherished Sertorius: the troops who had come with him from Italy were no less devoted to him. At any rate, when Perpenna Vento, who belonged to the same political party as Sertorius, arrived in Spain with a strong force and large sums of money and decided to fight Metellus independently, his soldiers quickly became dissatisfied with this plan and there was much talk in his camp about Sertorius. This angered Perpenna, who was intensely conceited because of his noble birth and his wealth. But when the news arrived that Pompey was crossing the Pyrenees, Perpenna's soldiers snatched up their standards, seized their arms, and raised an outcry against their general. They demanded that he should lead them to Sertorius, and threatened that if he did not

* Probably the modern Huesca in Aragon. Alexander the Great had instituted a similar custom by arranging for 30,000 Persian boys to be taught Greek.

they would go without him and put themselves in the hands of a general who could protect both himself and the men under his command. So Perpenna gave way and led them off to join Sertorius, thus bringing him a reinforcement of fifty-three cohorts.*

16. Sertorius's strength was now rapidly increasing, for all the tribes between the Ebro and the Pyrenees came over to his side, and troops came flocking daily to join him from every quarter. At the same time he was troubled by the lack of discipline and the over-confidence of these newly arrived barbarians, who would shout at him to attack the enemy and had no patience with his delaying tactics, and he therefore tried to win them over by argument. But when he saw that they were discontented and persisted in pressing their demands regardless of the circumstances, he let them have their way and allowed them to engage the enemy; he hoped that they would suffer a severe defeat without being completely crushed, and that this would make them better disposed to obey his orders in future. The event turned out as he expected and Sertorius came to their rescue, provided a rallying point for the fugitives, and led them safely back to his camp. His next step was to revive their dejected spirits, and so a few days later he summoned a general assembly. Before it he produced two horses, one of them old and enfeebled, the other large and lusty and possessing a flowing tail, which was remarkable for the thickness and beauty of its hair. By the side of the weak horse stood a tall strong man, and by the side of the powerful horse a short man of mean physique. At a signal the strong man seized the tail of his horse and tried with all his strength to pull it towards him, as if to tear it off, while the weak man began to pull the hairs one by one from the tail of the strong horse. The strong man, after tugging with all his might to no purpose and causing the spectators a great deal of amusement in the process, finally gave up the attempt, while the weak man quickly and with very little trouble stripped his horse's tail completely bare. Then Sertorius rose to his feet and said, 'Now you can see, my friends and allies, that perseverance is more effective than brute strength, and that there are many difficulties that cannot be overcome if you try to do everything at once, but which will yield if you master them little by little. The truth is that a steady continuous effort is irresistible, for this is the way in which Time

* Nearly twenty thousand men.

captures and subdues the greatest powers on earth. Now Time, you should remember, is a good friend and ally to those who use their intelligence to choose the right moment, but a most dangerous enemy to those who rush into action at the wrong one.' So by devising object-lessons like this from time to time and drawing the moral, Sertorius taught the barbarians to wait for their opportunities.

17. Of all his military exploits none has been more admired than his achievement in dealing with the tribe known as the Characitani. This people's territory lies to the north of the river Tagus. They do not live in cities or villages, but on a large and lofty hill, whose northern side is a steep cliff honeycombed with caves and hollows. The soil of the countryside at the foot of the hill consists of a white clay, which is porous and crumbles at a touch. It is not firm enough to bear a man's tread, and even if it is only slightly stirred, it scatters far and wide like ash or unslaked lime. Whenever the barbarians of these parts feared an attack, they would collect all their plunder, hide in these caves and stay quiet, and in this refuge it was impossible to capture them by force. At the time I am describing, Sertorius happened to have fallen back before Metellus and pitched his camp at the foot of this hill, and the savage inhabitants showed their contempt for him, as they supposed that he had only retreated there because he had been defeated. Sertorius, either out of anger or because he did not choose to be thought a fugitive, rode up to the hill and reconnoitred it. The heights were evidently impregnable, but as he rode idly around them, muttering empty threats, he noticed that great quantities of dust from the soil which I have described were being carried by the breeze in the direction of the barbarians' caves. The mouths of these, as I have explained, faced north, and the breeze which blows from that quarter – some people call it *Caecias* – is the strongest and most prevalent wind in that region. It takes its rise from marshy plains and snow-covered mountains, and at that season, which was the height of summer, its strength was increased by the melting of the northern snows, so that it blew a deliciously cool gale which refreshed both men and beasts throughout the day. When Sertorius had pondered over what he had seen and questioned the local inhabitants about the prevailing conditions, he ordered his soldiers to take some of this light and dusty soil, which I have de-

scribed, and pile it in a heap directly opposite the hill. The barbarians imagined this to be a mound which was being raised as a siege-work to attack them, and laughed at their enemy. Sertorius kept his soldiers working at this task until the evening, and then marched them back to their camp. At daybreak the next morning a gentle breeze sprang up, which stirred the lightest parts of the heaped-up soil, and scattered them like chaff. Then, as the sun rose higher and the north wind began to gather strength and cover the hills with dust, the soldiers came, stirred up the mound to the bottom, and broke up the heavy clods, while some galloped their horses back and forth through it, kicking up the loosened soil and throwing it high in the air. Then the wind caught the earth which had been stirred and broken up in this way, and flung it against the entrances of the barbarians' dwellings which faced northwards. The inmates, since their caves could only admit the air from the windward side, soon found their eyes blinded and their lungs choked, as they were forced to inhale a suffocating blast, which was laden with great quantities of dust. For two days they held out with great difficulty, but on the third they surrendered. Their submission strengthened Sertorius's reputation rather than his resources, because his ingenuity had won a victory which could never have been gained by force of arms.

18. So long as Sertorius was campaigning against Metellus, his success was generally attributed to his opponent's advanced age and natural slowness of movement; with these disadvantages Metellus was evidently no match for a daring leader, whose forces were believed to be composed of bandits rather than of regular soldiers. But when Pompey crossed the Pyrenees and Sertorius marched to oppose him, both men offered and accepted every possible challenge to their powers of generalship. In this contest Sertorius proved himself the master, both in devising schemes to outwit the enemy and in frustrating those that were launched against him. The result was that his fame spread even as far as Rome, where he was acknowledged by common consent to be the most expert commander of his time. It must be remembered that Pompey himself had already won great prestige, and by this time his reputation was at its height. He had achieved prodigies of generalship on Sulla's behalf, in return for which he had been given the title of The Great, and had been awarded a triumph before he had even grown his first beard. For this reason

many of the cities which were subject to Sertorius began to cast an eye in Pompey's direction and felt tempted to shift their allegiance, but after Pompey's totally unexpected defeat near Lauron* they quickly abandoned these intentions. This was a town which Sertorius was besieging, and Pompey marched with all his forces to relieve it. There was a hill nearby, the command of which was considered essential for an attack on the city, so that Sertorius was anxious to seize it in advance and Pompey to prevent him. Sertorius succeeded in occupying it first, whereupon Pompey, delighted at this move, halted his troops and drew them up in position, believing that he had trapped Sertorius between his army and the city. He also dispatched a messenger to the citizens of Lauron, encouraging them to take heart and seat themselves on their walls, where they could now witness the spectacle of Sertorius being besieged. When Sertorius heard this, he laughed and declared that he would teach Sulla's pupil – for this was his nickname for Pompey – a lesson, namely that a general needs to look behind him even more carefully than in front. As he said this, he pointed out to his beleaguered men the force of six thousand infantry, which he had left behind in their camp when he made his sortie to seize the hill: he had kept them there deliberately so as to attack Pompey's rear, in case he moved against the troops occupying the hill. Pompey did not discover this ruse until it was too late, but having done so he did not dare to attack Sertorius for fear of being encircled in his turn. At the same time he was ashamed to march away and leave the inhabitants of Lauron to their danger, and so he was forced to sit there and watch them being overcome, for the barbarians quickly gave up hope and surrendered. Sertorius spared their lives and let them all go free, but he burned their city to the ground. He did this neither out of anger nor cruelty, for he seems to have indulged such passions less than any other general, but rather with the object of disgracing and humiliating Pompey's supporters: he wanted to spread the word among the barbarians that although Pompey was almost close enough to warm his hands over the flames of a city which was one of his allies, yet he had done nothing to rescue it.

19. It is true that Sertorius experienced a number of setbacks during this campaign, but he always succeeded in keeping himself and his

* A town near the coast some fifty miles south of the modern Valencia.

own forces undefeated, and the reverses he suffered were all inflicted upon his subordinates. And in fact he displayed such skill in recovering from a defeat that he earned more admiration than his victorious opponents, as happened in the battle by the river Sucro* against Pompey, and again in the battle near Turia,* when he faced the combined forces of Pompey and Metellus. Pompey is said to have precipitated the battle of the Sucro so as to prevent Metellus from having any share in the victory. Sertorius was equally anxious to engage Pompey before Metellus came up, and he deployed his army and launched his attack just before darkness fell: he calculated that, as the Roman troops facing him were unfamiliar with the country, they would be as much hampered by the darkness whether they were in pursuit or in rout.

When the two armies closed, it happened that Sertorius, who was stationed on the right wing, found himself engaged not with Pompey but with Afranius, who commanded the Roman left. Sertorius then heard that the part of his army which faced Pompey was giving ground before his opponent's onslaught, and so he handed over the right wing to his subordinates, and hurried off to rescue his hard-pressed left. He succeeded in rallying the soldiers who were in retreat, and, after encouraging those who were still holding their ground, he launched a counter-attack against the oncoming Pompey, and threw his men back in rout. Pompey himself was wounded in this charge, and only escaped death by an extraordinary stroke of luck. This was because the Libyans who were fighting with Sertorius, after capturing Pompey's horse which was covered with gold ornaments and boasted a costly harness, became so engrossed in sharing out and quarrelling over the booty that they failed to press home the pursuit. But as soon as Sertorius had crossed over to rescue his left wing, Afranius broke throught the troops opposing him and drove them headlong back to their camp; indeed he was following so close on the heels of the fugitives that he entered it with them. By this time it was growing dark and he began to pillage Sertorius's camp, since he had heard nothing of Pompey's defeat and was unable to restrain his soldiers from looting. But meanwhile Sertorius returned from his victory on the other wing, attacked Afranius's troops who were scattered in disorder over the whole camp, and

* These place names have not been identified with certainty, but the campaign seems to have been fought in the neighbourhood of Valencia.

slaughtered them in great numbers. The following morning he again armed his troops and came out to fight, but then he learned that Metellus's army was close at hand. He therefore broke up his order of battle and marched away, declaring that 'If that old woman* had not come up, I would have given this boy† a good hiding and packed him off to Rome!'

20. Meanwhile, he was greatly distressed by the disappearance of his fawn, because this deprived him of a wonderful means of influencing the barbarians, who at this moment badly needed encouragement. By good fortune some men who were roaming about the country at night on other errands happened to see the fawn, recognized her by her colour, and caught her. When Sertorius heard of this, he promised the men a large reward if they would say nothing about her capture. Meanwhile he kept the fawn hidden and a few days later appeared in public smiling and cheerful, and declared to the barbarian chieftains that the gods had foretold a great stroke of good fortune to him in a dream; after which he mounted the tribunal and began to deal with the various petitions that were presented to him. At this moment the fawn's keepers released her close by. She caught sight of Sertorius, bounded up, and leaped on to the tribunal; then, laying her head on his lap, she licked his right hand as she had been accustomed to do in the past, whereupon Sertorius returned her caresses affectionately and even shed tears. The spectators were dumbfounded at first, and then, breaking into shouts of joy and loud applause, they escorted him to his house. They were convinced that he was beloved of the gods and possessed supernatural powers, and this assurance filled them with hope and confidence for the future.

21. Sertorius had blockaded the enemy so successfully in the plains around Saguntum that they suffered severe hardships, but when the Romans came out to plunder and forage he was forced to give them battle. Both armies fought magnificently. Memmius, the most skilful of Pompey's commanders, was killed where the fighting was hottest. Sertorius meanwhile was carrying all before him, and cutting down great numbers of the enemy who still held their positions, he pressed on steadily towards Metellus. In spite of his age, the Roman commander was holding his ground and defending himself valiantly,

* Metellus. † Pompey.

when he was struck by a spear. All the Romans who saw this happen or heard of it were filled with shame at the thought of abandoning their general, and were roused to anger against the enemy. They surrounded Metellus with their shields and carried him out of danger, then turned, launched a furious counter-attack, and drove back the Iberians. Victory had now changed sides, and Sertorius needed all his skill to disengage his troops and withdraw them to safety. He therefore retreated to a strong city in the mountains, where he could rebuild his army undisturbed, and although he had no intention of withstanding a siege, he set himself to repair the walls and strengthen the gates. This move completely deceived the enemy, who at once settled down to invest the city, which they expected to capture quite easily. In this way the retreating barbarians were allowed to escape without a pursuit, while the Romans took no notice of the reinforcements which were being mobilized for Sertorius in the meanwhile. And mobilized they were, for Sertorius had sent officers to the cities which were under his control with orders to send a messenger to him as soon as they had gathered a large enough body of troops. When the messengers duly reached him, he had no difficulty in breaking through the lines of the besieging troops and joining forces with his new recruits, and, with his army thus strengthened, he once more turned against the enemy and launched a double offensive. He harassed their supply routes on land by means of outflanking movements, ambushes, and surprise attacks from every quarter, and at sea by patrolling the coast with his light pirate craft. As a result of these tactics the Roman commanders were forced to separate, Metellus retreating into Gaul and Pompey spending the winter among the Vaccaei.* Here he suffered great hardships through lack of supplies, and wrote to the Senate that he would march his army out of Spain unless they sent him money, since he had already spent all his resources in the campaign he had fought to defend Italy. In fact the rumour was current in Rome that Sertorius would arrive in Italy before Pompey. Such was the measure of superiority which Sertorius had established over the ablest and most powerful generals of his time.

22. Metellus himself made it quite clear that he feared Sertorius and

* A tribe of north-western Spain, inhabiting a region north of the river Douro.

thought him a great leader, for he issued a proclamation that any Roman who killed Sertorius would receive a reward of a hundred talents of silver and twenty thousand *jugera** of land, and if he were an exile he would be granted permission to return to Rome. By this attempt to purchase Sertorius's death by treachery he plainly revealed that he had given up all hope of overcoming him in open war. And when on one occasion he did gain a victory over Sertorius, he felt so delighted and triumphant at his success that he had himself proclaimed Imperator, and the cities of Iberia received him with sacrifices on their altars when he visited them. It is said that he even allowed himself to be crowned with wreaths and accepted invitations to ceremonial banquets, at which he wore a triumphal robe as he drank his wine, while mechanical effigies of victory were lowered from the ceiling bearing golden crowns and trophies in their hands, and choirs of boys and women sang hymns of victory in his honour. It is not surprising that the people laughed at him, for it was surely ridiculous that he should show such extraordinary pleasure and vanity just because he had gained an advantage over Sertorius and forced him to retreat, while at the same time he referred to him as Sulla's runaway slave and the scum of Carbo's defeated party.

Sertorius, by contrast, showed his magnanimity in a number of ways. First of all he brought together the various senators who had fled from Rome to join his cause, and gave this body the title of Senate. From their number he appointed praetors and quaestors, and in all these arrangements he observed the forms of Roman tradition. Secondly, although he made use of the arms, the resources, and the cities of the Iberians, he never even discussed the idea of yielding up the authority of Rome in the smallest degree, but always appointed Romans to be their generals and commanders, believing that his task was to give his fellow-countrymen back their freedom, not to raise up the Iberians against them. For he was above all a man who loved his country and longed to return home from exile. And yet even when his fortunes were at their lowest, his courage never faltered and he never humbled himself before his enemies. On the other hand after his victories he several times sent word to Metellus and Pompey to tell them that he was ready to lay down his arms and live as a private citizen, on condition that he would be granted permission to return to Rome. He declared that he would rather live as the meanest

* Between twelve and thirteen thousand acres.

citizen in Rome than remain in exile, even if he were proclaimed the ruler of all the rest of the world.

It is said that his longing to return was largely inspired by his affection for his mother, who had brought him up after his father's death and to whom he was completely devoted. At the moment when his friends in Spain were pressing him to take up the command there* he had just learned of his mother's death, and his grief at the news almost killed him. He lay for seven days in his tent, during which time he would neither give out the password nor allow his friends to see him, and it was only with great difficulty that his fellow-commanders and brother-officers, after surrounding his tent, could prevail upon him to come out, mingle with the soldiers, and take part in their operations, which at that time were going well. All this led many people to suppose that Sertorius was a mild-tempered man, whose natural inclinations were for a life of quiet, but who was forced to accept commands quite against his wishes, and who, once he had been compelled by his enemies to resort to violence, took refuge in war as a necessary form of self-defence.

23. Yet another example of his magnanimity may be seen in his negotiations with Mithridates.† In spite of the fall which Sulla had given him, Mithridates had risen to his feet just like a wrestler ready for another bout, and made yet another attempt to seize the province of Asia. At this moment Sertorius's prestige was also at its height and his fame had spread to many countries, so that the traders who came from the west had filled the kingdom of Pontus with tales of his exploits like so much foreign merchandise. Mithridates was eager to send an embassy to him, and in doing this he was led on most of all by the foolish and exaggerated arguments of his flatterers. These men kept comparing Sertorius with Hannibal and Mithridates with Pyrrhus, and assured him that the Romans, if they were attacked on both fronts, would find it impossible to hold out against the combined strength of two such men, once the most powerful king in the world

* In 83 B.C.

† Mithridates, the ruler of the Black Sea kingdom of Pontus, invaded Asia in 88 B.C. and the inhabitants, long oppressed by Roman tax-gatherers, rose and massacred many of the Roman settlers. Sulla defeated Mithridates and made peace with him in 85 B.C. The negotiations with Sertorius took place in 75 B.C.

was joined by the ablest general. So Mithridates sent envoys to Spain carrying both letters and verbal proposals. The gist of these was that Mithridates promised to supply ships and money for a war against Rome, but in return he demanded that Sertorius should confirm his title to the sovereignty of the whole province of Asia, which he had renounced according to the terms of his treaty with Sulla. Sertorius assembled his council, which he called a Senate, and on this occasion the rest of his advisers urged him to welcome the king's proposals and accept them, since all that was being asked of their party was to grant a name and an empty title to a territory which they did not possess, while in return they would be provided with what they most badly needed. But Sertorius would on no account agree. He said that he had no objection to the king's taking possession of Bithynia and Cappadocia: these were territories which were accustomed to the rule of kings and were of no account to the Romans. But as for a province which Mithridates had seized and held when the Romans were in full and lawful possession of it, which he had lost in war to Fimbria and had given up according to a treaty with Sulla, this was a very different matter, and Sertorius declared that he could not consent to its falling into Mithridates's hands again. Such power as he himself wielded ought to be used to extend the authority of Rome, and he had no right to extend his own power at her expense. A man of noble spirit, he told them, welcomes victory if he can achieve it with honour, but he will not embrace dishonour even to save his own life.

24. When Mithridates heard this reply, his amazement was apparent to everyone, and we are told that he remarked to his friends: 'This Sertorius has been driven to the shores of the Atlantic, and from there he marks out the frontiers of our kingdom and threatens us with war. What terms do you suppose he will demand when he is sitting on the Palatine Hill?'* However, in spite of this a treaty was drawn up and ratified on oath. Mithridates was to take possession of Cappadocia and Bithynia, while Sertorius was to send him a general and troops and would receive in return three thousand talents and forty ships. Sertorius therefore sent as general to Asia Marcus Marius, one of the senators who had taken refuge with him. He was helped by Mithri-

* An anachronism. Plutarch was writing under the Empire, when the palace of the Caesars was situated on the Palatine Hill.

dates to capture certain cities in Asia, and when he entered them attended by the Roman fasces and axes, Mithridates followed him in person, voluntarily accepting second rank and the status of an inferior ally. Marius granted some of the cities their freedom and wrote to others to tell them that on Sertorius's authority they would be exempted from taxation. The result was that the province of Asia, which in the meanwhile had once more become infested with Roman tax-gatherers and oppressed by the greed and violence of the soldiers billeted there, was suddenly inspired by the prospect of better things and longed for the expected change of régime.

25. But meanwhile, in Spain, as soon as the senators and other patricians who had joined Sertorius felt confident that he was a match for their enemies, they forgot their fears, were filled instead by envy of Sertorius, and became foolishly resentful of his authority. They were encouraged by Perpenna, a man who because of his noble birth was consumed by empty ambitions to hold the supreme command. He began to organize secret meetings with his acquaintances and to rouse their feelings with such malicious questions as these: 'What evil genius has taken control of us all and is hurrying our affairs from bad to worse? We refused to stay at home and take orders from Sulla, when he made himself supreme over land and sea. Instead we banished ourselves to this miserable country, hoping to live as free men, and what have we become? We have turned ourselves into slaves in the bodyguard of this refugee, Sertorius. We call ourselves a Senate, and everybody who hears the title laughs at it, and we find ourselves subjected to the same orders and insults and hardships as these Iberians and Lusitanians.' These words had their effect on Perpenna's listeners. Most of them did not openly desert Sertorius, because they were still afraid of his power, but in secret they did their best to hamper his operations and ill-treated the barbarians by imposing heavy punishments and levying exorbitant taxes, always with the excuse that this was done on Sertorius's orders. The result was that the cities became restive and revolts broke out in several of them, while the men who were sent out to appease and settle these grievances only provoked more outbreaks before they returned, and inflamed the growing spirit of disobedience. It was at this point that Sertorius abandoned his original policy of clemency and moderation

and committed a terrible injustice against the sons of the Iberians, who were being educated at Osca. Some of them he had put to death and others were sold into slavery.

26. Meanwhile, Perpenna had won over a number of accomplices for his conspiracy against Sertorius, and he now added to their number a senior officer named Manlius. This Manlius was in love with a handsome boy, and as a proof of his attachment he told him about the conspiracy and said that he could now forget about his other admirers and give all his affections to Manlius, because in a few days' time his lover would be a great man. As it happened the boy preferred another of his admirers named Aufidius, and passed on to him everything that Manlius had said. Aufidius was astonished when he heard this, for although he had been enlisted in the conspiracy himself, he did not know that Manlius had been. But when the boy mentioned the names of Perpenna, Gracinus, and various others whom Aufidius knew to be engaged in the plot, he became seriously alarmed. He told the boy that there was nothing in the story and warned him to despise Manlius as a boastful liar; then he went to Perpenna, explained the danger of their situation, and urged him to make the attempt at once. The conspirators followed his advice, and they then prepared forged dispatches, arranged for a messenger to bring them, and introduced him into Sertorius's presence. The dispatches announced that one of Sertorius's generals had won a victory and inflicted heavy losses on the enemy. Sertorius was delighted and offered up a sacrifice to celebrate the good news. Thereupon Perpenna took advantage of the occasion to invite him to a banquet together with those of his own friends who were present – all of whom were in the plot – and after much pressing he persuaded Sertorius to accept. Now all the entertainments which Sertorius consented to attend were conducted in a well behaved and orderly fashion, since he refused to tolerate any indecency in word or action, and made it a rule that his companions' jokes and amusements should be restrained and inoffensive. But on this occasion, when the drinking was well under way, the guests became deliberately quarrelsome, used obscene language, and under the pretence of being drunk began to commit indecencies. All this was done in the hope of provoking Sertorius. It may have been that he was angry at their disorderly behaviour, or perhaps had guessed their intentions from the insolence of their talk

and their unusual disrespect for his wishes: at any rate he changed his position on his couch and threw himself on to his back, as if he were neither listening nor paying attention to them. Suddenly Perpenna took a cup of wine, and, as he was drinking it, let it fall with a clatter. This was the pre-arranged signal, whereupon Antonius, who was reclining above Sertorius on the couch, stabbed him with his sword. Sertorius swung round at the blow and tried to rise and grapple with his assailant, but Antonius threw himself on his chest and seized both his hands. Sertorius could make no move to defend himself and died beneath a hail of blows.

27. Most of the Iberians immediately deserted the conspirators, sent envoys to Pompey and Metellus, and surrendered to them. Perpenna tried to organize a resistance with those who remained, but he made just enough use of Sertorius's resources to cut a contemptible figure and prove conclusively that he was no better at giving orders than he was at obeying them. He attacked Pompey and was promptly defeated and taken prisoner, but he could not even endure his final misfortune as a leader should. He had Sertorius's private papers in his possession, and he offered to show Pompey a number of letters written in their own hands by men of consular rank occupying the highest positions in Rome. In these they invited Sertorius to come to Italy, where they assured him that there were many who wished to overthrow the present régime and change the constitution. Pompey dealt with this situation in a manner not at all to be expected of a young man, but rather of a statesman of mature and balanced judgement, and by his action he delivered Rome from the alarms and perils of revolution. He collected all the secret correspondence and Sertorius's other papers and had them burned, without either reading them himself or allowing anyone else to do so. He then had Perpenna executed at once, for fear that uprisings or civil war might break out if the names of Sertorius's correspondents were revealed.

Of Perpenna's fellow-conspirators, some were captured and put to death at Pompey's orders, while others fled to Africa and were killed by the spears of the Maurusians. Not one of them escaped except for Aufidius, Manlius's rival. Either because he could not be found, or because he was not considered worth looking for, he lived on into old age in some barbarian village, poor and detested by all.

8

BRUTUS

[85–42 B.C.]

* *
*

1. Marcus Brutus was a descendant of that Junius Brutus in whose honour the ancient Romans erected a statue of bronze and placed it in the midst of their kings. They represented him with a drawn sword in his hand in memory of the courage and resolution he had shown in dethroning the Tarquins. But the first Brutus possessed a character as unyielding as a sword of tempered steel. A hard man by nature, his disposition had never been humanized by education, and so his anger against the tyrants could even drive him to the terrible extremity of killing his own sons for conspiring with them. By contrast, the Brutus who is the subject of this Life took pains to moderate his natural instincts by means of the culture and mental discipline which philosophy gives, while he also exerted himself to stir up the more placid and passive side of his character and force it into action, with the result that his temperament was almost ideally balanced to pursue a life of virtue. So we find that even those men who hated him most for his conspiracy against Julius Caesar were prepared to give the credit for any redeeming element in the murder to Brutus, while they blamed all that was unscrupulous about it upon Cassius, who, although a relative and a close friend of Brutus, was neither so simple in character nor so disinterested in his motives.

Brutus's mother Servilia traced her descent from the celebrated Servilius Ahala, who, when Spurius Maelius* was plotting to secure the support of the people so as to make himself tyrant, took a dagger under his arm, went into the Forum, and walking up to Maelius as if he were about to start a conversation, chose his moment when the man inclined his head to listen, and then stabbed him to death.

* Spurius Maelius was a wealthy corn merchant, who plotted a *coup d'état* in 439 B.C. See Livy, IV, 13.

So much is generally admitted as regards his ancestry on his mother's side; but as for his father's, the people who bear him most hatred and ill will on account of Caesar's murder argue that it cannot possibly be traced back to the Brutus who drove out the Tarquins, because after he had killed his sons he was left without issue. According to them, Marcus Brutus was descended from a plebeian, who was the son of a steward of that name, and he had only recently risen to office. On the other hand, Poseidonius the philosopher maintains that the two grown-up sons of Junius Brutus were put to death, as the tradition has come down to us, but that there was yet a third son, an infant, who survived, and from whom the family thereafter traced its lineage. What is more, he mentions that there were a number of distinguished men of this house who were alive in his own day, and that some of them remarked on their physical resemblance to the statue of Brutus. So much for this subject.

2. Brutus's mother Servilia was a sister of Cato the philosopher. This was the man whom Brutus admired more than any other Roman alive, and whose daughter Porcia he later married. There was practically no Greek philosopher with whom Brutus was unfamiliar or unacquainted, but it was the writings of the disciples of Plato which attracted him most of all. He took no great interest in the theories of the New* or Middle Academy, as they are called, but devoted himself mainly to the Old. He was therefore always an admirer of Antiochus of Ascalon, whose brother Ariston he had made his close friend and companion. This was a man less gifted in learning than many philosophers, but one who in stability of character and sweetness of disposition was equal to the best. As for Empylus, who is often mentioned by Brutus and his friends in their letters as one of his guests, he was a rhetorician, who has left a short but well-written narrative of Caesar's assassination entitled *Brutus*.

In Latin Brutus was well trained both as an orator and as a pleader, but when he expressed himself in Greek, he practised the brevity of the apophthegm or epigrammatic maxim and the so-called Laconic style of address, and he gives some striking examples of these in his

* The Old Academy was founded by Plato. The Middle was founded by Arcesilaus in the middle of the 3rd century B.C. The most eminent names of the New Academy are those of Clitomachus and Carneades, who flourished in the 2nd century B.C. (see *Life of Cato*, chs. 22–3).

letters. For instance, when he had taken the field against Antony and Octavius, he wrote to the people of Pergamum: 'I hear that you have given money to Dolabella. If you did this willingly, you must confess that you have wronged me: but if you gave unwillingly to him, you can prove it by giving willingly to me.' On another occasion he wrote to the Samians: 'Your counsels are non-committal. Your contributions are non-existent. What do you think will be the end of this?' And in another letter: 'The Xanthians,* through their madness in rejecting my kindnesses, have made their country into their grave. The Patareans, by trusting in me, enjoy complete freedom to manage their own affairs. You have the opportunity to choose the judgement of the Patareans or the fate of the Xanthians.' This is the style which makes his letters memorable.

3. While he was still a young man,† he accompanied his uncle Cato to Cyprus on the expedition against Ptolemy. After Ptolemy had committed suicide, Cato, who was detained by business in Rhodes, sent one of his friends named Canidius to take charge of the king's treasure; but, since he did not trust Canidius's honesty, he wrote to his nephew ordering him to sail immediately for Cyprus from Pamphylia, where Brutus was recovering from a severe illness. Brutus set out with a good deal of reluctance, partly out of regard for Canidius, who he felt had been ignominiously superseded, and partly because he considered on principle that a task which demanded such minute attention to business was a mean occupation and distinctly unworthy of a young man such as himself, who was devoted to the things of the mind. However, he exerted himself so effectively that he was highly praised by Cato, and, after he had seen the king's property converted into money, he had the bulk of the treasure shipped with him and brought it to Rome.

4. When the Roman state split into two factions with Pompey and Caesar taking up arms against one another, and the whole empire was thrown into confusion, it was generally expected that Brutus would choose Caesar's side, especially as his father had been put to

* See chs. 31–2.

† In 57 B.C. when Brutus was twenty-eight. This Ptolemy, the brother of Ptolemy Auletes, Cleopatra's father, was at that time king of Cyprus.

death at Pompey's orders some years before.* But Brutus believed that he ought to put the public good before his private loyalties, and as he was convinced that Pompey had the better reasons for going to war, he attached himself to his party. He did this in spite of the fact that only a little while before he had refused to exchange a word with Pompey when he met him, since he thought it outrageous to be on speaking terms with the murderer of his father. But in the present situation he regarded Pompey as the leader of his country, and so put himself under his orders and sailed for Cilicia as legate to Sestius, who had been appointed the governor of this province. However, since he found no opportunity to distinguish himself there, and since Pompey and Caesar were now taking up their positions for the battle which was to decide the fate of the empire, he travelled of his own accord to Macedonia, to share the dangers of the cause he believed in. It is said that Pompey was so surprised and delighted at his arrival that he rose from his seat as Brutus approached, and in front of all his officers embraced him as though Brutus were his superior. During this campaign, whenever he was not in Pompey's company, he devoted himself to his books and his philosophical studies, not only in the weeks which led up to Pharsalus but on the very eve of the great battle.† It was then the height of summer, and the heat was overpowering, especially as Pompey's army was encamped near a marsh, and the soldiers who carried Brutus's tent were slow in arriving. He was exhausted by the lack of shade, but although it was almost noon before he had anointed himself and taken a little food, he spent the time until the evening – when his companions were either sleeping or brooding anxiously about the future – in writing out a summary of Polybius.

5. It is also said that Julius Caesar was so much concerned for his safety as to issue orders to his commanders that Brutus must on no account be killed in the fighting, but his life must be spared. If he gave himself up, he was to be taken prisoner, but if he resisted capture, they were not to offer him violence but let him go. All this, it is believed, he did for the sake of Brutus's mother. It seems that in

* In 77 B.C. Brutus's father was a supporter of Marius, and Pompey treacherously had him put to death after accepting his surrender (See *Life of Pompey*, ch. 16).

† August 48 B.C.

Caesar's youth he had had an affair with Servilia, who was madly in love with him, and as Brutus had been born at about the time when her passion was at its height, he had always cherished a suspicion that Brutus was his own son.* The story goes that when the great conspiracy of Catiline, which had come near to overturning the state, had been referred for judgement to the Senate, Cato and Caesar, who were opposing one another in the debate, were standing side by side. Just then a note was brought in and handed to Caesar, which he read over without divulging the contents. At this Cato shouted out that Caesar was acting outrageously in receiving communications from the enemies of the state. This created an uproar, whereupon Caesar handed the note just as it was to Cato, who read it only to discover that it was a love letter from his sister Servilia. 'Keep it, you sot!' were Cato's words, after which he threw the letter back to Caesar and returned to the debate. So notorious was Servilia's passion for Caesar.

6. After his defeat at Pharsalus, Pompey contrived to make his own escape by sea, but his camp was besieged. Meanwhile Brutus slipped out by a gate into the nearby swamp, which was waterlogged and covered with reeds, and after travelling through the night he arrived safely in Larissa. From there he wrote to Caesar, who was delighted to hear that he was alive, and invited Brutus to join him. Later Caesar not only pardoned him, but treated him as one of the most honoured members of his circle. At this moment nobody could give any account of the direction in which Pompey had fled, and since there were so many conflicting opinions, Caesar took a walk alone with Brutus and sounded him on the subject. Some of the arguments which he put forward convinced Caesar that Brutus's ideas concerning Pompey's movements came nearest to the truth, and so he put aside all other considerations and hurried towards Egypt. But before he could arrive, Pompey had landed in Egypt, as Brutus had guessed, and there met his fate.

Meanwhile Brutus even succeeded in allaying Caesar's anger against his friend Cassius. He also undertook the defence of the king of the

* The persistence of this legend is curious in view of the fact that Caesar was barely fifteen when Brutus was born. But he may well have been engaged in a love affair with Servilia at the time of the conspiracy of Catiline, which was twenty-two years later.

Libyans,* and although the weight of the charges against his client was more than he could overcome, still his appeals for clemency were so convincing that he saved a great part of his kingdom for him. It is said that when Caesar first heard Brutus speaking in public he remarked to his friends: 'I do not know what this young man wants, but everything that he wants, he wants very badly.' For the earnestness of his character and the fact that he could not easily be persuaded to lend an ear to mere appeals for favour, but acted only upon due reflection and a deliberate moral choice, made his efforts powerful and effective in whatever cause he undertook. No amount of flattery could induce him to grant an unjust petition, and he considered that to give way to shameless importunity, which some people regard as a kind of good-nature, is a most disgraceful weakness in a great man; indeed he used to say that in his opinion those who could refuse nothing must have been corrupted in their youth.

When Caesar was about to set out for his campaign against Cato and Scipio in Africa, he chose Brutus to be governor of Cisalpine Gaul, an appointment which proved to be a great stroke of good fortune for the province. While the peoples of the other provinces were plundered and treated with as much arrogance and greed by their governors as if they had been conquered in war, Brutus brought such relief to the Gauls that they felt consoled not only for their present but even for their earlier misfortunes. And not satisfied with this, he also made the people understand how much they owed to Caesar, so that when, after his return from Africa, the dictator made a tour of Italy, he was as delighted by the contentment of the cities as he was by the company of Brutus himself, who neglected nothing that could enhance his prestige, and treated him as a close friend.

7. At this time there were a number of praetorships vacant, and it was expected that the one which carried the greatest dignity, that is the praetorship of the capital, would be conferred upon Brutus or Cassius. According to some accounts this circumstance created still more disharmony between the two men, who had already found other causes for dispute, in spite of the fact that they were closely related, for Cassius had married Junia, one of Brutus's sisters. There

* This allusion seems to be either a textual corruption or an error of Plutarch's. In 47 B.C. Brutus pleaded unsuccessfully the case of Deiotarus, king of the Galatians.

are others, however, who say that this rivalry had been brought about by Caesar, who had secretly led on each man by hinting at his support, until with this measure of encouragement they found themselves in competition with one another. Brutus had little more than his honourable reputation and his record for upright dealings to set against Cassius's many brilliant exploits during Crassus's campaign against the Parthians. However, when Caesar had listened to each man's claims and was discussing the affair with his friends, he summed it up by saying: 'Cassius has the stronger case, but we must give Brutus the first praetorship.' Cassius was appointed to another praetorship, but he was more resentful about the post he had lost than grateful for the one he received. There were other ways too in which Brutus shared as much of Caesar's power as he wished. Indeed, had he chosen to do so, he might easily have become the most influential of all Caesar's friends and exercised the greatest authority, but his association with Cassius led him away from such a course. After their contest for office he was not yet personally reconciled towards Cassius; however, he listened to his friends who were constantly warning him that he must not allow himself to be charmed or won over by Caesar, but must make a point of refusing the dictator's favours, since these were designed not to reward his virtue, but to emasculate his proud spirit and weaken his strength of purpose.

8. On the other hand, Caesar was not without his suspicions of Brutus, and indeed there was no lack of informers against him, but while he feared the younger man's lofty spirit, his reputation, and his friends, he still had great faith in his character. When he was told that Mark Antony and Dolabella were plotting a revolution, he remarked, 'It is not these sleek, long-haired fellows who frighten me, but the pale, thin ones,' by whom he meant Brutus and Cassius. And again when various people were making accusations against Brutus and urging Caesar to be on his guard against him, he raised his hand to touch his body and asked, 'What? Do you imagine that Brutus cannot wait for this poor flesh to end its days?', so much as to say that no one but Brutus was fitted to succeed to such great power.

At any rate there seems to be little doubt that Brutus could easily have become the first man in Rome, if he had had the patience to serve for a time as Caesar's deputy and wait for his power to pass its zenith and the glory of his achievements to fade. But it was Cassius with his violent temper and his hatred of Caesar – which had its roots in personal animosity rather than in any disinterested aversion to tyranny – who inflamed Brutus's feelings and urged him on. Brutus, it is said, was opposed to the dictatorship, but Cassius hated the dictator, and among other grievances which he brought up against him was the matter of the removal of the lions, which Cassius had procured when he was about to take office as aedile. These animals had been left at Megara, and when the city was captured by Calenus,* Caesar appropriated them for himself. They are said to have brought disaster to Megara, because when the city was on the point of being captured, the Megarians broke open the cages and unchained them, hoping that they would attack the enemy as they entered the city. But, instead of this, the lions turned against the unarmed Megarians and tore them to pieces as they ran to and fro in terror, so that even their enemies were overcome with pity at the sight.

9. Some people have made out that Cassius's resentment at this affair was his principal motive in organizing the conspiracy, but to say this is a travesty of the facts. From his very earliest days Cassius was inspired by a peculiar bitterness and animosity towards the whole race of those who seek to dominate their fellows, and he revealed this even as a boy, when he went to the same school as Faustus, the son of Sulla. When Faustus began to throw his weight about among the other boys and boast of his father's absolute power, Cassius jumped up and gave him a thrashing. Faustus's guardians and relatives wanted to take the matter to court, but Pompey refused to allow this, brought the two boys together, and questioned them as to what had happened. Thereupon Cassius said, so the story goes, 'Come on then, Faustus, you can tell Pompey, if you dare, what you said that made me so angry, and I will knock your teeth in again.'

Such was Cassius's character. But in Brutus's case, it was not merely the arguments of his personal friends, but a whole succession of hints, appeals, and anonymous letters which urged him on. For example, an inscription appeared on the statue of his ancestor, that Junius Brutus who had overthrown the rule of the kings, which read, 'O that we had you now, Brutus', and 'Would that Brutus were alive'. And the tribunal upon which he sat as praetor began to be covered day after

* One of Caesar's officers who was engaged in pacifying southern Greece, while Caesar was campaigning against Pompey in 48 B.C.

day with writings which read, 'Brutus, are you asleep?' or 'You are no true Brutus'. Many of these outbursts of popular feeling were brought about by the actions of Caesar's flatterers, who, among the other invidious honours which they devised for him, went so far as to have crowns placed on his statues by night, in the hope that the people might be persuaded to salute him as king instead of dictator. But their efforts produced exactly the opposite effect to what was intended, as I have described in detail in my *Life of Caesar.**

10. Now when Cassius sounded out his friends about forming a conspiracy against Caesar, they all agreed to join him on condition that Brutus became their leader. Mere numbers, or daring, or a resolute spirit, they were convinced, were not enough. What the enterprise needed most of all was the reputation of a man such as Brutus, whose presence would, as it were, consecrate the victim and ensure the justice of the sacrifice by the mere fact of his participation. Without him they would act with less conviction in carrying out the murder, and would attract more suspicion afterwards, since men would say that if their cause had been just, then Brutus would not have refused to support it. Cassius saw the truth of these arguments, and accordingly paid Brutus his first visit since the quarrel which I have already described. Then, as soon as they had made up their differences and exchanged friendly greetings, he asked Brutus whether he had decided to attend the meeting of the Senate which was due to be held on the Kalends of March, for he had heard that Caesar's friends intended on that day to introduce a motion to have him declared a king. When Brutus answered that he would not go, Cassius went on, 'Then what if they send for us?' 'In that case,' Brutus answered, 'it would be my duty not to remain silent, but to defend my country and to die for its liberty.' Cassius was encouraged by this answer and asked him: 'But do you think there is a single Roman who will allow you to sacrifice your life like this? Do you know nothing about yourself, Brutus? Do you think that all these appeals that have been scrawled over your tribunal were put there by weavers or shopkeepers, and not by the foremost men in Rome? They look to the other praetors for public doles and spectacles and gladiatorial shows, but they look to you to deliver them from tyranny. They count on this as a debt which you owe to your an-

* *Life of Caesar*, ch. 61.

cestry, and they are ready to suffer anything for your sake if you show yourself the man they believe and expect you to be.' He ended by throwing his arms around Brutus and embracing him, and after they had been reconciled in this way, each of them returned to their friends.

11. There was a man named Gaius Ligarius, who had been denounced as one of Pompey's supporters but had later been pardoned by Caesar. Ligarius, so far from feeling any gratitude for this act of clemency, was full of resentment at the power which had put his life in danger: he hated Caesar and was one of Brutus's closest friends. Brutus found him sick one day when he came to visit him, and remarked, 'Oh Ligarius, what a time this is to take to your bed.' Ligarius immediately raised himself on to his elbow, grasped Brutus's hand, and declared, 'No, Brutus, if you need me for any cause that is worthy of yourself, I am well enough.'

12. After this they secretly sounded the attitude of a number of other prominent Romans in whom they had confidence. They did not confine themselves to their own circle of friends, but approached all the men whom they knew to be adventurous and brave and to have no fear of death. For this reason they did not take Cicero into their confidence, even though they trusted him and knew that he was well disposed towards them. They were afraid that his natural timidity, combined with the caution that time and old age had laid upon him, and his insistence on eliminating the smallest element of risk from any plan, would blunt the edge of their resolution at a moment when speed might be essential. Among his other friends Brutus also passed over Statilius the Epicurean, and Favonius, who was an admirer of Cato. The reason for this was that he had tested their attitude a little while before by the roundabout method of a philosophical discussion. Favonius had replied that a civil war was a greater evil than an illegal monarchy, while Statilius declared that a man of sense and judgement ought not to plunge himself into mental turmoil or physical danger for the sake of insignificant and unthinking people. However Labeo, who was also present, opposed both these points of view. For his part Brutus kept quiet while this argument was in progress, on the ground that this was a complicated question and difficult to decide, but later on he confided his plans to Labeo, who was enthusiastic and agreed to join him. After this it was also decided to invite another

Brutus, surnamed Albinus. This man had no great reputation for enterprise or even physical courage, but he was important to the conspirators because of the number of gladiators whom he was training at this time for a public spectacle, and he also commanded Caesar's confidence. When he was sounded by Cassius and Labeo, he declined to give an immediate answer, but later he had a private interview with Brutus, and as soon as he discovered that he was the leader of the conspiracy, he readily agreed to join. Most of the remainder, and certainly those of most consequence, were likewise attracted by Brutus's reputation. And although they took no oath nor exchanged any sacred pledges to guarantee their loyalty, they succeeded so well in keeping the secret among themselves that in spite of the various divine warnings which appeared in the form of prophecies, prodigies, and sacrificial omens, no one would believe in the existence of the conspiracy.

13. Brutus had now reached a point at which the safety of many of the leading citizens of Rome – the men most prominent for their ancestry, their prestige, and their personal qualities – depended upon his conduct. And since he was well aware of the danger which this involved, he strove at any rate in public to keep his plans strictly to himself and his thoughts under control, but at home and especially at night he was no longer the same man. Sometimes his misgivings would make him start up involuntarily out of his sleep, and at other moments, when he was more than ever immersed in calculations and brooding over his difficulties, it became clear to his wife, as she lay by his side, that he was weighed down by some unusual anxiety and was turning over in his mind some difficult and intricate plan.

Porcia, as I have mentioned above,* was one of Cato's daughters. She had married Brutus, who was her cousin, when she was still very young, although she was by then already a widow, and had by her first husband a little son, whose name was Bibulus.† He later wrote a small book entitled *Memoirs of Brutus*, which is still extant. Porcia, who loved her husband deeply and was not only of an affectionate nature but full of spirit and good sense, did not press her husband to reveal his secrets until she had put herself to a test. She dismissed her

woman

* Ch. 2.

† Her first husband was Marcus Calpurnius Bibulus, who was consul with Caesar in 59 B.C.

attendants from her room, and then taking a little knife such as barbers use to cut finger-nails, she gave herself a deep gash in the thigh. She lost a great quantity of blood, after which the wound became intensely painful and brought on fits of shivering and a high fever. When she was in great pain and saw that Brutus was deeply distressed for her, she said to him: 'Brutus, I am Cato's daughter, and I was given to you in marriage not just to share your bed and board like a concubine, but to be a true partner in your joys and sorrows. I have no reproach to make to you, but what proof can I give you of my love, if you forbid me to share the kind of trouble that demands a loyal friend to confide in, and keep your suffering to yourself? I know that men think women's natures too weak to be entrusted with secrets, but surely a good upbringing and the company of honourable men can do much to strengthen us, and at least Porcia can claim that she is the daughter of Cato and the wife of Brutus. I did not know before this how either of these blessings could help me, but now I have put myself to the test and find that I can conquer pain.' At this she showed him her wound and explained what she had done. Brutus was amazed and lifting up his hands to heaven he prayed to the gods to help him to succeed in his enterprise and show that he was a worthy husband of such a wife. Then he did all that he could to bring back his wife to health.

14. A meeting of the Senate was now announced which it was expected Caesar would attend, and the conspirators agreed to seize this opportunity for their attempt. The occasion would enable them to muster their full strength without attracting suspicion; what was more, they would have all the men of the highest rank and character in the republic assembled in one place, and these, they hoped, once the great deed was accomplished, would immediately embrace the cause of liberty. Besides, the very place of the meeting seemed to have been chosen by providence so as to favour their purpose, for the session was to be held in one of the porticoes adjoining the theatre and containing a hall furnished with a number of benches in which stood a statue of Pompey. This had been erected at the public expense in Pompey's honour, when he had adorned that quarter of the city with the porticoes and the theatre.* Here the Senate was summoned

* This large and handsome building, the first permanent theatre that Rome possessed, had been completed in 55 B.C. It was situated in the Campus Martius, the north-west quarter of the city.

for its meeting in the middle of March – the Romans call the day the Ides of March – and it seemed that some divine power was drawing Caesar to the place to meet his punishment for the death of Pompey.

When the day arrived, Brutus put on a dagger, unknown to anybody except his wife, and went out. The rest of the conspirators met at Cassius's house and accompanied his son to the Forum, for the boy was due on that day to put on his manly gown or *toga virilis*, as the Romans call it. From there they all hurried to Pompey's portico, where they waited, expecting that Caesar would arrive immediately for the meeting of the Senate. It was at this moment, above all, that anybody who knew what was about to happen would have been amazed at the unshakeable calm and presence of mind which these men displayed as the moment of crisis drew near. Many of them were praetors who were obliged by virtue of their office to transact business, and they not only listened impassively to every application or dispute which was laid before them, as if they had no other preoccupation in the world, but they took infinite pains to pronounce an exact and considered judgement upon every case. And when one of the litigants refused to accept Brutus's verdict, and began to protest loudly and to appeal to Caesar, Brutus looked round calmly at the bystanders and declared, 'Caesar does not prevent me from acting in accordance with the laws, nor will he do so at any future time.'

15. At the same time there were many surprising and unforeseen happenings to upset their composure. First of all, although it was growing late, Caesar had still failed to arrive. The sacrificial victims had been pronounced unfavourable, so that he was kept at home by his wife and forbidden to go out by the soothsayers. Next, a man walked up to Casca, one of the conspirators, took him by the hand, and remarked: 'You kept this a secret from us, Casca, but Brutus has told me everything.' As Casca stood there speechless, the other smiled and said, 'You must tell me, my dear fellow, how you made a fortune so quickly that you can stand for the aedileship.' Another moment, and because of the ambiguity of the man's words, Casca would have let out the secret of the conspiracy. About the same time Brutus and Cassius were greeted more effusively than usual by one of the senators, Popilius Laenas, who whispered to them, 'My prayers are with you. May your plan succeed, but whatever you do, make haste. Everyone is talking about it by now.' With these words

he walked away, leaving them full of suspicion that the plot had been discovered.

At this moment too a messenger came running from Brutus's house with the news that his wife was dying. Porcia had been almost beside herself at the thought of the murder. She found herself overwhelmed by the weight of her anxiety and could hardly bear to sit indoors. Every distant noise or cry would make her start up suddenly like a woman possessed with the Bacchic frenzy, and she would rush outside to ask every passer-by from the Forum what was happening to Brutus, and meanwhile she sent messenger after messenger to learn the news. As the day dragged on her strength sank lower and lower, and at last, as her tormenting doubts and fears multiplied, it deserted her utterly. There was no time for her to reach her room before suddenly, sitting as she was among her servants, she was seized by an overpowering faintness and stupor, her colour vanished, and she could not utter a word. Her maids shrieked aloud at the sight, her neighbours came running in a crowd to the door, and the rumour soon spread far and wide that she was dead. However, under the care of her women she revived after a little, and her senses returned. Brutus was deeply affected by the sudden news, as was natural enough, but he did not forget his duty, nor did he allow his anxiety to make his mind dwell on his private concerns.

16. And now the news arrived that Caesar was on his way, carried in a litter. He had been discouraged by the unfavourable omens, and had decided not to settle any important business on that day, but to postpone it on the pretext of being indisposed. As he stepped down from his litter, Popilius Laenas hurried up to him – the very man who not long before had wished Brutus success with his plans – and spoke for a few moments while Caesar stood and listened to him. The conspirators, as I shall now call them, could not hear what he was saying, but their suspicions naturally made them conclude that the object of Laenas's conversation was to warn Caesar of the plot. Their spirits sank, and in the glances that passed between them they silently agreed that they should not wait to be arrested, but should die by their own hands. Cassius and some of the others were already clutching the hilts of their daggers beneath their robes and were on the point of drawing them, when Brutus noticed that Laenas's whole manner made it obvious that he was urging a petition, not making an

accusation. Brutus did not utter a word, because he was surrounded by strangers who knew nothing of the plot, but he succeeded by the cheerfulness of his expression in reassuring Cassius and his friends. Then after a little while Laenas kissed Caesar's hand and took his leave, and it was clear that his interview with Caesar had been concerned with some personal matter which affected nobody but himself.

17. After the senators had entered the debating chamber ahead of Caesar, the rest of the conspirators grouped themselves around Caesar's chair, as if they were about to present a petition to him, while Cassius is said to have turned towards Pompey's statue and uttered a prayer to it, as though it could hear his words. At the same time Trebonius engaged Mark Antony in conversation by the door and kept him outside. When Caesar entered, the whole Senate rose in his honour, but as soon as he was seated the conspirators crowded around his chair, and brought forward Tullius Cimber to plead on behalf of his brother who had been banished. The others all supported this appeal and went on to clasp Caesar's hands and kiss his breast and his head. At first he simply refused their petition, but then when they would not let him go, he tried to rise and shake them off by force. Thereupon Tullius wrenched Caesar's robe off his shoulders with both hands, while Casca, who was standing behind him, drew his dagger and gave him the first stab, wounding him slightly near the shoulder. Caesar grasped the handle of his dagger and shouted loudly in Latin, 'Casca, you villain, what are you doing?' while Casca, speaking in Greek, called out to his brother to help him. By this time Caesar found himself being attacked from every side, and as he glanced around to see if he could force a way through his attackers, he saw Brutus closing in upon him with his dagger drawn. At this he let go of Casca's hand which he had seized, muffled up his head in his robe, and yielded up his body to his murderers' blows. Then the conspirators flung themselves upon him with such a frenzy of violence, as they hacked away with their daggers, that they even wounded one another. Brutus received a stab in the hand as he tried to play his part in the slaughter, and every one of them was drenched in blood.

18. At last, when Caesar had been done to death, Brutus stepped into the midst of the debating chamber and did his best to reassure the

senators and persuade them to stay. But they took to their heels in confusion and crowded panic-stricken through the doors, although nobody made any move to pursue them. For it had been firmly decided that one man and one only was to be killed, and the rest of the people were to be invited to take up their liberty. When they had discussed the execution of their plan, all the other conspirators had thought it necessary to kill Mark Antony as well as Caesar. They regarded him as a man who despised the law, favoured autocratic rule, and had acquired great power through his ability to mix familiarly with his soldiers and command their loyalty; and, lastly, his natural arrogance and ambition had become more dangerous than ever, because he had been raised to the dignity of the consulate and was at that time a colleague of Caesar. Brutus, however, opposed this idea. He insisted in the first place that they should act only with strict justice, and he also held out the hope that Antony might undergo a change of heart. He still cherished the idea that once Caesar was out of the way, Antony's generous nature, ambition, and love of glory would respond to the noble example set by the conspirators, and that he would join them in helping their country to achieve her liberty. In this way Brutus actually saved Antony's life, but in the general alarm which followed the murder, Antony put off his senator's toga, disguised himself in plebeian dress, and made his escape.

Brutus and his companions then went up to the Capitol, and with their hands smeared with blood and brandishing their naked daggers, they called upon the citizens to assert their liberty. At first they were greeted only by cries of fear, and the general confusion was increased by people wildly running to and fro in the terror which followed the news of the assassination. But since there was no more bloodshed and no looting of property, the senators and many of the people took courage and went up to the conspirators in the Capitol. When a large crowd had assembled, Brutus made a speech which was calculated to suit the occasion and please the people. His audience applauded him loudly and called upon him to come down from the Capitol, and the conspirators, their confidence returning, now made their way to the Forum. The rest of them walked together, but Brutus found himself surrounded by many of the most distinguished men in Rome, who escorted him in their midst with great honour from the Capitol, and conducted him to the rostra. The crowd which faced him was an audience of mixed sympathies and had come prepared to raise a riot, but at the sight of Brutus it was overcome with awe and awaited his words in orderly silence. When he came forward to speak, they listened intently to what he said, but the moment that Cinna took his place, and began to denounce Caesar, it became clear that many of his listeners were far from pleased with what had been done. The crowd's anger began to rise, and they abused Cinna so violently that the conspirators were obliged to take refuge again in the Capitol. Thereupon Brutus sent away the most distinguished of the citizens who had accompanied him, as he was afraid that they might be besieged there, and he did not think it right that they should run such a risk, considering that they had no share in the deed.

19. On the following day, however, the Senate held a meeting in the temple of the goddess Tellus, and Antony, Plancus, and Cicero spoke in favour of a general reconciliation and of passing a decree of amnesty.* A motion was then approved according to which not only was no action to be taken against the conspirators, but the consuls were to propose a measure conferring honours upon them, and after passing these decrees the Senate adjourned. Then, after Antony had sent his son to the Capitol as a hostage, Brutus and his companions again came down, and both parties exchanged greetings and salutations without reserve. Antony invited Cassius to his house, Lepidus received Brutus, and the rest were similarly entertained by their various friends or associates. At daybreak the senators met again, and their first action was to pass a vote of thanks to Antony for having averted the outbreak of a civil war: next they commended the action of Brutus and his friends who were present, and after this they proceeded to the distribution of the provinces. Crete was allotted to Brutus, Africa to Cassius, Asia to Trebonius, Bithynia to Cimber, and Cisalpine Gaul to Brutus Albinus.

20. Finally, the question of Caesar's will and of the arrangements for his funeral were debated. Antony and his supporters demanded that the will should be read in public, and that Caesar's body should not

* This was a compromise. The Senate, which was now the supreme constitutional authority, might have been expected to pronounce the murder of the chief magistrate to be an act of treason. It did not, but at this meeting it ratified all Caesar's edicts, as the presence of so many of his veteran soldiers in Rome virtually forced it to do.

be buried in private but with the customary honours, otherwise the people's indignation might break out again. Cassius opposed these demands with all his might, but Brutus gave way and agreed to them, and here again his judgement seems to have been seriously at fault. In the first place, by sparing Antony's life he had laid himself open to the charge of raising up a most bitter and formidable enemy against the conspirators, and now, by allowing Caesar's funeral to be conducted in the way that Antony proposed, he committed a fatal blunder. The first consequence of this was that, when it became known that according to the terms of his will the dictator had presented to every Roman citizen seventy-five drachmas, and had bequeathed them the use of his gardens beyond the Tiber where the temple of Fortune now stands, a great wave of affection for Caesar and a powerful sense of his loss swept over the people; and the second was that, after the dead man had been brought to the Forum, Antony delivered the customary funeral oration over his body. As soon as he saw that the people were deeply stirred by his speech, he changed his tone and struck a note of compassion, and picking up Caesar's robe, stiff with blood as it was, he unfolded it for all to see, pointing out each gash where the daggers had stabbed through and the number of Caesar's wounds. At this his audience lost all control of their emotions. Some shouted aloud to kill the murderers, others, as had happened in the riot in which Clodius the demagogue had lost his life,* dragged out benches and tables from the neighbouring shops and piled them on top of one another to make an enormous pyre. On this they laid Caesar's corpse and set fire to it, and indeed the spot was perfectly chosen for a funeral pyre, since it was surrounded by many temples, sanctuaries, and holy places. Then, as the flames began to mount, people rushed up from all sides, seized burning brands, and ran through the city to the murderers' houses to set them alight.

The conspirators had already barricaded themselves in and were able to fend off the danger, but there was a man named Cinna, a poet, who had had no connexion with the crime, and was actually a friend of Caesar's. He dreamed that he had been invited by Caesar to supper and had declined, but that Caesar had pressed him to come, and had finally taken him by the hand and led him to a vast and gloomy place, into which he had followed his host reluctantly and

* Clodius had been killed in a street fight with Milo, a rival demagogue, in 52 B.C.

with a feeling of horror. After the vision had left him, he found himself attacked by a fever which lasted all night. However, when morning came and Caesar's body was being carried out to his funeral, he felt ashamed not to be present and went out to join the crowd, who were by now in a savage mood. There he was seen, and since the crowd did not know who he was, but mistook him for the Cinna who had recently denounced Caesar in his speech, they tore him to pieces.

21. This episode more than anything else, except perhaps Antony's change of attitude, so alarmed Brutus and his party that they left the city. At first they waited for some time at Antium, in the hope of returning to Rome as soon as the people's fury had subsided. They expected this to happen as a matter of course, since city mobs are notoriously fickle and unstable in their impulses, and they knew that the Senate was well disposed towards them: for although it had allowed the men who had lynched Cinna to go free, it had made inquiries and arrested those who had attacked the conspirators' houses. By this time too, the people were becoming discontented with Antony, who was establishing himself in a position which was hardly to be distinguished from a dictatorship: they longed for Brutus's return and it was expected that he would appear in person to supervise the public games,* which it was his duty as praetor to provide. Brutus then discovered that many of Caesar's veterans, who had been settled on the land and in the cities by their commander, were plotting to assassinate him and were making their way into Rome in small groups, and so he was afraid to come back. However, the public games were given in spite of his absence and were presented with great expense and magnificence. Brutus had previously purchased large numbers of wild beasts, and he now gave orders that all of these should be used and none sold or left behind. He also travelled to Naples where he engaged many players and singers, and he wrote to his friends about Canutius, an actor who was especially popular at that time, and asked them to persuade him to visit Rome, as he did not approve of any Greek being compelled to go there.

* These were the *Ludi Apollinares*, held in July, which it was Brutus's task as *praetor urbanus* to supervise. Mark Antony's brother Lucius did so in his place.

Besides this he wrote to Cicero and asked him on no account to fail to attend these games.

22. This was the situation at Rome when the appearance of the young Octavius Caesar gave a completely new turn to events. He was the son of Caesar's niece, but the dictator's will revealed that Caesar had formally adopted him and made him his son and heir. At the moment when Caesar was murdered, Octavius had been pursuing his studies at Apollonia on the Illyrian coast, where he intended to join the expedition which Caesar had planned to lead almost immediately against the Parthians. As soon as he had learned of Caesar's fate, he came to Rome, and his first move to win the people's support was to assume Caesar's name, and to distribute to the entire citizen body the money which had been left them in Caesar's will. In this way he not only ousted Antony from the people's favour, but he also succeeded by a lavish use of these funds in rallying many of Caesar's veterans to his side. Cicero was also persuaded by his hatred of Antony to attach himself to Octavius's party, and for this he was indignantly reproached by Brutus. He noticed, he wrote, that Cicero did not really object to a tyrant, but was only afraid of a tyrant who hated him, and that when he declared in his letters and speeches what a good man Octavius was, his policy was really to recommend a painless form of slavery. 'But our forefathers,' he reminded Cicero, 'would not tolerate even easygoing tyrants.' As for himself, his mind was not yet fully made up whether to choose war or peace, but on one thing he was utterly resolved, that he would never be a slave. It astonished him, he went on, that Cicero should be so afraid of a civil war with all its dangers, but not of a dishonourable and ignominious peace, and that as a reward for getting rid of the tyranny of Antony he should ask for the privilege of setting Octavius up in his place.

23. This was the gist of Brutus's first letters to Cicero. But already by this time the Roman state was beginning to divide into two factions, the one supporting Octavius and the other Antony, and the soldiers, as though they were part of an auction, sold their allegiance to the highest bidder. In this situation Brutus despaired of events turning out as he had once hoped. He therefore resolved to abandon Italy and

travelled overland through Lucania to the seaport of Velia.* His wife Porcia was obliged to return from there to Rome. She tried to conceal her distress at parting from Brutus, but the sight of a painting broke down her noble resolve. The subject was drawn from Greek legend – the parting of Hector and Andromache – and the picture showed her taking from his arms their little son, while her gaze was fixed upon her husband. As Porcia looked at it, the image of her own sorrow which it conjured up made her burst into tears, and she went to see the picture time after time each day, and wept before it. On this occasion Acilius, one of Brutus's friends, quoted the verses from Homer which Andromache speaks to Hector:†

> Hector, to me you are all: you have cared for me as a father,
> Mother and brother and loving husband . . .

Brutus smiled at him and said, 'But I shall not give Porcia the answer that Hector gave,'‡

> Work at your loom and your distaff, and give your commands to your servants.

'She may not have the strength for the exploits that are expected of a man, but she has the spirit to fight as nobly for her country as any of us.' We have this story from Porcia's son, Bibulus.

24. After leaving Velia Brutus sailed to Athens, where he was received with great enthusiasm by the people and granted various public honours. He stayed in the city with a friend, attended the

* Brutus and Cassius finally left Italy in June, 44 B.C. But in this analysis of the political situation and its effect upon Brutus's state of mind Plutarch is running ahead of events. The conspirators left Italy not as political refugees, but with commands and commissions formally voted by the Senate. At this date the question of which type of régime would succeed the Caesarian remained in the balance, the allegiance of the armies in Italy and the provinces was still in doubt, and a long struggle lay ahead of Octavius before he could challenge Antony. The power of the Senate reached its height at the end of 44 B.C. with the election of two Republican consuls, Hirtius and Pansa. The turning-point came in the early summer of 43, when the two were killed at Mutina, and soon afterwards the army which Lepidus was bringing back from Spain went over to Antony, an event which completely altered the balance of power in Italy and led to the alliance of Octavius, Antony, and Lepidus (see *Life of Antony*, chs. 18–19).

† *Iliad* VI, 429–30. ‡ *Iliad* VI, 491.

lectures of Theomnestus of the Academy and Cratippus of the Peripatetic school, discussed philosophy with them, and appeared to be completely engrossed in literary pursuits. But all this while, without anybody suspecting it, he was making preparations for war. He planned to win over the commanders of the Roman armies in Macedonia, and for this purpose sent Herostratus there, and at the same time he rallied to his cause all the young Romans who were studying in Athens. One of these was Cicero's son, whom he praised in enthusiastic terms, saying that whether awake or dreaming he could not but admire a man who displayed such a noble spirit and such a detestation of tyranny. Later he began to act more openly, and when he found out that some Roman ships carrying money were sailing from Asia, and that their commander was an agreeable man and known to him by reputation, he went to meet him in Carystus, a city in Euboea. After conferring with him and persuading him to hand over the ships, Brutus arranged a splendid entertainment, for the occasion happened to be his birthday. Then, after they had begun drinking and proposed the toast of *Victory to Brutus*, and *Liberty for Rome*, Brutus, wishing to encourage the company still further, called for a larger bowl. As he held it in his hand, he recited, for no apparent reason, this verse from Homer, the last words of the dying Patroclus,*

> Fate turned against me first, then Apollo the son of Leto.

Some writers have added, in explanation of this, that when Brutus was going out to fight his last battle at Philippi the password which he chose for his troops was 'Apollo', and they conclude that the sudden impulse which led him to quote this line sprang from a foreboding of his defeat.

25. After this Antistius gave him half a million drachmas out of the money which he was carrying to Italy, and the remnants of Pompey's army, who were still roaming about Thessaly, gladly rallied to his standard. He also took from Cinna a force of five hundred cavalry, which Cinna was conducting to Dolabella in Asia. Next he sailed to Demetrias, a port in Thessaly, where he seized a large quantity of arms, which Julius Caesar had ordered to be collected for his Parthian campaign, and which were about to be delivered to Antony. Horten-

* *Iliad* XVI, 849. There is a pun on the name Apollo, which can also signify *destroyer*.

sius, the governor of Macedonia, now handed over the province to him, and the neighbouring kings and rulers declared their support and offered him assistance. Then news arrived that Gaius, Mark Antony's brother, had crossed from Italy and was on his way to join the troops commanded by Vatinius in Epidamnus and Apollonia.* Brutus decided to anticipate his arrival and capture his army before it could be reinforced. He therefore set out immediately with the troops he had ready and marched across difficult country, harassed by snowstorms and moving far ahead of his supply train. As he reached the neighbourhood of Epidamnus he began to suffer from the disease known as *boulimia*, which is brought on by cold and exhaustion. This is a malady which attacks both men and beasts, especially when they are fighting their way through the snow and are weakened by fatigue. It may be that the natural heat of the body, when it finds itself frozen in and thickened by the surrounding cold, quickly exhausts its nourishment, or else possibly that the sharp and subtle vapour which arises from the snow penetrates the body and annihilates the warmth as it emanates from the pores. For the body's sweat is evidently generated by this inward warmth, and a counter-action is set up by the cold which it meets as soon as it reaches the skin. However, I have discussed this subject at greater length elsewhere.

26. Brutus now found himself overcome by faintness. None of his soldiers had a morsel of food to give him, so that his attendants were obliged to appeal to their enemies, and, going up to the gates of the city, they asked the sentinels for some bread. When these men heard of Brutus's sickness, they came to him of their own accord and brought food and drink. In return, when Brutus captured the city later, he not only showed kindness to them, but to all the rest of the inhabitants for their sake.

When Gaius Antonius arrived at Apollonia, he ordered all the soldiers who were encamped near the city to join him. Instead they went over to Brutus, and at the same time it became clear to him that the people of Apollonia were also on Brutus's side, and he therefore left the city and advanced against Buthrotum.† First of all he lost three cohorts, which Brutus cut to pieces while his opponent was on the march, and later when he offered battle in the attempt to force the

* Ports in north-western Greece on the Adriatic coast.

† On the coast of the Greek mainland opposite Corfu.

lines surrounding Byllis, which his opponents had already occupied, he was defeated by the young Cicero, whom Brutus had entrusted with a command and who gained many successes for his general. However, when Brutus himself caught Gaius on marshy ground with his forces widely scattered, he would not allow his troops to attack. Instead he rode round his opponent's army and gave orders for their lives to be spared, as he was convinced that before long they would be fighting on his side. And this was exactly what happened: they surrendered both themselves and their general, so that Brutus found himself in command of a powerful force. He treated Gaius with full military honours for a long while and allowed him to keep his badges of rank, in spite of the fact, so we are told, that many people including Cicero wrote from Rome urging him to have Gaius executed. But when Gaius began to enter into secret negotiations with Brutus's officers and attempted to stir up a mutiny, Brutus had him transferred to a ship and kept him under close arrest. When the soldiers whom Gaius had seduced from their loyalty escaped to Apollonia and invited Brutus to visit them there, he answered them that this was not a Roman custom, but that they themselves must come to their commander and beg him to forgive their offence. This they did, and when they asked for pardon Brutus granted it.

27. As he was on the point of setting out for Asia, news reached him of the situation which had developed in Rome. For in the meanwhile* Octavius Caesar had secured the support of the Senate against Antony and driven his rival out of Italy. It was Octavius whom Brutus now had to fear most, since he was pressing to have himself appointed consul contrary to the law, and was maintaining large armies of which the state had no need. However, when he saw that even the senators were beginning to disapprove of these proceedings and to turn their eyes abroad towards Brutus, and had passed a decree confirming him in command of his provinces, Octavius became alarmed. He therefore sent messengers to Antony to propose a reconciliation. At the same time† he brought up his army to surround Rome and proceeded to force through his own appointment as consul, although he was a mere boy and still only in his twentieth year, as he himself has recorded in his *Commentaries*. One of his first actions was

* Early in 43 B.C.

† In the summer of 43 B.C.

to institute a prosecution for murder against Brutus and his fellow-conspirators on the charge of having put to death without a trial the first man in the state who was holding its highest offices, and he appointed Lucius Cornificius as the prosecutor of Brutus and Marcus Agrippa of Cassius. The accused were then condemned by default, the jurors being compelled to record their votes. It is said that, when the herald in the traditional fashion mounted the rostra and summoned Brutus to appear, the crowd uttered a deep groan and the patricians bowed their heads in silence. Publius Silicius was seen to burst into tears and for this reason his name was soon afterwards added to the list of the proscribed. A little later Octavius Caesar, Antony, and Lepidus became reconciled with one another, formed a triumvirate,* divided the provinces between them and drew up a list of proscribed persons, as a result of which two hundred men were to be put to death.† Among these was Cicero.

28. When the news of these events reached Macedonia, Brutus felt obliged to send orders to Hortensius that Gaius Antonius should be executed as a reprisal for the deaths of Cicero and Brutus Albinus, the one of whom was his close friend and the other his kinsman. This was the reason why, when Hortensius was captured at the battle of Philippi in the following year, Antony had him executed over the tomb of his brother. Brutus remarked that he felt more shame at the cause of Cicero's death than sorrow for the fact of it, and he blamed his friends in Rome for what had happened. He said it was not their oppressors but their own actions that had made slaves of them, and that they had allowed themselves to look on tamely at deeds which they should have considered it intolerable even to hear of.

Brutus now‡ crossed into Asia with his army, which was already an imposing force. He gave orders for a fleet to be fitted out in Bithynia and at the neighbouring port of Cyzicus, while he himself, travelling through the provinces by land, settled the affairs of the various cities and gave audiences to the local rulers. He also

* In October 43 B.C.

† This number refers merely to the senators sentenced to death. There were also some three thousand knights. The Senate varied considerably in size at different periods. Up to the beginning of the first century B.C. it was less than 200. Sulla increased it to some 500 and Julius Caesar to about 1,000. Augustus stabilized it at about 600.

‡ Late summer of 43 B.C.

sent messengers to Cassius in Syria to recall him from his intended expedition to Egypt. He reminded him that they were not roaming about the provinces to carve out an empire for themselves: their purpose was to gather an army with which they could overthrow the tyrants and restore liberty to their country. They should keep this purpose constantly before them, and so far from wandering a long way from Italy, they should hurry back and rescue their fellow-countrymen.

Cassius obeyed, and as he marched back Brutus went to meet him. When they were reunited at Smyrna this was the first time the two had seen each other since they had separated at Piraeus, the one on his way to Syria, the other to Macedonia, and so they could feel great pleasure and confidence at the forces which each of them now led. They had set out from Italy like the most despised of exiles, without money or arms, without so much as a single ship equipped with oars, a soldier to follow them, or a city to give them shelter, and now within a few months they were reunited with a fleet, money, and an army of horse and foot at their backs, and had become formidable contenders for the empire of Rome.

29. Cassius was anxious that Brutus and he should be treated with equal honours, but Brutus often forestalled his intentions by coming to visit him, since Cassius was an older man and could not endure the same degree of physical hardship. Cassius had the reputation of being a formidable soldier, but also a man of violent temper who maintained his authority chiefly through fear, although with his intimate friends he was rather too apt to descend to jesting or buffoonery. Brutus's virtues, on the other hand, made him popular with the rank and file, beloved by his friends, and admired by the nobility, while even his enemies found it impossible to hate him. He was a man of a singularly gentle nature and a lofty idealism, who stood unmoved by the temptations of anger, greed, or self-indulgence, but was upright and inflexible in defence of what he thought honourable and just, so that the reputation and affection which he earned were based above all on the confidence which men felt in his principles. In the case of Pompey the Great, for example, nobody had imagined that if he had conquered Caesar he would have disbanded his armies in obedience to the laws: it was generally assumed that he would retain the supreme power, but would pacify the people by adopting the style of consul

or dictator or some other more acceptable title of authority. Again, Cassius was known to be a man of violent and uncontrolled passions, whose craving for money had often tempted him to stray from the path of justice, and it therefore seemed natural that his motive for fighting, wandering about the empire, and risking his life was not to win liberty for his fellow-countrymen, but to secure some great place for himself. The leaders of the generation that preceded Pompey and Cassius, men such as Cinna and Marius and Carbo, had all treated their country as a prize of war, and had all but openly proclaimed that they fought to secure absolute power. But even Brutus's enemies never accused him of betraying his principles in this way, and indeed Antony was heard by many people to declare that Brutus was the only one of the conspirators who was moved by the splendour and what he believed to be the nobility of the deed, while all the rest plotted against Caesar because they envied and hated him. It is plain too from Brutus's letters that he put his trust in the virtue of his cause rather than in armed force. Just before the final crisis in his fortunes, he wrote to Atticus that his affairs stood in the best situation that fortune could devise, since he would either conquer and restore freedom to the Roman people, or die and be released from slavery, and that, while all other issues had been safely settled for him and his supporters, one thing alone remained uncertain, whether they would live and be free, or die. He added in the same letter that Mark Antony was paying a just penalty for his folly, since at the moment when he had the choice of taking his place in history beside such men as Brutus, Cassius, and Cato, he had preferred to make himself a mere appendage of Octavius, and he foretold that, if the two were not defeated together, they would soon be fighting one another. In this he seems to have been an excellent prophet.

30. While they were at Smyrna, Brutus asked Cassius to give him a part of the large sums of money which they had collected, since his own funds had been spent in building a fleet large enough to enable them to control the whole of the Mediterranean. But Cassius's friends opposed his giving anything to Brutus. Their argument was that it was unfair for the money which he had saved by his own frugality and at the cost of much ill feeling among his troops to be taken by Brutus and used to reward his own men and so increase his popularity with them. In spite of this Cassius handed over to him

a third of the whole sum. After this the two armies parted again to pursue their various operations. Cassius captured Rhodes, but he acted there with quite unnecessary severity, and this behaviour was certainly inconsistent with the reply which he gave to the citizens who had saluted him as their lord and king when he entered the city, for he told them, 'I am neither lord nor king, but I have punished and killed the man who would have been both.' Brutus, on the other hand, demanded money and troops from the people of Lycia.* Naucrates, the popular leader, responded by persuading the cities to revolt, and the inhabitants occupied certain heights which barred Brutus's line of march. Brutus first of all sent out a force of cavalry, who surprised the enemy as they were eating their morning meal and killed six hundred of them. Next he captured their strongholds and villages, but released all his prisoners without ransom in the hope of winning the people over by moderation. But the Lycians were obstinate and chose to nurse their resentment at their injuries and to despise Brutus's humanity and kindness, until he forced the most warlike of them to take refuge in the city of Xanthus, and then besieged it. The people tried to escape by swimming under the surface of the river which flowed past the city. But they were caught by nets which had been stretched across the channel and fastened to the bottom, while the tops had bells attached to them, which gave the alarm as soon as anyone became entangled. After this the Xanthians made a sortie at night and set fire to some of the siege-engines, but they were seen by the Romans and forced back to the walls. Then, when a strong wind began to blow the flames back towards the battlements and some of the adjoining houses caught fire, Brutus, who was afraid that the whole city would be destroyed, ordered his men to help put out the blaze.

31. However, the Lycians were suddenly seized with a terrible and indescribable mood of despair, which can best be defined as a passionate longing for death. Every inhabitant of the city, women and children, free men and slaves, people of every age and condition hurled missiles from the walls at the Romans, as they struggled to help the citizens to overcome the flames; and meanwhile the Xanthians with their own hands brought up reeds, wood, and every kind

* A province on the south coast of Asia Minor, in the neighbourhood of Rhodes.

of inflammable material and so spread the fire throughout the city, feeding it with all the fuel they could find and doing everything possible to increase the strength and fury of the conflagration. As the fire rushed onwards, encircled the city on every side, and wrapped it in a sheet of flame, Brutus in deep distress rode round the walls, and in his eagerness to help implored the Xanthians with outstretched hands to spare themselves and save their city. Not a soul listened to him, but men and women alike sought only for the means to destroy themselves, so that even the little children with cries and shrieks leaped into the flames or flung themselves headlong from the walls, or offered themselves up to their fathers' swords, baring their throats and begging them to strike. After the destruction of the city a woman was seen hanging in a noose. She had a dead child fastened to her neck and was holding a lighted torch to set fire to her house. The sight was so tragic that Brutus could not bear to look at it, and burst into tears when he heard of it; he also proclaimed that a reward would be given to any soldier who succeeded in saving a Lycian. All but one hundred and fifty, we are told, escaped the Romans' efforts to save them. So it came about, after a long lapse of time, that the Xanthians had the courage to repeat the disaster which their ancestors had suffered, as though they were fulfilling some predestined cycle of destruction: for the same people in the time of the Persian Empire had likewise burned down their city and destroyed themselves.*

32. Soon afterwards, when Brutus found that the city of Patara was offering a stout resistance to him, he hesitated to attack it and was at a loss what to do next, for fear that the people might be seized by the same frenzy as the Xanthians. But as his prisoners included some of the women of Patara, he set them free without demanding a ransom. These were the wives and daughters of the most prominent citizens, and they at once extolled Brutus's virtues and reported that he was a most just and moderate man, and finally persuaded their compatriots to surrender and hand over the city. As a result, all the rest of the inhabitants of Lycia followed their example, submitted themselves to his authority, and found that his kindness and humanity surpassed all their hopes. For while Cassius at about the same time compelled the Rhodians to surrender all the gold and silver which each of them

* Herodotus, I, 176, describes the destruction of Xanthus at the hands of the Persian general Harpagus.

possessed, thus collecting about eight hundred talents, and on top of this fined the city as a whole a further five hundred talents, Brutus demanded from the Lycians no more than a hundred and fifty talents, and then set off for Ionia without harming them in any other way.

33. Brutus performed a great many other memorable acts of justice in meting out rewards or punishments to those who deserved them, but I shall mention only one which gave especial satisfaction both to himself and the most distinguished Romans of the time. When Pompey the Great landed as a fugitive at Pelusium in Egypt, after being completely stripped of his great power in consequence of his defeat by Caesar, the guardians of the boy Pharaoh held a council with their friends at which their opinions were divided. Some took the view that they should give Pompey asylum, and others that they should expel him from Egypt. Then a man named Theodotus of Chios, who had been hired as a tutor in rhetoric for the young king, and who at that time was considered worthy, for lack of better men, to be a member of the council, declared that both parties, those in favour of admitting and of sending him away, were equally mistaken. In the present situation one policy and one only was expedient, and that was to receive him and then put him to death. He rounded off his speech with the proverb, 'A dead man does not bite'. The council followed his advice, and thus fell Pompey the Great, a victim of the rhetorical virtuosity of a sophist, as Theodotus afterwards used to boast, and an example of the unexpected and incredible mutability of fortune. When Caesar arrived in Egypt soon afterwards, the other assassins received their just reward and died the disgraceful death which they deserved. Theodotus continued to borrow from fortune enough time to eke out a vagabond, penniless, and ignominious existence, but he was discovered by Brutus during his travels in Asia, brought before him, and punished, and in this way his death became more memorable than anything in his life.

34. Brutus now invited Cassius to join him at Sardis. As he approached, Brutus went out to meet him with his friends, and their combined forces drawn up in full array saluted both men as *imperator*. But as often happens in great enterprises in which a large number of friends and commanders are engaged, there had been some sharp differences and mutual accusations had been exchanged.

So immediately after their journey their first action was to meet in a room face to face. The doors were shut, and with no one else present the two men first began blaming one another and then fell to recriminations and counter-charges. These soon led to indignant reproaches and tears, and their friends, who were amazed at the vehemence and bitterness of their anger, were afraid that the quarrel might end in violence. They had been strictly forbidden to enter, but in spite of this, Marcus Favonius, who had been an admirer of Cato, and who pursued philosophy with an impulsive fanaticism rather than in a spirit of reason, tried to enter the room but was prevented by their servants. However, once he had committed himself to any action it was not easy to stop him, for he was always a man of impulses and extremes. He attached very little importance to the dignity of his rank as a Roman senator, and by cultivating a cynical and outspoken manner he contrived to soften the offence which his words might otherwise have caused, and consequently men were prepared to treat his impertinence as a joke. So on this occasion he forced his way through the bystanders and burst into the room, where he proceeded to quote in a theatrical tone the words which Homer makes Nestor use to Achilles and Agamemnon*

> Be ruled by me, young men, I have more years and wisdom than you have

and so on. At this Cassius broke out laughing, but Brutus pushed Favonius out of the room, telling him that he might profess the philosophy of a Cynic,† but that all he really had was the impudence of a dog. However, this episode broke up their quarrel for the moment and they parted at once. Later Cassius gave a supper to which Brutus invited his friends. As the guests were just taking their places on their couches, Favonius arrived, fresh from the bath. Brutus called out to him, told him that he had not been invited, and ordered the servants to show him to the couch at the end of the room, but Favonius pushed his way past them and proceeded to take his place at the central couch.‡ Then gradually, as they drank, the entertainment

* *Iliad* I, 259.

† Followers of this philosophical school were known as Cynics (dog-like), because of the uncouth manners which they affected.

‡ The Romans placed three couches round their dinner-tables, leaving the fourth side open. The central couch was the seat of honour.

became more genial, and their talk was seasoned with wit and philosophy.

35. On the following day, Brutus publicly condemned and disgraced Lucius Pella. He was a Roman who had held the office of praetor and enjoyed Brutus's confidence, but had been accused by the Sardians of embezzling public money. Cassius bitterly resented this action, because only a few days before, when two of his friends had been found guilty of the same offence, he had privately reprimanded them but acquitted them in public and continued to employ them. He therefore blamed Brutus for administering the letter of the law too meticulously, at a moment when it would have been advisable to show more leniency. But Brutus retorted that Cassius should remember the Ides of March, the day on which they had killed Caesar, not because he was plundering mankind, but because his power enabled others to do so. If we are going to find excuses for neglecting justice, he argued, it would have been better to put up with Caesar's friends than to allow our own to do wrong. For in that case we should only have been called cowards, but as things are, after all the toils and dangers we have undergone, we shall now find ourselves called unjust into the bargain. These were the principles that Brutus kept before him.

36. When they were on the point of leaving Asia for Greece, Brutus is said to have seen an extraordinary portent. He was a light sleeper and by practice and self-discipline he had cut down his period of rest to only a few hours. He never lay down during the day, and at night only when, as a result of everyone having gone to bed, it was impossible for him to discuss or transact any more business. At this moment, when the war had begun and the whole management of the campaign rested in his hands and he was giving anxious thought to the future, it was his habit to take his first sleep in the evening after supper, and spend the rest of the night dealing with urgent business. If ever he succeeded in dispatching these affairs in a shorter time, he would read a book until the third watch, when the centurions and tribunes would come to him for orders. One night, just before the army crossed over to Greece, he was sitting alone in his tent, which was dimly lit; the hour was late, and the whole camp was wrapped in silence. In the midst of his meditations, he thought he heard some-

one enter the tent, and as he turned his eyes towards the entrance he caught sight of a strange and horrible apparition, a monstrous and terrifying figure standing silently by his side. Summoning up his courage to question it, he asked, 'What man or god are you, and what do you want with me?' The phantom answered, 'I am your evil spirit, Brutus: you shall see me at Philippi.' Brutus kept his self-control and replied, 'I shall see you then.'

37. When the ghost had vanished, Brutus called his servants, but they assured him that they had neither heard a voice nor seen anything. Brutus stayed awake for the rest of the night, but as soon as it was morning he visited Cassius and described what he had seen. Cassius, who was a follower of the doctrines of Epicurus, and who used frequently to dispute with Brutus on subjects of this kind, said to him; 'Our opinion, Brutus, is that by no means everything that we see or experience is real or true. In the first place, the perceptions that come to us through the senses are deceptive and unstable, and, secondly, our intelligence is quick to transform the experience itself, which may be quite illusory, into a whole variety of forms. What the senses actually register is like wax, and the human soul, which includes both the plastic faculty and the material upon which it works, can shape and adorn the objects of the senses at will. We can see this process at work in our dreams, where the imagination transforms some quite insubstantial experience into all kinds of emotions and shapes. It is the nature of the imagination to be eternally active, and this action expresses itself in fancy or in thought. Now in your case you have passed through a great many hardships, which have imposed a severe strain on your body, and this condition both stimulates and distorts the intelligence. As for spirits, I do not believe that they exist, or, if they do, that they can take on the appearance and speech of men, or that they can exert a power which is capable of affecting us. For my part, I could even wish that this were true. If it were, we could put our trust not only in our army and our horses and our ships, which are strong enough, but also in the help of the gods, since we are the leaders of a most righteous and sacred cause.' These were the arguments which Cassius used to reassure Brutus.

As the soldiers were embarking to cross to Greece, two eagles perched on the leading standards, and were carried along with them on the march. They were fed by the soldiers and accompanied the army as far as Philippi. But there on the day before the battle they flew away.

38. Brutus had already subdued most of the people through whose territory they passed on the march. But now, as they advanced along the Thracian coast, they brought over the remaining cities and rulers to their side. When they reached a point which is opposite the island of Thasos, Norbanus was encamped with his army at the narrows, near Symbolum, but they outflanked him and forced him to retire and abandon his position. In fact they came near to capturing his whole force – since Octavius Caesar's advance was delayed by his sickness – and they would have done so if Antony had not hurried to the rescue with such astonishing speed that Brutus could not believe it possible. Octavius arrived ten days later and pitched his camp opposite Brutus, while Antony faced Cassius.

The ground which lay between the two camps was known to the Romans as the plains of Philippi, and these were the two largest Roman armies which had ever faced one another in battle. Brutus's force was considerably smaller in numbers than Octavius Caesar's, but the superb quality of its weapons and equipment made it a magnificent sight. Most of his men's armour was embossed with gold and silver which Brutus had lavished on his soldiers. He had trained his officers to adopt a modest and austere standard of living in other respects, but he believed that the wealth which a man held in his hands or wore on his back lent courage to an ambitious soldier, while those who thought most of gain would fight all the harder, since they clung to their armour as their principal possession.

39. Octavius Caesar and Antony now carried out a review and a ceremony of purification in their entrenchments, and then distributed a little meal and five drachmas to each man for a sacrifice. Brutus and Cassius, on the other hand, showed their contempt for their opponents' poverty and meanness first of all by carrying out their purification in the open field, as is the normal custom, and then by distributing large numbers of cattle to every cohort for sacrifice and fifty drachmas to each man, and in this way they raised the goodwill and fighting spirit of their troops far above the enemy's. At the same time Cassius met with what was considered an unlucky omen during the ceremony, for the lictor brought him the garland which he was to wear turned

upside down. It is also said that, on an earlier occasion during a procession at some festival, a golden statue of Victory which belonged to Cassius and was being carried before him suddenly fell to the ground when its bearer lost his footing. Besides this, a great number of birds of prey were seen circling over the camp each day, and swarms of bees collected at a certain place within the lines. The diviners fenced off the spot, so as to dispel by means of their rites the superstitious fears which by this time had quite cowed the spirits of their troops, and were beginning to undermine even Cassius's Epicurean beliefs.

It was for these reasons that Cassius did not wish to put their fortunes to the test by fighting a battle at that moment, but was in favour of prolonging the war, since their party's strength lay in its resources, while in arms and manpower they were comparatively weak. Brutus, on the other hand, even before this had been eager to decide the issue with the least possible delay, so that he could either restore his country's freedom or deliver from their miseries all those peoples who were oppressed by the demands of military service, requisitions, and the vast expenses of war. It happened at this moment that his cavalry won some successes in the preliminary skirmishing and so his spirits rose. At the same time there were a number of desertions to Octavius's camp and a host of rumours and suspicions that more would follow, and at their council of war this factor persuaded many of Cassius's friends to support Brutus's opinion. However, one of Brutus's friends, Atillius, opposed his plan and advised that they should wait at least until the winter was over before fighting a battle. Brutus asked him how he thought he would be better off in a year's time, whereupon Atillius retorted, 'At least I shall have lived that much longer, if nothing else!' Cassius was not at all pleased with this answer, while the rest of the council were greatly offended and it was finally decided to give battle on the following day.

40. That evening at supper Brutus showed himself full of confidence, took part in philosophical arguments with his friends, and afterwards went to rest. Cassius, by contrast, so Messala tells us, dined in private with a few of his closest friends and appeared silent and thoughtful, contrary to his usual custom. After their meal he pressed Messala's hand earnestly, and speaking in Greek, as he was in the habit of doing

when he wanted to show affection, he declared, 'I call on you to witness, Messala, that I have been placed in the same difficulty as Pompey the Great, by being compelled to risk my country's fate on the issue of a single battle. But let us show a stout heart, and look fortune steadily in the face as we await her verdict. For even if our own plans are at fault, we should not distrust her.' These were the last words, so Messala tells us, that Cassius spoke to him, after which the two men embraced. Cassius had already invited Messala to supper on the following day, which was his own birthday.

Next morning, as soon as it was light, a scarlet tunic, which was the signal for battle, was hung out in front of Brutus's and Cassius's camps, and the two generals came out and met in the space between their armies. On this occasion Cassius said to Brutus, 'May this day bring us victory, Brutus, and may we share our success for the rest of our lives. But since the greatest of human affairs are the most uncertain, and since we may never see one another again if the battle goes against us, what have you decided to do if you have to choose between flight and death?' Brutus answered, 'When I was young, Cassius, and knew very little of the world, I was led, I do not know how, into making a rash judgement in philosophy. I blamed Cato for taking his own life, because I thought it was impious and unmanly to try to evade the divine course of things and not to accept fearlessly whatever may befall, but to run away from it. But now in the present state of my fortunes, I see things differently. If the gods do not give their verdict in our favour, I have no desire to try other hopes or plans. I shall die content with my destiny. On the Ides of March I gave up my life to my country, and since then for her sake I have lived another life which is free and glorious.'

At this Cassius smiled. Then he embraced Brutus and said, 'Now that our minds are made up, let us march against the enemy, for either we shall conquer, or, if we lose, we have nothing to fear.' After this they discussed the order of battle before their friends. Brutus asked Cassius to allow him to command the right wing, although it would normally have been Cassius's privilege by virtue of his years and experience to take this position. Cassius not only agreed but ordered Messala, who commanded the best troops in his army, to station himself on the right. Brutus immediately led out his splendidly equipped cavalry, and formed up his infantry in battle order equally promptly.

41. Meanwhile, Antony's soldiers were engaged in digging trenches from the marshes, where they were encamped, into the plain, so as to cut off Cassius from the sea. Octavius's troops, whose commander was absent at this moment because of sickness, were following out his policy of remaining on the defensive. They had never expected that the enemy would risk a pitched battle, but supposed that they would do no more than make occasional sorties to disturb the men who were digging the trenches by shouting at them and discharging light missiles. As they were not watching the troops posted opposite them, they were bewildered by the uproar and confused shouts which now began to reach them from the trenches. In the meanwhile, Brutus had sent out messages to his officers with the code word for immediate action written on them, while he himself rode along the line of the legions encouraging his men. Only a few actually heard the watchword as it was passed along. The great majority, without waiting for it, acted on a single impulse, and shouting their battle-cry as one man, hurled themselves forward against the enemy. This disorderly charge threw the troops out of line, so that they lost contact with one another, and first Messala's legion, and then the others adjoining it, overlapped Octavius Caesar's left wing and were carried past it. They engaged the soldiers at the end of the line for a short while and killed no more than a few, but then found their way round the flank and burst into the camp. Octavius Caesar has written in his Commentaries how one of his friends, Marcus Artorius, had seen a vision in his sleep, in which Octavius was urged to get up from his sick-bed and leave the camp. Acting on this warning, he had himself carried out only a short while before the attack began, and the rumour went round that he had been killed, for the enemy riddled his empty litter with their spears and javelins. When the camp was captured, those of his men who were found there were slaughtered, and two thousand Lacedaemonians who had recently arrived as allies were cut to pieces with them.

42. The part of Brutus's army which had not outflanked their opponents but engaged the main body, easily routed them and annihilated three legions in hand to hand fighting. Then, swept along by the impetus of their success and carrying Brutus with them, they rushed into the camp on the heels of the fugitives. But at this point the victors made a blunder, and their retreating adversaries were quick

to seize their opportunity. Brutus's right wing had moved up in pursuit and detached itself from his main body, leaving the centre broken and exposed, and it was here that the enemy counter-attacked. The centre resisted stoutly and held its ground, but the left wing, where the troops had lost their formation and did not know what had happened elsewhere, was routed, and Octavius's men drove them back to their camp and sacked it. Neither of the generals happened to be present during this action. Antony, we are told, had retired to the marsh to avoid the fury of the first charge, and Octavius Caesar had disappeared after escaping from his camp. In fact, a number of soldiers claimed to have killed him, and they showed Brutus their blood-stained swords and described Octavius Caesar's youthful appearance. But now Brutus's centre forced back their opponents with tremendous slaughter, and it became clear that Brutus had triumphed in his section of the battlefield, just as Cassius had been utterly defeated. And this turned out to be the fatal mischance which ruined their cause, namely that Brutus believed that Cassius had been victorious and did not come to his rescue, while Cassius believed that Brutus had been killed and did not wait for his help to arrive. At any rate Messala believes it to have been a conclusive proof of victory that Brutus captured three eagles and many standards from the enemy, while they took none of his.

After Brutus had sacked Octavius Caesar's camp, and was riding back from the pursuit, he was surprised not to see Cassius's tent, which was higher than the rest, nor the others in their usual places, for most of them had immediately been destroyed when the enemy broke into the camp. But those of his companions who possessed the keenest sight told him that they could pick out the flashes of helmets and of many silver breast-plates moving about in Cassius's camp, and that, judging by their strength and the appearance of their armour, this was not the garrison which they had left behind. At the same time they said that they could not see the numbers of dead bodies which they would expect to be there if so many legions had been overrun. This was what gave Brutus the first hint of disaster, and so, leaving a guard in the enemy's camp, he called off the pursuit and rallied his forces to hurry to Cassius's help.

43. Cassius's situation had been as follows. At the beginning of the battle he had watched with disapproval, as Brutus's troops launched

their first charge without waiting for the watchword or the order to attack, nor was he any better pleased when, after the success of their onslaught, they immediately rushed off to loot and plunder the enemy's camp without a thought of surrounding their opponents. But his own manoeuvres were hesitant and ponderous rather than swift and decisive, and he found himself enveloped by the enemy's right wing. His cavalry at once turned and galloped off towards the sea, and when he saw his infantry also falling back he tried to rally them. He seized the standard from a standard-bearer who had taken to his heels, and planted it on the earth in front of him, although by now even his bodyguard were showing signs of wavering. At last he was forced to retreat with a few followers to a hill which overlooked the plain. Because of his short sight he could scarcely make out his own camp being plundered, but the few horsemen who were with him saw a large body of cavalry riding towards them, which had in fact been sent by Brutus. Cassius believed that this was an enemy force sent to pursue him, but he sent one of his companions, Titinius, to reconnoitre. The horsemen saw him riding towards them, and when they recognized him as one of Cassius's trusted friends they shouted for joy. Some of his own comrades leaped off their horses, flung their arms about him, and clasped his hand, while the rest rode around him, singing, shouting, and clashing their weapons to show their overwhelming delight, and so it was their very joy that brought about the tragedy. For Cassius at once assumed that Titinius had been captured by the enemy. He cried out, 'I have loved life too much, and now I have clung to it until my friends are made prisoner before my very eyes,' and then retired into an empty tent, forcing one of his freedmen named Pindarus to accompany him. Ever since the disaster of the Parthian campaign, when he had served under Crassus, Cassius had trained this man to play his part in just such an emergency. Cassius had escaped the Parthians, but now he drew his cloak over his head and, baring his neck, offered it to the sword. Later his head was found severed from his body. But after his master's death Pindarus was never seen again, and for this reason some people have suggested that he killed Cassius without waiting for the order. Soon after this, Brutus's horsemen were recognized and Titinius, whom they had crowned with garlands, rode up to report to Cassius. But as soon as he learned from the weeping and lamentations of Cassius's friends of the fate which had overtaken the general, he reproached himself bitterly for his slowness which had been the cause, and then drew his sword and fell upon it.

44. Brutus had already learned of Cassius's defeat and was riding back towards him, but the news of his death reached him just as he arrived at the camp. He mourned over his friend's body, and called Cassius the last of all the Romans, by which he meant that so noble a spirit could never again be bred in Rome. He had the body wrapped for burial and sent it to Thasos, as he did not wish the army to be overcome with grief at the funeral rites. But he himself rallied Cassius's troops and cheered their dejected spirits. He saw that the sacking of their camp had deprived them of the simplest necessities of life, and so he promised each man the sum of two thousand drachmas to make good what they had lost. They were astounded at the size of the gift, took heart again at his words, and sent him on his way with cheers, acclaiming him as the only one of the four generals who had not been defeated in the battle. And indeed the event proved that he had good cause to be confident of victory, for with only a few legions he had put all his opponents to flight. If he had only concentrated the whole of his strength into his attack, and if so many of his men had not charged past the enemy and then fallen to plundering their possessions, it seems certain that he would have crushed the whole of his opponents' army.

45. Brutus's losses were eight thousand men, including his slaves and camp followers, who were known as the Briges, but, according to Messala, Antony and Octavius Caesar lost more than twice as many. For this reason they felt even more discouraged, until one of Cassius's servants, whose name was Demetrius, came that evening to Antony with the clothes and the sword which he had stripped from his master's dead body. This raised their spirits so much that at daybreak they led out their forces in battle order. On the other hand both of the camps which Brutus now commanded were dangerously disorganized. His own was filled with prisoners of war, which obliged him to detach a strong guard, while Cassius's troops were upset by the change of command, and at the same time, as often happens with defeated troops, they were full of jealousy and resentment towards their victorious comrades. Brutus therefore decided to keep his troops under arms, but not to risk a battle. He noticed that large

numbers of the slaves whom he had captured were moving about in a suspicious fashion among the prisoners of war, and so he ordered them to be executed. On the other hand he released some of his free-born prisoners and declared that it was really the enemy who had deprived them of their liberty, for under their command these men were captives and slaves, whereas with him they were free men and citizens of Rome. Then when he saw that his friends and officers were determined to take revenge on them, he saved their lives by hiding them and helping them to escape.

Among these prisoners there were an actor and a clown, the one named Volumnius and the other Saculio. Brutus regarded both these men as beneath his notice, but his friends had them brought before him and denounced them, because even in captivity they could not resist making insolent and derisive jokes. Brutus, who had his mind on other matters, said nothing, but Messala Corvinus gave his opinion that they should be sentenced to a public flogging and then sent back naked to the enemy's generals, as being exactly the right comrades and drinking companions for such commanders. At this some of the onlookers burst out laughing, but Publius Casca, the man who had been the first to stab Caesar, said, 'Do you think it is right, Brutus, that we should celebrate Cassius's funeral rites with laughter and fooling like this? But we shall soon see what regard you have for his memory, according to whether you punish or protect these men who abuse and dishonour him.' Brutus was furious and answered, 'Then why do you ask my opinion, Casca, instead of doing what you think best?' This answer was taken as signifying Brutus's consent to the punishment of these wretched men, and they were led off to execution.

46. After this, Brutus gave his soldiers their promised reward, and when he had mildly reprimanded them because they had not waited for the watchword, but launched themselves without orders into a haphazard attack, he promised to hand over two cities, Thessalonica and Lacedaemon, for them to plunder, provided that they fought well in the coming battle. In the whole of Brutus's life this is the one charge to which no defence can be found. It is true, of course, that Antony and Octavius Caesar committed far greater cruelties than this in extorting rewards for their soldiers, and drove the inhabitants from their ancestral lands throughout the length and breadth of Italy to

enrich their supporters with cities and estates to which they had no right. But to these men conquest and supreme power were the acknowledged ends of war. Brutus, on the other hand, enjoyed such a reputation for virtue among the people that in their minds he was not free to conquer or to save himself unless he employed just and honourable means; this was more than ever the case now that Cassius was dead, because in the past he had been accused of leading Brutus astray into various acts of violence. The truth was that just as at sea, when a vessel's rudder is shattered, the crew try to fit and fasten other timbers in its place, and in their effort to overcome the danger do not achieve a perfect repair, but simply the best they can contrive, so Brutus, being left in sole command of such a great army at a moment of crisis, and having no commander of the same capacity as himself, was obliged to make use of such subordinates as he possessed and to fit many of his actions and words to what they found acceptable. This was why he decided to do whatever they considered necessary to restore the spirit of Cassius's army, for these troops had now become very difficult to handle. Their lack of a personal commander made them undisciplined in camp, while their defeat made them afraid to face the enemy.

47. At the same time Octavius Caesar and Antony were no better off. Their supplies were scarce and, with their camp pitched as it was on low ground, they dreaded the harsh winter they must suffer. They were huddled together on the edge of the marshes, and the autumn rains that fell in torrents after the battle flooded their tents with mud and water, which immediately froze because of the coldness of the weather. In the midst of these hardships news arrived of the disaster which had overtaken them at sea. Brutus's fleet had attacked and destroyed a large convoy of reinforcements which had been sent out on Octavius Caesar's orders from Italy, and the few survivors who escaped the enemy were compelled by hunger to eat the sails and tackle of their ships. When Antony and Octavius Caesar heard of this, they were eager to force an action and decide the issue before Brutus discovered how great a success he had won. It so happened that the battles at sea and on land had been fought on the same day, but by some mischance rather than by the fault of the naval commanders no news of their victory reached Brutus's camp until twenty days after the event. If he had known this, he would not have

ventured upon a second battle, since his army was well stocked with supplies for a long while, he held the advantage of the ground in that his camp was not exposed to the wintry weather and was almost impregnable on the side facing the enemy, and besides all this the knowledge that he held complete control of the sea and had defeated the troops opposed to him on land had filled him with confidence and high hopes.

But the day of the Republic was past, it would seem, and it was necessary that the rule of a single man should take its place, and so the gods, wishing to remove from the scene the only man who could oppose the destined master of the world, kept from Brutus the knowledge of his success, although even so it almost reached him in time. On the very evening before the final battle, a man named Clodius deserted from the enemy and brought word that Octavius Caesar had heard of the destruction of his fleet, and that this was the reason for his haste to join battle. However, no one believed his story and he was not even admitted into Brutus's presence, but was generally despised as a rumour-monger who had either heard some idle report or had deliberately invented a falsehood to win himself favour.

48. On that night, it is said, the ghost again visited Brutus: it appeared in the same shape, but departed without a word. Publius Volumnius, who was a philosopher and who served with Brutus in all his campaigns makes no mention of this portent, but he says that the leading standard was covered with a swarm of bees, that the arm of one of the officers exuded oil of roses, and that although they often rubbed it and wiped the moisture away, this had no effect. He also reports that just before the battle two eagles met and fought in the space between the two camps, that both armies gazed at them while an extraordinary silence descended upon the plain, and that finally the eagle on Brutus's side gave up the fight and flew away. There is also the well-known story of the Ethiopian who encountered the standard-bearer just as the gate of the camp was thrown open, and who was cut down by the soldiers, because they believed his appearance signified a bad omen.

49. After Brutus had led out his forces in battle order and formed them up against the enemy, he waited for some time because, as he was reviewing the troops, he began to feel suspicious of some and

heard accusations made against others. He also noticed that the cavalry showed no great enthusiasm to begin the attack, but waited to see what the infantry would do. Then suddenly a man named Camulatus, a fine soldier whom Brutus had decorated for his courage, rode out of the ranks and went over to the enemy. Brutus was heartbroken at the sight, and partly out of anger, partly because he was afraid of treachery or desertion on an even greater scale, launched his attack at about three o'clock in the afternoon. In his own sector of the battlefield he immediately overcame the enemy and pressed forward, driving his opponents' left wing before him. His cavalry also moved up in support of the infantry, and as soon as they saw the enemy in disorder charged against them. His other wing, however, was extended by its commanders to prevent its being outflanked by the enemy who outnumbered it, and the result was to leave the centre so thinly manned that it could not hold its ground, but broke and fled. The enemy cut their way through the left wing, and then at once encircled Brutus's troops. Faced with this crisis, he showed all the virtues of a general and a soldier, both in his personal prowess and in his handling of the battle, as he fought to wrest victory from the enemy. But the factor which had told in his favour in the earlier engagement now worked against him. On that occasion the part of the enemy's army which had been defeated had been quickly annihilated, but this time when Cassius's troops were routed only a few of them were killed, and the fugitives, who had become quite demoralized by their earlier defeats, now infected the greater part of the army with their own terror and confusion. It was in this action that Marcus, the son of Cato the philosopher, was killed, fighting among the bravest of the young patricians. He fought on until he was exhausted and refused to surrender or to fly, but still wielding his sword and shouting aloud that he was the son of Marcus Cato, he fell dead upon the heap of enemies he had slain. The bravest men in the army were also killed sacrificing their lives to defend Brutus.

50. Among Brutus's close friends was a man of exceptional courage named Lucilius. When he saw a group of barbarian horsemen paying no attention to any other quarry but riding at full speed for Brutus, he determined to stop them at the risk of his own life, and so, letting himself fall a little way behind, he shouted to them that he was Brutus. He convinced the barbarians, because he asked them to lead

him to Antony, and pretended that he had confidence in him but was afraid of Octavius Caesar. They were delighted at their discovery, and thinking themselves fortunate beyond belief, they led Lucilius along, and as it was now growing dark, they sent ahead some messengers to warn Antony. Antony was also pleased at the news and went to meet the escort, and the rest of his troops, when they heard that Brutus was being brought in alive, ran up to see him, some of them pitying his ill-fortune, and others thinking him unworthy of his reputation in yielding so far to his love of life as to let himself be taken prisoner by barbarians. As they approached, Antony halted, as he felt uncertain as to how he should receive Brutus. But Lucilius, when he was led forward, spoke out boldly and declared, 'Antony, no enemy has taken Marcus Brutus prisoner, and none ever will. Fortune must never gain that victory over virtue. When you find Brutus, whether he is alive or dead, he will be worthy of himself. I tricked your soldiers into bringing me here, and however you decide to punish me, I am ready.' When Lucilius had confessed this to the amazement of his hearers, Antony turned to the men who had captured him and said, 'I expect you are angry at your mistake and think you have been made to look fools. But believe me you have laid hands on a prize that is worth far more than the man you were hunting. You went out to look for an enemy, and you have brought me back a friend. By the gods, I do not know how I could have treated Brutus if you had brought him here alive, but I know that I would rather have such a man as Lucilius for a friend than an enemy.' With these words he embraced Lucilius and entrusted him to the care of one of his friends. Later on he employed him and found him for ever afterwards a loyal and faithful comrade.

51. Meanwhile, Brutus had crossed a stream which was shaded by trees and overhung by steep banks, and since it was already dark he would go no farther, but sat down with a few officers and friends around him, in a place where the ground had been hollowed out and had a great rock in front of it. Then he gazed above him at the star-filled heavens, and recited two verses, one of which Volumnius has recorded,*

* Euripides, *Medea*, 334. Appian considers that in quoting this line, where the heroine is cursing her unfaithful husband Jason, Brutus was invoking the curse of Jupiter on Antony.

O Zeus, remember the author of these ills

but the other he says he has forgotten. Then after a little he uttered the names of each of his friends whom he had seen killed defending him in the battle, and he sighed most heavily when he came to Labeo and Flavius, the first of whom was his legate and the second his chief of engineers. Just then one of his attendants felt thirsty, and seeing that Brutus was in the same plight, he picked up a helmet and ran down to the stream. Suddenly they heard a noise from the opposite direction and Volumnius went out to reconnoitre, taking Dardanus his shield-bearer with him. After a while they came back and asked for some water to drink. 'It has all been drunk,' replied Brutus and smiled significantly, 'but we shall fetch you some more.' The same man who had brought it at first was sent out again, but this time he almost fell into the enemy's hands, was wounded, and only escaped with great difficulty.

Now Brutus still believed that he had not lost many men in the battle, and another of his friends, Statyllius, offered to make his way through the enemy's lines to Brutus's camp, for there was no other way of reaching it. There he would reconnoitre the position, and if all was well he would raise a blazing torch and return. He arrived there safely and the torch was raised. After this a long time passed and there was no sign of him, but Brutus said, 'If Statyllius is alive, he will come back.' But it appears that on his way back he fell into the enemy's hands and was killed.

52. The night was now far spent, and as Brutus sat on the ground, he leaned across to his servant Cleitus and spoke to him quietly. Cleitus made no reply but burst into tears, whereupon Brutus took his shield-bearer Dardanus aside and spoke to him in private. Lastly, he turned to Volumnius and, addressing him in Greek, appealed to the memory of the years they had spent together as students of philosophy, and begged him to hold his sword and help him drive it home. But Volumnius refused and so did all the rest, and one of them declared that they must wait no longer, but make their escape. At this Brutus jumped up and answered, 'Yes, we must escape, but this time with our hands, not our feet.' Then, after taking each one of them by the hand, he smiled, and said that he was filled with a great joy because not one of his friends had failed him, and as for fortune,

he blamed her only for his country's sake. He believed that fate had been kinder to him than to the victors, and not only in the past but in the present, since he was leaving behind him a reputation for virtue which his conquerors, for all their arms or their wealth, could never rival, and the world would come to know that wicked and unscrupulous men who put to death the good and the just were themselves unfit to rule. Then, after urging them to save themselves, he walked a little distance away with two or three of his companions, among whom was Strato, who had been one of his closest friends ever since they had studied rhetoric together. He placed Strato next to him, and then, grasping his naked sword by the hilt with both hands, he threw himself upon it and died. Some say that it was not Brutus himself but Strato who at his insistence held the sword in front of him, turning his eyes away, and that Brutus then ran upon it with such force that it transfixed his breast, killing him instantly.

53. Messala, who had been one of Brutus's friends, but had made his peace with Octavius Caesar, found occasion some time afterwards to present Strato to his new master, and said with tears in his eyes, 'This is the man, Caesar, who did the last service for my dear friend Brutus.' Octavius took him into his service and found that Strato, like other Greeks in his entourage, showed great courage in the wars that followed, especially at the battle of Actium. And the story goes that Messala himself was later warmly praised by Octavius: for whereas at Philippi nobody had fought harder against the Caesarians for Brutus's sake, at Actium he proved himself utterly devoted to his new master. At this Messala is said to have replied, 'Caesar, I have always fought on the better and juster side.'

When Antony found Brutus's body, he ordered it to be wrapped in the most costly of his scarlet cloaks, and afterwards when he discovered that the garment had been stolen, he had the thief put to death. The ashes he sent home to Servilia, Brutus's mother. As for Porcia, Brutus's wife, both Nicolaüs the philosopher and Valerius Maximus tell the story that she now longed to end her life, but was prevented by her friends who sat with her and continually watched her. So she contrived to snatch up some live coals from the fire and swallowed them, keeping her mouth closed, and so suffocated herself and died. And yet there is also in existence a letter from Brutus to his friends, in which he mourns Porcia's fate and reproaches them for it, because their neglect of her must have made her prefer death to the continuance of her illness. It would seem then that Nicolaüs is mistaken at any rate in the date of her death, for this letter, if Brutus really wrote it, tells us of Porcia's sickness, of her love for her husband and of the manner of her death.

9

MARK ANTONY

[83–30 B.C.]

* *
*

1. Mark Antony's grandfather was Antony the orator, who took the side of Sulla in the civil wars and was put to death by Marius. His father, who received the surname Creticus,* did not become famous nor make any great mark in public life, but was remembered rather for his benevolence, his honesty, and especially his generosity, as may be judged by the following episode. He was by no means rich, and for this reason his wife was inclined to restrain his philanthropic impulses. So when one of his intimate friends came to ask him for money, he had none to offer: instead, he ordered a young slave to fetch some water in a silver bowl, and when it arrived he moistened his face as though he were about to shave. He then dismissed the slave on some other pretext, presented his friend with the bowl, and urged him to make what use he could of it. Later, when he saw that a thorough search was being made among the slaves, and that his wife was angry and intended to question them one by one, Antony confessed what he had done and begged her forgiveness.

2. His wife Julia belonged to the family of the Caesars and could take her place among the most nobly born and admirable women of her time. It was under her care that Antony was brought up, and after his father's death she married Cornelius Lentulus, who was executed by Cicero as one of the ringleaders of Catiline's conspiracy. This seems to have been the origin and the reason for the bitter animosity which Antony felt towards Cicero. At any rate Antony

* This surname was given him ironically. He was entrusted with the command of a fleet against the pirates, lost a large part of it in action against the Cretans in 74 B.C., and died soon afterwards, leaving three sons, of whom Mark Antony was the eldest.

used to maintain that Cicero refused even to hand over Lentulus's body for burial until Julia had begged this concession from his wife. But this accusation is obviously false, since none of those who were executed at that time by Cicero was denied burial.

In his youth, it is said, Antony gave promise of a brilliant future, but then he became a close friend of Curio and this association seems to have fallen like a blight upon his career. Curio was a man who had become wholly enslaved to the demands of pleasure, and in order to make Antony more pliable to his will, he plunged him into a life of drinking bouts, love-affairs, and reckless spending. The consequence was that Antony quickly ran up debts of an enormous size for so young a man, the sum involved being two hundred and fifty talents. Curio provided security for the whole of this amount, but his father heard of it and forbade Antony his house. Antony then attached himself for a short while to Clodius, the most notorious of all the demagogues of his time for his lawlessness and loose-living, and took part in the campaigns of violence which at that time were throwing political affairs at Rome into chaos. But he soon grew tired of Clodius's crazy intrigues and alarmed at the strength of the opposition which they aroused, and he therefore left Italy for Greece, where he devoted himself to military training and to the study of public speaking, adopting what was known as the Asiatic style. This type of oratory was just then at the height of its popularity, and indeed had much in common with Antony's own mode of life, which was boastful, insolent, and full of empty bravado and misguided aspirations.

3. During his stay in Greece he was invited by Gabinius, a man of consular rank, to accompany the Roman force which was about to sail for Syria. Antony declined to join him in a private capacity, but when he was offered the command of the cavalry he agreed to serve in the campaign. His first operations were directed against Aristobulus,* who had incited the Jews to revolt. On this occasion Antony was the first man to scale the highest part of the enemy's fortifications, and he drove Aristobulus from all his positions. Then he engaged him, routed a greatly superior force with a handful of men, and killed all but a few of his opponents. Aristobulus and his son were both taken prisoner.

* Aristobulus was king and high priest of the Jews. Pompey had captured him in 63 B.C. and sent him to Rome. He escaped in 57 B.C.

After this campaign was over, Gabinius was approached by Ptolemy Auletes,* who appealed to him to join forces, invade Egypt, and recover his kingdom, for which services he offered a bribe of ten thousand talents. The majority of the Roman officers were opposed to the plan, but Gabinius, although he had no liking for the campaign, was captivated by the vision of the ten thousand talents. Antony, on the other hand, who longed to undertake some ambitious enterprise, was eager to gratify Ptolemy's request and so he threw his weight on to the king's side and persuaded Gabinius to join him. The general opinion was that the greatest danger lay not so much in the fighting as in the march to Pelusium, since the Romans would have to pass through deep sand and a completely waterless region as far as the Ecregma and the Serbonian marshes.† The Egyptians call this region Typhon's breathing-hole, but it is probable that the swamp consists of water which was originally left behind by the Red Sea, or else infiltrated from it at the point where the isthmus dividing it from the Mediterranean is at its narrowest. However, when Antony was ordered to advance with the cavalry, he not only occupied the isthmus, but also seized the large city of Pelusium and captured its garrison, thus securing the line of march for the main Roman force and laying a foundation for the campaign on which his commander could base confident hopes of victory. And on this occasion even the enemy profited from Antony's love of honour. As soon as king Ptolemy arrived in Pelusium, he was so overcome by his anger and resentment that he was about to carry out a massacre of the Egyptians, but Antony stepped in and prevented him. There followed a whole series of hard-fought battles, in which time and again Antony gave proof of his courage and his gifts of leadership. The most remarkable

* The father of Cleopatra. He had been obliged to flee to Ephesus because of the Egyptians' resentment of the high taxes he had imposed. He used these to bribe Roman officials in order to have himself declared a friend and ally of Rome. He was restored to the Egyptian throne in 55 B.C.

† Pelusium lay at the easternmost mouth of the Nile, on the site of the modern Damietta. Typhon, a brother of Isis and Osiris, was the evil deity of the Egyptians and was believed to lie buried beneath the Serbonian marshes, which began a few miles east of Pelusium. Milton refers to them in *Paradise Lost*, II.

> A gulf profound as that Serbonian bog,
> Betwixt Damiata and Mount Casius old,
> Where armies whole have sunk . . .

and Herodotus also describes them (Book III, ch. 5).

of these exploits was the operation in which by wheeling his own force he succeeded in outflanking the enemy and enveloping them from the rear, and so enabled the Roman troops who were attacking from the front to win the battle. He received suitable decorations and honours for all these feats, and the Egyptian people were especially impressed by the humanity which he showed to the dead Archelaus.* Although Antony had been his personal friend and guest, circumstances had forced him to make war upon this prince during his lifetime, but when he had been killed, Antony sought out his body and had it buried with royal honours. In consequence, he left a great name behind him among the Alexandrians, while his comrades in the Roman army looked up to him as a brilliant soldier.

4. Besides these qualities there was a noble dignity about Antony's appearance. His beard was well grown, his forehead broad, his nose aquiline, and these features combined to give him a certain bold and masculine look, which is found in the statues and portraits of Hercules. In fact there was an ancient tradition that the blood of the Heracleidae ran in Antony's family, since they claimed descent from Anton, one of the sons of Hercules, and Antony liked to believe that his own physique lent force to the legend. He also deliberately cultivated it in his choice of dress, for whenever he was going to appear before a large number of people, he wore his tunic belted low over the hips, a large sword at his side, and a heavy cloak. And indeed it was these same 'Herculean' qualities that the fastidious found so offensive – his swaggering air, his ribald talk, his fondness for carousing in public, sitting down by his men as they ate, or taking his food standing at the common mess-table – which made his own troops delight in his company and almost worship him. His weakness for the opposite sex also showed an attractive side of his character, and even won him the sympathy of many people, for he often helped others in their love-affairs and always accepted with good humour the jokes they made about his own. Besides this, his open-handed nature and the generosity with which he showered rewards upon his friends

myth

Character

* Archelaus was the son of Mithridates's general of the same name who had surrendered to Sulla. The son was married to Ptolemy Auletes's daughter Berenice, who had become Queen of Egypt when her father was expelled. Antony's first meeting with Cleopatra may well have taken place during this visit to Alexandria: she was then aged fourteen.

and his soldiers alike laid a splendid foundation when he first set out upon the road to power, and when he had established himself, these qualities raised his authority to still greater heights, even after he had begun to undermine it by innumerable acts of folly. I cannot refrain from quoting one example of his liberality. He had given orders for two hundred and fifty thousand drachmas to be presented to one of his friends, a sum which the Romans call a *decies*. His steward was dumbfounded at this command, and in order to make Antony understand the sheer size of the gift, he had the money laid out in full view of his master. As Antony passed by, he asked what this heap of coins represented, and the steward then explained that this was the gift he had ordered for his friend. Antony saw that the man grudged the expense, and so he remarked: 'I thought a *decies* amounted to more than that. This is just a trifle: you had better double it!'

5. These episodes belong to a later date. At the time of which I am now speaking the affairs of Rome had reached the brink of civil war, with the senatorial party ranging itself under the leadership of Pompey, who was in the capital, while the popular party sought the help of Caesar, who was then commanding the Roman armies in Gaul. At this point Curio, the friend of Antony's younger days, who had himself changed sides and was now one of Caesar's supporters,* persuaded Antony to join him. Curio's gifts as an orator gave him a powerful hold over the masses, and by making lavish use of the funds provided by Caesar, he secured Antony's election as tribune and later as augur, that is to say a priest whose duty it is to observe the flight of birds.† Once in office, Antony quickly found ways to use his powers for the benefit of those who were managing affairs on Caesar's behalf. First of all he found that the consul Marcellus was proposing not only to place the forces which had already been raised under Pompey's command, but also to grant him powers to conscript new levies. Antony opposed this plan by introducing a decree that the soldiers who had already been mobilized should sail for Syria to reinforce the army of Bibulus, who was engaged in a campaign against the

* Caesar had won over Curio by paying off his debts.

† Plutarch's chronology is vague at this point. Antony returned from Egypt in 54 and visited Caesar at his winter quarters in Gaul. He was in Rome again in 53, was elected quaestor in 52, and went out to Gaul. In 50 he returned to Rome and was appointed an augur, and in the following year was elected tribune.

Parthians, and that those whom Pompey was then recruiting should not serve under his command. On another occasion, when the Senate refused either to receive Caesar's letters or to allow them to be read, Antony employed the powers vested in his office to read them out aloud himself, and in this way he won many more supporters for Caesar's cause, because people were enabled to judge from these letters that his demands were no more than moderate and just. Finally, when two questions were laid before the Senate, the first whether Pompey should disband his army, and the second whether Caesar should do the same, and when only a small minority voted that Pompey should disarm and the great majority that Caesar should do so, Antony then rose and asked whether it was the Senate's opinion that both Pompey and Caesar should dismiss their troops. This suggestion was received with great enthusiasm, and amid shouts of applause for Antony the senators demanded that the motion should be put to the vote. But the consuls rejected this procedure, and thereupon Caesar's supporters put forward a fresh set of proposals which they believed to be reasonable. These in turn were overruled by Cato, and then Lentulus, exercising his authority as consul, had Antony ejected from the Senate. Antony responded by delivering a violent attack on his opponents, after which he left the house. He disguised himself in a slave's clothes, and in the company of Quintus Cassius* hired a chariot and set out to join Caesar. As soon as they arrived they reported angrily to Caesar that affairs at Rome were now in chaos, that even the tribunes of the people had been deprived of their freedom of speech, and that anyone who raised his voice on behalf of justice was persecuted and went in danger of his life.

6. When this news reached him, Caesar broke camp and invaded Italy, and it was for this reason that Cicero in his *Philippics* wrote that Antony had been the cause of the civil war, just as Helen had been of the Trojan war. But this is an obvious falsehood, for Caesar was by no means easily influenced, neither was he the man to abandon his calculations on account of anger. The mere sight of Antony and Cassius dressed in rags and arriving at his camp in a hired chariot would never have persuaded him to make war upon his country on the spur of the moment, unless he had planned such an action long before. On the contrary, Caesar had long been anxious to open

* A brother of the conspirator against Julius Caesar.

hostilities, and this episode merely provided him with the occasion and a plausible excuse. The real motive which drove him to make war upon mankind, just as it had urged Alexander and Cyrus before him, was an insatiable love of power and an insane desire to be the first and greatest man in the world, and this ambition could not be attained without subduing Pompey.

So Caesar advanced upon Rome, captured it, and drove Pompey out of Italy. He decided first of all to attack Pompey's forces in Spain, and later, when a fleet had been organized in his absence, to cross the sea to Greece, where his enemy was established. Meanwhile he left Rome to be governed by Lepidus, who was praetor, while the command of the troops and the administration of Italy were entrusted to Antony, who was one of the tribunes of the people. Antony quickly won the affections of the soldiers by joining them in their exercises, spending much of his time amongst them, and providing gifts for them whenever the opportunity arose. The rest of the population, however, saw him in a very different light. He was too lazy to deal with complaints and too impatient to listen to those who wanted to enlist his help, while at the same time he became notorious for his intrigues with other men's wives. In short, Caesar's régime, which appeared to be anything but tyrannical when he conducted it himself, was made unpopular by his friends, and of these it was Antony who wielded the greatest power, and hence was considered the worst offender.

7. In spite of this, when Caesar returned from Spain he ignored all the accusations that were brought against Antony, and, in so far as he found him a capable leader of men who had shown courage and energy in his prosecution of the war, his judgement was correct. Caesar himself now sailed from Brundisium with a small force,* crossed the Ionian sea, and sent back his transports with orders to Gabinius and Antony to embark their troops and join him as quickly as possible in Macedonia. Gabinius, however, was afraid to attempt the crossing, which was difficult in winter, and began to march his army round by the long route overland. Antony, on the other hand, was becoming more and more concerned that Caesar would find himself surrounded by superior forces. He managed to drive off Libo, who was blockading the harbour at Brundisium, by attacking

* Early in 48 B.C.

his galleys with a large number of small boats, and he then embarked a force of twenty thousand infantry and eight hundred horsemen and put out to sea. The enemy sighted and pursued him, but he was rescued from this danger by a strong south wind, which raised such a heavy swell that Libo's galleys wallowed in the trough of the waves and could make no headway. Antony, on the other hand, found that his ships were being driven towards a rock-bound shore and cliffs with deep water under them, from which there seemed to be no hope of escape. But suddenly the wind veered to the south-west, and the swell began to move towards the open sea and allowed him to change his course. As he sailed proudly along he could see the beach strewn with wreckage, for the wind had driven his pursuers ashore, and many of their ships had been destroyed. A great quantity of booty and many prisoners fell into Antony's hands. He then went on to capture the town of Lissus and inspired Caesar with great confidence by arriving at the critical moment with such large reinforcements.

8. There followed a long period of continuous fighting, and in all these engagements Antony distinguished himself brilliantly. Twice when Caesar's troops were in headlong retreat he met them, stemmed the rout, forced them to turn and charge their pursuers, and won a victory. In consequence, his reputation with the army was second only to Caesar's, and Caesar left no doubt as to his own opinion of Antony. When he was about to engage in the final and decisive battle at Pharsalus, Caesar took charge of the right wing and gave the left to Antony as the most able commander in his army. And after the victory, when he had been proclaimed dictator, he himself pressed on to pursue Pompey, but he chose Antony as his master of horse and sent him to Rome. This appointment is the second in rank when the dictator is in the city, but when he is absent it represents the supreme and almost the only authority, for once a dictator has been chosen there remains only the tribunate; all the other offices of state cease to function.

9. One of the tribunes at this time was Dolabella, a young man and a newcomer to politics, who was ambitious to change the existing order. He therefore proposed a law for the cancellation of debts and approached Antony – who was his friend and usually favoured any measure designed to appeal to the masses – to enlist his support. But

Asinius and Trebellius advised Antony against the scheme, and it so happened that at this moment he had reason to suspect that Dolabella had seduced his wife. Antony was enraged at this, drove his wife out of his house – she was his cousin, her father being the Gaius Antonius who had been Cicero's colleague during his consulship – and prepared for an open clash with Dolabella. Meanwhile Dolabella had already occupied the Forum so as to force his measure through the Assembly, and accordingly Antony, as soon as the Senate had passed a resolution authorizing him to take up arms, advanced on the Forum, killed a number of Dolabella's men, and lost some of his own. Through this action Antony forfeited his popularity with the people, while at the same time his course of life earned him the contempt of all men of principle; indeed, as Cicero explains, they positively detested him. They were disgusted at his ill-timed drunkenness, his extravagant spending, his gross intrigues with women, his days spent in sleeping off his debauches, or wandering about with an aching head and befuddled wits, and his nights spent in revels, or watching lavish spectacles, or attending the wedding feast of some actor or buffoon. The story goes that he once attended a banquet given for the wedding of Hippias the actor, ate and drank all night, and then, when he was summoned to attend a political meeting early in the morning at the Forum, he appeared in public surfeited with food and vomited into his toga, which one of his friends held ready for him. Sergius, the mime, was one of his friends who had the greatest influence over him, and also Cytheris, a woman from the same school of acting, to whom he was much attached. When he visited the cities of Italy she accompanied him in a litter, which was followed by a retinue of attendants as large as his own mother's.

Besides this, there was much else in Antony's way of living which caused great offence. People were scandalized, for example, at the sight of the golden drinking cups which were carried before him when he left the city, as if they were part of some religious procession; at the pavilions which were set up on his journeys; at the lavish meals which were spread in groves or on the banks of rivers; at his chariots drawn by lions and at his habit of billeting courtesans and sambuca-players in the homes of honest men and women. Most people thought it outrageous that while Caesar was sleeping under the open sky far away from Italy, and undergoing great hardships and dangers as he fought out the final campaigns of the civil war, his supporters should profit by his exertions to wallow in luxury and insult their fellow-citizens.

10. This kind of behaviour is also believed to have intensified the bitterness of the civil war and to have encouraged the soldiers to indulge in looting and other acts of violence. So when Caesar returned to Rome he pardoned Dolabella, and when he was elected consul for the third time, he chose Lepidus as his colleague but not Antony. At this moment also Pompey's house happened to be put up for sale and Antony bought it, but when he was asked to hand over the money for it he became angry. Antony himself makes out that the reason why he did not take part in Caesar's African campaign was that he felt aggrieved at not having been rewarded in any way for his earlier successes. But in spite of this, it appears that Caesar cured Antony of much of his extravagance and folly by not allowing his faults to pass unnoticed. At any rate, he now reformed his whole manner of living, turned his thoughts towards marriage, and chose Fulvia,* the widow of Clodius the demagogue. She was a woman who took no interest in spinning or managing a household, nor could she be content to rule a husband who had no ambition for public life: her desire was to govern those who governed or to command a commander-in-chief. And in fact Cleopatra was indebted to Fulvia for teaching Antony to obey a wife's authority, for by the time he met her, he had already been quite broken in and schooled to accept the sway of women.

However, Antony did his best by means of practical jokes and other boyish pranks to import a little gaiety into his relationship with Fulvia. For example, when Caesar returned after his victory in Spain, Antony, like many others among his supporters, went out to meet him. Suddenly the rumour began to spread that Caesar had been killed and that his enemies were about to invade Italy, whereupon Antony turned back to Rome. He disguised himself as a slave, made out that he was carrying a letter to Fulvia from Antony, and was admitted to her presence with his face all muffled. Fulvia was distracted and before taking the letter asked him whether Antony was

* Fulvia's first husband was Clodius, and her daughter by this marriage became Octavius Caesar's first wife in 43 B.C. (see ch. 20). Her second husband was Antony's friend Curio, who died in Africa in 49 B.C. Antony was her third husband, by whom she had two children. She died in 39 B.C.

alive. He handed it to her in silence, and no sooner had she opened it and begun to read it than he flung his arms around her and kissed her. I mention this story as a single example of many such actions of his.

11. When Caesar returned from Spain,* everybody of importance in Rome travelled for several days to meet him, but it was Antony whom he singled out for especial honour. As he passed through Italy, it was Antony who shared Caesar's chariot. After them rode Brutus Albinus and Octavius, the dictator's great-nephew who afterwards took the name of Caesar and ruled Rome for many years. And when Caesar had been elected consul for the fifth time, he immediately chose Antony for his colleague. He had intended to resign his office and entrust it to Dolabella, and he announced this plan to the Senate. But Antony violently opposed the scheme and poured abuse upon Dolabella, who returned it with interest, until Caesar became so ashamed of this wrangling among his supporters that for the time being he put the idea aside. Later, when Caesar appeared in public to nominate Dolabella as consul, Antony cried out that the omens were unfavourable,† whereupon Caesar gave up the attempt, much to Dolabella's indignation. In fact, it would appear that Caesar was as much disgusted with Dolabella as he was with Antony. The story goes that when someone was accusing them both of plotting against Caesar, he remarked: 'It is not the fat, sleek-headed men I am afraid of, but the pale, lean ones' – and here he pointed to Brutus and Cassius, the men who were to conspire against him and murder him.

12. It was Antony who quite unintentionally supplied the conspirators with their most plausible pretext. The occasion was the festival of the Lycaea, which the Romans call the Lupercalia, and Caesar, dressed in a triumphal robe and seated upon the rostra in the Forum, was watching the runners as they darted to and fro. This is a ceremony at which many of the young nobles and holders of the offices of state are anointed with oil, and, carrying leather thongs in their hands, they run about and strike in sport at everyone they meet. Antony was one of these runners, but instead of carrying out the traditional ceremony, he twined a wreath of laurel round a diadem and ran with it to the

* After his victory at Munda, in the autumn of 45 B.C.

† In his capacity as augur.

rostra. There he was lifted up by his fellow-runners and placed the diadem on Caesar's head, implying by this gesture that he deserved to be made king. At this Caesar made a show of declining the crown, whereupon the people were delighted and clapped their hands. Again Antony pressed it upon him, and again Caesar waved it aside. This pantomime continued for some time, with a few of Antony's friends encouraging his attempts to force the crown upon Caesar, while the crowd greeted every refusal with shouts of applause. Yet perhaps the most curious aspect of this affair was that while the people were ready to submit to the fact of being ruled by a king, they still shrank from the title, as though it signified the destruction of their liberty. At last, Caesar, who had been vexed by the whole episode, rose from the rostra, pulled open his toga, and called out that anyone who wished to cut his throat might do so there and then. The wreath was placed upon one of his statues, whereupon some of the tribunes of the people tore it down. The people followed them home with loud applause and cries of approval, but at Caesar's orders they were deposed from their office.

13. This episode encouraged Brutus and Cassius in their plot, and when they began to consider which of their friends could be trusted to help them, they discussed the question of whether or not to approach Antony. The rest of the conspirators were in favour of enlisting him, but Trebonius opposed the idea. He mentioned that at the time when many people had left Rome to meet Caesar on his return from Spain, Antony had travelled with him, and Trebonius had then sounded him unobtrusively and cautiously. Antony had understood his drift, he maintained, but had given him no encouragement: at the same time he had not reported the conversation to Caesar, but had faithfully kept it secret. It was then proposed that they should kill Antony at the same time as Caesar, but Brutus objected to this, arguing that if they were undertaking to kill a man for the sake of justice and the laws, then the deed must be kept pure and free from any taint of injustice. The others were afraid of Antony's physical strength and the influence which he commanded through his office, and some of the conspirators were detailed to keep watch for him, so that when Caesar entered the Senate-house and they were about to carry out the assassination, Antony should be engaged in conversation about some urgent matter and kept outside the chamber.

14. These plans were duly put into effect and Caesar fell in the Senate-house. Antony immediately disguised himself as a slave and went into hiding. But when he learned that the conspirators had merely assembled on the Capitol and had no further designs against anyone, he persuaded them to come down into the city and sent them his son as a hostage. He even went so far as to entertain Cassius in his house, and Lepidus did the same for Brutus. He also arranged a meeting of the Senate, at which he moved that an amnesty should be declared and that provinces should be allotted to Brutus and Cassius and their supporters. The Senate passed this proposal, and also voted that no change should be made in the measures which Caesar had taken. So when Antony left the Senate on this occasion, his reputation had never stood higher, for it was felt that he had delivered Rome from civil war and had succeeded in resolving an exceptionally difficult and confused situation in a most prudent and statesmanlike fashion.

However, these counsels of moderation were soon swept away by the tide of popular feeling which was now running in Antony's favour, and which inspired him with the hope that if Brutus could be overthrown, he himself would be sure to become the first man in Rome. It so happened that when Caesar's body was carried out for burial, Antony delivered the customary eulogy over it in the Forum. When he saw that his oratory had cast a spell over the people and that they were deeply stirred by his words, he began to introduce into his praises a note of pity and of indignation at Caesar's fate. Finally, at the close of his speech, he snatched up the dead man's robe and brandished it aloft, all bloodstained as it was and stabbed through in many places, and called those who had done the deed murderers and villains. This appeal had such an effect upon the people that they piled up benches and tables and burned Caesar's body in the Forum, and then, snatching up firebrands from the pyre, they ran to the houses of his assassins and attacked them.

15. Because of these events Brutus and his party left the city, while Caesar's friends allied themselves with Antony. Meanwhile, Caesar's widow Calpurnia entrusted him with the greater part of Caesar's treasure, which she removed from her house and delivered into Antony's hands. This amounted in all to four thousand talents. Antony also took charge of Caesar's papers, which contained written

memoranda of many of his plans and decrees. Antony made a number of insertions into these documents and so appointed many magistrates and senators according to his own wishes, and he also recalled some men from exile and released others from prison, as though all these actions represented the will of Caesar. The Romans by way of mockery nicknamed all those who had benefited in this way *Charonites*,* because if they were called upon to substantiate their case, they appealed to the records of the dead. In short, Antony at this period handled everything in an autocratic fashion, since he himself held the consulship, while his brothers had also been appointed to high office, Gaius as praetor and Lucius as tribune.

16. This was the situation in Rome which the young Octavius found when he arrived. He was, as I have mentioned above,† a son of Caesar's niece, who had been left the heir to the dead man's property, and at the time of the assassination he had been living at Apollonia. He at once paid his respects to Antony as the friend of his family, and then reminded him of the money which had been placed in his charge, since according to the terms of Caesar's will Octavius was bound as the legal heir to pay every Roman citizen the sum of seventy-five drachmas.‡ Antony was at first inclined to despise Octavius as a mere boy, and told him that he must be out of his mind, adding the warning that a young man who possessed few influential friends and little experience of the world would find it a crushing burden to accept the inheritance and act as Caesar's executor. Octavius was quite unmoved by this argument and continued to demand the money, while Antony for his part did everything possible to humiliate him. First of all he opposed him when Octavius stood for election as tribune, and then when the young man attempted to dedicate a golden chair in honour of Caesar, as the Senate had decreed,

* Plutarch gives the Greek word, derived from Charon, the legendary ferryman of Hades. The Latin word was *Orcini*, derived from Orcus the god of the underworld.

† See ch. 11.

‡ Octavius was not bound by law to accept the inheritance. Caesar's estate was so great that there was no danger of inheriting debts. The risk lay rather in inheriting the wealth and the odium which might attach to the dead man's name and in the difficulties of administering debatable legacies. Octavius was left three quarters of the estate. The remainder was left to Quintus Pedius, another great-nephew.

Antony threatened to have him imprisoned, unless he stopped trying to ingratiate himself with the people. Octavius's next move was to join forces with Cicero and all the rest of Antony's bitterest enemies: with their help the support of the Senate was secured, while he himself won the goodwill of the people and also succeeded in mobilizing many of Caesar's veterans from the colonies to which they had retired. By now Antony was becoming alarmed at these manoeuvres, and he met Octavius for a conference on the Capitol at which the two men were reconciled. On the same night after their meeting Antony experienced a strange dream, in which it seemed to him that his right hand was struck by a thunderbolt. A few days later a report reached him that Octavius was plotting against his life. Octavius did his utmost to justify himself, but he could not succeed in removing Antony's suspicions, and so the hostility between the two men flared up as intensely as ever. Both of them hurried all over Italy and vied with one another in offering lavish pay and rewards to recruit the veterans, who by now had settled on the land, and in being the first to secure the allegiance of the legionaries who were still under arms.

17. At this time Cicero still commanded more influence than any other man in Rome. He now devoted all his efforts to arousing public opinion against Antony and he succeeded so far as to persuade the Senate to declare him a public enemy, to confer the fasces and other insignia of a praetor upon Octavius, and to dispatch Hirtius and Pansa, the consuls, to drive Antony out of Italy. The two armies met near Mutina* and Octavius was present and fought on the side of the consuls. Antony was defeated, but Hirtius and Pansa were both killed. Antony's army experienced terrible hardships in their retreat, and they suffered most of all from hunger. But it was characteristic of Antony to show his finest qualities in the hour of trial, and indeed it was always when his fortunes were at their lowest that he came nearest to being a good man. It is a common experience for men who have suffered some reverse to understand what virtue is, but it is rare indeed for them to find the strength to emulate the qualities they admire and to rid themselves of the vices they condemn: on the contrary, many people become so discouraged by adversity that they give way to their habits all the more and allow their judgement to

* The modern Modena.

collapse. At any rate, on this occasion Antony set a wonderful example to his soldiers. In spite of all the luxury and extravagance of his recent life, he could bring himself without difficulty to drink foul water and eat wild fruits and roots. And during the crossing of the Alps, we are told, the army was reduced even to devouring the bark of trees and creatures that no man had ever tasted before.

18. They were anxious to make contact with the army commanded by Lepidus, for he was believed to be friendly to Antony, and like him he had benefited greatly from his association with Caesar. But when Antony arrived and encamped close by, there was no sign whatever of a welcome, and so he decided to risk everything on a bold move. His hair was long and uncombed, his beard had been left to grow ever since his defeat, and he now put on a dark cloak, walked up to the palisade which surrounded Lepidus's camp, and began to speak to the soldiers. Many of them were immediately touched by his appearance and stirred by his words, whereupon Lepidus became alarmed and ordered all the trumpets to be sounded so as to drown Antony's voice. But this only increased the soldiers' pity for him, and they then disguised Laelius and Clodius in the dresses of two of the prostitutes who followed the army and sent them to confer with Antony in secret. These two urged him to take courage and attack their camp at once, and told him that there were many who would not only welcome him but would kill Lepidus if he wished. Antony would not allow them to touch Lepidus, but the next day he began to cross the river with his army. He himself was the first to set foot in the water and waded over to the opposite shore, where he could already see many of Lepidus's troops stretching out their hands to welcome him and pulling down the fortifications of their camp. After he had entered and made himself master of the camp, he treated Lepidus with the greatest kindness. He embraced him, addressed him by the title of father, and, although he was in complete control of his rival's army, he insisted that Lepidus should retain the rank and honours of a general. His behaviour persuaded Munatius Plancus, who was encamped close by with another large body of troops, to join forces with him, and so with his army now restored to a formidable strength, he recrossed the Alps and marched into Italy with seventeen legions of infantry and ten thousand cavalry at his back. In addition to these he left six legions to garrison Gaul:

this force was under the command of Varius, one of his intimate friends and drinking companions, who was nicknamed Cotylon.*

19. By this time Octavius Caesar had quarrelled with Cicero, who, he realized, was determined to restore the liberties of the old Republic, and he now sent his friends to Antony and invited him to come to terms. So Antony, Lepidus, and Octavius met on a small island in the middle of a river,† and here their conference lasted for three days. They found no difficulty in agreeing on a great range of subjects, and they divided the rule of the whole world between them as easily as if it had been a family inheritance. The most troublesome of their problems turned out to be the question of which men were to be put to death, since each of them demanded the right to rid himself of his respective enemies and spare his own flesh and blood. In the end the hatred which each of them felt towards their enemies overcame their sense of honour towards their kinsmen and even their loyalty towards their friends, so that Octavius sacrificed Cicero to Antony, while Antony in his turn abandoned Lucius Caesar, who was his uncle on his mother's side. Lepidus was given the privilege of having his own brother Paulus executed, although some say that he gave up Paulus to Antony and Octavius who had demanded his death. However that may be, I can conceive of nothing more savage or vindictive than this trafficking in blood. At the end of all this bartering of one death for another, they were just as guilty of the murder of the men whom they abandoned as of those whom they seized; but the wrong which they did to their friends was the more revolting of the two, since they killed them without even hating them.

20. To complete this reconciliation the soldiers crowded round the three leaders and demanded that Octavius should cement the alliance by marrying Clodia, the daughter of Antony's wife Fulvia by her first husband. This was likewise agreed, after which the triumvirs proceeded to proscribe and put to death three hundred men:‡ Cicero was among the first, and after he had been slaughtered, Antony gave

* Derived from the Greek measure, *kotyle*, a half-pint.

† Near the modern Bologna in November 43 B.C.

‡ According to Appian, some three hundred senators and two thousand knights lost their lives. As in the Sullan proscriptions, the object was not only to eliminate political opponents, but also to raise money.

orders that his head and his right hand, with which Cicero had penned his invectives against him, should be cut off. When these were brought to him he gazed at them in triumph and burst into peals of delighted laughter. Then, after he had taken his fill, he had them nailed up above the rostra in the Forum, as if he had succeeded in inflicting a humiliation on the dead man, and not merely made a spectacle of the abuse of his power and of his own arrogance in the hour of good fortune. His uncle, Lucius Caesar, who had also been proscribed, found himself hunted down by his persecutors and took refuge with his sister, Antony's mother. When the murderers broke into her house and tried to force their way into her room, she stood in front of the door barring their entrance, and stretching out her hands, cried aloud, 'It was I who brought Antony, your general, into the world, and you shall not kill Lucius Caesar unless you kill me first.' By this action she succeeded in getting her brother Lucius out of the way and saved his life.

21. The Roman people came to detest the rule of the triumvirs, but it was Antony who earned the greatest share of the blame. He was older than Octavius and more influential than Lepidus, and yet no sooner had he shaken off his immediate troubles than he plunged once more into his old life of pleasure and debauchery. His general reputation was bad enough, but he aroused still more hatred on account of the house in which he lived. It had previously belonged to Pompey the Great, a man who was admired no less for his sobriety and his modest, orderly, and democratic way of life than for the fact of his having earned three triumphs. People were indignant when they saw that this house was most often barred to generals, magistrates, and ambassadors, who found themselves insolently turned away from the doors, and filled with actors, jugglers, and drunken parasites, upon whom Antony squandered most of the money which he had wrung with such violence and cruelty from his victims. For the triumvirate were not content with selling the properties of the men they proscribed, laying false accusations against their widows and relatives, and imposing extortionate taxes of every kind; when they learned that various sums had been deposited with the Vestal Virgins not only by Roman citizens but by foreigners, they went and seized the money by force. It was not long before Octavius Caesar discovered that Antony's appetite was insatiable, and he then demanded

that the money they confiscated should be shared between them. They also shared the command of the army and led their combined forces into Macedonia to attack Brutus and Cassius, leaving Lepidus in charge of Rome.*

22. However, when they crossed the Adriatic, launched their campaign, and encamped near the enemy with Antony facing Cassius's troops and Octavius those of Brutus, Octavius achieved nothing worth mentioning: it was Antony who seized the initiative and triumphed in every engagement. At any rate, in the first battle Octavius suffered a crushing defeat from Brutus, his camp was taken, and he himself barely managed to escape, although he makes out in his memoirs that he withdrew before the battle because of a dream which one of his friends experienced. Antony, on the other hand, overcame Cassius's army, although according to some accounts Antony was not present at the battle, but only joined in when his men were already in pursuit of the enemy. Cassius knew nothing of Brutus's success and was killed at his own command by Pindarus, one of his trusted freedmen. A second battle was fought a few days later and in this Brutus was defeated and took his own life. Here again Antony earned most of the credit for the victory, since on this occasion Octavius was ill. As he stood over Brutus's body, Antony uttered a few words of reproach for the fate of his brother Gaius, whom Brutus had put to death in Macedonia in revenge for the murder of Cicero. But he declared that Hortensius was more to blame for this action than Brutus and gave orders for him to be executed over his brother's tomb. Then he threw his own scarlet cloak, which was of great value, over Brutus's body and commanded one of his freedmen to make himself responsible for its burial. When he discovered later that this man had never burned the cloak with Brutus's body and had stolen most of the money which should have been devoted to the funeral, he had him put to death.

23. After this, Octavius was carried back to Rome, and it was generally believed that his sickness would prove fatal. Antony now marched across Greece with a large army to levy money from all the eastern provinces. The triumvirs had promised each of their soldiers a bounty of five hundred drachmas, and so they now found themselves

* In the late summer of 42 B.C.

obliged to adopt a harsher policy both in imposing taxes and collecting tribute. In his dealings with the Greeks, Antony's behaviour was moderate and courteous enough, at least in the beginning, and for his entertainment he was content to attend games and religious ceremonies and listen to the discussions of scholars. He was lenient in his administration of justice, and took pleasure in being addressed as a lover of Greece, and still more as a lover of Athens, where he showered gifts upon the city. But when the people of Megara wanted to show him something to rival the beauty of Athens and invited him to see their senate-house, he duly travelled there and looked it over. Then they asked him to tell them what he thought of it, to which he replied, 'Of course it is not very large, but then it is very ruinous!' He also had the temple of the Pythian Apollo surveyed so as to complete it: at least he promised the local senate that he would do this.

24. Soon after, he left Lucius Censorinus in charge of Greece,* crossed into Asia, and at once began to help himself to the wealth of the province. Obsequious rulers would flock to his door, while their wives would vie with one another in offering gifts and exploiting their beauty, and would sacrifice their honour to his pleasure. So while Octavius Caesar in Rome was wearing himself out in the never-ending struggle of party politics and civil war, Antony was revelling in the delights of peace and infinite leisure, and soon allowed his passions to sweep him back into his accustomed mode of life. Lute-players like Anaxenor, flute-players like Xanthus, the dancer Metrodorus, and a whole horde of Asiatic performers, who far surpassed in insolence and buffoonery even the pests who had come out with him from Italy, now descended upon him and took control of his household, and more and more people began to find it intolerable that all Antony's resources should be squandered on extravagances like these. For the whole province of Asia, like the Thebes of Sophocles's *Oedipus Tyrannus*, was now filled with incense,

The sound of paeans and despairing cries.†

At any rate, when Antony made his entry into Ephesus, women dressed as Bacchantes and men and boys as satyrs and Pans marched in procession before him. The city was filled with wreaths of ivy and

* In 41 B.C. † *Oedipus Tyrannus* 1, 4.

thyrsus wands, the air resounded with the music of harps, pipes, and flutes, and the people hailed him as Dionysus the Benefactor and the Bringer of Joy. Certainly this was how some people saw him, but to the majority he came as Dionysus the Cruel and the Eater of Flesh,* for he stripped many noble families of their property and gave it away to rogues and flatterers. In other cases men were allowed to steal fortunes from owners who were still living by making them out to be dead. And in Magnesia Antony presented a man's house to a cook, whose reputation, we are told, had been earned on the strength of a single dinner. But at last when Antony imposed a second levy on the cities, Hybreas, speaking on behalf of the whole province of Asia, summoned up the courage to say this; 'If you can take tribute from us twice a year, no doubt you can give us two summers and two harvests'. He expressed himself with a certain rhetorical flourish which appealed to Antony's taste, but then he added in blunter language that Asia had already raised two hundred thousand talents for Antony. 'If you have never received this money,' he went on, 'you should ask for it from the men who collected it. But if you did receive it and no longer have it, we are ruined.' These words made a deep impression upon Antony, for he was completely ignorant of much that was done in his name, not merely because he was of an easygoing disposition, but because he was simple enough to trust his subordinates.

His character was, in fact, essentially simple and he was slow to perceive the truth. Once he recognized that he was at fault, he was full of repentance and ready to admit his errors to those he had wronged. Whenever he had to punish an offence or right an injustice, he acted on the grand scale, and it was generally considered that he overstepped the bounds far more often in the rewards he bestowed than in the punishments he inflicted. As for the kind of coarse and insolent banter which he liked to exchange, this carried its own remedy with it, for anyone could return his ribaldry with interest and he enjoyed being laughed at quite as much as laughing at others. And in fact it was this quality which often did him harm, for he found it impossible to believe that the real purpose of those who took liberties and cracked jokes with him was to flatter him. He never

* Dionysus was credited with many different names and qualities, and the primitive and savage element in his cult was quite as typical as the genial and beneficent.

understood that some men go out of their way to adopt a frank and outspoken manner and use it like a piquant sauce to disguise the cloying taste of flattery. Such people deliberately indulge in bold repartee and an aggressive flow of talk when they are in their cups, so that the obsequious compliance which they show in matters of business does not suggest that they associate with a man merely to please him, but seems to spring from a genuine conviction of his superior wisdom.

25. Such being Antony's nature, the love for Cleopatra which now entered his life came as the final and crowning mischief which could befall him. It excited to the point of madness many passions which had hitherto lain concealed, or at least dormant, and it stifled or corrupted all those redeeming qualities in him which were still capable of resisting temptation. The occasion on which he lost his heart came about as follows. While he was preparing for the campaign against the Parthians, he sent word to Cleopatra, ordering her to meet him in Cilicia to answer the charge that she had raised money for Cassius and sent him help in his war against the triumvirs. Dellius, who carried out this mission, was struck by the charm and subtlety of Cleopatra's conversation as soon as he set eyes on her, and he saw at once that such a woman, so far from having anything to fear from Antony, would probably gain the strongest influence over him. He decided to pay his court to the Egyptian queen and urged her to go to Cilicia dressed in 'all the splendour her art could command', as Homer puts it,* and to have no fear of Antony, who was the gentlest and most chivalrous of generals. Cleopatra was impressed by what Dellius told her. She had already seen for herself the power of her beauty to enchant Julius Caesar and the younger Pompey, and she expected to conquer Antony even more easily. For Caesar and Gnaeus Pompey† had known her when she was still a young girl with no experience of the world, but she was to meet Antony at the age when a woman's beauty is at its most superb and her mind at its most mature.‡ She therefore provided herself with as lavish a supply of gifts, money, and ornaments as her exalted position and the

* The quotation is from *Iliad* XVI, 162, a passage which describes how Hera decked herself out to seduce Zeus.

† The son of Pompey the Great.

‡ In 41 B.C. Cleopatra was twenty-eight.

prosperity of her kingdom made it appropriate to take, but she relied above all upon her physical presence and the spell and enchantment which it could create.

26. She received a whole succession of letters from Antony and his friends summoning her to visit him, but she treated him with such disdain, that when she appeared it was as if in mockery of his orders. She came sailing up the river Cydnus in a barge with a poop of gold, its purple sails billowing in the wind, while her rowers caressed the water with oars of silver which dipped in time to the music of the flute, accompanied by pipes and lutes. Cleopatra herself reclined beneath a canopy of cloth of gold, dressed in the character of Venus, as we see her in paintings, while on either side to complete the picture stood boys costumed as Cupids, who cooled her with their fans. Instead of a crew the barge was lined with the most beautiful of her waiting-women attired as Nereids and Graces, some at the rudders, others at the tackle of the sails, and all the while an indescribably rich perfume, exhaled from innumerable censers, was wafted from the vessel to the river-banks. Great multitudes accompanied this royal progress, some of them following the queen on both sides of the river from its very mouth, while others hurried down from the city of Tarsus to gaze at the sight. Gradually the crowds drifted away from the market-place, where Antony awaited the queen enthroned on his tribunal, until at last he was left sitting quite alone and the word spread on every side that Venus had come to revel with Bacchus for the happiness of Asia.

Antony then sent a message inviting Cleopatra to dine with him, but she thought it more appropriate that he should come to her, and so, as he wished to show his courtesy and goodwill, he accepted and went. He found the preparations made to receive him magnificent beyond words, but what astonished him most of all was the extraordinary number of lights. So many of these, it is said, were let down from the roof and displayed on all sides at once, and they were arranged and grouped in such ingenious patterns in relation to each other, some in squares and some in circles, that they created as brilliant a spectacle as can ever have been devised to delight the eye.

27. On the following day Antony returned her hospitality with another banquet, but although he had hoped to surpass her in

splendour and elegance he was hopelessly outdone in both, and was the first to make fun of the crude and meagre quality of his entertainment. Cleopatra saw that Antony's humour was broad and gross and belonged to the soldier rather than the courtier, and she quickly adopted the same manner towards him and treated him without the least reserve. Her own beauty, so we are told, was not of that incomparable kind which instantly captivates the beholder. But the charm of her presence was irresistible, and there was an attraction in her person and her talk, together with a peculiar force of character which pervaded her every word and action, and laid all who associated with her under its spell. It was a delight merely to hear the sound of her voice, with which, like an instrument of many strings, she could pass from one language to another, so that in her interviews with barbarians she seldom required an interpreter, but conversed with them quite unaided, whether they were Ethiopians, Troglodytes, Hebrews, Arabians, Syrians, Medes, or Parthians. In fact, she is said to have become familiar with the speech of many other peoples besides, although the rulers of Egypt before her had never even troubled to learn the Egyptian language, and some of them had even given up their native Macedonian dialect.

28. At any rate, Cleopatra succeeded in captivating Antony so completely that, at the very moment when Fulvia his wife was carrying on war in Italy against Octavius Caesar in defence of her husband's interests, and a Parthian army under Labienus* (whom the king's generals had appointed commander-in-chief) was hovering threateningly on the frontier of Mesopotamia and was about to invade Syria, he allowed the queen to carry him off to Alexandria. There this veteran indulged himself in the amusements and diversions of a young man with all his future before him, and was content to squander on idle pleasures what Antiphon calls the most precious of all commodities, that is time. Antony and Cleopatra gathered around them a company of friends whom they called the Inimitable Livers,

* This Labienus was a son of the Titus Labienus who had been one of Caesar's officers in Gaul, joined Pompey's side, and was killed at the battle of Munda in 45 B.C. The son was sent by Brutus and Cassius to seek help from Orodes, the king of Parthia, and was there when the conspirators were defeated at Philippi. Labienus invaded Syria in 40 B.C., but was driven out by Antony's general Ventidius and later captured in Cilicia.

and each day they gave banquets for one another of an almost incredible extravagance. Philotas, a physician who lived at Amphissa, used to tell my grandfather that he was studying his profession in Alexandria at this time,* and that, having made the acquaintance of one of the royal cooks, he was persuaded, as was natural enough in a young man, to come and see the lavish preparations which were made for a royal dinner. He was introduced into the kitchens of the palace, and, after he had seen the enormous abundance of provisions and watched eight wild boars being roasted, he expressed his astonishment at the size of the company for which this vast hospitality was intended. The cook laughed aloud and explained that this was not a large party, only about a dozen people, but that everything must be cooked and served to perfection, and that the whole effect could be ruined by a moment's delay. It might happen that Antony would call for the meal as soon as the guests had arrived, or a little later he might postpone it and call for a cup of wine, or become absorbed in some conversation. 'So we never prepare one supper,' he explained, 'but a whole number of them, as we never know the exact moment when they will be sent for.' This is the story Philotas used to tell, and he also mentioned that in later years he treated Antony's eldest son by Fulvia as one of his patients, and was in the habit of dining with him at his house with his friends, when the young man did not dine with his father. On one occasion there was a physician present, who had been talking boastfully and had annoyed the company at supper, until Philotas managed to silence him with the following piece of sophistry: 'In some states of fever the patient should take cold water. Everyone in a fever is in some state of fever: therefore everyone in a fever should take cold water.' The man was nonplussed by this argument and could say nothing in reply. Antony's son was delighted and said with a laugh, 'All this is yours, Philotas', and pointed to a table which was laden with large drinking cups. Philotas appreciated his host's desire to show his gratitude, but gave himself leave to doubt whether so young a boy could possibly have the authority to give away a present of this size. But not long afterwards one of the slaves brought the cups to him in a sack and asked him to put his seal on it. And when Philotas waved them aside and was afraid to accept the present, the man said, 'Don't be a fool! Why do you hesitate? Don't you know that this is Antony's son, who has the right to give you all

* Alexandria possessed a famous school of medicine.

these things in gold if he wants to? But if I were you, I should exchange the whole lot with us for cash. Some of these cups are old, and the workmanship is considered very valuable, and it is quite possible the boy's father might miss them.' According to my grandfather, Philotas was fond of telling stories like these at every opportunity.

29. Plato speaks of four kinds of flattery, but Cleopatra knew a thousand. Whether Antony's mood were serious or gay, she could always invent some fresh device to delight or charm him. She engrossed his attention utterly and never released him for an instant by day or by night. She played dice with him, drank with him, and hunted with him, and when he exercised with his weapons, she watched him. At night, when he liked to wander about the city, stand by the doors or windows of ordinary citizens' houses, and make fun of the people inside, she would dress up as a maidservant and play her part in any mad prank that came into Antony's head, for it was his custom to go out disguised as a slave. On these occasions he was always received with torrents of abuse, and sometimes even found himself beaten up before he returned to the palace, although most people guessed who he was. The fact was that the Alexandrians had a weakness for his buffoonery and enjoyed taking part in these amusements in their elegant and cultivated way. They liked him personally, and used to say that Antony put on his tragic mask for the Romans, but kept the comic one for them.

Now it would be a great waste of time for me to describe all the details of Antony's childish amusements, but a single instance may serve as an illustration. One day he went out fishing, had no luck with his line, and was all the more enraged because Cleopatra happened to be present. So he ordered some fishermen to dive down and secretly to fasten on to his hook a number of fish they had already caught. Then he proceeded to pull up his line two or three times, but the queen discovered the trick. She pretended to admire his success, but then told her friends what had happened and invited them to come and watch on the next day. A large party got into the fishing boats, and when Antony had let down his line, Cleopatra ordered one of her own servants to swim immediately to his hook and fix on to it a salted fish from the Black Sea. Antony, believing that he had made a catch, pulled up his line, whereupon the whole company burst out laughing, as was natural, and Cleopatra told him: 'Emperor, you had better give up your rod to us poor rulers of Pharos and Canopus. Your sport is to hunt cities and kingdoms and continents.'

30. In the midst of these follies and boyish extravagances Antony was surprised by two reports. The first was from Rome to the effect that his brother Lucius and Fulvia had quarrelled with one another and then joined forces to make war against Octavius Caesar, but had been defeated and forced to flee from Italy. The second, which was no less disturbing, announced that Labienus in command of a Parthian army was making himself master of Asia, from the Euphrates and Syria as far west as the provinces of Lydia and Ionia. Then at last,* like a man who has been roughly awoken after sleeping off a heavy debauch, Antony took the field against the Parthians and advanced as far as Phoenicia. There, however, he received a letter from Fulvia full of lamentations at her plight and so he decided to change his plans and sail for Italy with his fleet of two hundred ships. On his way he picked up a number of his supporters who were in flight from Italy, and from them he learned that it was Fulvia who had been the principal cause of the war with Octavius. She was a headstrong woman who enjoyed meddling in politics, and she had hoped that the quickest way to make Antony leave Cleopatra would be to stir up hostilities in Italy. But it so happened that Fulvia, as she was on her way to meet Antony, fell ill and died at Sicyon. This event greatly improved the prospects of a reconciliation with Octavius, for when Antony arrived in Italy it soon became clear that Octavius had no intention of holding him responsible for the war, while Antony himself was ready to blame Fulvia for any accusations that might be made against himself. At any rate, when they met,† their friends on both sides refused to allow time to be spent in probing too closely into Antony's excuses. Their first concern was to reconcile the two men personally, and then to divide up the empire. They made the Ionian sea the boundary between them and gave the eastern territories to Antony and the western to Octavius, while Lepidus was assigned the province of Africa. It was also agreed that when neither of the two men wished to be consul themselves, their supporters should hold this office in turn.

* Early in 40 B.C. † In October 40 B.C.

31. These arrangements were generally considered fair on both sides, but it was felt that a closer tie would also be desirable, and for this fortune now provided the opportunity. Octavius Caesar had a half-sister, Octavia, who was older than himself and was the daughter of Anchoria, while he was the child by a later marriage of Atia. Octavius was deeply attached to his sister, who was, as the saying is, a wonder of a woman. Her husband, Gaius Marcellus, had died only a short while before and she was now a widow, while Antony, since Fulvia's death, was also regarded as a widower. He did not deny his connexion with Cleopatra, but he did not admit that she was his wife, and in this matter he was still torn between his reason and his love for the Egyptian queen. Meanwhile, on the Roman side, everybody was anxious that this marriage should take place, for it was hoped that if only Octavia – who in addition to her beauty possessed great dignity of character and good sense – could become united to Antony and win his love, as such a woman could hardly fail to do, this alliance would prove the salvation of their own affairs and would restore harmony to the Roman world.* Accordingly, when the two men had agreed upon terms, they went up to Rome and celebrated Octavia's wedding. The law did not allow a woman to marry until ten months had elapsed after her husband's death, but in this instance the Senate passed a decree to dispense with the usual time limit.

32. At this time Sextus Pompeius's forces were still in control of Sicily. He was also ravaging the Italian coast, and with the help of a pirate fleet under the command of Menas and Menecrates was able to threaten shipping throughout the whole central Mediterranean area. Nevertheless, he had given help to Antony's mother when she had fled from Rome with Fulvia and was believed to be well disposed towards Antony himself, and so the triumvirs decided to negotiate with him. They met at the promontory of Misenum† by the mole

* There is evidence that it was this union and the hope that a son would be born from it which inspired Virgil's famous Fourth Eclogue, with its prophecy of the coming of a divine infant who would inaugurate a golden age.

† This conference at Misenum, the northern tip of the gulf of Naples, took place in the spring of 39 B.C. Sextus was the younger son of Pompey the Great, and his control of the sea enabled him to cut off corn supplies from Rome. This had produced famine and a number of riots in the capital which had been brutally suppressed.

which runs into the sea. Pompey's fleet was anchored close by, and Antony's and Octavius's troops were drawn up on the shore. There it was agreed that Pompey should hold Sardinia and Sicily, in return for which he undertook to keep the sea clear of pirates and send a specified quantity of grain to Rome: then, after they had reached agreement, they invited one another to dine. They cast lots to decide who should be host, and it fell to Pompey to entertain the company first. When Antony inquired where the banquet would be held, Pompey replied 'There', and pointed to his flagship with its six banks of oars, 'it is the only ancestral home that is left me.' This retort was by way of reproach to Antony, who had taken possession of the house which had belonged to Pompey the Great.* At any rate, Pompey anchored his ship close inshore, constructed a pontoon between it and the headland, and warmly welcomed his guests on board. But later, when the company had become thoroughly convivial, and jokes concerning Antony's passion for Cleopatra were being bandied freely about, Menas the pirate came up to Pompey and whispered to him out of the guests' hearing, 'Shall I cut the cables and make you master not just of Sicily and Sardinia but of the whole Roman empire?' Pompey thought over this remark for a moment, and then burst out, 'Menas, you should have acted, not spoken to me about this beforehand. Now we must be content with things as they are. I do not break my word.' After this Pompey was entertained in his turn by Antony and by Octavius, and later he sailed back to Sicily.

33. After this treaty had been concluded, Antony sent Ventidius† ahead of him into Asia to check the Parthian advance. Meanwhile, to please Octavius, he accepted the office of Pontifex Maximus, which Julius Caesar had held, and during this period they consulted one another and acted in harmony in their handling of political problems and other affairs of state. Nevertheless, Antony was vexed by the fact that in their various diversions and amusements he always found himself worsted by Octavius. He kept in his house an Egyptian soothsayer who was skilled in casting horoscopes, and this man, either

* See ch. 21.

† P. Ventidius Bassus was what the Romans called a *novus homo*, that is the first member of his family to win distinction. His talents as a commander were originally discovered by Julius Caesar.

to oblige Cleopatra or because he wished to tell Antony the truth, made no secret of his conviction that Antony's fortune, although great and brilliant by any other standard, was constantly eclipsed by that of Octavius; and so he advised Antony to keep as far away from his young colleague as he could. 'Your guardian spirit,' he warned Antony, 'stands in awe of his, and although by itself it is proud and full of mettle, it becomes cowed and daunted in the presence of Caesar's.' And indeed the turn of events seemed to bear out the Egyptian's words, for we are told that whenever the two men cast lots or threw dice, whether by way of amusement or to decide some matter on which they were engaged, it was always Antony who came out the loser.

Antony contrived to hide his annoyance at such incidents, but they made him pay more attention to the Egyptian's warnings, and, after placing the management of his household in Octavius's hands, he left Italy and took Octavia, who had meanwhile given birth to a daughter, with him to Greece. He spent the winter in Athens and it was there that the news reached him of the first successes of Ventidius,* who had defeated the Parthians in a pitched battle and killed not only Labienus, but also Pharnapates, who was king Hyrodes' ablest general. In honour of this victory Antony gave entertainments for the Greeks and organized an athletic festival in Athens, at which he presided. He left at home his insignia of rank as a Roman general, and appeared in public wearing the robes and white shoes and carrying the rods of a gymnasiarch, and he acted as referee in some of the contests, taking the young wrestlers by the neck and parting them.

34. When the time came for him to set out for the Parthian campaign, he took a wreath from the sacred olive tree of Athena, which stands on the Acropolis, and in obedience to an oracle had a vessel filled with water from the sacred spring of the Clepsydra, and took it with him. Meanwhile Pacorus, king Hyrodes's son, had again invaded Syria with a large army of Parthians, but he was engaged

* In 39 B.C. Ventidius defeated the Parthians at the Cilician Gates and Mt Amanus. In these campaigns the Parthians abandoned the long-range attacks by mounted archers, which had won them the battle of Carrhae against Crassus, and relied, unsuccessfully, upon their armoured cavalry, manned by the feudal nobility. By the time that Antony invaded Parthia this lesson had been learned.

and defeated by Ventidius at Gindarus in the region of Cyrrhestica,* and the greater part of his force was annihilated, Pacorus himself being one of the first to be killed. With this victory, which came to be regarded as one of their most brilliant military achievements, the Romans gained their full revenge for the disaster which they had suffered under Crassus, and the Parthians, who had now been decisively defeated in three successive battles, were driven back behind the frontiers of Media and Mesopotamia. Ventidius decided not to pursue them any farther, however, for fear of arousing Antony's jealousy at his success. Instead, he attacked and subdued the tribes which had revolted against Rome, and laid siege to Antiochus of Commagene in the city of Samosata. When Antiochus offered to pay a thousand talents and make his submission to Antony, Ventidius told him that he must send his offer to Antony himself, who had advanced into the neighbourhood and had refused to allow Ventidius to conclude a settlement directly with Antiochus.† He was anxious that at least one achievement should be credited to his own name and did not wish every success to be attributed to Ventidius. However, the siege dragged on and the townspeople, when they found that they had no hope of obtaining terms, defended themselves stoutly. Antony could achieve nothing, and as he had now begun to feel ashamed and repentant at having refused the original offer, he was content to make peace with Antiochus and accept a payment of three hundred talents. He went on to settle some minor affairs in Syria, and then returned to Athens, and at the same time conferred appropriate honours on Ventidius and sent him home to be given his triumph.

Ventidius is the only man up to the present time who has ever celebrated a triumph over the Parthians. His origins were humble, but his friendship with Antony gave him the opportunities to achieve great things, and he made such effective use of these that he confirmed the general verdict which has been passed on both Antony and Octavius Caesar, namely that their victories were more often won

* In 38 B.C., according to Dio Cassius, Pacorus was killed on 9 June, the same day on which Crassus had lost his life fifteen years earlier.

† Other evidence suggests that Ventidius accepted a bribe from Antiochus not to press the siege with any vigour, and Antony was obliged to finish off the operation himself. Ventidius was allowed to return to Rome to celebrate his triumph, but thereafter he disappears from the scene.

by their subordinates than by themselves. Certainly Sossius, another of Antony's commanders, won important victories* in Syria, while Canidius not only conquered the Armenians† when Antony left him in their territory, but also subdued the kings of the Iberi and the Albani‡ and advanced as far as the Caucasus. As a result of these campaigns the fame and the prestige of Antony's power spread far and wide among the barbarians.

35. Meanwhile, Antony had again been angered by various slanders which Octavius had been spreading against him, and he sailed with three hundred ships for Italy. The people of Brundisium closed their harbour against him, and he therefore sailed round the coast to Tarentum. There he was prevailed upon by Octavia, who had accompanied him from Greece, to allow her to visit her brother. She had already borne Antony two daughters and was now again pregnant. She met Octavius on her way to him, and, after taking aside his two friends Agrippa and Maecenas and winning their sympathy, she appealed to her brother with tears and passionate entreaties not to make her the most wretched of women after having been the happiest. As it was, she told him, the eyes of the whole world were upon her, since she was the wife of one of its masters and the sister of the other. 'If the worst should happen,' she said, 'and war break out between you, no one can say which of you is fated to conquer the other, but what is quite certain is that my fate will be miserable.' Her words touched Octavius and he came to Tarentum in a mood to make peace.§ There the inhabitants witnessed a truly noble spectacle, an immense army, peaceably encamped on land, and an equally

* He took the island and town of Aradus in Phoenicia in 38 B.C. and also captured Jerusalem.

† In 37 B.C., the year before Antony's invasion of Parthia, Canidius led an advance expedition into Armenia.

‡ Tribes living to the south of the Caucasus.

§ This meeting at Tarentum took place in the spring of 37 B.C. From Antony's point of view there were two most pressing problems. First, although both triumvirs had an equal right to recruit troops in Italy, he found that his were repeatedly held back or diverted on various pretexts. Secondly, the appointed term for the triumvirate would shortly expire and it was important to renew his powers. By this pact he abandoned Sextus Pompeius and supplied Octavius with ships to use against him. In return, since his right to recruit was proving valueless, he demanded troops. The triumvirate was extended for a further five years.

powerful fleet lying quietly off shore, while between these two great armaments there passed nothing but friendly greetings and expressions of goodwill. Antony took the initiative by entertaining Octavius Caesar, who accepted the invitation for his sister's sake, and they arrived at an agreement whereby Octavius was to transfer two legions to Antony for his Parthian campaign, and Antony in return a hundred galleys armed with bronze rams. Besides these concessions Octavia persuaded her husband to make over twenty light vessels to her brother, and her brother a thousand infantrymen to her husband. In this way they parted friends, and Octavius, who was anxious to secure Sicily, lost no time in launching his campaign against Sextus Pompeius.* Antony, on the other hand, after entrusting Octavia and her daughters together with his children to Caesar's charge, set sail for Asia.

36. But now the fatal influence, that is his passion for Cleopatra, which for a long while had lain dormant in his heart, and which appeared to have been charmed away or at least lulled into oblivion by wiser counsels, suddenly gathered strength and blazed once more into life as he approached the coast of Syria. And finally, just like the rebellious and unmanageable horse which Plato describes when he compares the human soul to a chariot team,† so Antony flung away all those nobler considerations of restraint which might have saved him, and sent Fonteius Capito to escort Cleopatra to Syria. And when she arrived, the presents he showered upon her were no mere trinkets. To the dominions she already possessed he added Phoenicia, Coele Syria,‡ Cyprus, and a large part of Cilicia. He also gave her the region of Judaea which produces balsam and the coastal strip of Arabia Nabataea, which stretches down to the Red Sea. The gift of these territories aroused deep resentment among the Romans. In the past, Antony had bestowed tetrarchies and even the sovereignty of great peoples upon private individuals; he had deprived many rulers of their

* In effect, he spent the rest of 37 preparing for this operation. Pompeius was finally defeated and driven from Sicily in the autumn of 36. He fled to Asia and was there captured and put to death by one of Antony's officers.

† In the *Phaedrus* Plato compares the soul to a winged chariot with a charioteer, Reason, a white horse, which represents Honour, and a black, Pride and Insolence.

‡ The central region of Syria which extends eastwards from the Lebanon mountains and includes Damascus and Palmyra.

kingdoms, as for example Antigonus,* whom he had brought out of prison and beheaded, although no king before him had ever been punished by the Romans in this way, but nothing caused so much offence to his own countrymen as the shame of these honours conferred upon Cleopatra. He went on to make the scandal worse by acknowledging his twin children by her, one of whom he named Alexander and the other Cleopatra, and surnamed them the Sun and the Moon. However, Antony was well versed in the art of putting the best possible face on disreputable actions, and he used to declare that the greatness of the Roman empire was manifested in its power to bestow kingdoms rather than to take them, and that a noble line should be extended by leaving a succession born of many sovereigns. At any rate it was on this principle, he said, that his own ancestor had been begotten by Hercules, who did not limit his posterity to any single womb, nor allow himself to be overawed by any Solonian laws to regulate conception. He never feared the audit of his copulations, but let nature have her way, and left behind him the foundations of many families.

37. Not long after this, Phraates put his father Hyrodes to death and seized possession of the kingdom of Parthia. Many of the Parthians fled the country, and one of them named Monaeses, a man of high rank and considerable power, took refuge with Antony. It occurred to Antony that this man's situation was rather like that of Themistocles, and, as he also saw a flattering parallel between his own abundant wealth and generosity and those of the Persian kings, he presented him with three cities, Larissa, Arethusa, and Hierapolis which was previously called Bambyce.† However, when the Parthian king summoned Monaeses to return, sending him a right hand,‡ as the saying is, Antony gladly took the opportunity of sending him back.

* Antigonus was in fact a High Priest of the Jews, a usurper, not a king, and he had risen to power with the support of the Parthians during their invasion of Syria. He was executed in 37 B.C. Herod, whom Antony now made ruler of Judaea, had been a loyal adherent of his, and according to Dio Cassius it was at Herod's request that Antigonus was put to death.

† It was an oriental custom to grant a man of a certain eminence a town or a district. It maintained him and he administered it. He was then expected to show loyalty on the feudal principle.

‡ An expression used among the Persians and Parthians to signify an offer of peace and friendship.

In reality his plan was to deceive Phraates* by pretending that he had no intention of fighting, and the only demand he made was for the return of the Roman standards, which had been captured when Crassus was defeated, and the release of any of his men who might still be living. Antony himself, after sending Cleopatra back to Egypt, at once marched through Arabia and Armenia to a place where he had arranged for his own forces to be joined by those of the various kings who were his allies. There were many of these rulers, but the most powerful of them was Artavasdes, the king of Armenia, who provided six thousand cavalry and seven thousand infantry. Here Antony held a review of his army. The Romans themselves numbered sixty thousand, together with the cavalry which was classed at that time as Roman, in this case ten thousand Spaniards and Celts. The other nations contributed a total of about thirty thousand men, including cavalry and light-armed troops.

And yet we are told that this immense concentration of strength, which alarmed even the Indians beyond Bactria and made all Asia tremble, was rendered useless to Antony because of his attachment to Cleopatra. Such was his passion to spend the winter with her that he took the field too early in the season and conducted the whole campaign in a disorderly fashion. It was as if he were no longer the master of his own judgement, but rather under the influence of some drug or magic spell, for he gave the impression that his eyes were constantly drawn to her image and his thoughts fixed upon hastening his return rather than upon conquering the enemy.

38. In the first place, then, his best plan would have been to spend the winter in Armenia, to rest his men who were worn out by a march of a thousand miles, and after this to occupy Media in the early weeks of the spring, before the Parthians had moved out of their winter quarters. As it was, he was too impatient to wait and immediately led his army forward, leaving Armenia on his left and traversing the province of Atropatene, which he ravaged. Secondly, his haste was so great that he refused to wait for the engines needed for siege operations, which were transported on three hundred wagons, and included a battering ram eighty feet long. If any of these machines

* The deception worked rather against Antony, since it seems unlikely that Monaeses ever needed to seek refuge. His purpose was to spy out Antony's plans and report them.

were destroyed, it would be impossible to replace them in time for the campaign, because none of the provinces of upper Asia produce timber which is sufficiently long or hard for these purposes. Nevertheless, Antony gave orders for this equipment to follow in the rear, on the ground that it hindered the speed of his advance: he therefore detached a large force under the command of Statianus to escort it, while he himself began the siege of Phraata, a large city which was the residence of the wives and children of the king of Media. But the difficulties of this operation quickly showed him what a blunder he had made in leaving his siege-train behind. Accordingly, he moved his troops close up to the city wall and began to build a mound against it, which his men could only heap up slowly and with great labour. In the meanwhile Phraates had marched down from Parthia with a large army, and as soon as he discovered that the wagons with the siege-train had been left in the rear he despatched a strong force of cavalry to attack it. Statianus found himself surrounded,* he and ten thousand of his men were killed, and the barbarians captured the siege-engines and destroyed them. They also took a large number of prisoners, among whom was Polemon, one of the kings of Pontus.

39. Antony's army, as was natural, was deeply discouraged at suffering this unexpected disaster at the very beginning of their campaign. To make matters worse, Artavasdes, the king of Armenia, decided that the Romans' prospects were hopeless, withdrew his forces, and departed,† although he had been the prime mover of the war in the first instance. The Parthians now came up to the besieging army and used their finest troops to make a demonstration in full armour, during which they shouted insulting threats at the Romans. Thereupon Antony, who was anxious that his army should not lose its offensive spirit and become utterly demoralized by remaining inactive, took with him ten legions, three cohorts of the praetorian guard, and all his cavalry, and led them out on a foraging expedition, in the hope that this would be the best way to draw the enemy into a pitched battle.

* He was defeated by the same tactics that had been used against Crassus – hordes of mounted archers, constantly supplied with fresh quivers by pack animals, who stayed out of reach of the legions and poured in a destructive hail of arrows upon them.

† Artavasdes in fact deserted Statianus's force. It was his cavalry which had formed a large part of the escort, and their defection contributed greatly to the annihilation of the siege-train.

After he had advanced one day's journey, he noticed that the Parthians were beginning to envelop him and were evidently watching their opportunity to fall upon him as he marched. He therefore hung out the signal for battle inside his camp, but had the tents taken down, as though his intention were not to fight but to retreat, and he then marched past the line of barbarians who were drawn up in a crescent-shaped formation. But he had given orders that, as soon as the legionaries were close enough to attack the enemy's leading ranks, the cavalry should launch a charge. To the Parthians drawn up in a parallel line the steadiness of the Roman discipline seemed indescribably impressive, as they watched them march past, rank upon rank, maintaining their exact intervals in perfect order and silence and with their spears at the ready. But when the signal was given and the Roman cavalry wheeled and charged with loud shouts, they received their onslaught and repelled it, even though the enemy were upon them so quickly that they could not use their bows. However, when the legionaries joined in the attack, shouting and clashing their weapons, the Parthian horses took fright and backed away, and the Parthians fled before the infantry could get to close quarters.

Antony pursued them hard, for he had great hopes that he had put an end to the war, or at any rate won a decisive victory in that one battle. His infantry kept up the pursuit for over six miles and his cavalry for twenty, and yet when the Parthian losses were reckoned up they amounted to a mere thirty prisoners and eighty dead. This news spread dismay and despondency throughout the army, and it came as a terrible shock to the men to discover how few of the enemy they had killed in winning this victory, compared with the crushing defeat they had suffered when the wagons were captured. The next day they broke camp and started back towards their base at Phraata. On the way they encountered at first only a few scattered troops of the enemy, then larger groups and finally the whole body, who immediately challenged and attacked them from all sides, as if they were a completely fresh army which had never been defeated. The Romans were hard pressed, but at last after much heavy fighting they forced their way through to their camp. Soon afterwards the Medes made a sortie from the town, attacked the Romans' mound, and put its defenders to flight. This enraged Antony, and he carried out the punishment which is known as decimation against the troops who had been guilty of cowardice. This meant that they were divided into groups of ten and one man out of each ten, chosen by lot, was put to death. He ordered the rest to be issued with rations of barley instead of with wheat.

40. This was a campaign of great hardship for both sides, and the future looked even more disturbing. Antony had now to reckon with the prospect of famine, since it was no longer possible to maintain his army by foraging without suffering heavy losses in killed and wounded. On the other hand, Phraates knew that his men would do anything rather than endure the hardships of a winter campaign and months of bivouacking in the open, and he was afraid that if the Romans held out and stayed in their camp, his own men would desert him, for the air was already growing sharp now that the autumn equinox was past. He therefore tried the following trick. He arranged that those of the Parthians who were most familiar with the Roman troops should not harry them so strenuously on their foraging expeditions and other encounters, but should allow them to obtain some provisions: at the same time they should take every opportunity to praise their courage and let them know that the Parthians considered them first-rate soldiers, and that they were admired with good reason by the king. After this they would ride up closer, and, drawing their horses unobtrusively alongside the Romans, they would begin to blame Antony, saying that although Phraates was anxious to come to terms and save the lives of so many brave men, Antony would give him no chance to do so. Instead, he insisted on staying there and waiting for those two powerful and formidable enemies, famine and winter, which they would find it difficult to escape, even if the Parthians escorted them on their way. These tactics were reported to Antony from many different sources, but, although his hopes prompted him to open negotiations, he did not send heralds to the Parthians until he had inquired from the barbarians who had assumed this friendly attitude whether their words expressed their king's sentiments. When they assured him that this was so and that he need have no fear nor suspicion of their offer, he sent some of his companions to repeat his request for the return of Crassus's standards and the Roman prisoners of war, for he did not wish the king to suppose that all his demands would be satisfied if he could make his escape in safety. However, the Parthian king's reply was that he should not press this matter of the prisoners, but that if he now withdrew his

troops he would be guaranteed a safe and unmolested journey, and so within a few days Antony packed up his baggage and broke camp. But although he was an orator who could always dominate a popular audience, and knew better than any man of his time how to produce the kind of speech which would inspire his troops, he found himself too much weighed down by shame and melancholy to make the customary speech of encouragement to the army, and he deputed Domitius Ahenobarbus* to do it. Some of the soldiers resented this and felt that they were being treated with contempt, but most of them were touched to the heart and understood the reason, and indeed felt that they ought to show all the more respect and obedience to their commander on that account.

41. Antony had planned to lead his troops back by the same road that he had come, which ran through level country and was completely bare of trees. But a man of the Mardian tribe from the southern shores of the Caspian, who was thoroughly familiar with Parthian customs and had already proved his loyalty to the Romans during the battle for the siege-train, now came forward and urged Antony to keep close to the hills on his right during his retreat: above all he must not expose an army of infantrymen heavily burdened with equipment to the attacks of such a large force of mounted archers by marching across open country which did not offer a vestige of cover. This was exactly what Phraates had intended, he said, when he had used these friendly approaches to persuade Antony to raise the siege. But if Antony agreed to his plan, he offered to guide the army by a route which was shorter and better supplied with provisions. When he heard this, Antony thought over what the tribesman had told him. Now that a truce had been arranged, he did not wish to give the impression that he distrusted the Parthians. But as he himself favoured the shorter route and preferred to follow a road which would take them past inhabited villages, he asked the Mardian for a pledge of his good faith. The man offered to let himself be put in chains until he had conducted the army into Armenia. This was done

* This officer, who plays so important a part in Shakespeare's tragedy, had fought on Brutus's side at Philippi, and then, after sailing part of the Republican fleet to the Adriatic, joined forces with Antony in 40 B.C. An outspoken opponent of Cleopatra and her influence, he remained with Antony up to Actium, but deserted on the eve of the battle.

and he proceeded to guide them for two days without meeting any opposition. But on the third day, by which time Antony had dismissed the enemy from his thoughts, and, because of the confidence he felt, had allowed the column to march in a somewhat ragged fashion, the Mardian noticed that the embankment of the river beside them had been recently demolished, and that the stream was pouring over the road directly across their line of march. He saw at once that this was the work of the Parthians, who had diverted the river to obstruct and delay the Romans' retreat, and he warned Antony to keep a sharp look-out and be on his guard, as the enemy must be close at hand. Sure enough, just as Antony had deployed the heavy infantry and was arranging for the slingers and javelin-throwers to pass through the ranks and advance against the enemy, the Parthians appeared and began to gallop round them, so as to encircle the army and throw it into confusion on all sides. They were at once attacked by the Roman light-armed troops, who were severely harassed by their arrows, but, as the Parthians suffered just as many casualties from the sling-shot and javelins of their opponents, they fell back. They rallied, however, to make a second attack, which continued until the Celts, massing all their horses together, charged and scattered them, whereupon the Parthians vanished for the rest of that day.

42. This engagement taught Antony a number of tactical lessons. He now covered not only his rear but his flanks with strong detachments of javelin-throwers and slingers, and arranged his order of march in the form of a hollow square. He also gave orders to the cavalry that they must drive off the enemy when they attacked, but that, after routing them, they must not pursue them far. As a result, the Parthians during the four days that followed suffered many more casualties than they inflicted, their ardour became noticeably cooler, and they began to think of returning home, making the excuse that the winter was now well advanced.

However, on the fifth day Flavius Gallus, one of Antony's senior officers and an exceptionally daring and spirited commander, came and asked permission to take a detachment of light-armed troops from the rear and some of the cavalry from the vanguard, as he felt confident that he could achieve an important success. Antony let him take these troops, and when the Parthians attacked, Gallus drove them off. But he did not gradually give way and draw them on to the legions, as had been done on the preceding days, but held his ground and engaged them more boldly. The officers in charge of the rear-guard could see that he was in danger of becoming cut off from them and sent runners to call him back, but he refused to listen to them. Then Titius, the quaestor, it is said, seized hold of his standards, turned them round as if to order the troops to fall back on the main body, and blamed Gallus for throwing away the lives of so many brave men. Gallus retorted equally angrily, and ordered his soldiers to stand firm, whereupon Titius turned back alone. But as Gallus continued to push forward, he failed to notice that large numbers of the enemy had now encircled him from the rear. Then at last, when he found himself shot at from all sides, he appealed for help. At this point the officers of the legions – among them Canidius, for whom Antony had an especially high regard – are generally considered to have made a serious blunder. They ought to have wheeled so as to engage the enemy with their whole line at once, but instead they sent only small groups to help Gallus, and waited until each was overwhelmed in turn before sending out reinforcements; and so before they were aware of it they came near to involving the whole army in the defeat and rout of these units. Fortunately, Antony hurried back from the vanguard with his heavy infantry to stem the retreat, and his third legion forced its way through to face the enemy and check any further pursuit.

43. The Romans lost no less than three thousand killed, and five thousand men were brought back wounded to the camp: among them was Gallus, who had been pierced in front by four arrows. He died of his wounds soon after, but Antony visited the rest of the wounded men, and his affection for them brought tears to his eyes even as he tried to raise their spirits. For their part, the men greeted him with cheerful faces and gripped his hand as he passed: they begged him not to let their sufferings weigh upon him, but to go and take care of himself, and they hailed him as their Imperator and told him that they knew they were safe so long as he was unharmed. Altogether it would be true to say that no other commander of that age ever gathered together an army of such superb fighting qualities, composed as it was of soldiers in the prime of their young manhood, who were capable of great feats both of

courage and of endurance. But most impressive of all was the respect, the obedience, and the goodwill which they showed towards their general, together with the feeling shared by every man – those with the greatest reputation and those with none, commanders and privates alike – that they preferred Antony's good opinion to their own lives and safety: in short, this was an army which could not have been excelled even by the soldiers of ancient Rome. There were many reasons to inspire this devotion, as I have already mentioned, namely Antony's noble birth, his eloquence, his simplicity, his generosity which amounted to extravagance, and the familiar and genial manner which he showed in his amusements and his social intercourse. On this occasion the sympathy with which he treated his men and his readiness to share their distress and attend to their wants had the effect of making the wounded and the sick even more ready to serve him than those who were well and strong.

44. However, the enemy, who only the day before had been exhausted and ready to give up fighting, were now so exultant at their victory and so contemptuous of the Romans that they spent the night close by, expecting that they would soon be able to plunder the empty tents and abandoned baggage of a routed army. At daybreak they gathered to attack in far greater strength, and at this moment their forces are said to have numbered forty thousand horsemen, as the king had sent even the royal bodyguard to join in the battle. This action proved that he now felt completely confident of success, because the Parthian king is never present in person at any battle. Antony decided to address the troops, and at first he called for a dark robe, as he wanted to make this speech as moving as possible. His friends opposed this idea, and so he appeared in a general's scarlet cloak and spoke to the army, praising the troops who had driven back the enemy and reproaching those who had fled. The former urged him to have confidence in them, while the latter in the effort to excuse their conduct told him that they were ready to suffer decimation and any other punishment he thought fit, if only he would forget their disgrace and cease to distress himself at it. In reply Antony lifted up his hands and prayed to the gods that, if some retribution were in store for him to balance his former good fortune, they would allow it to fall upon him alone and grant safety and victory to the rest of the army.

45. On the next day the Romans covered their advance more effectively, and when the Parthians attacked they met with a severe shock. They rode up expecting to have nothing to do but pillage and plunder their enemies, but when they were greeted with a hail of missiles and saw that the Romans were fresh, resolute, and eager for battle, they once more grew tired of the struggle. However, when the Romans were obliged to descend a steep slope, the Parthians made another attack and poured their arrows into the column as it wound slowly downhill. At this the infantry, who carried heavy shields, wheeled so as to enclose the light-armed troops within their ranks. Then the legionaries in front dropped on to one knee and held their shields in front of them. Those in the second rank held their shields out over the heads of the first, and those behind them took up the same position towards the second rank. This formation, which looks like the tiled roof of a house, makes a striking spectacle and provides the most effective defence against arrows, which merely glance off it. The Parthians, however, when they saw the Romans dropping on to one knee, imagined that they were exhausted, and so they put down their bows, gripped their spears by the middle, and advanced to close quarters. Then the Romans suddenly leaped to their feet and, joining all together in one great battle-cry, lunged forward with their javelins, speared the front ranks of the Parthians, and put the rest to flight. The days that followed saw a series of similar engagements, so that the retreat could proceed only in short stages.

The army was also beginning to suffer severely from hunger, since it could only find small quantities of grain even by fighting, and it was not well supplied with implements for grinding it. Most of these they had been obliged to abandon, since some of the pack animals had died, while many others were needed to carry the sick and wounded. It is said that at this time an Attic *choenix** of wheat cost fifty drachmas, while loaves of barley were sold for their weight in silver. The Romans had no choice but to fall back on vegetables and roots, but since they could find very few to which they were accustomed, they were obliged to try some they had never tasted before and it was in this way that they came to eat a herb which first drove men mad and then killed them. Those who ate of it lost their memory and became obsessed with the task of moving and turning over every stone they could see, as if they were accomplishing some-

* About a bushel: fifty drachmas is roughly the equivalent of £2.

thing of immense importance. All over the plain men could be seen stooping to the ground, digging around stones and removing them, and finally they would vomit bile and die, since they had no stores of wine which is the only remedy against this sickness. The Romans lost many men in this way, and all the while the Parthians kept up their attacks, while Antony, so the story goes, often exclaimed, 'O, the Ten Thousand!' This was to show his admiration for Xenophon's army, which made an even longer march from Babylon to the sea and succeeded in forcing its way through against even stronger opposition.

46. All this time the Parthians had still been unable to throw the Roman army into confusion or break up its formation. So, after being defeated and put to flight in many engagements, they began once more to fraternize with the legionaries as they went out to look for fodder or grain, and pointing to their unstrung bows, they would say that they had now given up their pursuit and were returning home. A few Medes would continue to follow the Romans for one or two days' march, but would cause them no trouble, as their only purpose was to protect the outlying villages. These professions of friendship were accompanied by greetings and various acts of goodwill, so that once again the Romans' spirits rose, and when he heard these reports, Antony was tempted to direct his march through the plains, as the route through the mountains was said to be waterless. But just as he was about to do this, a man named Mithridates arrived in his camp from the enemy: he was a cousin of the Monaeses who had taken refuge with Antony and been presented with the three cities.* Mithridates asked for somebody who could speak the Parthian or the Syrian language and interpret for him, and Alexander of Antioch, who was a close friend of Antony's, went out to meet him. After Mithridates had announced who he was, and explained that they must thank Monaeses for the information he was now going to give them, he asked Alexander whether he could see a range of lofty hills lying ahead of them. When Alexander replied that he could, Mithridates told him, 'Under those mountains the whole Parthian army is waiting in ambush for you. The great plains stretch right up to the foot of the range, and the Parthians expect that you will be deceived by their friendly advances into

* See ch. 37.

leaving the road through the mountains and marching in that direction. It is true that if you cross the heights you will have thirst and exhaustion to contend with, but you are accustomed to these by now: on the other hand if Antony tries to march across the plains he can expect to meet the same fate as Crassus.'

47. After he had given this information, the man departed. Antony was greatly disturbed at what he had heard and called together his friends and his Mardian guide, who took the same view as Mithridates. He considered that, even if they had no enemy to reckon with, the route across the plains involved the risk of much arduous wandering about with no certainty of finding their way because of the absence of clearly marked tracks, and he pointed out that the way through the mountains, although it was rough, offered no other danger than the lack of water for a single day. So Antony chose this route, and, after ordering his men to carry water with them, led the march by night. Most of his men, however, had no containers, and some actually filled their helmets and carried them, while others took water in skins.

As soon as Antony set off, his movements were reported to the Parthians, and contrary to their usual custom they started in pursuit while it was still dark. Just as the sun was rising they made contact with the Roman rear-guard, who were already tired out with hard marching and lack of sleep, for they had covered thirty miles during the night. The spirits of the Romans sank, for they had never expected that the enemy would overtake them so quickly, and, worse than this, the fighting increased their thirst, for they continued to march on at the same time as they tried to beat off the enemy's attacks. At length the vanguard arrived at a river, the water of which was clear and cool, but turned out to be salty in taste and poisonous in its effects. As soon as it was drunk, it produced painful spasms in the bowels and increased the men's thirst, but although the Mardian guide had warned them of this danger, the soldiers thrust aside anyone who tried to restrain them, and drank from the stream. Antony went along the column begging his men to hold out for a little longer, and telling them that not much farther on they would come to a river whose water was drinkable, and that the track ahead of them was too rocky for cavalry, so that in any case the enemy would be forced to turn back. At the same time he ordered the troops who were engaged in fighting to break off the action, and gave the signal to pitch tents, so that the men might at least be refreshed by the shade.

48. Accordingly, the Romans set to work pitching their tents, and the Parthians, following their usual tactics, immediately began to fall back. At this moment Mithridates appeared again, and after Alexander had been sent to receive him, he offered the advice that Antony should allow the army only a short spell of rest and should then resume his march and press on to the next river, for his opinion was that the Parthians would not cross this, but were determined to pursue the Romans until they reached it. Alexander conveyed this message to Antony, and by way of reward brought back from him a large number of golden drinking-cups and bowls. Mithridates stuffed as many of these as he could hide under his clothes and rode away. Then, while it was still daylight, the Romans broke camp and continued their march. The enemy did not attack them, but by their own actions they contrived to make this the most disastrous and terrifying night they had yet experienced. Those who were known to possess gold and silver were murdered and robbed, many private possessions were stolen from the pack animals, and finally Antony's own baggage-train was attacked and his drinking-cups and expensive tables broken up and divided among the thieves.

This outbreak of looting produced great confusion throughout the army, and some of the troops began to lose touch and stray from the main body, for the rumour went round that the enemy had attacked, caused a rout, and so broken up the army's formation. At this Antony called for one of his bodyguard named Rhamnus and made him swear that when he gave the order the man would run him through with his sword and cut off his head, for he was determined neither to be taken alive by the enemy nor to be recognized when he was dead. Antony's friends burst into tears, but the Mardian did his best to raise his master's spirits, assuring him that they had now almost reached the river, for there was moisture in the breeze that was blowing from that direction and the cooler air in their faces made it easier to breathe. He explained too that the time they had been on the march proved that the river must be close by, for the hours of darkness were now almost past. At the same time others arrived with the news that the uproar had been caused by the greed and violence of their own troops.* Antony therefore gave the signal to pitch camp, so as to bring his army back to its proper formation after this collapse of discipline and organization.

49. It was now daylight and a certain degree of order and tranquillity had been established, when the arrows of the Parthians began to fall upon the rear-guard, and the light-armed troops were given the signal to engage. The infantry took up the same defensive formation as before, so as to cover one another with shields, and succeeded in holding off their attackers, who did not venture to move in to close quarters. Following these tactics the head of the column slowly moved on, and at last the river came into sight. When they reached the bank, Antony drew up his cavalry to face the enemy and had his sick and wounded carried over first. But before long even the troops who were holding off the enemy were left free to drink at their ease, for as soon as the Parthians caught sight of the river, they unstrung their bows, told the Romans they could cross over without fear, and shouted to them praising their courage. In this way they reached the other side unmolested, and after resting for a while they resumed their march, but at the same time they put no faith whatever in the Parthians' assurances. On the sixth day after their last engagement they arrived at the river Araxes, which forms the frontier between Media and Armenia. This river is so deep and its current so violent that they expected to find it difficult to ford, and there was a rumour that the enemy were waiting in ambush there, and would attack them as soon as they tried to force a passage. At any rate, as soon as they had made their way over safely and set foot in Armenia, they kissed the ground and threw their arms around one another for joy, as if they were storm-tossed mariners who had just sighted land. But as they marched through this region, which abounded in provisions of every kind, and took to eating and drinking freely after the hardships they had suffered, they began to succumb to dropsy and dysentery.

50. Here Antony held a review of his army, and found that he had lost twenty thousand of his infantry and four thousand of his cavalry,

* This episode seems curiously inconsistent with the supposed devotion of Antony's troops, and it has been conjectured that the plundering of his possessions may have been caused by a report of his despair or a false rumour of his death.

more than half of whom had died not at the hands of the enemy but through disease. They had marched for twenty-seven days from Phraata and had defeated the Parthians in eighteen battles, but their victories had been indecisive and had failed to secure them against attack, because they could never follow them up effectually nor pursue the enemy for more than a short distance. This fact more than any other makes it clear that it was the defection of Artavasdes the Armenian* which deprived Antony of the power to finish off the war. For if the sixteen thousand† horsemen which he withdrew from the expedition when it was in Media had been available, armed as they were like the Parthians and accustomed to fighting them, and if they, after the Romans had routed the enemy in pitched battles, had pursued and cut down the fugitives, the Parthians would never have been able to rally their forces and return to the attack as often as they did. For this reason the army was furious with Artavasdes and urged Antony to take revenge on him. However, Antony, since his army had been so much weakened both in manpower and in supplies, refrained for reasons of policy from blaming Artavasdes for his treachery, or from treating him with any less goodwill, friendship, or respect than he had shown before. But afterwards, when he carried out a second invasion of Armenia, he sent Artavasdes a succession of invitations and tempting promises, managed to persuade him to come to a meeting, and then had him arrested, put into chains, and brought to Alexandria. There Antony organized a triumph and led the king in it, an action which caused particular offence to the Romans, because it was felt that he was celebrating the honourable and solemn rites of his own country for the benefit of the Egyptians and for the sake of Cleopatra. These events, however, took place at a later date.

51. Antony now pressed on, for the winter had already set in sharply, and he encountered incessant snow-storms and lost eight thousand men on the march. He himself went down to the Mediterranean coast with a small escort, and at a place between Berytus and Sidon called the White Village he waited for Cleopatra to join him. When she was slow in coming he became distraught and soon gave himself up to heavy drinking, and yet he could not endure the tedium of the

* In 30 B.C. Artavasdes was put to death by Cleopatra after the battle of Actium.

† In ch. 37 Plutarch mentions six thousand, which is a more probable figure.

table, but would jump to his feet and run out to see if she were coming, until at last she arrived by sea, bringing with her large quantities of clothing and money for the soldiers. But according to some accounts, while Cleopatra presented the clothes, it was Antony himself who took the money from his private funds and distributed it to the army as a gift from her.

52. At this date* a quarrel arose between the king of the Medes and Phraates of Parthia. This had arisen, so it is said, over the division of the spoils captured from the Romans, but it aroused the suspicions of the Median king, who now feared that his throne might be taken from him. For this reason he invited Antony to come to his help and promised to support him with his own forces in a war against Parthia. This offer greatly raised Antony's hopes, for the one factor which, as he believed, had prevented him from conquering the Parthians, that is the lack of a strong force of cavalry and archers, was now to be supplied to him, and on such terms that if he accepted he would be conferring a favour rather than asking one. He therefore made preparations to march once more into upper Asia through Armenia, and there to join forces with the Median king at the river Araxus and reopen the war.

53. Meanwhile, at Rome, Octavia was becoming anxious to sail east and join Antony. It is generally agreed that Octavius allowed her to do this not so much to give her pleasure, but rather to give himself a plausible pretext for declaring war, if she were neglected or insulted by her husband. When Octavia arrived in Athens† she received letters from Antony in which he told her to stay there and explained the plans for his new expedition. Octavia, although she was hurt by this news and saw through Antony's excuses, nevertheless wrote asking him where he wished to have the things sent which she was bringing him, for she had come out with large stores of clothing for his troops, many pack animals and money and presents for Antony's staff and his friends, and besides all this two thousand picked men splendidly equipped with full armour to serve as praetorian guards.‡

* Late in 35 B.C. † In the summer of 35 B.C.

‡ Under the Roman Republic, while the consuls were the commanders-in-chief of its armies, the praetors were often its generals: hence the praetorian guard was originally a picked body of cavalry and infantry who served as the general's personal bodyguard.

Octavia sent one of Antony's friends whose name was Niger to give him this news, and in delivering it he praised and complimented her, as indeed she deserved.

Cleopatra now saw that her rival was preparing to challenge her influence at close quarters. She was afraid that if to her natural dignity and her brother's power Octavia could once add the charm of her daily society and her affectionate attention, she would win complete control of her husband and make her position unassailable. So she pretended to be consumed with the most passionate love for Antony, adopted a rigorous diet, and succeeded in making her body waste away. Whenever Antony came near her she would fix her eyes on him with a look of rapture, and whenever he left she would appear to languish and be on the verge of collapse. She took great pains to arrange that he should often see her in tears, and then she would quickly wipe them away and try to hide them as if she did not wish him to notice, and she kept up this elaborate performance all the time that he was preparing to march from Syria and join the king of Media. Her flatterers also worked hard upon Antony at this time. They told him that he must be an insensitive brute with a heart of stone, for here was a mistress who was utterly devoted to him alone, and he was killing her. Octavia, they made out, had married him as a matter of political convenience to suit her brother's interests, and she enjoyed the title of his wife: but Cleopatra, who was the sovereign of many nations, had been content to be called his mistress, and she did not shun this name nor think it unworthy of her so long as she could see him and spend her life with him, but if he drove her away it would be the death of her. In the end they so melted and unmanned him, that he began to believe she would take her own life if he left her. And so he returned to Alexandria and put off his Median expedition until the summer, in spite of the fact that Parthia was said to be greatly weakened by internal dissensions. Later, however, he made a journey to Media and restored his friendly relations with the king. Then, after arranging the betrothal of one of the king's daughters, who was still only a young child, to one of his sons by Cleopatra, he returned to Egypt, but by this time his thoughts were taken up by the impending war between Octavius Caesar and himself.

54. When Octavia returned from Athens Octavius considered that Antony had insulted her outrageously, and he told her that she must

now set up her own household. But she refused to leave her husband's house, in fact she even begged Octavius, unless he had already made up his mind to declare war for quite different reasons, to ignore Antony's behaviour towards her, for it would be intolerable, she pleaded, to have it said of the two greatest Imperators in the world that they had plunged the Roman people into civil war, the one out of love and the other out of jealousy for the rights of a woman. These were her words and her actions added weight to them. She went on living in her husband's house as if he were at home, and she looked after Antony's children, not only those whom she had borne him but also Fulvia's, with a truly noble devotion and generosity of spirit. She also entertained any friends of Antony's who were sent to Rome either on business or to solicit posts of authority, and she did her utmost to help them obtain whatever they wanted from Octavius. But in this way she unintentionally did great harm to Antony's reputation, since he was naturally hated for wronging such a woman.

Antony also aroused great resentment because of the division of his inheritance which he carried out in Alexandria* in favour of his children. People regarded this as an arrogant and theatrical gesture which seemed to indicate a hatred for his own country. Nevertheless, he assembled a great multitude in the athletic arena there, and had two thrones of gold, one for himself and one for Cleopatra, placed on a dais of silver, with smaller thrones for his children. First, he proclaimed Cleopatra Queen of Egypt, Cyprus, Libya, and Coele Syria† and named Caesarion as her consort. This youth was believed to be a son of Julius Caesar, who had left Cleopatra pregnant. Next he proclaimed his own sons by Cleopatra to be Kings of Kings. To Alexander he gave Armenia, Media, and Parthia, as soon as he should have conquered it, and to Ptolemy Phoenicia, Syria, and Cilicia. At the same time he presented his sons to the people, Alexander in a Median costume which was crowned by a tiara, and Ptolemy in boots, a short cloak, and a broad-brimmed hat encircled by a diadem. The latter wore Macedonian dress like the kings who succeeded Alexander the Great, and the former the dress of the Medes and Armenians. After the children had embraced their parents, the one

* This pronouncement was no mere gesture but a deliberately conceived political settlement, known as the Donations of Alexandria (see Appendix, p. 356).

† See note in ch. 36.

was given a guard of honour of Armenians and the other of Macedonians. Cleopatra not only on this but on other public occasions wore the robe which is sacred to Isis, and she was addressed as the New Isis.

55. Octavius Caesar reported these actions to the Senate,* and by repeatedly denouncing Antony in public he did his utmost to rouse the Roman people's anger against him. Antony for his part made a number of counter-accusations against Octavius. The most important of these were, first that after capturing Sicily from Sextus Pompeius he had not given Antony any share of the island; secondly, that after borrowing some of Antony's ships for this campaign he kept them for his own use; thirdly, that after removing his colleague Lepidus from his position as triumvir and degrading him, he took possession himself of the troops, the territories, and the revenues which had been assigned to Lepidus, and, finally, that he had distributed almost all the available land in Italy to his own soldiers and left nothing for Antony's. Octavius Caesar's retort to these charges was that he had deprived Lepidus of his authority because he was misusing it, and that as for his conquests in war he was willing to divide these with Antony as soon as Antony offered to share Armenia with him. He added that Antony's soldiers had no claim upon any lands in Italy. Their rewards lay in Media and Parthia which they had added to the Roman empire by their gallant campaigns under their Imperator.

56. Antony was in Armenia when this answer reached him, and he at once ordered Canidius to march to the coast with sixteen legions. Meanwhile, he travelled with Cleopatra to Ephesus, where his naval force was assembling from all quarters. It numbered eight hundred warships together with merchant vessels: Cleopatra provided two hundred of these, as well as twenty thousand talents and supplies for the whole army during the campaign. On the advice of Domitius Ahenobarbus and several other friends, Antony told Cleopatra to sail to Egypt and to wait there for the outcome of the war. But the queen was afraid that Octavia might again succeed in reconciling the two

* Octavius brought matters to a head by surrounding the Senate with soldiers when he delivered his accusations. Antony still had many supporters in Rome, for at this point both the consuls for 32 B.C. and some four hundred senators left Rome to join him in the East.

antagonists, and so she bribed Canidius to plead for her with Antony, pointing out that it was unjust to refuse a woman who contributed so much to the expenses of the war the privilege of being present at it, and unwise for Antony to depress the spirits of the Egyptians who formed so large a part of their naval force. Besides, there was no indication as far as he could see that Cleopatra was inferior in intelligence to any of the kings who were taking part in the expedition: on the contrary, she had for many years ruled a large kingdom by herself, and her long association with Antony had taught her many lessons in the management of great affairs. And so, since fate had decreed that everything should fall into Octavius Caesar's hands, these arguments won the day, and when all their forces had been assembled, the two sailed together to Samos and there gave themselves up to pleasure.* For just as the order had gone out that all the kings, princes, tetrarchs, nations, and cities from Syria to the Mareotic Lake and from Armenia to Illyria should bring or send their quota of equipment for the war, so all the dramatic artists were commanded to present themselves at Samos, and, while almost the whole world round about was filled with sighs and lamentations at the impending war, this single island echoed for many days with the music of strings and flutes, the theatres were packed and choirs competed with one another. Every city sent an ox for sacrifice, and the kings who accompanied Antony vied with one another in the magnificence of their gifts and entertainments, until the word went round, 'If these people spend so much on festivals just to prepare for war, what will the conquerors do to celebrate a victory?'

57. At the end of these entertainments Antony arranged for the dramatic artists to be settled in the city of Priene as their permanent residence. Then he sailed on to Athens, and allowed himself to be diverted by a further round of amusements and theatrical spectacles. Cleopatra for her part felt jealous of the honours which the city had paid to Octavia – for the Athenians were particularly devoted to her – and tried to make herself popular with the citizens by heaping lavish benefactions on them. The Athenians responded by conferring various public honours upon the queen and sent a delegation to her

* It is also possible that these ceremonies were not organized for pleasure but for a religious purpose: in a similar fashion Alexander organized gatherings in honour of Dionysus before several of his campaigns.

house to present her with the public decree to this effect. Antony himself accompanied them in his capacity as an honorary citizen, and standing before her he delivered a ceremonial address on behalf of the city of Athens. At the same time he sent men to Rome with instructions to turn Octavia out of her house. We are told that, when she left it, she took with her all of Antony's children except Antyllus, the eldest son of his marriage to Fulvia, who was with his father, and that she wept tears of anguish at the thought that she would be regarded as one of the causes of the war. Yet it was not she whom the Romans pitied so much as Antony for his folly, especially those who had seen Cleopatra and knew that she had neither Octavia's youth nor her beauty.

58. Octavius Caesar was dismayed when he learned of the speed and the scope of Antony's preparations, since he was afraid that he would be forced to embark that very summer* upon the campaign that would decide the war, and for the time being he was not only very short of supplies but had made himself thoroughly unpopular on account of the taxes he had imposed. Full citizens were obliged to pay over one quarter of their income and freedmen one eighth of their property, with the result that there was a violent outcry from both classes against Octavius and disturbances broke out all over Italy. For this reason Antony's postponement of the war is now considered to have been one of his greatest errors of judgement, since it gave Caesar the opportunity to complete his preparations and allowed time for the indignation aroused by his measures to subside. People felt rebellious at the moment when the money was extorted from them, but, once they had paid it, their anger cooled off. At the same time Cleopatra went out of her way to insult two of Antony's friends, Titius and Plancus, both of them men of consular rank, who strongly opposed the idea that she should remain with the expedition. They made their escape and passed on to Octavius some information about the contents of Antony's will of which they knew the details. This will had been deposited with the Vestal Virgins,† and when Octavius Caesar asked for it, they refused to send it to him, but told

* 32 B.C.

† This was apparently a common custom with men of rank. But Octavius's action was resented, because a will deposited with the Vestal Virgins was regarded as especially sacred, and it was still in Antony's power to change its provisions.

him that if he wished to have it he should come and take it himself, which he proceeded to do. First of all he read it through privately and marked the passages which would serve best to discredit Antony, and later he summoned a meeting of the Senate and read it aloud to them. Most of the senators had little sympathy for this performance, since they thought it an extraordinary and intolerable procedure that a man should be called to account while he was still alive for what he wished to have done after his death. Octavius singled out for especial emphasis the clause which dealt with Antony's burial, for he had left instructions that even if he were to die in Rome, his body should be carried in state through the Forum and then sent to Cleopatra in Egypt. Besides this, Calvisius, one of Octavius's friends, accused Antony of a number of other excesses in his behaviour towards Cleopatra: he had presented her with the libraries at Pergamum which contained two hundred thousand scrolls; at a banquet with a large company present he had risen from his place and anointed her feet, apparently to fulfil some compact or wager; he had allowed the Ephesians to salute Cleopatra as their sovereign in his own presence, and on many occasions, while he was seated on the tribunal administering justice to kings and tetrarchs, he would receive love-letters from her written on tablets of onyx or crystal and read them through in public; and on another occasion when Furnius, a man of great distinction and the foremost orator in Rome, was pleading a case, Cleopatra happened to pass through the Forum in her litter, whereupon Antony leaped to his feet from his tribunal, walked out of the trial, and accompanied Cleopatra on her way, hanging on to her litter.

59. However, Calvisius was generally believed to have invented most of these accusations. Meanwhile, Antony's friends also canvassed the people and appealed to them on his behalf, and they sent one of their number named Geminius to urge Antony not to sit by and allow himself to be voted out of authority and declared an enemy of Rome. But as soon as Geminius landed in Greece, he was suspected by Cleopatra of being an agent working for Octavia, and she arranged that he should be humiliated by being seated in the least distinguished place at the dinner table and having practical jokes played on him. Geminius endured all these insults with great patience and waited for an opportunity to speak to Antony. But when he was called upon to

explain the reason for his presence, they were seated at dinner, and so Geminius answered that he would keep the rest of his message for a more sober occasion, but that he had one thing to say, sober or drunk, and this was that all would go well if Cleopatra were sent back to Egypt. Antony was furious at this reply, but Cleopatra put in, 'You have done well, Geminius, to confess the truth without being put to the torture.' At any rate Geminius escaped a few days later and returned to Rome.* Cleopatra's parasites succeeded in driving away many other friends of Antony's, who found these creatures' drunken antics and ribald buffoonery more than they could tolerate. Among those who left him at this time were Marcus Silanus and Dellius the historian. Dellius also mentions that he was afraid of a plot against his life, which Glaucus the physician warned him had been organized by Cleopatra. It appears that he had offended her on one occasion at supper by remarking that Antony's friends were served with sour wine, while at Rome Sarmentus, Octavius Caesar's little page, one of his boy favourites or *deliciae*, as the Romans call them, was drinking Falernian.

60. As soon as Octavius Caesar had completed his preparations, he had a decree passed declaring war on Cleopatra and depriving Antony of the authority which he had allowed a woman to exercise in his place. Octavius Caesar also gave it out that Antony had allowed himself to fall under the influence of drugs, that he was no longer responsible for his actions, and that the Romans were fighting this war against Mardian the eunuch, Potheinus, Iras, who was Cleopatra's hairdresser, and Charmian, her waiting-woman, since it was they who were mainly responsible for the direction of affairs.

Here I may mention a number of prodigies which are said to have heralded the outbreak of war. Pisaurum, a city near the Adriatic which Antony had colonized, was suddenly engulfed by an earthquake. One of the marble statues of Antony near Alba was seen to ooze with sweat, and the moisture in spite of being wiped away continued to flow. At Patras the temple of Hercules was destroyed by

* Matters had gone too far for any reconciliation with Octavia to be likely. It is more probable that Cleopatra feared Geminius to be one of those who, like Ahenobarbus, were pressing Antony to break off his connexion with her and restore his position in the west. The fact that she could threaten a free-born man with torture was the final provocation for some of Antony's friends.

lightning, and in Athens the figure of Dionysus in the group known as the Battle of the Giants was torn loose by the wind and hurled down into the theatre. Now Antony, as I have mentioned earlier in this Life, claimed to be descended from Hercules, and because he liked to associate himself with Dionysus in his manner of living he had been given the name of the New Dionysus.* The same storm also fell upon the colossal statues of Eumenes and Attalus at Athens, on which Antony's name had been inscribed, and overturned them, while the other sculptures nearby remained undisturbed. Besides this, Cleopatra's flagship was named Antonias, and here too an alarming portent was observed. A number of swallows had built their nests under the stern, but other swallows attacked them, drove them out, and killed their young.

61. When the two sides had mobilized for the war, Antony's fleet numbered no less than five hundred warships, including many vessels which carried eight or ten banks of oars, and were fitted out with elaborate decorations as though they were intended for a triumph, while his army consisted of a hundred thousand infantry and twelve thousand cavalry. Among the subject kings who came to his support were Bocchus the king of Libya, Tarcondemus the king of Upper Cilicia, Philadelphus of Paphlagonia, Mithridates of Commagene, and Sadalas of Thrace. These rulers accompanied his forces, while other contingents were sent him by Polemon of Pontus, Malchus of Arabia, Herod of Judaea, and Amyntas of Lycaonia and Galatia, while the king of the Medes also provided an auxiliary force. Octavius Caesar on the other hand had two hundred and fifty warships, eighty thousand infantry, and about twelve thousand cavalry. Antony's dominions stretched from the Euphrates and Armenia to the Ionian sea and Illyria, and Octavius Caesar's from Illyria to the Atlantic ocean and from there back to the seas which bordered Etruria and Sicily. On the African shore of the Mediterranean, the coast which lies opposite Italy, Gaul and Iberia as far as the Pillars of Hercules belonged to Caesar, while Antony controlled the region that extends from Cyrene to Armenia.

62. By this time Antony had become so much of a tool in Cleopatra's hands that, although he was far stronger than Octavius on land, he

* See chs. 4 and 24.

was determined that his victory should be gained by his fleet; he insisted on this merely to please the queen; even though he could see that he was so short of seamen that his trierarchs were impressing travellers, muledrivers, reapers, and boys not yet of military age from the exhausted provinces of Greece. Even then his crews were still below strength, with the result that the vessels were undermanned and wretchedly handled. Octavius Caesar's fleet, by contrast, consisted of ships which had not been built to an ostentatious height nor designed for show, but were fully manned, fast sailing, and easy to manoeuvre. He had concentrated his fleet at Tarentum and Brundisium, and now sent a message to Antony challenging him not to waste any more time, but to come with his forces: Caesar would then leave the roadsteads and harbour free for his fleet to enter and would withdraw his army the distance of a day's ride inland, until Antony had safely disembarked and established his camp. Antony retorted in equally boastful language, challenging Octavius to meet him in single combat, even though he was the older man. If Octavius declined this, Antony demanded that they should fight out the issue at Pharsalus, as Julius Caesar and Pompey had done before them. However, while Antony's fleet was anchored off Actium, where the city of Nicopolis now stands, Octavius stole a march on him by crossing the Ionian sea and seizing a town in Epirus named Toryne, the name of which means 'ladle'. When Antony's friends showed alarm at this, as their own army had not yet come up, Cleopatra made a joke of it and asked mockingly, 'What is so terrible about Caesar's having got hold of a ladle?'

63. A little later the enemy sailed against Antony's fleet at daybreak and he was afraid that his ships might be captured before his soldiers could arrive to go aboard them. He therefore armed his oarsmen and paraded them on the decks so as to make the best possible show. Then he drew up the vessels near the mouth of the gulf of Actium with their banks of oars raised out of the water and held in readiness for the strike, and with their bows pointing towards the enemy, as if they were fully manned and ready to engage. Octavius Caesar was outwitted by this manoeuvre and retired. Antony was also considered to have made a skilful move by erecting some earthworks to cut off the enemy from the supply of drinkable water, since there were few springs in the neighbourhood, and even these were of poor quality.

It was also at this time that he behaved with great generosity – although quite against Cleopatra's inclinations – to Domitius Ahenobarbus. Domitius, who was already suffering from fever, put off in a small boat and went over to Octavius Caesar; but Antony, although he was deeply grieved by his friend's desertion, sent not only his baggage but all his friends and servants after him, whereupon Domitius died almost immediately, as if he longed to repent as soon as his treachery and disloyalty were discovered.

Some of the subject kings also chose this moment to change sides, and Amyntas and Deiotarus went over to Octavius Caesar. Moreover, since his fleet proved unsuccessful in every one of its operations and always arrived too late to give any help, Antony was obliged to pay more attention to his land forces. Canidius too, now that he recognized the danger in which they stood, reversed the attitude he had taken up before and advised Antony to send Cleopatra away, withdraw his troops into Thrace or Macedonia, and trust to a land battle to decide the issue. Dicomes, the king of the Getae, had promised to support him with a powerful army, and there would be no disgrace, Canidius urged, in giving up the control of the sea to Octavius, since his forces had been trained in naval operations during the Sicilian campaign against Sextus Pompeius. On the other hand, it would be absurd for Antony, who was as experienced in fighting on land as any commander living, not to take advantage of the superior numbers and equipment of his legions, but to distribute his fighting men among the ships and so fritter away his strength.

But in spite of anything that Canidius could say, it was Cleopatra's choice that the war should be decided at sea which finally prevailed. And yet the truth was that her thoughts were already turning towards flight, and the real purpose of the battle order which she drew up for her forces was not to win a victory but to ensure her escape in the event of defeat. It happened also that there were two long walls which stretched from Antony's camp down to the naval base, and Antony was in the habit of walking between these without suspecting any danger. Octavius was informed by a slave that Antony could be captured as he passed down this route, and so he sent a patrol to ambush him. The soldiers almost achieved their purpose, but they jumped to their feet a moment too soon and seized a man who was in front of Antony, while Antony himself ran off and just succeeded in escaping.

64. When he had finally decided to fight at sea, Antony had all but sixty of the Egyptian ships burned.* He then manned the best and largest which carried between three and ten banks of oars and embarked in them twenty thousand heavy infantry and two thousand archers. It was on this occasion, we are told, that one of the centurions from the legions, who had fought in innumerable battles under Antony and whose body was seamed with scars, suddenly burst out as Antony was passing by, 'Imperator, how can you distrust this sword and these wounds of mine and put all your hopes in rotten timbers? Let these Egyptians and Phoenicians do their fighting at sea. Give us the land, where we know how to stand foot to foot and conquer our enemies or die.' To this Antony could make no reply. All he did with a look and a gesture of his hand was to encourage the man to take heart, and then he passed on. And in fact it seemed that he had little enough confidence himself, because when the captains of his ships proposed leaving their sails behind,† he gave orders that they should be put aboard on the pretext that they must not allow a single one of the enemy to escape.

65. On that day and throughout the three that followed, a strong wind blew and the sea ran so high that it was impossible to engage. But on the fifth day the wind dropped, the sea grew calm, and the two fleets met. Antony together with Publicola took command of the right wing, Coelius was in charge of the left, and Marcus Octavius and Marcus Insteius of the centre. Octavius Caesar posted Agrippa on the left and took the right wing himself. Antony's army was commanded by Canidius and Octavius's by Taurus, but both generals drew up their forces along the shore and remained inactive. As for the two commanders, Antony made the round of all the ships in a small rowing boat. He urged the soldiers to rely on the weight of their vessels and to stand firm and fight exactly as if they were on land, and at the same time he ordered the sea captains to receive the

* This seems to have been done for fear that they might desert. The sixty were reserved to guard Cleopatra.

† Antony is said to have hoped to take advantage of the following wind to drive the opposing fleet down the coast. However, in battle, warships normally relied on their oars, not their sails, and his order inevitably created the impression that his real intention was not to fight but to escape: this was strengthened by the fact that his treasure, which could have been guarded by the army, was in fact embarked with the fleet.

shock of the enemy's warships as if they were lying quietly at anchor, and to hold their positions at the mouth of the gulf which was a narrow and difficult passage. Octavius Caesar, so the story goes, had left his tent while it was still dark and was on his way to visit his fleet when he met a man driving an ass. He asked his name and the man, who recognized him, replied: 'My name is Fortunate and my ass is named Conqueror.' After the battle, when Octavius Caesar set up many of the beaks of the captured ships to decorate the place, he also erected a bronze statue of a man and an ass. After he had inspected the dispositions of the rest of his fleet, he was rowed in a small boat to the right wing, and there he saw to his astonishment that the enemy were lying motionless in the narrows, for their ships looked as though they were riding at anchor. For some while he believed that this was really the case and kept his own ships at about a mile's distance. But about noon a breeze sprang up from the sea. By this time Antony's men had become impatient at waiting so long for the enemy, and since they felt confident that the height and the size of their ships made them invincible, they got the left wing of the fleet under way. Octavius Caesar was overjoyed to see this and ordered the rowers of his right wing to back water, so as to lure the enemy out of the gulf and its narrow entrance. His plan was to surround them with his more agile craft and fight at close quarters, where he was confident that he would have the advantage over his opponents' large and undermanned galleys which were slow and difficult to manoeuvre.

66. When the opposing battle lines first met, the ships did not attempt to ram or crush one another at all. Antony's vessels, because of their great weight, were not making the speed which is required to stave in an opponent's timbers. Octavius Caesar's, on the other hand, deliberately avoided a head-on collision with their enemies' bows, which were armoured with massive plates and spikes of bronze, nor did they even venture to ram them amidships, since their beaks would have been easily snapped off against hulls which were constructed of huge square timbers bolted together with iron. And so the fighting took on much of the character of a land battle, or, to be more exact, of an attack upon a fortified town. Three or four of Octavius's ships clustered round each one of Antony's and the fighting was carried on with wicker shields, spears, poles, and flaming missiles, while

Antony's soldiers also shot with catapults from wooden towers. Agrippa then began to extend his left wing, so as to feel his way round the enemy's flank. Publicola to counter this manoeuvre was obliged to advance against him and so became separated from the centre, which was thrown into confusion and was promptly engaged by Arruntius, who commanded the centre of Octavius's fleet. At this moment, while neither side had gained a decisive advantage, Cleopatra's squadron of sixty ships was suddenly seen to hoist sail and make off through the very midst of the battle. They had been stationed astern of the heavy ships, and so threw their whole formation into disorder as they plunged through. The enemy watched them with amazement, as they spread their sails before the following wind and shaped their course for the Peloponnese. And it was now that Antony revealed to all the world that he was no longer guided by the motives of a commander nor of a brave man nor indeed by his own judgement at all: instead, he proved the truth of the saying which was once uttered as a jest, namely that a lover's soul dwells in the body of another, and he allowed himself to be dragged along after the woman, as if he had become a part of her flesh and must go wherever she led him. No sooner did he see her ships sailing away than every other consideration was blotted out of his mind, and he abandoned and betrayed the men who were fighting and dying for his cause. He got into a five-banked galley, and taking with him only Alexas the Syrian and Scellius, he hurried after the woman who had already ruined him and would soon complete his destruction.

67. Cleopatra recognized him and hoisted a signal on her ship, whereupon Antony came up and was taken on board, but he neither saw her, nor was seen by her. Instead he went forward by himself into the bows and sat down without a word, holding his head between his hands. Presently several light Liburnian vessels from Octavius's fleet were seen coming up in pursuit. Antony ordered the ship to be turned to face them and held them all off except for the vessel commanded by Eurycles the Spartan, who came in close and stood on the deck brandishing a spear, as though to hurl it at Antony. When Antony stood up in the bows and shouted out, 'Who is it who pursues Antony?' the answer came back, 'I am Eurycles, the son of Lachares, and I come armed with Caesar's fortune to avenge my father's death.' This Lachares had been involved in a charge of robbery

and had been beheaded on Antony's orders. Eurycles did not attack Antony's vessel, but he rammed the other admiral's galley – for there were two of them – and swung her round with the shock, and as she fell away from her course captured her, and soon after another ship, which contained valuable plate and furniture. When Eurycles had sailed off, Antony flung himself down in the same position and refused to move. For three days he stayed by himself in the bows of the ship; all this time he felt either too angry or too ashamed to see Cleopatra, and he then put in at Taenarum.* It was here that Cleopatra's waiting women first persuaded the two to speak to one another, and then later to eat and sleep together.

By this time several of their heavy transports and some of their friends began to rally to them from the general rout. Their news was that the fleet had been utterly destroyed, but they believed that the army still held together. When he heard this, Antony sent messengers to Canidius with orders to withdraw as quickly as he could through Macedonia into Asia. As for himself, he intended to sail from Taenarum to Libya, but at the same time he picked out one of the transports which carried a great quantity of money and a number of precious utensils of silver and gold which belonged to the royal household: this ship he presented to his friends, and urged them to divide up the treasure and save themselves. They refused his offer with tears in their eyes, but Antony comforted them with all the warmth and kindness imaginable and entreated them to accept his gift. Finally he sent them away, after writing to Theophilus, his steward in Corinth, with instructions that he should give them refuge and keep them hidden until they could make their peace with Octavius Caesar. This Theophilus was the father of Hipparchus, who was the most influential of all Antony's followers: yet he was the first of Antony's freedmen to go over to Octavius's side, and he afterwards settled in Corinth.

68. This was how matters stood with Antony. At Actium his fleet continued to hold out for several hours against Octavius, and it was only after the ships had been severely battered by a gale, which blew head on against them, that his men unwillingly surrendered at about four in the afternoon. Not more than five thousand lost their lives, but three hundred ships were captured, as Octavius has re-

* The modern Cape Matapan, the most southerly point in the Peloponnese.

corded. Up to this moment only a few people knew that Antony had fled, and those who heard the news at first found it impossible to believe that he should have run away and left them, when he had nineteen legions of infantry and twelve thousand cavalry, all of them undefeated. After all, Antony had had plenty of experience of fortune in all her moods, and was inured to the reverses and vicissitudes of innumerable campaigns. His soldiers longed to see him and were confident that he would appear from one quarter or another: indeed, such was their loyalty and courage that, even after his flight had become common knowledge, they still held together for seven days and ignored every approach made to them by Octavius. It was only when their general Canidius left the camp and stole away at night that the soldiers, finding themselves completely destitute, cut off from their supplies, and betrayed by their commanders, finally went over to the conqueror.

After these events Octavius sailed to Athens and made a settlement with the Greeks. He found that the cities were suffering great hardship, because they had been stripped of money, slaves, and pack animals, and he proceeded to arrange for the distribution of all the supplies of grain which had not been used in the war. My great grandfather Nicarchus used to relate how all the citizens of our native town of Chaeronea were forced to carry on their shoulders a certain quantity of wheat down to the sea at Anticyra, and how they were urged on by the whip. They had carried down one consignment in this fashion, when the news that Antony had been defeated arrived just in time to save the city from further hardships, for all Antony's agents and soldiers immediately fled, and the inhabitants were left to share out the wheat among themselves.

69. When Antony landed on the coast of Libya, he sent Cleopatra ahead into Egypt from Paraetonium,* and was able to enjoy all the solitude he could desire. He wandered about the country attended by only two friends, the one a Greek named Aristocrates, who was a rhetorician, and the other a Roman, one Lucilius, whom I have already mentioned in my *Life of Brutus*.† This man fought at Philippi, and in order to help Brutus escape he impersonated him and gave himself up to Brutus's pursuers. Because of this action Antony spared his life, and Lucilius remained faithful and loyal through all his

* Near the modern Sollum. † See ch. 50.

misfortunes to the very end. When Carpus,* whom Antony had put in command of the troops in Libya, also went over to Octavius, Antony tried to kill himself, but was prevented by his friends who persuaded him to come to Alexandria. There he found Cleopatra on the point of embarking upon a perilous and ambitious enterprise. The isthmus, which divides the Red Sea from the Mediterranean and is generally regarded as the boundary between Africa and Asia, measures at its narrowest point less than forty miles† across. It was here that Cleopatra intended to raise her ships out of the water and haul them overland. Her plan was then to embark a large sum of money and a strong escort, launch the vessels in the Red Sea, and settle beyond the frontiers of Egypt, leaving the dangers of war and captivity far behind her. But the Arabs of the kingdom of Petra set fire to the first ships that were brought across,‡ and, since Antony still imagined that his army at Actium had remained loyal, Cleopatra abandoned the attempt and posted her troops to guard the approaches to Egypt. Meanwhile, Antony abandoned the city and the company of his friends and went to live on the island of Pharos,§ in a house which he had built on a jetty running into the sea. There he shut himself away from all human society, and said that he asked for nothing better than to follow the example of Timon, since his own fate had been so similar. Like Timon he had been wronged and treated with ingratitude by his friends, and for this reason he distrusted and hated the whole human race.

70. Timon had been a citizen of Athens who lived about the time of the Peloponnesian war, and he is mentioned in the comedies of Aristophanes and of Plato.|| These writers represent him as a gloomy and misanthropic character, but although he took pains to avoid or repel almost every kind of human contact, yet he enjoyed the society of Alcibiades – who was at this time an insolent and aggressive young man – and used to embrace and kiss him affectionately. When Apemantus expressed his amazement at this and asked the reason,

* One of Antony's officers who had fought with him at Philippi.

† In fact, about seventy.

‡ The subjects of Malchus of Nabatea. This ruler had had a grudge against Cleopatra ever since his territory had been given her under the settlement drawn up by Antony in 37 B.C. (see ch. 36).

§ The island opposite Alexandria, which contained the famous lighthouse.

|| The comic dramatist, not the philosopher.

Timon told him that he was devoted to Alcibiades because he knew that he would be the cause of infinite mischief to Athens. This Apemantus was the only man whom he sometimes admitted into his company, since the two had much in common, and Apemantus sometimes tried to model his way of living upon Timon's. On one occasion during the Festival of the Two Pitchers,* as it is called, Apemantus remarked, 'Timon, what an excellent party we are having!' 'We would be,' Timon retorted, 'if you were not here.' There is another story that when the Athenians were holding a public assembly, Timon mounted the rostra, and this in itself was such an extraordinary event that the audience immediately fell silent and strained their ears to catch what he would say. Then Timon announced: 'I have a small plot of building land, men of Athens, and on it there stands a fig-tree. Many of my fellow-citizens have already hanged themselves on its branches, but as I propose to build a house on the site, I thought it best to give public notice, so that if any of you are anxious to hang yourselves, you may do so before the tree is cut down.' After Timon's death, he was buried at Halae by the edge of the sea, but part of the shore in front of his tomb subsided and the sea flowed over it and made it impossible to approach. The inscription on his tomb read as follows:

Here, after snapping the thread of a wretched life, I lie buried.
  Seek not to know my name: I have nothing for you but my curse.

This epitaph he is said to have written himself, but the version which is more generally known was composed by Callimachus, and this is how it runs:

Here lies Timon who hated mankind: let no passer-by linger.
  Curse me if that is your wish, but pass, that is all I entreat.

71. These are a few of the many anecdotes which have come down to us about Timon. It was Canidius who broke the news to Antony that his entire army at Actium had melted away, and soon afterwards Antony learned that Herod of Judaea† had declared for Octavius and taken a number of legions and cohorts with him, that the rest of his

* The second day of the wine festival held in honour of Dionysus. It was a day of libations to the dead.

† Herod the Great, until then an ardent supporter of Antony. He had sent a contingent to Actium but had not been present there.

client-kings were deserting him, and that nothing now remained of his power outside Egypt. But by this time such news could no longer affect him, and he seemed happy to rid himself both of his hopes and of his cares at once. He left his retreat by the sea, which he had called the Timoneum, was welcomed by Cleopatra into the palace, and once more plunged the city into a round of banquets, drinking-parties, and lavish distributions of gifts. He had Caesarion, the son of Julius Caesar and Cleopatra, enrolled in the list of ephebes, and conferred the *toga virilis* without the purple hem on Antyllus,* his own son by Fulvia, and the entertainments, banquets, and revels which were given to celebrate these honours engaged the whole city for days on end. Cleopatra and Antony now dissolved their celebrated society of Inimitable Livers and instituted another, which was at least its equal in elegance, luxury, and extravagance, and which they called the Order of the Inseparable in Death. Their friends joined it on the understanding that they would end their lives together, and they set themselves to charm away the days with a succession of exquisite supper parties. Meanwhile, Cleopatra collected together many kinds of deadly poisons, and tested these on prisoners who had been condemned to death, to discover which was the most painless. When she found that the drugs which acted most quickly caused the victim to die in agony, while the milder poisons were slow to take effect, she went on to examine the lethal qualities of various venomous creatures which were made to attack one another in front of her. She carried on these experiments almost every day, and after trying almost every possibility, she discovered that it was the bite of the asp alone which brought on a kind of drowsy lethargy and numbness. The venom caused neither groans nor convulsions, but only a light perspiration on the face, while the senses were gradually dulled and deprived of their power, and the sufferers resisted any attempt to awake or revive them, as people do when they are in a deep natural sleep.

72. At the same time the pair also sent a delegation to Octavius Caesar in Asia. Cleopatra asked that her children should inherit the

* Caesarion was to be educated as a Greek – hence his enrolment among the *ephebes* – Antyllus as a Roman. A Roman boy assumed the *toga virilis* at about fourteen, which signified that he had attained full legal capacity; up to that date he wore the *toga praetexta*, which had a broad purple border. Both these boys were put to death by Octavius.

throne of Egypt, and Antony that he should be allowed to retire into private life in Athens, if he were forbidden to stay in Egypt. But since they had been deserted by many of their friends and scarcely knew any longer whom they could trust, they sent Euphronius, who was their children's tutor. This was because of the action of Alexas of Laodicea. Timagenes had originally introduced this man to Antony in Rome, and he had come to enjoy more influence with him than any other Greek. He had also worked most effectively upon Antony on Cleopatra's behalf, and had persuaded him to reject all the considerations which might have reunited him to Octavia. Antony had sent him to Herod of Judaea in the hope of preventing the king from changing sides. But then, after Alexas had stayed with Herod for some time, and had betrayed his master, he had the impudence to appear before Octavius Caesar, relying on Herod's influence to protect him. However, Herod could do nothing to help. Alexas was arrested and brought in chains to his own country, where he was executed on Octavius's orders. This was the penalty which Alexas paid for his treachery while Antony was still alive.

73. Octavius Caesar rejected Antony's petition, but he sent back word to Cleopatra that she would be granted any request within reason, on condition that she would put Antony to death or expel him from Egypt. At the same time Octavius also sent to Cleopatra one of his freedmen named Thyrsus.* He was an intelligent man, and Octavius calculated that he might use his powers of persuasion effectively in delivering a message from a young general to a woman who was conscious and intensely proud of her personal beauty. When the delegation returned to Cleopatra, this man was granted a longer audience than the others and was so conspicuously honoured that Antony at once became suspicious. He had the man seized and flogged and sent him back to Octavius with a letter explaining that Thyrsus's insolent and arrogant airs had enraged him at a moment when his misfortunes made him all the more easy to provoke. 'If you are displeased at what I have done,' he went on, 'you have my

* Antony and Cleopatra had sent several emissaries to Octavius without success, including Antony's son Antyllus with a large sum of money. Octavius kept the money but dismissed Antyllus. It seems likely that Thyrsus was sent to keep the prospect of negotiations sufficiently alive to prevent the royal treasure of the Ptolemies from being destroyed. This was of immense value and Octavius was badly in need of money.

freedman Hipparchus as a hostage. You can string him up and whip him and we shall be quits.' After this Cleopatra tried to redeem her fault and calm Antony's suspicions by showing him the greatest tenderness and affection. She passed her own birthday in a way which was appropriate to their fallen fortunes, but she celebrated his with such a dazzling display of luxury and extravagance that many of the guests came to the banquet as paupers and went away rich men. Meanwhile, Octavius Caesar was recalled to Italy by Agrippa who kept writing from Rome to remind him that his presence there was urgently needed.

74. For the moment, then, the war remained at a standstill, but when the winter was over, Octavius marched against Antony from Syria, while his other generals advanced from Libya. When Pelusium was captured, it was rumoured that Seleucus had surrendered the city with Cleopatra's consent, but at the same time she allowed Antony to put to death Seleucus's wife and children. Not long before, Cleopatra had built for herself a number of high monuments and tombs of great beauty near the temple of Isis, and she now collected here all the most precious items of the royal treasures, gold, silver, emeralds, pearls, ebony, ivory, and cinnamon, and also a great quantity of firewood and tow. Octavius Caesar became alarmed at these preparations, and as he drew nearer to the city with his army he continued to send her messages and hints of generous treatment, for he was afraid that Cleopatra might set fire to all this wealth in a fit of despair. However, after he had encamped near the Hippodrome of Alexandria, Antony made a sortie and delivered a brilliant attack in which he routed Octavius's cavalry and pursued them as far as their camp. Elated by his victory, he marched back in triumph to the city, entered the palace, embraced Cleopatra just as he was, in full armour, and presented to her one of his soldiers who had fought most gallantly. Cleopatra gave the man a golden breastplate and helmet as a reward for his valour. He accepted them and the very same night deserted to Octavius Caesar.

75. Antony now sent Octavius another challenge to meet him in single combat, but all he received was the retort that Antony might find many other ways to end his life. This answer brought it home to Antony that to die in battle was the most honourable end left to

him, and he determined to attack by land and sea at once. It is said that at dinner he told his slaves to fill his cup and serve him more generously than usual, for no man could say whether on the next day they would be waiting on him or serving other masters, while he himself would be lying dead, a mummy and a nothing. But when he saw that his friends were weeping at these words, he told them that he would not lead them into action, since he did not expect that he would come out of the battle victorious or safe, but rather looked to it to assure him of an honourable death. That evening, so the story goes, about the hour of midnight, when all was hushed and a mood of dejection and fear of its impending fate brooded over the whole city, suddenly a marvellous sound of music was heard, which seemed to come from a consort of instruments of every kind, and voices chanting in harmony, and at the same time the shouting of a crowd in which the cry of Bacchanals and the ecstatic leaping of satyrs were mingled, as if a troop of revellers were leaving the city, shouting and singing as they went. The procession seemed to follow a course through the middle of the city towards the outer gate, which led to the enemy's camp, and at this point the sounds reached their climax and then died away. Those who tried to discover a meaning for this prodigy concluded that the god Dionysus, with whom Antony claimed kinship and whom he had sought above all to imitate, was now abandoning him.*

76. As soon as it was light, Antony posted his infantry on the hills in front of the city and watched his ships as they put out and advanced against the enemy. Then, as he still believed that his fleet might carry the day, he stood and waited for the issue of the battle at sea. But his crews, as soon as they drew near the enemy, raised their oars in salute, and, when their greeting was returned, they went over to Octavius as one man, and so the two fleets, now combined into one, changed their course and headed straight for the city. No sooner had Antony witnessed this than he found himself abandoned by the cavalry, which likewise deserted to the enemy, and finally when his infantry was routed he retreated into the city, crying out in his rage that Cleopatra had betrayed him to the very men he was fighting for her sake. Then the queen, in terror at his fury and despair, fled to her monument, let down the hanging doors which were strengthened with bars and

* There was a familiar legend that the gods abandoned a doomed city before its fall.

bolts, and sent messengers to tell Antony that she was dead. Never doubting the message, he said to himself, 'Why delay any longer, Antony? Fate has taken away the one excuse which could still make you desire to live,' and went into his room. There, as he unbuckled his armour and laid the pieces aside, he exclaimed, 'O, Cleopatra, it does not hurt me to lose you, for I shall soon be with you, but I am ashamed that an Imperator such as I have been should prove in the end to have less courage than a woman.'

Now Antony had a faithful servant, whose name was Eros. He had long ago made this man swear to kill him if the need arose, and he now ordered him to carry out his promise. Eros drew his sword and raised it as if he were about to strike his master, but suddenly turned away and killed himself. As he fell at his master's feet, Antony cried out, 'That was well done, Eros. You have shown me what I must do, even if you had not the heart to strike the blow yourself.' Then he stabbed himself with his own sword through the belly and fell upon the bed. But the wound did not kill him quickly. Presently, as he lay prostrate, the bleeding stopped and he came to himself and implored the bystanders to put him out of his pain. But they ran out of the room and left him writhing in agony and crying for help, until Cleopatra's secretary, Diomedes, arrived with orders from the queen to bring him to the monument.

77. When he understood that Cleopatra was still alive, Antony eagerly ordered his slaves to lift him up, and they carried him in their arms to the doors of the tomb. Even then Cleopatra would not allow the doors to be opened, but she showed herself at a window and let down cords and ropes to the ground. The slaves fastened Antony to these and the queen pulled him up with the help of her two waiting women, who were the only companions she had allowed to enter the monument with her. Those who were present say that there was never a more pitiable sight than the spectacle of Antony, covered with blood, struggling in his death agonies and stretching out his hands towards Cleopatra as he swung helplessly in the air. The task was almost beyond a woman's strength, and it was only with great difficulty that Cleopatra, clinging with both hands to the rope and with the muscles of her face distorted by the strain, was able to haul him up, while those on the ground encouraged her with their cries and shared her agony. When she had got him up and laid him upon a

bed, she tore her dress and spread it over him, beat and lacerated her breasts, and smeared her face with the blood from his wounds. She called him her lord and husband and emperor, and almost forgot her own misfortunes in her pity for his. Antony calmed her lamentations and called for a cup of wine, either because he was thirsty or because he hoped it might hasten his death. When he had drunk it, he urged her to think of her own safety, if she could do this without dishonour, and told her that of all Caesar's associates she would do best to put her trust in Proculeius. Last of all, he begged her not to grieve over this wretched change in his fortunes, but to count him happy for the glories he had won and to remember that he had attained the greatest fame and power of any man in the world, so that now it was no dishonour to die a Roman, conquered only by a Roman.

78. The breath was scarcely out of his body when Proculeius arrived from Octavius Caesar. After Antony had stabbed himself and while he was being carried to Cleopatra, one of his bodyguard named Dercetaeus snatched up Antony's sword, hid it, and slipped out of the palace. Then he ran to Octavius and was the first to bring him the news of Antony's death, while at the same time he showed him the sword covered with blood. When Octavius heard what had happened, he retired into his tent and wept, for Antony was not only related to him by marriage, but had been his colleague in office and his partner in many great enterprises and battles. Then he brought out the letters they had exchanged, and calling in his friends, he read them aloud to let them hear in what moderate and conciliatory terms he had written, and how contemptuously Antony had always replied. After this he dispatched Proculeius with orders to make every possible effort to capture Cleopatra alive, for he was afraid, as I have already mentioned, that the queen would set fire to her treasure, and he also felt that her presence would greatly enhance the splendour of his triumphal procession in Rome. Cleopatra refused to surrender herself into Proculeius's hands, but she consented to talk to him when he came to the monument and stood outside one of the doors at the ground level. This door was strongly secured with bolts and bars, but it was possible to speak through it. There they held a parley in which Cleopatra asked that her children should be allowed to succeed to her kingdom, while Proculeius urged her to take courage and trust Octavius Caesar in everything.

79. Meanwhile, Proculeius took careful note of the monument, and, when he had made his report to Octavius Caesar, Gallus* was sent to hold a further interview with the queen. Gallus walked up to the door and engaged Cleopatra in conversation, while Proculeius fixed a scaling ladder against the monument and entered by the window through which the women had lifted Antony. Then he ran down with two servants to the door where Cleopatra was standing with her attention fixed on Gallus. One of the waiting women caught sight of him and screamed aloud, 'Unhappy Cleopatra, you are caught!' In the same instant the queen turned, saw Proculeius, and tried to stab herself, for she carried in her girdle a dagger of the kind which robbers wear. But Proculeius rushed up, flung both his arms around her, and said, 'Cleopatra, you do yourself and Caesar a great injustice. Do not refuse him this opportunity to show his generosity towards you. He is the gentlest of commanders, but you are acting as if he were a treacherous and implacable enemy.' At the same time he snatched away the weapon and shook out her dress to see whether she had hidden any poison. Octavius Caesar also sent one of his freedmen named Epaphroditus, whose orders were to allow her every concession which might comfort or give her pleasure, but to take the strictest precautions to keep her alive.

80. Meanwhile, Octavius Caesar made his entry into Alexandria with Areius the philosopher at his side. He gave him his right hand and kept up a conversation with him, so as to increase Areius's importance in the eyes of the Alexandrians and make him respected on account of this signal honour which he was being shown by Caesar. When he entered the public gymnasium and mounted a tribunal which had been erected there, the people were beside themselves with fear and fell on their faces before him. But Octavius told them to rise and assured them that he had no intention of holding their city to blame, first because it had been founded by Alexander, secondly because he himself admired its beauty and spaciousness, and lastly because of his regard for Areius. This was a special mark of honour which he conferred upon Areius, and at his request Octavius also granted a number of individual pardons. Among these was Philo-

* A Roman knight in command of the forces which had been advancing on Egypt from Libya. He later became governor of Egypt and was a friend of Virgil, who dedicated the tenth Eclogue to him.

stratus, a man who as an extempore speaker was the superior of the sophists of any age. Unfortunately he had made a completely unfounded claim to be a philosopher of the Academy, and for this reason Octavius, who detested the man's whole manner of life, refused to pardon him. So Philostratus allowed his white beard to grow, and then, dressing himself in black, he made a point of following close behind Areius and constantly repeating this verse,

The wise, if they are wise, will save the wise.

When Octavius heard of this, he granted the man a pardon, though he was more concerned to spare Areius embarrassment than to relieve the fears of Philostratus.

81. As for Antony's children, Antyllus, his son by Fulvia, was betrayed by his tutor Theodorus and executed. When the soldiers beheaded him, the tutor contrived to steal a precious stone which the boy wore around his neck, and sewed it into his belt, but although he denied the theft, he was found guilty and crucified. Cleopatra's children and their servants were kept under guard, but otherwise they were generously treated. However, Caesarion, who was supposed to be Cleopatra's son by Julius Caesar, was sent away by his mother with a large sum of money to travel to India by way of Ethiopia. Before long his tutor Rhodon, a man of the same type as Theodorus, talked him into believing that Octavius would make him king of Egypt and persuaded him to return. It is said that while Octavius was making up his mind how to treat him, Areius, parodying Odysseus's famous verse in the *Iliad*,* remarked to him,

It is bad to have too many Caesars . . .

82. After Cleopatra's death Octavius acted on his advice and had Caesarion executed. But as for Antony, although a number of kings and generals petitioned Octavius to allow them to perform the last rites for him, he would not take the body away from Cleopatra, and she buried it with her own hands and gave it a funeral of royal

* *Iliad* II, 204. Odysseus, striving to restore discipline in the Greek army, remarked

It is bad to have too many rulers . . .

splendour and magnificence, for which she was granted all the resources she needed. Because of the grief and pain she had suffered – for her breasts were inflamed and lacerated from the blows she had given them – she gladly seized upon her illness as a pretext to refuse food and so release herself without further interference from the burden of living. One of her trusted attendants was a physician named Olympus to whom she confided her true intentions: it was on his advice and help that she relied to bring about her death, and he confirms the fact in a history of these events which he has published. Meanwhile, Octavius Caesar had become suspicious and began to frighten her by uttering threats about the fate of her children. By applying these pressures in much the same way as a general uses siege-engines, he quickly undermined her resistance, so that she gave up her body to be treated and nourished as he desired.

83. A few days later Octavius paid a visit to talk to Cleopatra and try to reassure her. She had abandoned her luxurious style of living, and was lying on a pallet bed dressed only in a tunic, but, as he entered, she sprang up and threw herself at his feet. Her hair was unkempt and her expression wild, while her eyes were sunken and her voice trembled uncontrollably: her breasts bore the marks of the cruel blows she had inflicted on herself, and in a word her body seemed to have suffered no less anguish than her spirit. And yet her charm and a certain reckless confidence in her beauty were still by no means extinguished, and despite her sorry appearance they shone forth from within and revealed themselves in the play of her features. At any rate after Octavius had urged her to lie down and seated himself close to her, she tried at first to justify her part in the war, making out that her actions had been forced upon her by necessity and through her fear of Antony. But as Octavius contradicted her on every point and demolished her excuses, she quickly changed her manner and began to appeal to his pity with prayers and entreaties, as if she still clung above all else to the hope of saving her life. Finally, she handed to him a paper, which was supposed to be a complete inventory of her treasures, but when Seleucus, one of her stewards, made it clear that she was concealing and making away with a number of her possessions, she leaped to her feet, seized him by the hair, and pummelled his face. Octavius smiled at this episode and at last restrained her, whereupon she said, 'But is it not outrageous,

Caesar, when you do me the honour to come and speak to me in my wretched condition, that I should be accused by my own servants of putting aside a few women's trinkets like these? They were not meant for my poor self, you may be sure, but simply to have some little present by me for Octavia and your wife, Livia, so that I could appeal to them to make you kinder and more merciful.' Octavius was pleased at this speech, because it convinced him that Cleopatra still wished to live. He told her that she could settle any details of this kind as she pleased, but that in most important matters he would treat her more generously than she could possibly expect. Then he took his leave, feeling confident that he had deceived the queen, but the truth was that she had deceived him.

84. One of the members of Octavius's staff was a young aristocrat named Cornelius Dolabella.* He was by no means insensible to Cleopatra's charms, and now when she pressed him, he contrived to warn her secretly that Octavius was planning to march through Syria with his army, and had decided that she and her children were to be sent away within three days. When the queen heard this, her first action was to beg Octavius to allow her to pour her last libations for Antony, and when this request was granted, she had herself carried to the tomb. She was accompanied by the women who usually attended her, and there at the tomb she clasped the urn which contained his ashes and said, 'My beloved Antony, it is only a little while ago that I buried you with these hands. Then they were free, but now, when I come to pour libations for you, I am a prisoner, guarded so that I shall not disfigure this body of mine by beating it or even by weeping. It has become a slave's body, and they watch over it only to make me adorn their triumph over you. But after this you must expect no more honours or libations; these are the last that Cleopatra the captive can bring you. For, although in our lives nothing could part us, it seems that death will force us to change places. You, the Roman, have found a grave in Egypt, and I, unhappy woman, will receive just enough of your country to give me room to lie in Italy. But if there is any help or power in the gods of Rome, for mine have betrayed us, do not abandon your wife while she lives, and do not let me be led in triumph to your shame. Hide me and let me be buried here with you, for I know now that the thousand griefs

* The son of the politician mentioned in ch. 9.

I have suffered are as nothing beside the few days that I have lived without you.'

85. So Cleopatra mourned Antony, and she crowned his urn with a garland and kissed it. Then she ordered a bath to be made ready, and, when she had come from the bath, she lay down and was served with an exquisite meal. Presently, there arrived an Egyptian peasant carrying a basket, and when the guards asked him what was in it, he stripped away the leaves at the top and showed them that it was full of figs. The guards were astonished at the size and beauty of the figs, whereupon the man smiled and invited them to take some, and in this way their suspicions were lulled and they allowed him to bring in his fruit to the queen. When Cleopatra had dined, she took a tablet on which she had already written and put her seal, and sent this to Octavius Caesar. Soon afterwards she dismissed all her attendants except for two faithful waiting women, and closed the doors of the monument.

Octavius Caesar opened the tablet, and as soon as he read Cleopatra's prayers and entreaties that she should be buried with Antony, he immediately guessed her intention. His first thought was to go himself to save her life, but he restrained this impulse and sent messengers to hurry to the queen and discover what had happened. But the tragedy had moved too swiftly for them. The messengers rushed to the monument and found the guards still unaware that anything was amiss, but when they opened the doors, they found Cleopatra lying dead upon a golden couch dressed in her royal robes. Of her two women, Iras lay dying at her feet, while Charmian, already tottering and scarcely able to hold up her head, was arranging the crown which encircled her mistress's brow. Then one of the guards cried out angrily, 'Charmian, is this well done?' and she answered, 'It is well done, and fitting for a princess descended of so many royal kings,' and, as she uttered the words, she fell dead by the side of the couch.

86. According to one account, the asp was carried in to her with the figs and lay hidden under the leaves in the basket, for Cleopatra had given orders that the snake should settle on her without her being aware of it. But when she picked up some of the figs, she caught sight of it, so the story goes, and said, 'So here it is', and, baring her arm,

she held it out to be bitten. Others say that it was carefully shut up in a pitcher and that Cleopatra provoked it by pricking it with a golden spindle, until it sprang out and fastened itself upon her arm. But the real truth nobody knows, for there is another story that she carried poison about with her in a hollow comb, which she kept hidden in her hair, and yet no inflammation nor any other symptom of poison broke out upon her body. And indeed the asp was never discovered inside the monument, although some marks which might have been its trail are said to have been noticed on the beach on that side where the windows of the chamber looked out towards the sea. Some people also say that two faint, barely visible punctures were found on Cleopatra's arm, and Octavius Caesar himself seems to have believed this, for when he celebrated his triumph he had a figure of Cleopatra with the asp clinging to her carried in the procession. These are the various accounts of what took place.

Octavius Caesar was vexed at Cleopatra's death, and yet he could not but admire the nobility of her spirit, and he gave orders that she should be buried with royal splendour and magnificence, and her body laid beside Antony's, while her waiting women also received an honourable funeral. When Cleopatra died she was thirty-nine years of age, she had reigned as queen for twenty-two of these, and been Antony's partner in his empire for more than fourteen.* Antony was fifty-six according to some accounts, fifty-three according to others.† All his statues were torn down, but those of Cleopatra were allowed to stand, because Archibius, one of her friends, gave Octavius Caesar two thousand talents to save them from the fate of Antony's.

87. Antony left seven children by his three wives, and of these the eldest son, Antyllus, was the only one to be put to death by Octavius. Octavia took all the rest into her household and brought them up with her own family. For Cleopatra's daughter who bore the same name she arranged a marriage with Juba, the king of Numidia, one of the most gifted rulers of his time, and she brought Antony, another of Fulvia's children, into such high favour with Octavius that, while Agrippa held the first place of honour in his estimation, and the sons

* This figure is difficult to understand. The famous meeting at Cydnus did not take place until 41 B.C., a bare ten years before Actium.

† Antony was born on 14 January 82 or 81 B.C.: he thus died in his fifty-second or fifty-third year.

of Livia the second, Antony was generally regarded as holding the third, and this was no more than the truth. By her first husband, Marcellus, Octavia had two daughters and a son, also named Marcellus. Octavius married his daughter Julia to this boy and adopted him as his son, and he gave one of Octavia's daughters in marriage to Agrippa. But, as the young Marcellus died soon after his marriage, and as Octavius Caesar found it difficult to choose from among his friends a son-in-law in whom he could have full confidence, Octavia proposed that Agrippa should divorce her own daughter and marry Julia himself. First of all she persuaded Octavius Caesar, and then finally Agrippa gave way, whereupon she took her daughter back into her house and married her to her half-brother, the young Antony, while Agrippa married Julia. Antony left two daughters by Octavia, one of whom became the wife of Domitius Ahenobarbus,* while the other, Antonia, who was celebrated for her beauty and her virtue, married Drusus, who was the son of Livia and stepson to Octavius Caesar. Among the children of this marriage the most famous were Germanicus and Claudius. Claudius later became emperor, while of Germanicus's children, Gaius, also known as Caligula, ruled with distinction for a short time before being assassinated with his wife and child, and Agrippina, who had a son by Ahenobarbus named Lucius Domitius, later became the consort of the emperor Claudius. This Lucius Domitius was adopted by Claudius, who gave him the name of Nero Germanicus. He was the Nero who became emperor in my lifetime, murdered his mother, and through his folly and madness brought the Roman empire to the verge of destruction. He was the fifth in descent from Antony.†

* The son of Antony's friend who deserted before Actium.

† Thus the struggle between Octavius and Antony continued, in a sense, to the end of Nero's reign (68 A.D.) when, in the year of the four emperors, the ruling house of the Julian, Claudian, and Antonian families was wiped out.

APPENDIX

★ ★
★

ANTONY AND CLEOPATRA: PLUTARCH AND SHAKESPEARE: MYTH AND HISTORY

Plutarch, as we have seen elsewhere, is more interested in pointing a moral, composing a striking portrait, and creating a dramatic pattern of events than in investigating historical fact. He is consistently more hostile towards Antony than towards most of his heroes (possibly because of the harsh treatment suffered by his great-grandfather*), and his attitude towards Cleopatra is scarcely more sympathetic, at least until after the battle of Actium, when he draws upon material supplied by Olympus, the queen's physician. Shakespeare naturally follows Plutarch's historical outline – so far as we know he had no other – but he gives it quite another emphasis. Where the biographer, looking for examples of the public virtues in action, sees only the infatuation of a great soldier, the dramatist, whose play is not only a tragedy but a love poem, proclaims that

> the nobleness of life
> Is to do thus, when such a mutual pair
> And such a twain can do't . . .

The grandeur of Rome, which Plutarch still finds embodied in the person of Octavius Caesar, is seen as hollow, kingdoms are clay, it is paltry to be Caesar, and the splendour of the poetry is reserved for the lovers. In this way Shakespeare discovers in Antony's passion a depth of self-sacrifice of which we should never otherwise have believed him capable. Plutarch's account, on the other hand, depended, as was inevitable when he wrote, on the strongly biased evidence provided by the imperial historians. Thus we are confronted as it were with a triptych of the subject – the partial portrait of Plutarch, the dramatized portrait of Shakespeare, and the shadowy but far from identical portrait of history.

* See the Life, ch. 68.

CLEOPATRA

Cleopatra is one of those women whose image the world has always preferred to fashion out of myth rather than fact. Shakespeare's 'lass unparalleled' has been the general verdict, and she lives for posterity not as a ruler with a career to be chronicled, but as a symbol of the power of woman over man. Plutarch, and to an even greater extent Shakespeare, depict her not merely as a queen of infinite fascination – which could scarcely be disputed – but as an enchantress and a voluptuary, a woman preoccupied above all with the life of the emotions and the senses. Historical evidence suggests that ambition rather than sex was the key to her character. She was descended from the proud, rigorously in-bred Macedonian dynasty founded by Alexander's general Ptolemy, and incidentally possessed not a drop of Egyptian blood. To the Romans her territory, which was still nominally independent, represented the most tempting prize in the Mediterranean world. It was the only considerable Oriental state which had not been plundered in the civil wars, and apart from its natural wealth it contained the immense hereditary treasure of the Ptolemies, which plays an important part at the end of the story. For Cleopatra, on the other hand, the possibility of raising herself above the position of a client-queen lay in the hands of the Roman governor of the East. It was therefore no accident that her two lovers should have been Julius Caesar and Mark Antony, for her supposed connexion with Gnaeus Pompey is almost certainly mythical. She was highly cultivated, beloved by her subjects, and a very capable, if unscrupulous, ruler and diplomat. At most points of her career she displayed a courage which Shakespeare allows only to appear at the very end of it, and it seems probable that she conquered Antony much less by the commonplace arts of seduction than by her intelligence, her gaiety, and her indomitable spirit. Certainly her ambitions extended beyond the sphere of personal conquests: the question is how much farther. Some historians believe that she would have been content to regain and secure the possessions of her ancestors, others that she aspired to the imperial throne herself – she is quoted as using as a favourite oath the phrase, 'So may I deliver my edicts upon the Capitol'. In this context we must remember that the Mediterranean world of the first century B.C. was convulsed not only by political but by spiritual uncertainty. There was a general belief that one world-epoch was passing away and another coming into being, and the desire for a universal ruler who would dispense justice and security to suffering mankind was becoming more and more widespread. Certainly, Cleopatra had no reason to love the Romans, who had sapped the strength and exploited the rivalries of the Hellenistic monarchies of the Near East. On their side, the Romans had long been haunted by a terror of a mass uprising, such as Mithridates had already brought about half a century before, of the Asiatic peoples against their oppressors. There were many Messianic prophecies current in the Levant, which foretold that a great host would come out of Asia, that the power of Rome would be cast down to the dust and raised up again by a woman's hand, and that thereafter East and West would at last live side by side under a reign of justice and love. Whatever the influence or the following of these predictions, they made it easy for Octavius Caesar to play upon the fears of the Romans, and they partly explain the extraordinary outburst of hatred which was directed against Cleopatra before the campaign of Actium, for it was the queen of Egypt, not Antony, who was declared the enemy of the state. In one sense, this surge of national feeling certainly represents a triumph for Octavius Caesar's propaganda, but in another, perhaps, a tribute to the strength of Cleopatra's unaided genius. As the Cambridge Ancient History sums up this episode, 'Rome, who had never condescended to fear any nation or people, did in her time fear two human beings; one was Hannibal, and the other was a woman.'

CYDNUS

In spite of Plutarch's inspired description, it is by no means certain that Antony lost his heart upon the river at Cydnus in the autumn of 41 B.C., nor in the winter that followed, spent among the Inimitable Livers in Alexandria. Cleopatra certainly needed to exert her charms upon him, partly to account for her dealings with Cassius, and partly to enlist his help in ridding herself of her sister and rival Arsinoe. Antony, it seems more likely, was merely enjoying the fruits of victory as the new conqueror of the East, and still regarded himself as a free agent in his dealings with Fulvia and the Triumvirate. At any rate, when in the spring of 40 he received the news of Fulvia's clash with Octavius and of the Parthian invasion of Asia Minor, he left Cleopatra abruptly and did not see her again for three and a half years.

ANTONY'S MARRIAGES

Antony married Octavia in the autumn of 40 B.C. and remained with her for the three succeeding winters. The crucial date in his relationship with Cleopatra is the year 37. In that spring, thanks to Octavia's diplomacy, Antony and Octavius had patched up their differences to the extent of signing the pact of Tarentum (ch. 35), and joining forces against Sextus Pompeius. Six months later, while Antony had supplied the ships he had promised, Octavius had still failed to provide the legions which were urgently needed for the invasion of Parthia. Whether or not Antony had tired of his wife, he seems to have decided that further co-operation with her brother was impossible. It was at this point that he left Octavia and joined Cleopatra in Antioch.

Historians still disagree as to whether Antony contracted a marriage at this moment, and, if so, what was its significance. The important point to recognize (Shakespeare gives no hint of it) is that for Antony the Parthian adventure represented a supreme, if also supremely dangerous, opportunity. It was an enterprise bequeathed by Julius Caesar, one of the few legacies which Octavius had not succeeded in securing, and it offered Antony his best chance of restoring his status as an Imperator. Antony had already lost two years, partly through his own self-indulgence, but partly also because he had responded to Octavius's appeals for help, and the campaign could be delayed no longer.

Accordingly, some authorities maintain that he now married Cleopatra as a diplomatic manoeuvre to obtain help for the war, that he gave her in return the territories mentioned in chapter 36, which included some of the former possessions of the Ptolemaic Empire, and that if he had succeeded in Parthia he would still have been free to return to Octavia. Certainly, in Roman eyes he remained Octavia's husband, and his marriage to Cleopatra had no legal validity whatever outside the East. The Cambridge Ancient History, however, concludes that Antony had now made his final choice. Its authors consider that he could have laid his hands on the wealth of Egypt, and that nothing but his love for Cleopatra prevented him from doing so. If he had chosen Fulvia or Octavia, so the argument runs, he could have ruled half the Roman world without difficulty. Instead he chose the one woman who saw him as the instrument of her ambition. He, if not Cleopatra, lost the world for love.

THE PARTHIAN CAMPAIGN

Plutarch almost certainly goes astray in attributing the impatience and carelessness of Antony's strategy to the desire to return to Cleopatra. His haste is far more likely to have been brought about by the various delays which for two years had obstructed the campaign. It is true that Canidius was sent out early in 37 B.C. with an advance expedition to secure Armenia as a base for operations. But although Artavasdes made a formal submission, no guarantees were demanded, hostages taken, nor garrisons posted, and the optimistic trust which was placed in the king proved fatal. Similarly, after the withdrawal from Armenia, it was not romance which prompted Antony to hurry on ahead of his main body and join Cleopatra at the White Village. He feared that the Parthians might already have invaded Syria (as they had successfully done in 40 B.C.), hence the arrangement to meet at a small port where Cleopatra could force a landing if necessary. Antony was also in desperate need of the supplies and clothing which she brought, so as to get his army settled into winter quarters: after such a disaster he was by no means certain of its loyalty.

It is the Parthian campaign which probably marks the turning-point in the struggle between Antony and Octavius. During the same summer that Antony was advancing into Parthia (36 B.C.) Octavius was on the verge of committing suicide, having narrowly escaped defeat at the hands of Sextus Pompeius. But in September Pompeius's fleet was defeated at Naulochus, and having overcome this adversary Octavius never looked back. Antony, by contrast, had lost over 20,000 legionaries whom he could never replace, more than a third of the finest army he had ever commanded. Octavius had never sent the four legions he had promised at Tarentum, and henceforward it was evidently his policy to starve his opponent of manpower. At any rate, whatever the state of Antony's feelings in the past, it was now that he took the decisive step of turning back Octavia from Athens and rejecting her help. Neither adversary was yet ready for the final clash, but from this point it became increasingly easy to represent Antony as dominated by Cleopatra's ambitions.

A further link in the chain is suggested by the naming of Antony's children, conceived three and a half years before. The elder of his twin sons by Cleopatra, whom he now saw for the first time, he named Alexander the Sun. Antony himself had aspirations to be known as a new Alexander: at the end of the battle of Philippi he had emulated Alexander's gesture towards the dead Darius by covering Brutus's body with his purple cloak, and henceforth he made the sun his coin emblem. The name of Alexander likewise foreshadowed Antony's grand design of eastern conquest, which was to begin with the invasion of Parthia. Finally, since Octavia had borne him only daughters, it seems possible that in Antony's mind the dedication of Virgil's Fourth Eclogue (see note in ch. 31) was now transferred to Cleopatra. She was the new Isis, at once the daughter and mother of the Sun, who had given birth to the divine boy, the Sun-child, who would inaugurate a golden age, and inherit the peace won by his father's sword.

THE DONATIONS OF ALEXANDRIA

To redeem his shaken prestige, Antony invaded and subdued Armenia in the spring of 34 B.C. That winter he returned to Egypt with king Artavasdes as his prisoner and celebrated a triumphal procession in Alexandria. This was an almost unprecedented action, since a triumph was traditionally held in honour of Jupiter Capitolinus, the protector and presiding deity of Rome, and whether or not it antagonized moderate opinion in Italy it certainly provided Octavius with some excellent material for propaganda. This ceremony was followed by the so-called Donations of Alexandria, at which Antony publicly recognized Cleopatra and Caesarion (her son by Julius Caesar) as Queen of Kings and King of Kings, joint sovereigns of Egypt and overlords of the various realms of Cleopatra's children. Of his twin sons by her he proclaimed Ptolemy Philadelphus to be sovereign of all the kingdoms from the Hellespont to the Euphrates, and Alexander sovereign of those east of the Euphrates. These dynastic pronouncements made very little difference to the actual business of administering the Asiatic provinces. Here Antony had generally shown sound judgement in his choice of subject rulers, and the greater part of his settlement of the eastern empire was left unchanged by Octavius after Actium. On the other hand, to recognize Caesarion as the true heir of Julius Caesar was to assail the legality of Octavius's inheritance. In the last resort, of course, the whole grandiose structure of the Donations rested upon nothing but the loyalty of the legions, and hence Antony's own status was deliberately left unspecified. In the eyes of the Greeks or Asiatics he was Dionysus or Osiris, the consort of the goddess queen of Egypt, but to his Roman supporters he was still Marcus Antonius, pro-consul and triumvir. It was here that Antony's position was most ambiguous and vulnerable to the attacks of his enemies.

Octavius was quick to see the threat to his own situation and the weakness of Antony's. Antony made a final appeal in 33 B.C. for Octavius to allow him to recruit troops in Italy and provide allotments of land for his veterans, which Octavius refused. Antony then wrote to the Senate asking for ratification of his whole eastern settlement, including the Donations, and offering to lay down his office as triumvir. The new consuls for 32 B.C., although both supporters of Antony, did not venture to make this letter public for fear of the indignation it would arouse, and confined themselves to censuring Octavius's actions. Octavius coerced the Senate into submission, whereupon both consuls and some three hundred senators, nearly a third of the whole body, took refuge with Antony. It must be remembered that in the decade which had elapsed since Philippi many political allegiances had shifted. Antony had been a trusted friend of Julius Caesar, but he was not dedicated, as Octavius was, to the avenging of the dictator and the creation of a new form of Caesarism. Thus, over the years many former Republicans or supporters of Cato or Pompey, such as Ahenobarbus, had gravitated to Antony's camp, including even two of the surviving murderers of Caesar, and he still commanded a considerable following in Italy. On the other side, Octavius seized the opportunity to exploit the desertion of Plancus (see ch. 58). Although Octavius was no doubt well informed of the Donations, he had no documentary proof of them, and hence he welcomed the opportunity to publish Antony's will. He was able to play not only upon the apprehensions mentioned earlier of a mass uprising of the East against Roman domination, but also upon the fear that a victorious Antony would transfer the capital of the Empire from the Tiber to the Nile. Nevertheless, Octavius was careful to concentrate hostility upon the foreign enemy, and when in the autumn of 32 B.C. he ceremonially flung the spear into the soil before the temple of Bellona, he was declaring war upon Cleopatra alone.

ACTIUM: THE PRELIMINARIES

The true story of Actium and of Antony's conduct in the battle has vanished beyond recall. The riddle lies not so much in the details of the fighting – for, considering the size of the forces involved, it was a remarkably bloodless campaign – but rather in the minds of the combatants. Here some preliminary explanations are required. Plutarch's criticism of Antony for not attacking Octavius sooner is easily met. To have attempted an invasion of Italy with Cleopatra would have united the entire population against him, but she would not allow him to fight the war without her. Indeed, the question of the queen's presence dominated the strategy of the campaign and determined the actions of Antony's followers. These had, at best, been united by personal loyalty, not by a cause, and were by now deeply divided. The most clearheaded, such as Ahenobarbus, considered that Antony could only lead his men against Romans as a Roman, not as a Hellenistic monarch, and therefore wanted Cleopatra to be left behind in Egypt. Some of Antony's officers such as Canidius would follow him anywhere, others, such as the newly arrived senators, only if they approved of his policy. The rank and file of the legions no doubt thought in terms of a victorious return to Italy and of the soldier's traditional reward of a grant of land, and it was their attitude which ultimately decided the issue.

Antony had the superiority in ships, some 500 against 400: he could muster about 60,000 legionaries against Octavius's 80,000, and some 70,000 Asiatic troops. Octavius moved into western Greece first and secured the better strategic position. Antony's forces depended for their supplies on convoys from Egypt, but Agrippa, by capturing their naval stations in the Peloponnese, succeeded in cutting his opponent's communications, so that Antony was forced to rely upon provisions brought overland from Boeotia. A cavalry action launched against Octavius's water supply failed, and some of the Oriental mounted troops went over to the enemy. Antony seems to have regarded this reverse as decisive for operations on land and withdrew to Actium. As the summer advanced his troops began to suffer from malaria, food grew more scarce and desertions more frequent: it was at this point that Ahenobarbus left him.

ACTIUM: THE BATTLE

A council of war was held. Canidius's advice was to abandon the fleet, move into Macedonia, and engage the enemy in the open field, probably an impossible task, in view of the deteriorating condition of Antony's troops. Cleopatra wished to man the fleet with part of the army and fight a way out. If they were defeated, they could still escape to Egypt and defend the East against Octavius, leaving the rest of the army to make its way back. Antony, according to Professor Tarn's brilliant reconstruction of the battle,* may have conceived a more ambitious scheme. His plan was to sail out, and then, when the wind shifted at noon, as it regularly did on this coast, to turn Agrippa's left with his own right wing and drive the enemy's fleet away from its base. If this manoeuvre succeeded, the tables would be turned and Octavius's camp would be blockaded. This would explain the order to ship the sails (ch. 64), since it would be impossible to pursue the enemy if the galleys relied only on their oarsmen. There may well have been a secret plan whereby in the event of failure Antony and Cleopatra would break through with whatever ships they could take, leaving Canidius to extricate the army. Plutarch does not make it very clear, and Shakespeare still less so, that Antony needed to use a large proportion of his legionaries even to fight a naval battle. At any rate, the decision to embark the sails – and still more the royal treasure, which could safely have been left with the army – seems to have had a disastrous effect on the spirit of Antony's Roman troops.

After burning his surplus shipping, Antony was left with seven squadrons of sixty vessels each, in which he embarked over half his legionaries. He sailed out on 2 September, himself in command of the right wing, with Cleopatra's squadron bringing up the rear to prevent any desertions. Whether the main body of Antony's fleet was driven back into harbour or whether it refused battle from the outset is uncertain: what is clear is that it was the resistance of the Roman, not the Egyptian, formations which collapsed. Cleopatra's ships succeeded in breaking through the line and standing out to sea, and

* Journal of Roman Studies, vol. 21.

were followed by Antony with the remnants of his squadron. The story of the prolonged struggle carried on by the rest is apocryphal. Canidius tried to withdraw the army, but could not persuade the men to march, and was finally forced to fly for his own life. Thus the naval battle of Actium was virtually lost before it was fought, and Antony's defeat was brought about not by the cowardice imputed to him by Plutarch, but by a fatal weakness of judgement which led him to suppose that his supporters could not see through the disguises of his policy and the confusion of his aims, and so cost him the loyalty of his troops. At any rate, his flight to Egypt made his position clear and further deception impossible.

ACTIUM: THE SEQUEL

After the surrender Antony's legions were broken up, some of the troops being posted to various parts of the empire, while the veterans of both armies were settled in Italy. Not long after, these veterans mutinied in protest at being deprived of the expected plunder from Egypt. Octavius was obliged to return to Brundisium to pacify them, and one of his promises was that they would receive a share of the treasure of the Ptolemies. Henceforth it became a matter of life and death to secure this prize.

Cleopatra sailed back into Alexandria with her ships garlanded as if for victory, and promptly suppressed any signs of disaffection. She herself was full of plans and resources, but Antony's will to resist had gone. He travelled to Cyrene to rally the legions there, but found that they had already declared for the enemy. Since he now despaired of the loyalty of all his troops, he made no attempt to defend the naturally strong line of the Nile, and Cleopatra forbade her people to fight for her, as they were otherwise prepared to do. In taking this course she may have calculated that there was still a chance that Octavius would accept her children as client rulers, and as a last resource she could always bargain with him for the preservation of the treasure, which she had made preparations to burn if necessary. In the summer of 30 B.C. the advance on Egypt was resumed, Octavius marching from Syria, and Gallus from Libya. Antony sent a message to Octavius offering to kill himself on condition that Cleopatra should be spared, but received no reply. On 31 July the Roman advance guards reached the outskirts of Alexandria, and Antony scattered them. The story of his desertion that night by his patron deity Dionysus, which inspired Shakespeare's famous 'music under the earth' scene, is an echo of the tradition, familiar from the tale of Troy, that the gods abandon a doomed city on the eve of its fall. The next day the remainder of Antony's troops and Cleopatra's mercenaries went over to the enemy. There seems to be little likelihood that Antony was betrayed on this occasion, except by the false news of Cleopatra's death. But in any event the last moment had now arrived at which it was still possible for him to die with honour.

The remainder of the drama was quickly played out in the immediately succeeding weeks. Octavius secured the treasure, and it is reported that when it arrived in Rome the current rate of interest dropped from twelve to four per cent. Octavius allowed Antony to be buried with honour and in other respects his reprisals were carefully chosen: they consisted of four men and two boys. These included the two surviving murderers of Julius Caesar, Antony's marshal Canidius, and the luckless children, Caesarion and Antyllus.

As for Cleopatra's meeting with Octavius and her suicide, the question of which outwitted the other has inspired an infinity of rival theories. It is not easy to believe that, if Octavius had seriously intended to keep Cleopatra alive for his triumph, he would have been so simply duped: it seems possible that he was more concerned to allow her the opportunity to die in circumstances for which he could not be blamed. He may, for example, have hinted that he intended to annex Egypt, thus depriving her children of their inheritance and the queen of any further desire to live. However this may be, Cleopatra's death was a fitting culmination both to her life and her legend, a scene which poetry may be allowed to take over from history. If the asp was really the means of her death, its choice, we are told, would have carried a religious significance. To the Egyptians it was the divine minister of the Sun-god, and its effigy encircled the crown of Egypt to protect the royal line. The asp deified its victims, and the symbolic meaning of its bite was that the Sun-god had rescued his daughter from humiliation and taken her to himself. So died the last queen of the Ptolemies, 'all fire and air'; perhaps, in the words of a modern historian, 'the only one of all the successors of Alexander whom his fire had touched'.

GALLIA
AQUITANIA
GALLIA NARBONENSIS
Rhodanus F.
Arausio
Massilia
Narbo
GALLIA CISALPINA
Mediolanum
Placentia
LIGURIA
Genua
Pisae
Tiberis F.
Roma
Capua
GALICIA
LUSITANI
HISPANIA
TARRACONENSIS
Numantia
Iberus F.
Osca
Tagus F.
Turis F.
Sucro F.
Saguntum
Castulo
Baetis F.
BAETICA
Gades
Carthago Nova
Pityussae
Baleares
CORSICA
SARDINIA
SICILIA
Tingis
Carthago
Zama
MAURETANIA
NUMIDIA
0
200 miles
GAETULIA
The Western Mediterranean

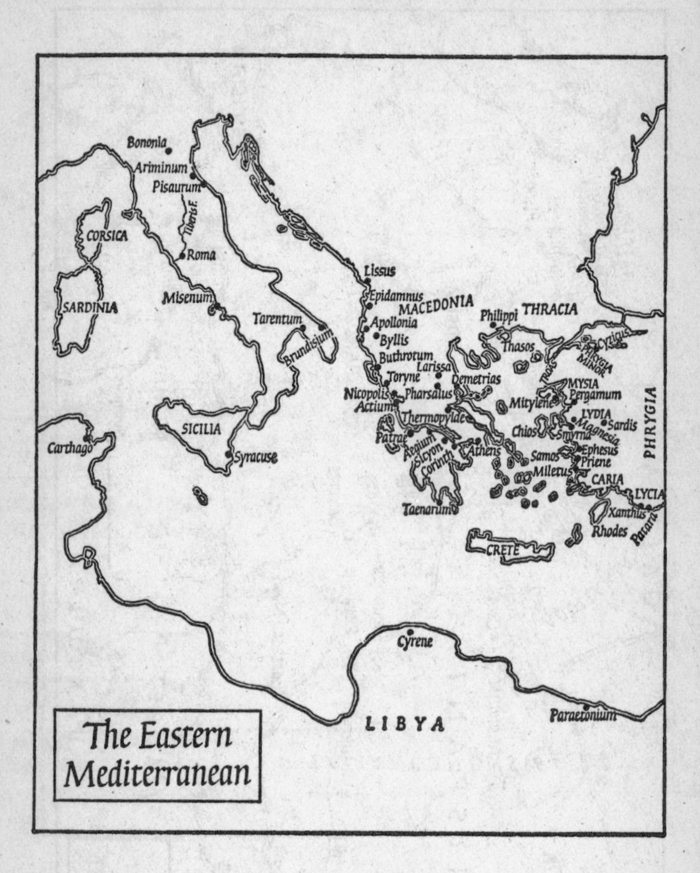

The Eastern Mediterranean

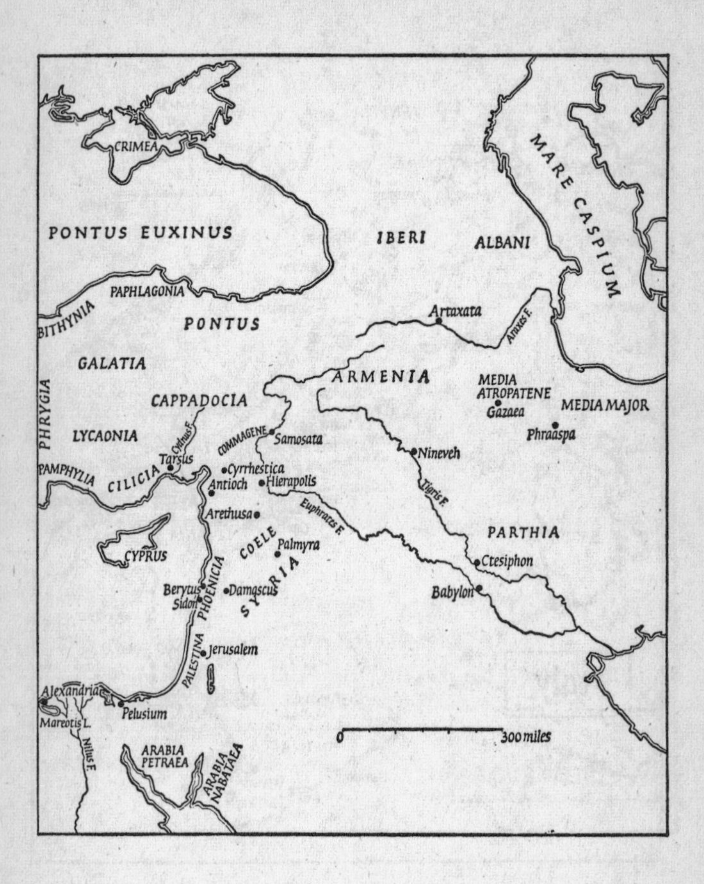
CRIMEA
PONTUS EUXINUS
IBERI
ALBANI
MARE CASPIUM
PAPHLAGONIA
BITHYNIA
PONTUS
Artaxata
Araxes F.
GALATIA
ARMENIA
MEDIA ATROPATENE
Gazaea
MEDIA MAJOR
Phraaspa
CAPPADOCIA
PHRYGIA
LYCAONIA
Cydnus F.
COMMAGENE
Samosata
Nineveh
Tarsus
PAMPHYLIA
CILICIA
Cyrrhestica
Antioch
Hierapolis
Tigris F.
Arethusa
Euphrates F.
PARTHIA
COELE
Palmyra
CYPRUS
SYRIA
Ctesiphon
PHOENICIA
Berytus
Sidon
Damascus
Babylon
PALESTINA
Jerusalem
Alexandria
Pelusium
Mareotis L.
0
300 miles
Nilus F.
ARABIA PETRAEA
ARABIA NABATAEA

GALLIA
Mediolanum
Acerrae
Placentia
VENETIA
Padus F.
LIGURIA
CISALPINA
Trebbia F.
Genua
Mutina
Bononia
Ravenna
Ariminum
1 AEQUI
2 MARSI
3 VESTINI
4 PAELIGNI
5 MARRUCINI
0
100 miles
Pisae
ETRURIA
UMBRIA
Tiberis F.
Ancona
PICENUM
Firmum
Trasimene L.
CORSICA
SABINI
Nussa
Falerii
Roma
LATIUM
Corioli
Velitrae
Toleria
Antium
Fregellae
VOLSCI
Casinum
Circeii
BRENTANI
SAMNIUM
APULIA
Cannae
Sinuessa
Capua
Casilinum
Cumae
Nola
Aufidus F.
Canusium
Misenum
Venusia
Bantia
Neapolis
Brundisium
CALABRIA
Capreae
Numistro
Tarentum
SARDINIA
LUCANIA
Metapontum
Petelia
BRUTTIUM
Italy
Panormus
Messina
Caulonia
Locri
Rhegium
SICILIA
Catana
Leontini
Agrigentum
Megara
Syracuse
Gela
Acrillae